Freedom's
Embrace

Freedom's Embrace

J. Melvin Woody

The Pennsylvania State University Press
University Park, Pennsylvania

"Right or Left At Oak Street"
Words and Music by Joe Nixon/Charlie Williams
© 1969 SONY/ATV SONGS LLC
Administered by EMI BLACKWOOD MUSIC INC. (BMI)
All Rights Reserved. International Copyright Secured. Used by Permission.

Library of Congress Cataloging-in-Publication Data

Woody, J. Melvin, 1933–
    Freedom's embrace / J. Melvin Woody.

      p.   cm.
    Includes bibliographical references and index.
    ISBN 0-271-01760-0 (cloth : alk. paper)
    ISBN 0-271-01761-9 (pbk. : alk. paper)
    1. Free will and determinism.   I. Title.
    BJ1461.W66   1998
    123'.5—dc21   97-48495
                                                CIP

It is the policy of The Pennsylvania State University Press to use acid-free paper for
the first printing of all clothbound books. Publications on uncoated stock satisfy the
minimum requirements of American National Standard for Information Sciences—
Permanence of Paper for Printed Library Materials, ANSI Z39.48-1992.

Contents

Prologue

Scattered along Second Avenue in New York are shops crowded with *objets d'art* and fine antiques. But the general public cannot gain access to the goods within, however valuable. They are available only to other dealers and professional decorators. A discreet sign at the door reads

> Open Only to the Trade.

Such a sign might well be posted at the entry to recent philosophical discussions of freedom, which have become so technical that they are only accessible to other professional philosophers. Yet the meaning of freedom is scarcely a parochial philosophical issue. Freedom is one of the central concerns of contemporary global politics. Although its articulation as a political value developed in the West, the expansion of Western culture has confronted all other societies with appeals to freedom as a social, economic, and political ideal. But these appeals invoke competing interpretations of the meaning of freedom. In the face of this popular importance and public disagreement, philosophy has an important role to play. The inaccessibility of the recent philosophical literature therefore seems especially lamentable.

I believe that the technical refinements of recent philosophical arguments about freedom cause another danger: that the process of refinement may produce a distillate so rarefied and volatile that the original meaning may dissipate in a haze of contrary-to-fact conditionals or a vapor of semantic distinctions. I fully appreciate the virtues of technical philosophy. The philosophical critique of abstractions requires both logical rigor and semantic precision. But when philosophers write only for one another, their discourse is liable to become ingrown. I find this true of recent discussions of freedom stemming from both the Anglo-American and the Continental European philosophical traditions. Within any such tradition, thought tends to move within a set of assumptions and methods of argument that define the tradition and give it its peculiar vitality and value. The very virtues of developing a technical vocabulary that sustains a community of professional discourse thus come, in time, to occlude the issues. Philosophy is not like science. It cannot sustain itself by perfecting a deductive system of technical terms. Every such technical vocabulary or method achieves precision and clarity at the price of divisions and exclusions that eventually eclipse, rather than illuminate, the questions that set us wondering.

Wittgenstein and Heidegger, the most seminal figures in these two contemporary traditions, have both called attention to this danger. And they resorted to very different, but parallel remedies. Each attempted to escape the limitations of his technical philosophical tradition from which he came by making a fresh beginning—by a return to ordinary language in the case of Wittgenstein and to everyday existence in the case of Heidegger. The insights gained by these strategies proved so provocative that they spawned new traditions, which have eventually become as ingrown and recondite as the logic of the *Principia Mathematica* or the phenomenological refinements of Husserl's *Ideen*.

In this book, I confront the question of the meaning of freedom afresh, and begin by restating in the most ordinary terms the issues surrounding disputes about the meaning of freedom. By beginning from an ordinary, everyday formulation of the problem, I hope to accomplish two ends: to avoid foreclosing important questions by assuming the techniques and perspective of any one philosophical tradition and to open the discussion to a wider audience, in hopes of restoring the easy communication between philosophy and the general public that American philosophy enjoyed in the heyday of American pragmatism.

Professional readers may be somewhat impatient at finding familiar philosophical arguments presented in such popular garb in the opening chapters. But they will also find they can sail through those passages with relative speed. I can only hope that they will find this formulation refreshing, that they will see that beginning all over from the way these issues arise in ordinary, everyday discourse will prove worth the trouble in the sequel. This, after all, has been a recurrent philosophical strategy—to place all the traditional "school philosophy" in doubt and go back to the beginning, whether to "build on a new foundation," as Descartes proposed, or to attack the very possibility of foundations, with more recent thinkers.

But this inquiry would be seriously impoverished if it did not also communicate with the rich resources available in the long historical tradition of philosophical debate about freedom. The inquiry therefore eventually ventures into a stricter mode of philosophical discourse. In the process, I must also reopen dialogue with the philosophical tradition that has devoted so much thought and ingenuity to this topic. In the main text, I have tried to invoke philosophers who should be familiar to anyone who has taken a standard course in the history of Western philosophy, confining references to more recent literature to the footnotes. Where I have had to discuss less familiar thinkers in the main text or to deal with major thinkers in greater depth, I have tried to explain their views in a way that will be accessible to a general audience. By so doing, I hope to produce a text that will be open to the general public, as well as to the trade, and that speaks to the interests of both.

Preface: A Simple Choice

Right or Left at Oak Street

When I reach the stop sign at Oak Street
The same thought crosses my mind,
Should I turn right, like I always have,
Or left and leave it behind?

Right or left at Oak Street
That's the choice I face every day
And I don't know which takes more courage,
The stayin' or the runnin' away.

A left turn would take me to somewhere
Leave alarm clocks and schedules behind,
And the world wouldn't care, if I'm not somewhere
At some particular time.

For a man can do what he wants to do
And no one expects him to give
All of his time to the same old routine
In the one life that he has to Live.
    —Charlie Williams and Joe Nixon

On a Monday morning in August, Domer Ringuette turned left. The *New York Times* reported:

> Mr. Ringuette—weekly newspaper owner, pillar of small business and local politician in Chicopee, Mass.—abruptly disappeared without a word to employees, bankers, customers, newspaper readers or even the mayor.

> When employees of his paper, *The Chicopee Herald,* went to his house to check on him, they found it empty except for an ironing board. Mr. Ringuette, at 53 years, had done what many people only dream of doing: he had simply driven away from position, responsibility and assets . . . worth as much as $750,000.[1]

According to the *Times,* people in Chicopee at first suspected foul play—or that Domer Ringuette had acted under duress: "One theory was that he had fled to escape huge gambling debts; another had him deep in debt to loan sharks, and it was whispered in Chicopee that he was last seen getting into a sinister black limousine." But when his relatives did not file a missing-person report, "everyone concluded that Mr. Ringuette had bolted of his own free will."

And indeed, that was Domer Ringuette's own view. When a newspaper reporter found him dealing poker in Las Vegas several months later, Ringuette's explanation seemed to echo the sentiments of the country-and-western song quoted above. "He said that he was fed up with 18 hour workdays, a recession-racked economy that had made money very scarce and the day-to-day frustrations of operating his newspaper, rental property and the Green Valley Country Store and Gas, the convenience store and gas station that he opened every day at 5 A.M. So he gave a friend all his furniture, piled some luggage into his Lincoln, and headed West."

"I had made up my mind to be free, so I became free," he told the *Times.* As for unpaid debts and wages back in Chicopee, "If anybody is concerned and wants to put me in jail, they're welcome to. I don't give a damn; I'm free."

But is he really free? Did Domer Ringuette act of his own free will? Was he free all along—or did he only become free on the day he left Chicopee behind? Now that he has made up his mind to be free, would he still be free even in jail?

A skeptical psychologist might object that Domer Ringuette's flight from Chicopee is not an exercise of free will, but an obvious product of circumstance. The skeptic would find a simple causal explanation for Domer's actions. The long hours of work, the failing economy, the day-to-day hassle of managing so many enterprises simply wore him down until he couldn't stand the pressure. So he broke and ran. He may think he chose to leave of his own free will, but his departure was really an event as inevitable as the fall of a tree whose roots have been undercut by a stream. He could

---

1. "In the Case of a Missing Publisher, All the Cards Are Now on the Table," *New York Times,* Monday, March 23, 1992. The quotations that follow come from this same article.

no more choose to stay than the tree could choose to cling to the bank after a spring flood has washed it "free" of the land.

Right or left at Oak Street? A simple choice. It seems obvious that a decision to turn one way or the other is an exercise of human freedom. Every morning, Domer Ringuette rose to a 4:30 alarm and opened his convenience store at 5:00. Surely, he could have chosen to do so again on the Monday that he turned left and drove away from Chicopee, leaving "alarm clocks and schedules behind." Yet, according to the *Times,* even the local chiropractor who took over the *Chicopee Herald* found a simple psychological formula to explain Ringuette's departure: "He was unhappy here, and he left." A more professional and doctrinaire psychologist might seize this occasion to go further and argue that no one ever acts or chooses freely, that actions that appear to be freely chosen are really only the necessary effects of earlier causes that shape our personalities and determine every action, every detail of our lives. He might compare Domer to a rat faced with similar alternatives in a laboratory maze. At first, the rat finds that there is always a little food at the end of the right-hand path of the maze, corresponding to the profit and satisfaction Domer Ringuette found in his businesses, whereas the left offers no such incentive. But then, suppose that the food rewards decline, and the rat receives a mild electric shock every time it reaches the end of the right-hand path. Once the shocks have been administered with sufficient frequency and intensity, the rat will turn left. We do not suppose that the rat turns left because of the exercise of "its own free will." The causes that make the rat turn left are too obvious. In most cases of human behavior, the operative causes are not so obvious, but they are plain enough in Domer Ringuette's case, and his flight from Chicopee is their necessary consequence.

Was Domer Ringuette's flight necessary and inevitable? Was he trapped like a rat in a maze? Is the rat's action inevitable and necessary? Someone might rise to the rat's defense and argue that, like Domer, the rat has simply had enough—what with being shocked every time it turns right—that it simply shows good sense in choosing the avoidance of pain over the declining rewards to be had by sticking to its old habits. But it is hard to take such a defense seriously. Our disdain and distaste for rats make us hesitate to elevate them to the status of free agents, and we rather suspect that such a defense is guilty of a specious anthropomorphism. We hesitate to defend human freedom at the price of conceding that the rat is free. But the parallel between the two cases is so obvious that to insist upon Domer's freedom while denying that of the rat would seem a transparent expression of prejudice.

Right or left at Oak Street? A simple choice. At first, it seems obvious that a decision to turn one way or the other is an exercise of human freedom.

But our skeptical psychologist speaks for a great many other students of human behavior and history, indeed for a whole tradition of thought that insists that human choices and deeds are, like all other events, the necessary effects of causal processes. And if every action is inevitable, the agent couldn't possibly have done otherwise, so there was never any real alternative to doing as he did. The very appearance that there is any choice is therefore deceptive. If an act appears to be free, that appearance is simply due to our ignorance of the causes that made the decision inevitable. Freedom of choice is only an illusion produced by ignorance of the true causes of action.

Can that be all there is to freedom? The question merits closer scrutiny. We may well hesitate to concede so much, to pass so readily from doubting the freedom of one choice to a blanket denial of human freedom. Is freedom a mere illusion, a by-product of our ignorance rather than the seat of human dignity? Is that what all the shooting is about? Is all the conflict and bloodshed in the name of freedom just a futile sacrifice dedicated to a blank spot in our knowledge, a tragic folly born of our ignorance of the true causes of our deeds? Is the modern, liberal effort to establish and protect freedom chasing a will-o'-the-wisp—a project born of confusion and ignorance about the actual causes of human behavior? Indeed, if human beings *are* ever free agents, is that freedom an original human capacity? Or is it something that we can gain or lose and that we can only enjoy thanks to favorable circumstances and institutions, an outer liberty that we are liable to forfeit if we don't vigilantly defend and foster those conditions? Or does personal freedom depend upon more intimate, inner conditions—upon self-mastery or moral integrity or stoic detachment?

These questions will not go away. And although they have plagued the West for centuries, they cannot simply be relegated to the realm of those perennial problems that can be tidily confined to the philosophy class or to dormitory debates. Freedom is one of the central values of modern economic and political life. Yet our political and economic and social theories, like psychology, have typically embraced determinism as their ideal—or assumed it as axiomatic to the very enterprise of a "scientific" understanding of human behavior. So far as that is so, we are caught in the absurd predicament of pursuing goals that our understanding declares impossible, or of seeking to enlarge our liberty through social engineering!

In this book, I attempt a radical reexamination of freedom. I rethink the idea of freedom from the ground up, in a fresh and independent inquiry that draws upon the long tradition of philosophical discussion of these issues without drowning the reader in historical erudition or technical philosophical discourse. The book begins with a closer look at some perennial and recalcitrant philosophical debates about human freedom. It seeks to break out of those disputes by showing how they arise from fragmentary conceptions of freedom and from convictions about ourselves and our world that may seem innocent enough but only create confusions that have trapped modern thought in an impasse that seems inescapable. Closer analysis shows that those convictions depend upon assumptions that are both unnecessary and untenable and that each of the partial conceptions of freedom that have long muddled debate has a legitimate place within a more comprehensive understanding of what it means to be free. In the process, the contradiction between freedom and necessity gives way to a discovery of the necessary conditions of freedom.

Once we understand the necessities of freedom, we must reconceive the relation between freedom and necessity. That means rethinking both the place of necessity in science and the place of freedom in nature. We must confront the neglected question of animal freedom and recognize that freedom is not a peculiarly human privilege. Still, human freedom does differ from animal freedom in ways reflected by the difference between natural evolution and human history. Symbolism and culture vastly expand the range of alternatives available for human choice. They raise human freedom from the level of immediate options to the level of strategies, norms, and rules. They also lead, eventually, to a self-awareness of freedom that seems lacking in animals. Only human beings seem able to establish freedom as an ideal.

But our advantage over the animals also exposes us to the threat of despair, as Kierkegaard observed. On the one hand, self-conscious freedom raises human choice beyond the confines of immediate opportunity and opens the way to deliberate social and political change and to responsible moral decision. Yet the discovery that we are responsible for our own actions, customs, and institutions also opens the way to nihilism by revealing the historicity of the very institutions and norms *for* which and *to* which we hold ourselves responsible.

If our mores and morals are not natural, but artificial—and therefore subject to historical modification, are they not also optional, leaving us sovereigns of a realm in which revolution is always legitimate? In the end, we must ask whether the ideal of freedom can fill the void opened by the recognition that our values and culture are neither natural nor sacred, but "human, all too human." Does our fresh understanding of the necessities of freedom also lead to a renewal of the liberal moral and social ideals? The final chapter seeks an answer to that question through reflection on the necessary conditions of a free community.

I conclude on the threshold of the ethics and politics of freedom. To cross that threshold would be to embark upon a second volume dealing with questions of social, economic, and political liberty. Those questions are far too numerous and complex to fit into this book, which closes with an epilogue that exploits the parallels between political liberty and individual freedom to review the entire argument and provide a final survey of why the several varieties of freedom belong together as parts of a single, coherent whole.

Introduction

Freedom and Determinism: A Frozen Maelstrom

Right or left at Oak Street: a simple choice, such as everyone makes every day. Yet it has plunged us into the midst of a stubborn and persistent dispute. Like the skeptical psychologist whose comments were described in the Preface, many philosophers, scientists, historians, and sociologists argue that all human choices are completely subject to causal laws, like any other events in the universe. Human actions are not exempt from the laws of nature, they argue, and this means that whatever any individual decides to do, his choice and act must be completely determined by prior events.

Not all advocates of this deterministic view dismiss freedom as altogether illusory, as did the skeptical psychologist. Some of them insist that there is no conflict between causal necessity and freedom, if only the nature of freedom is properly understood.[1] But they, too, argue that there is no such

---

1. This is sometimes called "soft" determinism, a name coined by William James. For a standard statement of this position, see Moritz Schlick, *Problems of Ethics*, trans. David Rynin

thing as freedom of choice. They insist that all human actions and decisions
are the necessary consequences of antecedent causes and would be precisely predictable if we knew enough about the antecedent conditions in
each individual case and the relevant laws of human behavior. Granted, we
usually do not know enough about the background of the particular case.
Granted, too, that the sciences that deal with human behavior do not
furnish all the laws that would be required in order to make such predictions or to explain exactly why a certain action or choice was necessary. But
we need not await further evidence and scientific progress to know that
there is no such thing as freedom of choice, say these determinists. To
suppose that any choice is not completely determined by antecedent causes
is to suppose it to be inexplicable, unintelligible. For to explain or understand an event is the same as to discover the causes sufficient to bring it
about. To attribute an act to "free will" is like attributing an event to
"chance" or fortune. Both only express ignorance of the causes that actually
necessitate what happened. Thus, the very nature of rational, scientific
explanation obliges us to insist that human actions must be determined by
causal laws and to deny that they are the result of free choices.

This is a vigorous and persuasive argument. But it has probably provoked
as much heated opposition to as agreement with the claim that human
choices are never free. Its opponents insist with equal vigor that the
universe is not a tightly knit system of causal relations in which the entire
future is completely determined by the past. They claim that *human*
choices, at least, are not necessarily predetermined in accordance with
causal laws and that human actions are not completely predictable either in
fact or in principle. They argue that the failure of science to discover
rigorous laws of human behavior that would make such predictions possible
is not simply due to the fact that the sciences of human behavior are still
relatively young, but is rooted in the very nature of their subject matter. The
fact that there is no exact science of human nature comparable to modern
physics is not a sign of our ignorance, but testimony to the fact that human
beings are not dominated by past events but are able to choose freely
between the alternatives that confront them. To attempt to "explain"
human actions without acknowledging this freedom of choice is to attempt
to explain away that which makes them human.

Thus runs the debate between advocates of determinism and champions
of free choice, or "free will," a dispute that has dominated reflection about

---

(New York: Prentice Hall, 1939), chap. 7. Cf. C. A. Campbell's critique of Schlick, "Is 'Freewill'
a Pseudo-Problem?" *Mind* 60, no. 240 (1951): 441–65. Both are reprinted in Bernard Berofsky,
Free Will and Determinism (New York: Harper & Row, 1966).

freedom far too persistently and profitlessly. The scientific trappings that lend the issue such an aura of modernity are somewhat misleading. For the modern version of the debate, which is formulated against a background of mechanistic physics and of historical, psychological, or sociological determinism, only reformulates the older problem of free will versus divine predestination, which can be traced back through Christian thought to Roman Stoicism, Democritean atomism, and Eleatic monism.[2] To this day, the most trenchant and formidable attack upon freedom of choice is not to be found in the writings of contemporary physicists or behavioral scientists, but among the works of Jonathan Edwards, the formidable American clergyman who is more often remembered for his sermon "Sinners in the Hands of an Angry God." Although Edwards's work on freedom of the will displays some influences of Locke and Newton, his arguments are rooted in Saint Augustine, and his purpose was to defend Calvinist theology, with its strict doctrine of divine predestination. If Edwards seems to us a strange bedfellow for contemporary scientific determinists, it may seem even more odd to find that the strange bedfellows were once combined in a single person. Joseph Priestley, perhaps the first distinguished modern physicist to develop the deterministic thesis in detail, was both a scientific materialist and a Nonconformist Christian minister rolled into one.

Anyone who surveys the history of the freedom-determinism controversy will be impressed, above all, by its monotony. The underlying issues and arguments have changed but little over the centuries. Whether the source of necessity is conceived as the Stoic *Logos*, as Christian divine providence, or as the laws of modern physics, the two sides of the argument remain remarkably constant. Arguments over the implications of the indeterminacy principle in contemporary physics invite comparison with Lucretius's introduction of a spontaneous swerve of atoms into the Democritean theory. In their critiques of the idea of free will, scientifically oriented positivists echo the arguments of Saint Augustine. Contemporary efforts to reconcile determinism with some form of freedom recall those of Calvinist theologians.

Aside from the sheer monotony of the debate, one is struck by the fact that the two sides of the dispute rarely seem to be talking about the same thing. The doctrine of freedom that strict determinists criticize and reject can scarcely be recognized in the writings of their opponents. Conversely, the complete rejection of choice for which the "libertarians" attack the determinists is vigorously denied by a number of authors who champion

2. For a lucid account of this derivation, see Milic Capek, "The Doctrine of Necessity Re-examined," *Review of Metaphysics* 5, no. 1 (1951): 11–54.

determinism but insist that choices are real even though they are not free. This impression that the parties to this dispute are not fighting on common ground is at least partially deceptive, however. It can be shown that the charges of each side do pertain to the assertions of the other. Yet, in the face of such a stubbornly persistent controversy, one cannot but wonder whether the dispute reflects some equally persistent failure of mutual understanding. The suspicion arises that perhaps the combatants are not altogether clear about the subject of their argument. The disputants themselves reinforce this suspicion by accusing one another of not understanding what they are talking about and of misconstruing the plain, ordinary meanings of the words employed.

Meanwhile, the dispute becomes tiresome. The issues grow stale; the central arguments become familiar through repetition; novel minor variations evoke more indifference and frustration than interest. This weariness and frustration combine with suspicion of the arguments' lack of clarity and reciprocal understanding to provoke us to turn our backs on the whole dispute and cast about for some other attack upon the problem of freedom. Perhaps if we could achieve some clarity about the nature of freedom, we might either escape this tedious controversy altogether or at least gain some notion why the dispute is so unproductive and why it so stubbornly resists resolution on its own terms.

After all, this conflict among thinkers about whether the will is free or determined is the most harmless, insipid, and academic of squabbles compared with the political conflicts fought in the name of freedom between the armies of opposing nation-states and by revolutionary movements scattered throughout the world. While academic thinkers retrace the same well-rutted arguments about causation and the will, and haggle over the relevance of the latest proclamations of physics or psychology, the rest of the world contends with the problem of freedom by exploding bombs and spilling blood in attempts to overthrow governments or transform societies. Indeed, it has become almost a matter of custom for both sides of any dispute to appeal to the cause of freedom. Such appeals have become so much a part of the accepted cosmetics of politics that no political movement or party would even think of appearing in public without decking itself out as the party of freedom. Where once men sought to prove that God was on their side, they now seek to consecrate the worthiness of their cause by invoking the name of freedom.

The result is that *these* struggles, too, grow wearisome, baffling, and frustrating, though for reasons different from those that so render the academic dispute over freedom and determinism. The danger arises that people may grow indifferent to freedom, turn their backs upon those struggles, and accept whatever social order may seem to promise stability and rest, however repressive of freedom it may be. But anyone who turned to the academic experts in search of some clue to the resolution of all this strife would find them still embroiled in an endless parochial conflict about determinism and free will that seems to have no bearing upon the problems of the world at large. That creates the impression that the academic controversy has no connection with the social and political conflicts of our day. But this impression is false. The deterministic thesis, in its Marxist form, has been at the center of modern political conflict, where it has contended with a democratic liberal tradition that invites comparison with the "libertarian" side of the debate over free will and determinism. Even the details of the academic dispute have their analogues in the political domain, where one party sets itself up as the champion of freedom, while its opponent undertakes to represent itself as the party of "law and order." In this case, of course, the "law and order" in question are political and social rather than natural and scientific, but the accusations and counteraccusations echo those employed in the academic debate. When the liberal sets out to defend this or that civil liberty, his conservative opponent accuses him of undermining the social order and of championing chaos and anarchy rather than genuine liberty. On the other hand, at the first mention of "law and order," the liberal is likely to accuse the conservative of fascism and of attempting to bring about a totalitarian, monolithic society.

In almost identical terms, the determinists argue as though the least hint of freedom as an ingredient in the universe entails complete chaos and the collapse of all regularity, certainty, and predictability in human knowledge. The libertarian counters with the accusation that the determinist is defending a monolithic, monistic, "block" universe, in which there is no room for diversity and change.[3] And, in both political and metaphysical controversies, each side typically denies the charges of the other.

These similarities between the academic and political levels of controversy about freedom are all the more striking because they are so unexpected. Can it be that the issue at stake in the academic debate is *not* a "purely academic question" after all? Philosophical disputation and political conflict seem to follow surprisingly parallel channels. But "parallel ruts" might be a better description, for the two forms of controversy also appear to be similarly fruitless and irresolvable. Surely, we need a clearer understanding of the *nature* of freedom—and for reasons that are not merely academic! But the most obvious and familiar approaches to this problem only lead us into a controversy so fixed in form that it reminds one of a battle carved in marble. Evidently the entire problem must be reexamined

3. See William James, "The Dilemma of Determinism," in *Essays in Pragmatism* (New York: Hafner, 1948).

in order to find some other route to its solution. What other avenues of approach are available that might offer some promise of resolution?

Experience, Science, and Language

When faced with a stubborn controversy of this sort, modern thinkers have appealed to three resources, or authorities, in hopes of finding a solution. We may turn to *experience* as the original source of all knowledge or as the final test of all theory. Or we may appeal to the authority of *science* as the most rigorous form of knowledge and the one that has achieved greatest success in developing methods for settling theoretical controversies. Finally, we may turn to an examination of *language,* to see whether we cannot trace the dispute in question to some merely verbal disagreement that may disappear once we have achieved clarity about the meanings of the terms at issue. Experience, science, language: these three resources are by no means mutually exclusive, yet they obviously provide the basis for three fairly distinct approaches to the problem of freedom. Can one of them furnish a pathway out of the sterile impasse presented by the conflict between freedom and determinism?

Indecisive Resources

The Appeal to Experience

When thought gets stuck fast in a tangle of theoretical controversy, it is always tempting to seek a way out by returning to experience, from which all thought must somehow draw its nourishment. Surely, a sufficiently careful and exacting scrutiny of experience will show which theory is correct or whether both have lost their way by losing touch with the solid ground of experience. Such is the strategy of both classical empiricism and modern phenomenology. Perhaps we can escape from the impasse about freedom by following their lead.

Unfortunately, when they deal with the issue of freedom and determinism, the two schools of thought that urge a return to experience lead us in opposite directions. Classical empiricism reached its zenith in the thought of David Hume, who sided with determinism. Hume points to our experience of regularity in human behavior, or to the "constant conjunction" of certain circumstances, motives, and actions, and concludes that human actions are as necessarily determined as the behavior of material things: "Whether we consider mankind according to the difference of sexes, ages, governments, conditions, or methods of education; the same uniformity and regular operation of natural principles are discernible. Like causes still produce like effects; in the same manner as in the mutual action of the elements and powers of nature."[4] Consequently, Hume later concludes, we cannot, without a manifest absurdity, attribute necessity to events and refuse to attribute it to human actions.[5]

More-recent empiricists have typically followed Hume's lead. But contemporary phenomenologists, who are certainly as insistent as empiricists upon methodically and scrupulously founding philosophy on experience, almost all take up the opposite side of this dispute. They reject determinism and insist upon freedom of choice. Indeed, it would be hard to imagine a more radical defense of freedom of choice than that which Jean-Paul Sartre develops in the course of his phenomenological investigations in *Being and Nothingness*. According to Sartre, freedom is not a characteristic of some human acts but not of others. Nor is it merely one human attribute among others, or a condition that men may or may not enjoy according to their character or circumstances. Human consciousness and freedom are inseparable, and that freedom defines man's very being:

> Thus freedom . . . is not a *property* which belongs among others to the essence of the human being. We have already noticed furthermore that with man the relation of existence to essence is not comparable to what it is for the things of the world. Human freedom precedes essence in man and makes it possible; the essence of the human being is suspended in his freedom. What we call freedom is impossible to distinguish from the *being* of "human reality." Man does not exist *first* in order to be free *subsequently;* there is no difference between the being of man and his being-free.[6]

So, Sartre concludes in a later passage, "I am condemned to be free. This means that no limits to my freedom can be found except freedom itself or, if you prefer, that we are not free to cease being free."[7]

Experience is evidently an ambiguous oracle, since those who consult it are led to such contradictory conclusions. Hume, the empiricist, and Sartre, the phenomenologist, reach opposite verdicts about whether hu-

---

4. *A Treatise of Human Nature* (Oxford: Oxford University Press, 1960), 401.
5. Ibid., 404.
6. *Being and Nothingness*, trans. Hazel Barnes (New York: Philosophical Library, 1956), 25.
7. Ibid., 439.

man actions are ever free. Like the oracles of antiquity, experience requires interpretation—and men are likely to find interpretations that suit their expectations. Philosophers may pour over their experience with all the painstaking exactitude of Talmudic scholars, yet still arrive at interpretations that are diametrically opposed to one another. The reason for this is not hard to find. Experience does not come to us all neatly trussed up, packaged and labeled regarding the correct theoretical conclusions to be derived from it. It does not obligingly sort itself out into reliable portions and deceptive portions. Thus, although Domer Ringuette may claim a direct experience of his own freedom in choosing to leave Chicopee and begin a new life, the skeptical psychologist dismisses that experience as deceptive, while Hume, who would test everything against experience, can write of *"a false sensation or experience"* of freedom![8] Experience must be analyzed and interpreted if it is to lend itself to the establishment or proof of theoretical claims—and it does not obligingly provide the terms or methods for its own analysis or interpretation. This is not to say that Hume and Sartre are both wrong, or that one analysis of experience may not be more apt or accurate than another. But it does indicate that we cannot hope to resolve the impasse about freedom by a simple appeal to experience. For, in order to choose between the two methods, empiricist and phenomenological, and their opposing sets of claims about freedom, we would have to become embroiled in yet another dispute about how experience is to be analyzed and interpreted. Clearly, *that* dispute cannot be resolved on experiential grounds, since it has to do with how experience is to be approached.

A few observations concerning Sartre's view will serve to illustrate these difficulties and will point to other problems that are implicit in any attempt to base a theory of freedom upon an appeal to experience. Sartre's discussion of freedom contains some extremely interesting and provocative analyses of experience. Sartre's analyses depend heavily upon his conceptions of consciousness (or "being-for-itself") and of being as it is apart from consciousness (or "being-in-itself"). His theory of human freedom is closely tied to these two concepts and to that of "nothingness." Yet no Humean empiricist would be likely to recognize any of these terms as empirically valid, and Sartre himself admits that neither consciousness nor being-in-itself is ever itself an item in experience. Sartre arrives at these key concepts,

---

8. *Treatise*, 408. This passage reappears almost verbatim as footnote 7 to section 8 of Hume's *Inquiry Concerning Human Understanding*. But in that case he qualifies the experience in question as only a "seeming" experience. In the passage that follows in both texts, he argues that the question of liberty and necessity has to do with inference rather than experience and is therefore not to be resolved by appealing to the authority of the agent's experience.

which are pivotal to his entire analysis, through deductive transcendental arguments. That is, he argues that consciousness and being-in-itself are necessary conditions of the very possibility of our experience. In order to assess the validity of Sartre's theory of freedom, then, we would have to weigh the validity of the conceptions that are central to his interpretation of experience against the transcendental arguments and key concepts of other phenomenologists and empiricists.

Moreover, the phenomenological method itself involves a danger for any theory that is founded upon it. Again, the example of Sartre may help to illustrate the danger in question. According to Sartre, there can be no consciousness without self-consciousness. He does not mean by this that we are always either embarrassedly or reflectively conscious of our own states of mind or thought processes, but only that every consciousness, however absorbed with objects in the world, also includes a *pre*reflective form of self-consciousness. But Sartre also argues that this form of self-consciousness entails freedom. Are we to understand, then, that animals are both self-conscious and free? Or are we to go to the opposite extreme and deny that animals are conscious? Even if we assume that Sartre's transcendental arguments are legitimate and establish that experience presupposes consciousness as he understands the term, it is hard to see how an appeal to human experience could settle the important issue about the freedom or consciousness of animals, which Sartre's view nevertheless raises. The problem points to a more general danger that is inherent in the phenomenological method, a method founded upon the phenomenologist's reflective examination of his own, human experience. The danger is that freedom may be understood in terms that *apply* only to human freedom, much as Sartre has defined consciousness in general in a way that may only apply to human consciousness. Once freedom is so defined, it becomes impossible to acknowledge freedom elsewhere in nature, since traits that may be specific to human freedom will have been taken to be definitive of freedom in general, so that any nonhuman variety of freedom is ruled out in advance by a definition derived from reflection only upon human experience.[9] Even if we assume that Sartre has shown that to be self-

---

9. A still more extreme form of this danger afflicts the extensive philosophical literature that narrows the field even further by conceiving the problem of freedom entirely in terms of disputes about the conditions of *moral responsibility*, thereby limiting the scope of inquiry to a mere subset of human activity. See, for example, Susan Wolf's *Freedom Within Reason* (New York: Oxford University Press, 1990) or the collection of essays in *Moral Responsibility*, ed. John Martin Fisher (Ithaca: Cornell University Press, 1986). But Harry Frankfurt, one of the chief contributors to that discussion, in the preface to *The Importance of What We Care About* (Cambridge: Cambridge University Press, 1988), rightly warns against identifying the two questions: "So far as freedom is concerned, it is of course true that freedom is commonly

conscious is to be free, he has not thereby shown that to be free is to be
self-conscious, or even that freedom necessarily presupposes consciousness.
I have already noted how the problem of Domer Ringuette's freedom can
become entangled with the question whether a rat would be free in parallel
circumstances. There are philosophers who hold that to be actual is to be
free in some degree,[10] so that freedom is not confined to human beings,
but can be found throughout nature. On the other hand, one of the chief
objections that determinists raise against human freedom of choice is that
it sets man apart from the rest of nature, which they believe to be ruled by
causal necessity. Insofar as the phenomenological method prejudices these
issues by focusing too narrowly on human experience and human freedom,
it may not provide the basis for a complete philosophy of freedom.

Thus, we see that the appeal to experience cannot of itself solve our
problem. The shortcomings of the appeal to experience complement one
another. On the one hand, experience has to be interpreted and analyzed,
and the *manner* of interpreting it depends upon the methods and conceptions with which it is approached. On the other hand, such an appeal runs
the risk of leading to a conception of freedom that is too narrow and biased.
In both cases, the problem is that of relating concept and percept, theory
and experience. There seems to be nothing about the return to experience
as such that guarantees that it will not lead to the kind of contradictory
theories reached by Hume and Sartre, by empiricists and phenomenologists respectively.

The Appeal to Science

But surely, science has achieved stunning success in overcoming these
problems of a simple appeal to experience by developing a rigorous
method for relating theory and experience. The scientist does not pretend
to approach experience without theoretical preconceptions. Instead, the

---

understood to be a necessary condition of moral responsibility. Moreover, the nature of
freedom is often investigated, as in several efforts of my own, in the light of that particular
connection. On the other hand, I do not think that it is mainly for the sake of moral
responsibility that we care as much as we do about being free. Nor am I convinced that it is
possible to illuminate what it means for us to be free only if we begin by construing freedom
specifically as a condition of being morally responsible" (viii).

The dispute about freedom and determinism certainly entails difficult questions about
moral responsibility, as Kant so vigorously argued. But anyone who identifies freedom with
moral responsibility will almost certainly be led, like Kant, to a rather controversial conception
of freedom that leaves no room for subhuman freedom or for irresponsible decisions that are
free.

10. E.g., Alfred North Whitehead and Paul Weiss.

scientist goes to experience with a precisely formulated theoretical hypothesis already in hand and subjects that hypothesis to the test of experience through carefully controlled experimental techniques. As a result, science has been able to reach authoritative and unequivocal conclusions that command common consent. It therefore provides exactly the resource we need in order to resolve the endless controversy over freedom and determinism.

Moreover, it seems quite obvious that science has already resolved this issue in favor of determinism. For it is just among scientists, social scientists, and scientifically oriented philosophers that one finds the deterministic view of man and nature most consistently and vigorously maintained. Contemporary determinists typically appeal to the authority of science in support of their stand and are likely to maintain that their rejection of freedom of choice is a necessary corollary of a scientific view of man and nature. Does science, then, decisively settle the long and tedious dispute over freedom of choice and relieve us of the burden of further inquiry by declaring that the theory of free choice is scientifically untenable?

Unfortunately, science provides no such convenient rescue. For, despite the number of scientists who advocate determinism, this is not one of those questions upon which scientists are universally agreed. It *may* be that the majority of scientists side with determinism, but the agreement is not unanimous. There are notable exceptions. The extreme counterexample is Alfred North Whitehead, the English mathematical physicist-turned-philosopher, who not only reserves a place in the universe for human freedom, but argues that there is a moment of free decision ingredient in every natural event. Modern developments in physics, such as Heisenberg's principle of indeterminacy and the substitution of probabilistic laws for the deductive necessities of classical Newtonian mechanics, have led many physicists and philosophers to serious doubts about the notion that science unambiguously entails determinism. The determinist sees these features of contemporary physics as merely due to defects or limitations in our *knowledge*, but insists that events themselves are strictly determined. But scientists differ over this very question. Indeed, according to Capek, "Contemporary physicists generally do not share this deterministic view. With a few exceptions, to which, paradoxically enough, both Einstein and Planck belonged, physicists today reject the assumption of the hidden strictly determined processes that would underlie the apparent contingency of the observed phenomena. In their view, the observed statistical laws are regarded as ultimate and irreducible features constituting the objective physical reality."[11]

11. M. Capek, *The Philosophical Impact of Contemporary Physics* (Princeton: Princeton Univer-

How is this lack of accord within the scientific community possible? Cannot science resolve this issue simply by treating freedom and determinism as alternative hypotheses and subjecting both to the test of experimental verification? The answer is somewhat surprising. The trouble is that neither of these "hypotheses" has ever been developed with sufficient clarity and articulation to make it scientifically testable. Major scientific hypotheses are almost never amenable to *direct* and *conclusive* experimental tests. In order to verify a scientific hypothesis, it is necessary first to work out its implications or deductive consequences in some detail. The original hypothesis is then tested by seeking to obtain experimental or empirical verification of these deductive implications. The standard example of this process is the verification of Einstein's general theory of relativity. The central theses of this theory cannot be directly tested. But some of the implications of the theory *can* be tested through such phenomena as tiny shifts in the orbit of the planet Mercury or the bending of light rays as they pass near the sun. No single test of this sort can conclusively prove that Einstein's theory is true. Consequently, the process of verification is still going on over half a century after the theory was first formulated, and no one can be sure that the theory will not finally be superseded, like Newton's theory before it.

Now, surprisingly enough, although scientific thinkers have advocated determinism for centuries, the deterministic hypothesis has never been subjected to this sort of disciplined scientific test. Indeed, as Isaiah Berlin has wryly suggested, the nature and implications of the deterministic theory have never been articulated with adequate clarity and detail to allow for such a process of verification. Berlin goes so far as to suggest that such a thoroughly thought-out determinism is well nigh impossible:

> My submission is that to make a serious attempt to adapt our thoughts and words to the hypothesis of determinism is an appalling task, as things are now, and have been within recorded history. The changes involved are too radical; our moral categories are, in the end, more flexible than our physical ones, but not much more so; it is not much easier to begin to think out in real terms, to which behavior and speech would correspond, what the universe of the genuine determinist would be like, than to think out, with the

---

sity Press, 1961), 297. See Ian Hacking, *The Taming of Chance* (Cambridge: Cambridge University Press, 1990), for a rich and fascinating account of how science arrived at this point of view. Hacking describes how the evolution of social statistics during the nineteenth century accomplished an "erosion of determinism" that opened the way for the scientific acceptance of irreducibly statistical "laws" in place of the deterministic conception of causation.

minimum of indispensable concrete detail (i.e., begin to imagine) what it would be like to be in a timeless world, or one with a seventeen-dimensional space.[12]

Whether or not Berlin is correct, it is true that the scientific verification of the deterministic hypothesis would be a prodigious undertaking. First of all, it would be necessary to develop the full implications of the hypothesis in detail. Second, it would be necessary to supply scientific laws that would make it possible to predict all of human behavior with considerable precision, since the deterministic hypothesis proposes that all of human behavior is inexorably governed by such laws. Moreover, these laws would have to be of the deductively necessary type that was characteristic of classical Newtonian mechanics rather than the statistical, probabilistic laws actually supplied by modern quantum mechanics, psychology, and social science. Statistical laws do not provide any basis for the verification of the deterministic hypothesis, since they only entail that a certain event is probable, not that it is necessary or that no alternative could possibly occur. But this necessity of the event is precisely what determinism asserts. The champion of free choice need find no difficulty in admitting that if we know enough about a person, we could predict with considerable reliability how

12. Berlin, Isaiah, *Historical Inevitability* (London: Oxford University Press, 1954), 34. Cf. Ernst Nagel's criticisms of Berlin's argument in "Determinism in History," *Philosophy and Phenomenological Research* 20, no. 3 (1960): 291–317. But Nagel only defends determinism as a methodological principle. On the other hand, Norman Malcolm carries Berlin's point even further in attacking mechanism ("The Conceivability of Mechanism," *Philosophical Review* 77, no. 1 [1968]: 45–72; reprinted in *Free Will*, ed. Gary Watson [Oxford, Oxford University Press, 1982], 127–49). After remarking that "[s]ome philosophers hold that if mechanism is true then a radical revision of our concepts is required," Malcolm adds: "I think these philosophers have not grasped the full severity of the predicament. If mechanism is true, not only should we give up speaking of 'asserting,' but also of 'describing' or even of 'speaking.' It would not even be right to say that a person 'meant' something by the noise that came from him. No marks or sounds would mean anything. There could not be *language*" (in Watson, 148, sec. 26). He concludes that mechanism "presents a harsh, and perhaps insoluble antinomy to human thought" (in Watson, 149). Malcolm may have overstated his case, however. For critics who argue that he has, see Alvin Goldman, "The Compatibility of Mechanism and Purpose," *Philosophical Review* 78 (1969): 468–82, and Daniel Dennett, "Mechanism and Responsibility," in Brainstorms (Cambridge, Mass.: MIT Press, Bradford Books, 1978).

Meanwhile, similar objections might also be raised about freedom, as we shall see below. Indeed, Ted Honderich, who has taken exceptional trouble to think through the full implications of determinism, complains that the alternative notion of freedom of will "has often been assumed and talked about, but hardly ever been set out explicitly. Perhaps it has never been set out by anyone who is really alive to its problems" (*How Free Are You?* [Oxford: Oxford University Press, 1993], 35). Honderich presents a fuller account of his version of determinism in *A Theory of Determinism* (Oxford: Oxford University Press, 1988).

he would choose in certain circumstances—while we could still reject the claim that he could not possibly choose otherwise.[13]

These prerequisites for a scientific verification of the hypothesis of determinism have never been met and *cannot* be met without great advances in the sciences of human behavior. But if the deterministic theory has never been scientifically verified, how does it happen that so many scientists have advocated the theory over such a long period of history? I have already touched upon the answer to this problem in my initial sketch of the deterministic view of man.[14] The scientific determinist may well argue that it is unnecessary to await the discovery of particular laws of human behavior or to seek empirical confirmation of the deterministic theory, because the very nature of rational, scientific knowledge and explanation obliges us to accept the truth of determinism. To admit that free choices occur would be to suppose that events occur that are uncaused, inexplicable. To accept the doctrine of freedom of choice would be to embrace irrationalism, since it involves accepting the notion that something can happen for which there is no adequate reason. In short, the real basis of the scientist's determinism is not to be found in an accumulation of scientific evidence, but in what Leibniz called "the principle of sufficient reason": that nothing happens without a reason why it should be so rather than otherwise. This is a fundamental principle of all rational thought and explanation. But it is an *axiom* that makes scientific inquiry *possible* rather than a *result* of scientific inquiry. The scientific determinist gives this methodological principle a more specific and substantive meaning by understanding "sufficient reason" to mean "adequate cause," and it is therefore that he insists that every *choice*, like every other event, must follow necessarily from its causes.

This root of scientific determinism explains why scientists have so often embraced determinism without demanding empirical proof of its truth. And, indeed, even the empiricist Hume closes out his initial case against freedom with this nonempirical argument: "According to my definitions, necessity makes an essential part of causation; and consequently liberty, by removing necessity, removes also causes, and is the very same thing with chance. As chance is commonly thought to imply a contradiction, and is at

13. Strictly speaking, then, Hume is not a determinist after all, or not a consistent one. According to his theory of causation, causal connections are never necessary, only probabilistic. Accordingly, we are never in a position to say, on Hume's view, that an individual chose as he did necessarily or that he could not possibly have chosen otherwise. The most we can say is that another choice was improbable or unlikely.

14. Cf. pages 1–2 above.

least directly contrary to experience, there are always the same arguments against liberty or free will."[15]

Certainly, if determinism is based upon the principle of sufficient reason rather than upon empirical evidence or experimental scientific inquiry, then it is easy to understand why the deterministic view of man antedates modern science and why modern, scientific determinism is so similar to earlier, theological formulations of the doctrine. Since determinism has its roots in a fundamental axiom of rational thought and explanation, it is not surprising that the theory is older than science and that the formal features of the arguments for the theory change very little in the course of history, so that, as Hume put it, "there are always the same arguments against liberty or free will." What does change, what distinguishes a theological determinism from a scientific version of the doctrine, for example, is the more specific way in which each defines what counts as a sufficient reason.

The passage from Hume also aptly illustrates the specific conception of freedom to which this line of thinking leads and helps to explain why the scientist is so apt to reject freedom as irrational and scientifically untenable. What the determinist means by freedom, typically, is what Hume calls "chance" and what is usually called "indeterminism": the notion that choices occur *without* sufficient causes or reasons. He embraces determinism because accepting freedom would seem to imply admitting that choices somehow pop into being out of nowhere by sheer chance, inexplicably, unintelligibly. And the scientist is methodologically debarred from entertaining this hypothesis.

But is this what freedom means? It is difficult to find a champion of freedom who will accept such a conception of it. The theory that freedom means "indeterminism" almost seems to be an invention of its determinist opponents. One suspects that the very few advocates of free choice who *do* accept the notion of indeterminism, such as William James, have been persuaded by their opponents that this is the necessary price of defending freedom. But others simply do not agree that their advocacy of free choice commits them to indeterminism and irrationalism. The result is that, as already noted, the two sides of the controversy seem not to be talking about the same thing when they argue about freedom.

The Appeal to Language

Many a long and fruitless argument has been brought to a happy conclusion by the discovery that the source of the disagreement was some

---

15. *Treatise*, 407.

misunderstanding about the meanings of words. One whole school of modern philosophy is founded upon an attempt to extend the recognition involved in this discovery into a systematic method for resolving philosophical problems and disputes. They argue that all substantive or factual issues should be turned over to science to be settled by empirical experiment. Once that is done, there will remain a number of persistent issues and controversies that have long perplexed philosophers and even scientists but that are not amenable to scientific solutions. But these are not factual issues, since otherwise science *could* settle them; they must therefore be semantic or linguistic in origin. The way to settle them, then, is through a careful analysis and clarification of language—either the language of ordinary speech or, in some cases, the specialized, technical vocabulary of science.

We have just found reasons to believe that the problem of whether there is any such thing as freedom of choice may arise out of just such a misunderstanding or disagreement about the meanings of the terms that are in dispute. Can this issue and the whole sterile controversy about freedom and determinism be resolved through an analysis of the meaning of ordinary language? Is the whole problem soluble simply by getting clear about what we mean by the word "freedom"? Let us see where this strategy leads and whether it promises to succeed where the appeals to experience and science have failed.

If the appeal to science seemed at first to prejudice this issue in favor of determinism, it would appear that an appeal to ordinary language must prejudice the issue in favor of freedom. Domer Ringuette certainly *thinks* and speaks as though he freely chose to leave Chicopee, and ordinary people often do speak in this way. The authority of ordinary usage of language might thus seem to support the doctrine that human actions may arise from free choices. But this really does nothing to resolve the dispute. For the fact that people commonly describe their actions as freely chosen in no way proves that they are *right*, that their choices *are* free rather than determined. Our skeptical psychologist was scarcely ready to concede that Domer was *actually* free simply because he *used that word* to describe himself. Nor is this a case of a difference between the meaning of a word in ordinary usage and a technical, scientific use of the same term. In fact, there is a clear-cut technical, scientific meaning of "freedom" as the term is used in physics, but that is certainly not the sort of freedom that the scientist rejects in embracing determinism. Rather, it is freedom as Domer Ringuette uses the word, as it appears in ordinary speech, which the determinist rejects and over which there is confusion and disagreement between determinists and "libertarians," or advocates of free choice.

Some clarification of the meaning of "freedom" is certainly called for, and that task of clarification begins by examining what the word "freedom" means in ordinary, everyday talk. But it is only fair to warn that it would be extremely optimistic to hope that this appeal to ordinary language will lead to a ready resolution of the dispute over the existence of free choice. One of the main lessons of recent linguistic philosophy is that it would be foolish to expect that an analysis of ordinary English usage will lead us to any single, univocal definition of "freedom." Ordinary language, by using one word to convey a variety of meanings, purchases an economy of words at the price of a sacrifice in scientific precision. These several meanings of a single word may be quite varied and, even at best, may bear only a "family resemblance" to one another. There is little reason to expect that "freedom" will turn out to be an exception. It is likely to prove to be as ambiguous as any other ordinary word, generously lending itself to a variety of interpretations. We must not expect, then, that a mere appeal to ordinary language will allow us to pin down the meaning of freedom in a way that will *settle* the dispute at hand.[16] And indeed, linguistic philosophers are no more in agreement on this issue than are those who appeal to experience or to science.

This brief review of the strategies usually employed for resolving stubborn theoretical disputes has not been encouraging. Because these strategies have not provided any ready solution in this case, the dispute over whether

16. Indeed, it is on just these grounds that Richard Double concludes that there is no such thing as freedom of will (*The Non-Reality of Free Will* [Oxford: Oxford University Press, 1991]). Double surveys a variety of linguistic intuitions and paradigms of "free action" and finds the diversity of meanings at work so great as to render philosophical disputes about the reality of freedom undecidable. Hence, he concludes, "The best strategy I can see is to admit that there are at least this many partially adequate notions of freedom and indeed as many as we find useful to distinguish. But since there is no single overriding sense of 'freedom' to be found, i.e., there can be nothing about non-linguistic reality that constrains our efforts to taxonomize freedom in one of the various ways rather than the others, the central theme of this book has been established. There can be no such thing as free will" (223).

In Chapter 1, I make my own survey of the meanings of "freedom" and find that, if anything, Double may *under*estimate the diversity of intuitions or conceptions to be found here (since he confines the field to *rational* choices). Yet Double may be too quick to despair of the reality of freedom, too readily dismayed by the sheer diversity of the phenomena. He admits, with some embarrassment, that his taxonomy of paradigms of freedom is "armchair speculation," that he hasn't seriously surveyed the history of philosophy to see if his paradigms are representative (115). Fortunately, a taxonomy based upon such a broad survey is available in Mortimer Adler's *Idea of Freedom,* and it reveals more conceptual order than Double discerns, as we will see in Chapter 2. In the sequel, I try to show how reflection upon that order opens the way to a coherent theory of the reality of freedom. See also Christine Swanton's *Freedom: A Coherence Theory* (Indianapolis: Hackett, 1992) for another, rather different way of finding coherence among these diverse meanings.

man is free may now appear to be at an even more stubborn impasse. Of course, this dispute would probably long since have been settled if a mere appeal to experience or science or linguistic clarification *were* all that was needed to resolve it. Instead, though advocates of *both* sides of the dispute have appealed to all of the resources of experience, science, and linguistic analysis in support of their positions, no resolution has come forth, and there are methodological reasons to doubt that any of these strategies can in the future lead to a resolution. Still, consulting these resources has not yielded entirely negative results. For the failure of each of these appeals suggests something about the requirements of a more fruitful inquiry. The appeal to experience, alone, cannot provide either the conceptual framework or the methods for interpreting experience and relating its contents to the theoretical issues involved in the dispute between freedom and determinism. Science does supply a rigorous methodology for relating theoretical hypotheses and experience. But science has never really resolved this issue, because it has never developed the competing hypotheses with sufficient clarity and detail to submit them to its own methods of verification. What stymies *both* of these appeals, then, is a lack of conceptual clarity about the nature of freedom.[17] In effect, if experience and science are to be helpful to us, then we must consult them with a clearly developed conception of freedom already in hand. In order to clarify our understanding of freedom, it is certainly necessary to examine the meaning of the word in ordinary speech. But ordinary language alone hasn't the authority to settle the factual issue of whether free choices exist. Ordinary people may *say* so, but they may be mistaken. Nor can analysis of ordinary language alone be expected to yield a clear and unequivocal theory or definition of freedom. It can only be expected to *expose* the ambiguities and confusions in our everyday understanding of freedom, not to *dispel* them. If we are to achieve an unambiguous conception of freedom, then, we must find some way to go beyond the vagaries of everyday speech.

---

17. Cf. David Wiggins, "Towards a Reasonable Libertarianism," in *Essays on Freedom of Action,* ed. Ted Honderich (London: Routledge & Kegan Paul, 1973): "One of the many reasons I believe why philosophy falls short of a satisfying solution to the problem of freedom is that we still cannot refer to an unflawed statement of libertarianism. Perhaps libertarianism is in the last analysis untenable. But if we are to salvage its insights we need to know what is the least unreasonable statement the position can be given" (33).

Summary and Prospect

Right or left at Oak Street? A simple choice between clearly opposed alternatives. But did Domer Ringuette have a genuine choice? Or was his action necessitated by prior events, so that it was actually impossible for him to stay and open his store that morning—as it presumably had been impossible on other mornings to turn left and leave Chicopee behind? That problem, too, seems to present two simple, clearly opposed alternatives: either he acted freely, or his act was determined by antecedent causes. But the controversy about freedom or determinism that this alternative poses has led to a dead end. Still, exploration of this blind alley has at least revealed the reasons for the impasse. Stated very simply, it has shown us that the two alternative positions are not so clear as they at first appeared and that it is impossible to settle the issue of whether freedom exists without first achieving clarity about the nature or meaning of "freedom." This sets the direction for further inquiry. But it also presents serious problems. For it demands an understanding of *what* freedom is prior to a determination of whether it exists at all. It requires that we develop a sufficiently clear and detailed conception of the nature and implications of freedom so as to furnish a basis for settling the question of fact. But the problem is to find a way to do this that will not already assume the answers to those questions of fact: Is man free? If so, does this distinguish the human species from the rest of nature? Or is freedom to be found elsewhere in nature as well, at least in the higher animals and perhaps even entering into every event that occurs? If we are to avoid begging these questions, then we must develop a notion of freedom that is not so singularly oriented to the human condition as to lead us to frame too narrow a conception of freedom, one that would prejudice the issues raised by those who argue that freedom is not peculiar to human beings.

But how are we to investigate the meaning or nature of freedom *without* begging these questions? Must the search for conceptual clarity be cut off entirely from the resources of human experience and from the science and philosophy of nature? Must we entirely forgo empirical examples and illustrations, to be left entirely dependent upon the analysis of ordinary language? If so, how is inquiry ever to get beyond cataloguing the ambiguities in the ordinary usage of the word "freedom" except through sheer stipulation or purely speculative conceptual fabrications?

Fortunately, we can sidestep these difficulties simply by proceeding *hypothetically*. When a scientist sets out to develop a theoretical hypothesis, he need not presuppose that he will find empirical evidence to validate it. He may *postulate* the existence of entities or relationships without committing himself to a belief in their *actual* existence. When Sherlock Holmes or Perry Mason, in setting out to solve the mystery of the sudden disappearance of a wealthy young heiress, says, "Let us assume that she was murdered," he is not begging the question whether a murder has been committed. He postulates the existence of a murderer, but does not thereby rule out the possibilities of suicide, accidental death, elopement, and amnesia. In the course of developing such hypotheses, neither scientists nor detectives need to forswear all reference to the evidence to which the theory is intended to pertain. They may enrich and direct their hypothetical reflections by constant references to pertinent experience, facts, or scientific data without prejudicing the hypothetical status of those reflections.

I employ just such a strategy in the inquiry that follows. Without presupposing that human beings *are* free, or that humans *alone* are free, or even that freedom *exists* at all, we can attempt to develop a clear account of the nature of freedom, an account that makes it possible to determine whether there *are* any free beings, whether human beings or any other beings satisfy that description of the nature and conditions of freedom. On the other hand, we need not abstain from all reflection upon the human condition or human experience or nature. For we can assume, hypothetically, that human beings *may* be free, that freedom *may* also be found elsewhere in nature, etc. This hypothetical inquiry must lead to a clearly developed and articulated conception of freedom if it is to be of any use. That is, the conditions, meaning, and implications of freedom must be worked out sufficiently to make the hypothesis that man is free testable against human experience. For, as we have seen, the perpetuation of the controversy over freedom and determinism is largely due to the lack of such clearly articulated conceptions of the competing hypotheses.

This description might suggest that the discussion should proceed deductively, like the development of a scientific proof. But, in fact, the inquiry develops through a series of definitions or conceptions of freedom, each of which proves to be untenable or inadequate and thereby leads to a further stage in an effort to reach an intelligible and adequate conception of freedom. In the course of the inquiry we will come to see that this format is not simply a method of argument or a rhetorically convenient way of organizing the materials, but is demanded by the subject matter and reflects the very nature of freedom itself.

Part I

The
Meanings
of Freedom

"Freedom's just another word for nothin' left to lose"
—Kris Kristofferson, "Me and Bobby McGee"

Is freedom *just* another word? Can it mean whatever we choose? Is that why there are so many competing versions of what it means to be free? At first, the word seems heavy with import. But perhaps that is because it has become freighted with so many different meanings, which it has accumulated in the course of a long history. Is the word so well used that it is beyond abuse, and hence at the brink of becoming meaningless? Or do all these meanings seek to capture a single idea—or spring from some original kernel of meaning so fertile that it has disseminated itself in such a motley and quarrelsome progeny?

We have to contend with this confusing crowd of meanings before we can even begin to rethink the question whether we are free, or whether freedom is a worthy ideal or an empty illusion. Otherwise, we will only lose our way among as many competing answers as there are meanings of freedom. The first two chapters plunge into the midst of this melee of meanings in search of some order. Chapter 1, "Doing As I Please," begins with the ordinary, commonsense understanding of freedom as "the ability to do what I want" and shows how other, competing conceptions of freedom arise out of reflection upon what that ability may imply or presuppose. Chapter 2, "Freedom and Constraint," analyzes the resultant variety of meanings and examines the differences between them in search of family resemblances among them. In the process, it leads beyond mere ordinary usage of words to reflection upon human desires and actions, which in turn reveals the motives for the different usages of "freedom" in light of the contrast between freedom and constraint.

✤ 1 ✤

Doing As I Please

Certainly, then, ordinary language is *not* the last word. In principle it can everywhere be supplemented and improved upon and superseded. Only remember, it *is* the *first* word.

—J. L. Austin, "A Plea for Excuses,"

The Ordinary Understanding of Freedom

On the eve of the battle of Shrewsbury, Shakespeare's Falstaff pauses to remind himself that he is being pricked into battle only by honor and that honor is only a word, "a mere scutcheon." A sensible reminder! So speaks the common sense of the ordinary Englishman—and English philosophy has drawn upon that good sense ever since William of Ockham, reminding itself time and again that, like Falstaff, we are often pricked into controversy by mere words. Recent English philosophy echoes Falstaff's reminder and would urge us to consider that "freedom," like "honor," is only a word, a word whose meaning is not to be snatched out of a heaven of pure ideas or grasped by the light of pure reason, but must be sought in the actual use of the word in everyday talk. The point is well taken. We must surely begin with the words we have in stock and with the meanings that we ordinarily attach to them. Philosophical inquiry into the nature of freedom must begin from general linguistic usage and ordinary understanding if it is not to lose itself in a recondite and apparently perverse technical language that is completely estranged from everyday speech.

What is the ordinary meaning of the word "freedom"? The word itself is common currency, the coin of politicians and journalists, revolutionaries and diplomats, adolescents and educators alike. Certainly, like coin much circulated, any word so widely used is bound to be worn somewhat thin and smooth in the course of exchange. Yet it seems equally certain that a term so widely employed must have some fairly simple, ordinary meaning or set of meanings that is equally widely recognized. Surely, ordinary people must know what they mean by the word "freedom," even though the average person probably can't produce an elegant definition upon demand.

Unfortunately, agreement about what it means to be free is far less common than the use of the word. I have already remarked upon how sharply people disagree about freedom, how often the term is involved in social and political controversies. They argue about whether each new law or government will enlarge or restrict their freedom. They risk their lives in wars and revolutions that are fought to "defend their freedoms." In legislatures and courtrooms, and in cafes, bars, and dormitories, they debate about which laws, methods of education, or other institutions will best promote, preserve, and protect freedom. Can there really be any common agreement about the meaning of a term that is so controversial?

Actually, these very disputes over how freedom can best be secured, over what fosters freedom and what threatens it, point to some minimal underlying accord about the meaning of the word. Evidently, the ordinary, everyday understanding of freedom regards it as something that can be protected or threatened, gained or lost. Disagreement about the best means of promoting, preserving, or defending freedom proves that there is agreement about the need for *some* such means. Indeed, the average person can probably describe the kinds of things that prevent and threaten freedom more readily than he can specify how to acquire it. The loss or curtailment of freedom may result from any kind of oppression, restriction, inhibition, hindrance, repression, constraint, or compulsion. And, in ordinary talk, freedom is often defined simply by contrast or opposition to these various sorts of limitations. To be free, we say, is to be *un*hampered, *un*constrained, *un*inhibited, *in*dependent. Or we call forth a more vivid image by contrasting freedom with slavery and imprisonment, which we regard as the most obvious examples of constraint and loss of freedom.

But the everyday understanding of freedom is not just the product of negation. Rather, the positive meaning of the word seems so *self-evident*, so immediately obvious, that ordinary discourse passes over it at once to dwell on what endangers or opposes freedom. Our negative definitions derive from our tendency to be preoccupied with what threatens and limits freedom. Negative definitions reflect the boundaries or exterior limits of freedom rather than its inner nature. Yet this ready store of contrary terms bears tacit witness to a more positive grasp of what it is that *is* limited or confined within these boundaries. Our language thereby betrays the fact that we all "know" what freedom is.

What we gain in the absence of opposition, what is enjoyed in the absence of these limitations and hindrances, is simply *the ability to do what we want*. It is this ability that distinguishes the free man from the slave or prisoner and that can be hampered, restricted, inhibited, and constrained in various ways. Clearly, too, it is this ability that is at issue and that serves as the common center of reference in all our talk of more specific forms of freedom. "Freedom of the press," for example, and "academic freedom" have to do with an individual's ability to publish or teach as he or she wants or sees fit, unhampered by public censorship and control.

This ordinary understanding of freedom seems perfectly simple and straightforward: To be free is to be able to do what I want to do. I believe that this is the meaning that informs most everyday discourse on the subject of freedom.[1] Most people take this understanding of freedom so much for granted that they are surprised and baffled when they first encounter moral and religious doctrines that define freedom in terms of the *limitation* or *control* of immediate wants and desires. Such definitions can only seem perverse to the person who assumes that freedom consists in the realization or satisfaction of those very desires. The ability to "do what I want" or "say what I think" or "go where I please" means the ability to fulfill the wants, desires, intentions, or thoughts that I actually feel or have *now*. What I *did* want before lunch, or yesterday, or last week, or what I *may* want tomorrow has no bearing on my present freedom except insofar as old plans or anticipated desires enter into or influence my *actual, present* intentions. More important, freedom as it is ordinarily understood has nothing to do with what I *might* want or intend "if only I knew better" or were less neurotic or "would just listen to reason." "The ability to do what I want" does not mean the abilities or wants I would have "if things were different" or "if I were different." And what is at stake is certainly *not* the desires or intentions that I *should* feel or *ought* to entertain. No one imagines that the so-called

---

1. This is only an opinion, of course. In general, the imputation of meanings to the general public or to the common man by philosophers should be regarded with suspicion. The present imputations are no exception. It is one thing to try to make contact with ordinary discourse and quite another to cite one's own opinion of its meaning as an authority. At any rate, *I* ordinarily and unreflectively understand "freedom" in this way and accept responsibility for this definition.

"free world" is a world in which everyone desires or does what he *ought*. It is only a world in which individuals enjoy relatively more freedom to do as they *please*. If freedom is "the ability to do what I want," then this "what I want" means what *I do in fact want here and now,* not what I *might* or *should* or *would* want.

Consequently, from the standpoint of this ordinary understanding of the meaning of freedom, those moralistic and religious and psychiatric doctrines that identify freedom with rational or ethical volition or make it depend upon faith or grace or completion of psychoanalysis all appear to be outright perversions of the meaning of freedom. Any suggestion that freedom is to be attained only through the *restraint* or *renunciation* of immediately felt personal desires seems to ignore and even to contradict what is meant by freedom in ordinary talk. For freedom, after all, is *the ability to do what I want,* and this means the realization or fulfillment of the desires, wants, and intentions that are *currently* and *immediately* felt. Ethical and religious requirements may have their legitimate place in life, but insofar as they require the inhibition and limitation of my ability to fulfill my actually felt, present wants and needs, moral standards represent restrictions *opposed* to freedom rather than conditions of *acquiring* it.

Evidently, freedom as it is ordinarily and immediately understood is—as might well have been expected—the freedom of immediacy. For the ability to do what I want means the ability to realize my desires and intentions here and now, at this immediate moment. That doesn't necessarily mean that freedom is confined to *pure* immediacy, to the realization of wants, impulses, or drives in the complete absence of any and all reflection. Moral or religious motives may well have influenced the wants and plans I entertain. Indeed, any amount of reflection *may* have entered into the formation of my intentions. Experience and a little thinking may even have taught me that the man with more moderate desires enjoys greater freedom in the end because his desires are more readily realized. None of this matters to the ordinary sense of freedom so long as the desires and intentions in question are the ones that *I actually feel* at the immediate moment when I try to realize them. Freedom depends solely upon whether I am able to realize my desires, whatever they may be.

We should be reluctant to deviate from this everyday interpretation of freedom, just because it *is* so popular and such a simple and direct definition. Why tamper with such a clear and straightforward view? Reflection should not create problems where none already exist. Unfortunately, this ordinary understanding of freedom creates problems of its own, and as the sequel will show, its attempts to resolve these lead toward that very inverted view of freedom that the ordinary understanding originally finds so perplexing.

The Limits of Freedom

Philosophers usually cite necessity and determinism as the very opposites of freedom. But the primary alternative to the form of freedom described above is not fatality, but *frustration*. We cannot do everything we want to do. Our hopes and plans are frequently thwarted, and we find ourselves engaged in some disagreeable course of action instead, and are therefore doubly frustrated. For the prisoner and the slave, this frustration may amount to a permanent condition, and that is why they represent the archetypal examples of unfreedom. Whatever mitigating pleasures and satisfactions they may retain are achieved against the background of a general curtailment of their ability to do as they please.

But slavery and imprisonment only represent the most striking and generalized instances of the curtailment of that ability. "Iron bars do not a prison make," and at a particular moment, my desires and plans may be frustrated as effectively by a coy mistress, an empty bottle, or a traffic jam as by prison bars. The ability to do what I want depends both upon what I happen to want and upon the circumstances in which I have to act. Fancy is always free because fancy sets its own stage and arranges for everything to cooperate in the attainment of the object, the success of the action. But the process of *realizing* our fancies is subject to the limitations of a less amiable and cooperative reality. The ability to do what I want is bound up with what the circumstances will *allow,* so that immediate freedom is a function of immediate circumstance.

Circumstance, then, is the source of frustration. Stubborn circumstances impose those restrictions, obstacles, and constraints that limit or even preclude my ability to do what I want. Now, if circumstances really oppose me, they must be external to me. As that which "stands around" me, the circumstantial seems readily definable as the *external.* But this apparent ease of definition is spurious. For the concrete meaning of this definition depends upon where we draw the line between internal and external. Insofar as freedom depends upon circumstance, the precise understanding of the nature of freedom also depends upon this distinction between internal and external. For what is at stake is as much a definition of the desiring and active self as a definition of the circumstances upon whose cooperation the freedom of that self depends. In short, we need a clear demarcation of the border between the *self* and the *not-self.*

There seems to be no immediate difficulty in making this distinction. External circumstance begins where my body leaves off. After all, doing what I want usually involves some overt, bodily action. Further, the body is the locus of the desiring self, with its needs, wants, appetites, and aversions.

There are other, more refined desires too, of course, but none more immediate or insistent than these bodily ones. And it is my *body* that directly contacts my environment and that immediately feels both the pleasures of satisfied desires and the resistance of external opposition. And it is the body of the slave or prisoner that is shackled or confined. All of this surely indicates that the frontier between internal and external lies at the surface of the skin. Thus the problem of locating the border between external and internal appears simple enough to solve.

Yet our wants are not always thwarted by *bodily* constraint, nor are we always coerced to perform unwanted actions by *physical* pressures. The man who surrenders his wallet at gunpoint is constrained only by *fear*, for example. Similarly, the prisoner is a prisoner still when under armed guard, though outside the walls of his prison cell, and the slave unshackled remains a slave when he obeys out of fear of his master. The loss of freedom in a police state is due more to psychological intimidation than direct physical coercion. In more everyday cases, the fears to which a man surrenders may be only financial or social: the loss of a job, the hostility of his community, the contempt of his peers. On the whole, fear and psychological duress seem to be more typical sources of constraint than bodily obstructions and pressures. How can this new wrinkle be ironed out so as to save the demarcation between internal and external?

Perhaps the solution is to treat fear and duress as mere extensions of threatening circumstances that *do* lie outside the body. They might even be described as mere anticipations of bodily coercion or constraint. The man facing a revolver can legitimately claim to be coerced, even if he is never pushed, or even touched, by the man wielding the gun. Very well, but to allow circumstances such an extension is to extend the realm of circumstances and to abandon the skin as the frontier between internal and external. The external, the circumstantial, can now dwell *within* the self's body and psyche. Whether the ordinary view can accommodate this modification remains to be seen.

Meanwhile, difficulties of a different sort suggest further doubts about the location of the body on the inner side of that frontier between the internal and the circumstantial. Even in the absence of duress, fear, or impediments outside the body, my ability to do what I want may be frustrated by some bodily *disability*. A sexually impotent man may nonetheless have sexual desires. But though all other circumstances may cooperate—including the woman he desires—he is nevertheless frustrated by his own bodily incapacity. A still more vivid and touching instance of desire thwarted by physical disability is that of the crippled child who longs to run and play with other children. Everyone is familiar with more ordinary and limited examples of this type of frustration. Combined with the general tendency of our imagination to exceed our physical capacity, these experiences of physical inability suggest the metaphor of the body as the prison or inadequate instrument of the psyche. Since my body often serves me very well, such metaphors are one-sided; but they nonetheless epitomize the difficulties that result from placing the body on the near side of the border between me and not-me. Since my body can be either a prison or a servant, can thwart as well as aid the realization of my wishes and plans, surely it belongs in the realm of external circumstances that may be favorable or unfavorable to the intentions of the inner self.

But if we surrender the body to the realm of circumstance, then the distinction between internal and external would seem to belong at the threshold between the mind, or psyche, and the body. Indeed, it now appears that this is how the distinction should have been specified at the outset. After all, it is really the mind that desires and wants, either with or without the prompting of the body. It is the mind that initiates actions, in which the body may or may not prove cooperative or adequate. If *I* can be constrained through the confinement of my body, this is only because the body acts as a circumstance to constrain the mind. Though the mind may roam at will, I, if my leg is shackled, am not free to go where I please. On the other hand, some forms of mental activity are not hampered by such bodily restraints. Though my leg be shackled, my mind is free to roam, and the deepest dungeon cannot confine memory or hope within its walls. The psyche, then, would seem to be the locus of the self, and everything outside it belongs to circumstance. Maybe, then, this is what the ordinary view of freedom meant all along.

Yet—why is it that I cannot banish this little fragment of melody from my mind? Let no one dare to say that I am secretly pleased by this scrap of an old singing commercial. It has been running through my head for days, and I loathe it and long to be rid of it. Yet it is my mind that repeats it so incessantly, that inserts it into the most urgent reflections and ruins the most cheerful mood with an awful ditty: "Winston tastes good, like a cigarette should."

An insignificant example? Perhaps, but many more dramatic examples could be set alongside it. We are well aware these days that not all constraints originate outside the psyche. We are acquainted with a wide range of behavior founded on mental suggestibility and compulsions, from my induced desire to smoke Winstons to heroin addiction, from a slight twitch or speech impediment to kleptomania or pyromania. A man may despise his compulsive acts as much as I do my scrap of tune—and yet be equally unable to stop repeating them. To these cases we might add examples of posthypnotic suggestion and a wide variety of neurotic thought patterns.

These cases are generally regarded as evidence of the constraining or compelling influence of unconscious forces upon the conscious mind. They may also be regarded as mental "disabilities," and are often so described. In either case, they seem to prove that psychic factors of which I am unaware, or very imperfectly aware, can obstruct my ability to do as I please and even force upon me an unwanted course of mental or physical action. But if my unconscious psyche can function to oppose me in such ways, then must it not be classed as circumstantial and the frontier between internal and external be changed accordingly?

Very well, the unconscious is a rather embarrassing annex of the mind anyway. Freud himself wrote that psychoanalysis demands that unconscious mental processes "must be judged as if they belonged to someone else and are to be explained by the mental life ascribed to that person."[2] Even my body seems more intimately familiar and tractable and closer to my self than this uncanny region of the psyche. It is only the conscious self with which I can identify, and what is really *internal* to the self is therefore only the conscious mind. The conception of freedom that results may no longer seem quite "ordinary," but the ordinary man is not likely to accept mental compulsions as part of what he means by freedom as "doing what I want." "The ability to do what I want" certainly refers only to desires and plans of which I am aware. Whatever desires and impulses may lie in my unconscious psyche do not really "belong" to me and must be kept separate from the conscious wants and plans that are at stake in immediate freedom. It is the conscious ego that should be identified with the self—and all else belongs to circumstance.

But this is not the end of the matter. For what are we to make of Swann's wretched and helpless passion for Odette in *Swann's Way*. This passion eventually smothers all of Swann's pleasures and practical interests. It prevents him from leaving Paris and disrupts or contaminates his every undertaking. Yet this is an unwanted passion, whose object doesn't even suit Swann's taste: "To think that I have wasted years of my life, that I have longed for death, that the greatest love that I have ever known has been for a woman who did not please me, who was not in my style."[3] And nonethe-

---

2. "The Unconscious" [1915], in *The Standard Edition of the Complete Psychological Works of Sigmund Freud,* trans. James Strachey (London: Hogarth Press, 1957), 14:169. Jacques Lacan has attracted attention to this description of the unconscious by his own description of the unconscious as "the Other" or "the language of the Other." But Lacan regards this language of the Other as expressing the authentic desires of the self and regards the conscious ego as the source of alienation and constraint. His view would lead to a doctrine of freedom directly opposite to the one under discussion. Later in this chapter, I consider such views briefly.

3. Marcel Proust, *Swann's Way,* trans. C. K. Scott Moncrieff (New York: Modern Library, 1956), 549.

less, Swann is thoroughly conscious of this passion, so much so that he tastes its every painful nuance.

Literature is full of similar cases of enthralling passion. But thralldom is slavery. Shaw's Don Juan offers a more humorous, but comparable, description of how he lost the illusion of being his own master, who had "never consciously taken a step until my reason had examined and approved":

> Do you not understand that when I stood face to face with Woman, every fiber in my clear critical brain warned me to spare her and save myself. My morals said No. My conscience said No. My chivalry and pity for her said No. My prudent regard for myself said No. My ear, practised on a thousand songs and symphonies; my eye, exercised on a thousand paintings; tore her voice, her features, her color to shreds. I caught all those tell-tale resemblances to her father and mother by which I knew what she would be like in thirty years time. I noted the gleam of gold from a dead tooth in the laughing mouth: I made curious observations of the strange odors of the chemistry of the nerves. The visions of my romantic reveries, in which I had trod the plains of heaven with a deathless, ageless creature of coral and ivory deserted me in that supreme hour. I remembered them and strove to recover their illusion; but they now seemed the emptiest of inventions: my judgement was not to be corrupted: my brain still said No on every issue. And whilst I was in the act of framing an excuse to the lady. Life seized me and threw me into her arms as a sailor throws a scrap of fish into the mouth of a seabird. . . . I saw then how useless it is to attempt to impose conditions on the irresistible force of life.[4]

Is the man who is enslaved by infatuation or lust less constrained than the one enslaved by fear? For that matter, don't the fear and duress already considered belong in the same category with such overwhelming passions as Swann's even though they are conscious? And what of those fits of childish rage in which I do things that, even at the time, I don't want to do, when I "cut off my nose to spite my own face" by destroying some treasured object or hurting some beloved person? These are all conscious emotions, feelings of which I am painfully aware; yet they seem capable of utterly smothering my ability to do what I want. These are the "overpowering" emotions—and it is *myself* that they overpower.[5] What has the spokesman

---

4. George Bernard Shaw, *Don Juan in Hell* (New York: Dodd, Mead & Co., 1952), 40.

5. Harry Frankfurt has explored cases such as Swann's and Don Juan's in a series of articles that are now collected in *The Importance of What We Care About* (Cambridge: Cambridge

for the ordinary view to say when faced with such challenges to his formula?

I suggested above that constraining fears should be treated as extensions of the threatening circumstance that occasion them. Other overwhelming passions tend to be more complex in origin, but seem to be born of some covert intercourse between unconscious influences and a provocative object or situation. As such, they too may be regarded as extensions of circumstances external to the conscious self. But here again, to concede such extensions of circumstance is really to extend the realm of circumstances and, in this case, to extend it into the citadel of the conscious mind.

Apart from the problem of such inordinate emotions, there is also a problem of conscious mental disabilities. I settle down at a lecture or concert, for example, eager and determined not to miss a word or note. I want to catch both the total structure and every nuance of the address or composition I have come to hear. But I don't. My mind wanders. My powers of concentration are inadequate, my mental discipline flabby. Or perhaps my memory will not retain the first parts through to the end. I may simply not know enough to be able to follow what I hear. In such cases, my desire is frustrated solely by some weakness of my conscious self. I can strive to conquer this weakness through sustained effort or training, much as I would try to overcome some physical obstacle or bodily weakness. Yet what can be thus conquered must be external to the conquering self, not a real component of its inner being. Where, in such cases, *is* the self that is free to do what it *wants* to do?

To bow to these considerations is to grant that overpowering emotions and certain conscious weaknesses are of a circumstantial character. But this admission in turn means that even the conscious psyche has its circumstantial aspect and that the threshold of consciousness is not the frontier between internal and external, since the struggle between self and circumstance is carried on within the citadel of consciousness. It is now the well-disciplined mind of mature and moderate emotional balance that appears to be the *real* self, and what does not belong to it belongs to circumstance.

University Press, 1988). In "Freedom of the Will and the Concept of a Person," Frankfurt argues that human freedom cannot be adequately described as the ability to do what one wants. Even animals may enjoy the freedom to do as they please, Frankfurt points out, but human beings also develop "second-order desires," desires about their own desires. If doing what I want means acting on a desire that I wish I didn't harbor—or even one that I didn't want to act upon under the circumstances—then my freedom of action does not issue from a free will. Frankfurt uses the example of the unwilling narcotics addict to illustrate his point, but anyone who has had to struggle to quit smoking will recognize this predicament. I spent years despising my stubbornly recurrent desire for cigarettes.

In order to formulate the most ordinary understanding of freedom clearly, I have had to try to specify the distinction between self and circumstance. This effort, however, has led to a progressive enlargement of the realm of circumstances at the expense of the self. This train of reflections has not been followed out to the end even yet. But from the point now reached it might proceed in several directions. For example, we could reflect upon the goals and taboos implanted in the individual by his society and question whether these do not stifle or inhibit his genuine emotional life. That would lead toward ascribing all culturally inherited or "imposed" values and patterns of thought and behavior to the social circumstances from which they derive. Or, we could extend the preceding line of reasoning about overwhelming passions and ask whether *all* emotions in any way connected with external objects do not "belong" to the circumstances that provoke them. That might lead to claims that the whole emotional life of the individual represents an insidious invasion of consciousness by circumstances, which thereby disrupt and pervert the activity of thought of the real, purely rational self. Or, it might be argued that *all* contents or features of consciousness that derive from the environing world, including cognitive contents as well as affective influences, represent a contaminating attachment of the psyche to alien material and temporal conditions. Accordingly, it would only be by purging itself of all such infectious contents and attachments that the self would be able to extricate itself from the bondage of circumstance in order to devote itself to activities and goals appropriate to the purity of its eternal nature.

Immediate Freedom Versus Ethical Freedom

In the effort to clarify the most common and immediate view of freedom, I have traversed a series of stages that form a dialectical progression. This dialectic is older than Athens. In varied forms, its movements and stages are the familiar stock in trade of moral and religious teachers. But they are *not* familiar to that ordinary understanding of freedom that I originally set out to clarify. Indeed, I have ended with that very inversion of the meaning of freedom that the ordinary man finds quite perverse. For regardless of which branch of this dialectic I follow at the end, I am led to the conclusion that freedom depends upon the attainment of some special state of the self, whether psychological, moral, or religious. Freedom no longer consists in the realization of whatever immediate desires or intentions an individual may happen to feel, but only in the realization of some limited, privileged class of desires or intentions deemed appropriate to the innermost self. Since only these represent the proper aims of the "true" self, they are also the "true goals" of the individual—those that he *ought* to pursue if he would be truly himself. "True freedom," then, is enjoyed by the individual who is as he ought to be, and may be designated *ethical* freedom to distinguish it from the immediate freedom that the analysis took as its point of departure.

Ethical freedom does not exclude immediate freedom, nor does immediate freedom exclude the attainment of ethical freedom. But advocates of these two views of freedom tend to collide in personal and philosophical conflict. Indeed, these are two of the fundamental and perennially competing ideas of freedom distinguished in *The Idea of Freedom,* that encyclopedic study of the concept produced by the Institute for Philosophical Research under the direction of Mortimer Adler. Adler and his associates conducted a thorough survey of philosophical literature and found that theories of freedom could be classified into three major alternatives.

What I have called "immediate freedom" corresponds to what Adler calls "the circumstantial freedom of self-realization." Adler attempts to formulate a philosophically neutral definition of this idea of freedom in the following terms: "To be free is to be able, under favorable circumstances, to act as one wishes for one's own individual good as one sees it."[6] This formula indicates schematically the three factors that Adler finds to be essential identifying elements of this type of view, and it is clear that they are also the essential ingredients in the dialectic just traversed. First, freedom is enjoyed only under favorable circumstances or in the absence of coercive or constraining circumstances.[7] Second, the freedom made possible by such circumstances consists in the actual execution of the individual's wishes, so that his actions proceed from himself rather than from the influence of external forces.[8] Third, the goals fulfilled by his action must be those that he actually wants and thus depend upon his personal estimate of what is good for him, regardless of how that may conform or conflict with any supposed social, objective, or universal good.[9]

This is exactly the view I have described as the idea of freedom implicit in most ordinary discourse. Moreover, my ascription of this view to the immediate understanding is reflected in Adler's list of the thinkers who champion this type of freedom to the exclusion of all others. They are predominantly philosophers who belong to the positivistic or empiricist

6. Mortimer Adler, *The Idea of Freedom* (Garden City, N.Y.: Doubleday, 1958), 1:606.
7. Ibid., vol. 2, chap. 4.
8. Ibid., 2:174–76.
9. Ibid., 183–89.

traditions, who argue that the primary source of meaning or truth or reality is to be sought in the immediate data of experience.[10]

On the other hand, I ended up with an ethical conception of freedom that corresponds roughly with what Adler calls "the acquired freedom of self-perfection." Adler's neutral formula for this conception of freedom is that "to be free is to be able, through acquired virtue or wisdom, to will or live as one ought in conformity to the moral law or an ideal befitting human nature."[11] Here again, Adler's formula is a schematic rendering of the essential characteristics of a whole class of views. First, this is a freedom that is acquired through the attainment of some special "state of mind, character or personality that marks one man as somehow 'better' than another."[12] Second, the goals sought in this freedom do not depend upon the idiosyncratic, personal desire of the individual, but involve standards that are valid for every person and so prescribe how any individual *ought* to act. As might be expected, philosophers who champion the freedom of self-perfection as the only true form of freedom also hold immediate experience to be a poor guide to the truth. They all hold that ultimate reality can be known only through the use of reason or by the benefit of revelation.[13]

These two forms of freedom appear sharply and unequivocally opposed to one another—an appearance that is borne out by the strife between philosophical proponents of the two views. In book VIII of Plato's *Republic,* for example, Socrates describes the freedom to do as one pleases as a state of license and anarchy. He attributes the evils and downfall of democracy to an excess of this sort of liberty, which leads to a condition of slavery in the individual and the state alike. These are the objections that the champions of ethical freedom characteristically direct against immediate freedom. The first step is to charge that such a freedom is merely *license,* which promotes

10. See ibid., 592. The list of these authors includes Hobbes, Hume, Priestly, Bentham, J. S. Mill, Kelsen, Laski, Nowell-Smith, Schlick, Ayer, and Stevenson.

11. Ibid., 606.

12. Ibid., 135. More cautiously, these might be described as "normative" theories, thereby leaving open the question whether the agent who acts in accord with his nature is therefore also acting *ethically*. This would accommodate those who might object that acting in accordance with one's true nature may mean violating repressive ethical standards. On the opposite tack, Richard Double argues that although freedom is a normative concept in the sense that the exercise of freedom involves satisfying normative standards of rationality, the rational act need not also be an *ethical* act. See "Does Freedom Require Morality?" chap. 3 in *The Non-Reality of Free Will* (Oxford: Oxford University Press, 1991).

13. See ibid., 592. The list of these authors, in toto: Saint Ambrose, Marcus Aurelius, Bosanquet, Bradley, Epictetus, Plato, Plotinus, Seneca, and Spinoza. For an admirably lucid recent presentation of this view, see Susan Wolf, *Freedom Within Reason* (Oxford: Oxford University Press, 1990). For a shorter version, see her "Asymmetrical Freedom," *Journal of Philosophy* 77 (March 1980): 151–66.

"a libertinism of the useless and unnecessary pleasures."[14] Second, they see in such license a more severe bondage of the individual than any chains could ever impose. Saint Ambrose describes this bondage vividly: "For he is a slave to his passions; he is slave to his own wishes; he cannot escape his rulers night or day because he has these rulers within him; within he suffers unbearable slavery. Slavery is twofold, one of the body and the other of the soul, men being masters of the body, but sin and passion masters of the soul, and from these only liberty of spirit delivers a man so that he is delivered from his servitude."[15]

The champion of immediate freedom regards such talk of the enslavement of the individual to his own desires as a vicious abuse of metaphor. He may object that impersonal and universal standards threaten to subject the individual to an unwanted and alien discipline, and he regards the idea of a "true" or "better" self as a needless confusion of fact and value on the part of the moralist.

Yet, despite this strife, the opposition between these two types of views proves superficial under closer scrutiny. First of all, the proponents of immediate freedom, or Adler's "circumstantial freedom of self-realization," differ among themselves over the nature of circumstance and, consequently, over what counts as a constraining external influence. At one extreme, Hobbes's version of this doctrine unequivocally specifies the nature of circumstances in terms of physical obstructions to bodily movement: "Liberty or Freedome signifieth (properly) the absence of Opposition; (by Opposition I mean external impediments to motion)."[16] Hobbes holds rigorously to this definition and insists that neither illness nor physical disability,[17] nor fear,[18] nor even madness[19] can constitute any curtailment of freedom.

Hume's terse assertion that freedom "is universally allowed to belong to everyone who is not a prisoner and in chains" suggests that he agrees with Hobbes.[20] But other advocates of this type of view do not concur. Moritz Schlick, for example, treats the alcoholic or the narcotic addict as unfree because external influences are at work on him through his body.[21] Schlick

---

14. *Republic* 561 (trans. Francis M. Cornford [Oxford: Oxford University Press, 1945]).

15. *Letters,* trans. Sister Mary Melchior Beyenka, vol. 26 of *The Fathers of the Church* (New York: Fathers of the Church, 1954), no. 54, p. 295.

16. *Leviathan* (Cambridge: Cambridge University Press, 1904), pt. 2, chap. 21, p. 147.

17. Ibid.

18. Ibid., 148.

19. Adler, *The Idea of Freedom,* 1:190 n. 56.

20. *An Inquiry Concerning Human Understanding* (New York: Liberal Arts Press, 1955), 104.

21. *Problems of Ethics,* trans. D. Rinan (New York: Prentice Hall, 1939), 150–51. Cf. Adler's discussion of this whole issue in *The Idea of Freedom,* 1:117–21.

also holds, as do A. J. Ayer and others, that fear and duress represent further influences of circumstances that curtail freedom. Ayer goes still further, arguing that cases of psychological compulsion, such as kleptomania, also involve the constraint of freedom.[22]

Clearly, we are back in the middle of the very dialectic discovered earlier. The differences between these thinkers over the nature of circumstances are exactly those encountered in the first stages of that dialectic. Ayer's denial that the kleptomaniac is free brings us to the point where the circumstantial freedom of self-realization borders on the acquired freedom of self-perfection.[23] If we turn now to those who claim that this latter is the only true freedom, it is not their differences that must claim our attention, but a point upon which they all agree. Despite their differences, these thinkers agree that *within* the acquired condition of ethical freedom the individual still is able to do what he wants and, indeed, that *only* within that condition can he be truly said to be unhindered by external influences. The classic expression of this conviction is the Socratic doctrine that no man knowingly chooses evil, that to know the objective good is to desire it, and that to be ruled by other desires is slavery.[24] The passage from Saint Ambrose cited above is in this same spirit. Similarly, Spinoza introduces his conception of the free man in the following terms: "[I]t will be easily seen in what consists the difference between the man who is led by affect or opinion alone and one who is led by reason. The former, whether he wills it or not, does those things of which he is entirely ignorant, but the latter does the will of no one but himself, and does those things only which he knows are of greatest importance in life, and which he therefore desires above all things. I call the former, therefore, a slave, and the latter free."[25]

This all amounts to saying, once again, that only in ethical freedom is the *true* self liberated from the influence of circumstances, and it is in these terms that F. H. Bradley states this doctrine: "Suppose I am a glutton and a drunkard; in these vices I assert my private will; am I then free so far as a glutton and a drunkard, or am I a slave—the slave of my appetites? The

22. *Philosophical Essays* (London: Macmillan, 1954), 280.
23. Cf. Adler's comments to the same effect: *The Idea of Freedom*, 1:120 nn. 35 and 36.
24. See *Meno and Republic* 430–31.
25. *Ethics* IV, prop. 66, scholia. See also IV, scholium 1 to prop. 37. The affinity of such passages in Ambrose and Spinoza with the Stoic doctrine of the wise man should be obvious. However, I do not agree with Adler's classification of the Stoics among those who regard self-perfection as the *sole* form of freedom. The Stoic doctrine of the freedom of judgment closely parallels that of Descartes, whom Adler rightly classifies among the proponents of a third type of view, which understands freedom as self-determination.

answer must be, 'The slave of his lusts is, so far, not a free man. The man is free who realizes his *true* self!'"[26]

For the advocate of ethical freedom the notion of the "true" or "better" self is clearly no mere metaphor, although the champion of immediate freedom levels just that charge. What is at stake in the quarrel between the two schools of thought is a genuine disagreement about the nature of the self. If the definition of the self given by the proponent of self-perfection be granted, then the remainder of the psyche constitutes an alien "opposition." So understood, this view of freedom exhibits the same fundamental form as that of Hobbes, since both say that to be free is to be able to do what I (= my true self) *want* to do. As Bradley goes on to say, everything depends on the answer to the question, "What is my true self?"[27]

The whole issue between ethical freedom and immediate freedom resolves itself into a conflict over the distinction between self and circumstance. Thus, we come full circle, returning to the by-now-familiar dialectic. We are now in a position to see that *the opposition between the two types of views is rooted in the same problem that provokes differences between the advocates of either view*. And that is the very same problem that gave rise to the dialectic: that of distinguishing between the internal and the external. Once their agreements and differences are carefully scrutinized, it is obvious that instead of populating two opposing camps, these philosophers are distributed along the route of that dialectic in accordance with the various specifications of that distinction which each of them adopts.

It must now be manifest that there is really nothing relentless about that dialectic, nothing that could force us inexorably to its furthest stage. You may call a halt at any stage you choose and find yourself in respectable philosophical company. It even seems quite possible to devise a reverse argument, leading from the most extreme or ascetic version of ethical freedom back to the freedom of immediacy. Since each stage represents a different specification of freedom, the exact nature of freedom seems to be an arbitrary matter, depending upon where you tire of the dialectical route, or perhaps even upon which direction you choose to travel it. Everything depends upon how much you are ready to concede to circumstance—or

---

26. *Ethical Studies* (Oxford: Oxford University Press, 1952), 57.

27. Ibid. Harry Frankfurt distinguishes between a genuine *person* and a "wanton" on rather similar grounds: "The essential characteristic of a wanton is that he does not care about his will. His desires move him to do certain things without its being true of him either that he wants to be moved by those desires or that he prefers to be moved by other desires. The class of wantons includes all nonhuman animals that have desires and all very young children. Perhaps it also includes some adult human beings as well" ("Freedom of the Will and the Concept of a Person," 16–17).

upon what you regard as the real self.[28] The dialectic seems to carry no necessity, and so to carry no one any further than he cares to go. Consequently, it has no historical force, so that despite its venerable antiquity, every stage of the dialectic has doubtless had its advocates in every period of history.[29]

But doesn't this whole survey of meanings of the word "freedom" simply prove that there is no single conception involved here, but only a diversity of meanings attaching to a single word? Doesn't my entire survey invite us to regard these different meanings of "freedom" as a mere plurality of uses, which have, at the most, only a *family resemblance* to one another? Is that Wittgensteinian verdict about the meanings of ordinary words also to be the last word about the nature of freedom?

28. "What *is* a self supposed to be? Do we not need more information?" Ted Honderich complains in *How Free Are You?* (Oxford: Oxford University Press, 1993) —and by now we can certainly sympathize with his complaint of a lack of clarity on this point in discussions of freedom. Indeed, the definition of "the self" seems pivotal to this whole attempt to understand freedom. But by now, it should also be obvious that any exact definition will prejudice the whole question of the nature of freedom. In order to keep that question open, I simply use "the self" to refer to *any* free entity. We need a noncommittal term for that purpose in any case, since it would be awkward constantly to refer to "a free entity" or "any free being." "The self" serves very handily in that role precisely because it is so ambiguously poised between reflexive pronoun and substantive noun and is the kernel of the competing descriptions of freedom as "*self-*realization," "*self-*perfection," or "*self-*determination." But we must beware of the temptation, of which Honderich warns, "to regard a self as a person within a person, a homunculus"—or to take the ambiguity of the term as occasion to freight it with *all* its various meanings at once.

29. Indeed, a comparison of the lists given in notes and 10 and 13 above will show that advocates of the later stages of the dialectic tend on the whole to antedate the advocates of its earlier stages. But Plato's discussion in book VIII of the *Republic* clearly shows that the more immediate view of freedom was common enough in his day.

❦ 2 ❧

Freedom and Constraint

Family Resemblances

A family resemblance is not a *chance* resemblance. Even though there may be no single feature that is common to all the members of a family, there must be some *recognizable* pattern or commonality of features, or we could not speak of a *family* resemblance. And a group of individuals who bear such a resemblance to one another is not a merely arbitrary collection. If a man resembles his father, we do not regard the similarity as a remarkable coincidence. And if a set of cousins all resemble one another, we are ready to explain their resemblance by tracing it to common progenitors, even if it would be difficult to specify any one common *feature* they all share. The notion of a family resemblance was introduced into the discussion of the meanings of words in order to dispel the notion that all the meanings of a single word must share in a common essence, or derive from a single concept or universal nature. But the metaphor was not an entirely happy choice. For to say of individuals—or of the meanings of words—that they bear a family resemblance to one another is hardly to dispel all hope of discovering an underlying nature or essence, since that metaphor directly evokes the classic Aristotelian doctrine of the natures or essences of things as epitomized in the biological transmission of form from one generation to another. If we recall the connection between the "nature" of a thing and its nativity—and that what is "native," or "innate," is what is acquired by birth—then there would seem to be nothing that is more *natural* than a family resemblance.

To detect a family resemblance among several individuals is to discover grounds for suspecting that there is some deeper connection among them than meets the eye—or deeper than the fact that they all bear the same surname. The family resemblance among the meanings of "freedom" suggests comparable doubts about whether they form a merely arbitrary collection, which would leave us with such insurmountable ambiguities that we could not hope to discover any nature of freedom that might allow us to resolve the differences and disputes explored in the last chapter. If family resemblances reflect the processes of biological generation, perhaps we should seek some comparable generative principle to explain the family resemblances among the meanings of freedom.

Of course, the meanings of words are not fixed *by nature*. But the processes of linguistic and biological generation are frequently compared. On the one hand, the structures that assure biological reproduction are described as a "genetic code" and thereby explicitly compared to a language, or system of symbols, employed to transmit information. On the other hand, recent linguistic theory employs the notion of generative principles or structures to explain how speakers can produce an endless series of novel utterances that nevertheless preserve the grammatical forms of the language, a process inviting comparison with the preservation of the form of a biological species through the generation of a series of novel individuals. The genetic and linguistic codes do not produce exact duplicates like Xerox photocopies, of course, but only family resemblances. And the structures that govern the generative process and assure the preservation of linguistic or organic form are not themselves displayed by the individual utterances or organisms as common features evident to the eye or ear. The point is that the superficial similarities and differences involved in family resemblance—or in the resemblance of all the members of a species or all standard English sentences—need not be accepted as ultimate and irreducible, since they may be traceable to deeper structures of which the obvious features, or "surface structures" in linguistics, are only so many permutations or transformations that spring from a common productive principle.

There is no need to pursue the details of these developments in linguistics and genetics. It is enough to heed the clear warning they convey: We cannot simply come to a halt by noting a family resemblance among the meanings of freedom and thereupon conclude that we are faced with insurmountable ambiguities. Instead, we must ask whether that resemblance can be traced to some deeper structure or generative principle that may explain both the similarities and differences among the members of the family.

Self and Circumstance

In fact, there does seem to be a "structure" or generative principle at work in the dialectic traversed in the last chapter. There may be many cases in which the meanings that accrue to a word through usage constitute only a rather vague, indeterminately related collection. And there may be still other usages of the word "freedom" that *are* only faintly related to those examined—distant cousins twice or thrice removed. But in the set of surveyed meanings, there was no *mere* diversity or resemblance, but an obvious development that placed them in relation to one another as earlier and later stages in a series. The mere attempt to specify the meaning of the most ordinary and obvious definition of freedom as self-realization, or "the ability to do what I want," generated the whole series of concepts, ending with ethical and religious views that appear entirely antagonistic to that initial definition.

Indeed, beyond the obvious differences, there is a single underlying notion of freedom at work. Throughout the entire series, freedom could be defined as the self's ability to realize its own proper desires and intentions. All the differences among these views stem from differences about the nature of the *self*, which result in disagreements over just which desires or intentions properly *belong* to the self. So the same *basic* conception of freedom as self-realization generates a whole series of different specifications simply by altering the definition of one of its terms: the self. This is a very simple and obvious example of a generative principle. Anyone familiar with formal logic and mathematics will recognize that it can be represented as a simple function: $f(x)$. Any such function will generate a series of different values by changing the definition of x, the "argument" of the function. For those who find such formalism helpful, then, the formula for the series of definitions of freedom would be Freedom = $f(s)$, where s stands for the nature of the self.

But we are confronted with an assortment of different conceptions of the self, to each of which there corresponds a different account of the specific import of freedom. How are we to decide which is the "real" self? The generative idea of freedom as self-realization, as the ability to realize my own proper desires and intentions, does not seem to offer any basis for deciding among these competing conceptions of the self. And unless that issue is decided first, we seem to be left at much the same impasse as before with regard to the specific import of freedom. Has the discovery that self-realization is the single generative idea behind all these competing versions of freedom really advanced our lot significantly? Or have we simply traded the enigma of freedom for another, more celebrated enigma, the Delphic riddle of self-knowledge? The ambiguity of freedom has been resolved only by being transmuted into the problem of determining the true nature of the self. But now we are left with the problem of deciding which is the "real" self. Is the real self the moral self who assumes responsibility for the life he has made? Or is it the spontaneous, uninhibited personality who feels most truly himself when his deeds issue directly from his feelings and when he can see his actions as genuine expressions of his deepest convictions and passions? Or does the real self lie somewhere between the two? Each alternative can offer weighty arguments for its view of the self. The champion of spontaneity insists upon taking the self just as it is, as it is immediately given in experience. In this way, he may well argue, the self is conceived and accepted as the whole person—body, emotion, and intellect together—rather than defined in terms of some privileged faculty or part to the exclusion of the rest. To dismiss this advantage is to sunder the personality into parts and set the putative "true" self in opposition to the rest. Yet the ethical view of freedom offers cogent reasons for doing just that, insisting that many of the properties of the whole person actually represent external influences and are more properly attributed to circumstances than to the self. Is the weight of my body really a part of myself, for example, when it is actually due to the gravitational attraction of the earth? And if my weight is not really part of me, then what are we to say of the thirst that is born of a scorching hot sun, or the anger evoked by an insult, or the desire provoked by a voluptuous woman? And, for that matter, what about the ambition nurtured by a competitive society that has made a virtue of this erstwhile vice? Surely, the ethical view of freedom has good reason to treat these as foreign influences—and to conceive of what properly belongs to the self in such a way as to exclude such foreign influences.

This effort to distinguish external influences from what genuinely belongs to the self is another theme that runs throughout the dialectic. At every stage freedom is conceived as *conditional*. It is not only a function of the nature of the self, but also depends upon favorable conditions, upon the absence of constraining circumstances or coercive external influence. If the competing views of freedom define these conditions very differently, that is because they disagree about the nature and range of circumstances. Since these disputes are the exact counterpart of disputes about the nature of the self, any attempt to *resolve* them would simply lead back to the same impasse as before. To decide what properly belongs to circumstances and to determine what properly belongs to the self are simply two sides of the same coin.

Where, then, does freedom belong? Not to the self alone, insofar as freedom is also a function of favorable circumstances. But not to circumstances alone either, for if freedom is *self*-realization, then it must also be grounded in the self. Even though this generative notion makes the exact definition of freedom a function of the nature of the self, it does not belong to the nature of the self to be free, since freedom is only available under special conditions. Freedom is understood here as the self's ability to realize its own desires and intentions, but that ability depends upon conditions that lie outside the self, upon the absence of coercive and constraining conditions. Yet external conditions alone cannot confer freedom upon an individual. No configuration of circumstances—democracy, "the free world," a naturally mild and dispassionate temperament—can be *intrinsically* free, according to this basic conception. The most that circumstances can offer is conditions favorable to the freedom of *most* individuals; but even the most favorable circumstances cannot guarantee the realization of the desires of *all* individuals at all times.

It does not belong either to the nature of the self or to the nature of circumstances to be free, then, but only to the *relation* between the two. Freedom requires a peculiar conjunction or combination of self and circumstances, organism and environment, event and world, according to this basic generative conception, and cannot be separately ascribed to *either* of these two poles alone. That is why the effort to distinguish between the two moves the dialectic generated by the idea of freedom as self-realization from stage to stage. Freedom so conceived must be recognized as a *relational concept*. For those who find such logical formalization helpful, we could say that the earlier representation of this conception of freedom as a function of the self, $f(s)$, is inadequate, after all, and that it would be similarly inadequate to represent it as a function of circumstance, $f(c)$. Rather, we need to employ the convention for representing any relation, R, between two terms, a and b, as $R(ab,)$ or a function with two arguments as $F(ab)$, and should represent the logic of this concept of freedom as the relation $F(sc)$.

Accordingly, although it is easy and conventional to attribute freedom to the self alone or to speak of a "free society," these usages tend to foster confusion insofar as they disguise this *relational* character of the concept.

Perhaps that is why Thomas Hobbes insists upon distinguishing between *freedom* and *power*. He ascribes power wholly to the self, leaving freedom entirely a function of favorable circumstances, after the manner of physical mechanics. But Hobbes's own examples may be used to show that what is really at stake is a single relationship rather than separable functions. For example, he describes freedom as "the absence of external impediments to motion." But of course, what will effectively impede a motion is *relative* to the power informing that motion. Or again, Hobbes says that a bedridden man "wants not the liberty, but the *power* to move."[1] Yet, of course, the sick man's weakened powers *would* enable him to move if it weren't for the impediment of external forces—in a weightless environment, for example.

Hobbes's liberty and power are the sundered halves of a single relational structure, and they betray their fragmentary character by their dependence upon one another. But Hobbes's examples serve as useful reminders that the particular relationship between self and circumstances required by freedom is very commonly described *negatively,* as the *absence* of impediment, obstruction, opposition, bondage, etc. All these terms may be summarized under the heading of *constraint,* and this basic idea of freedom as self-realization is often described simply as the absence of constraint or coercion. This description seems at first to define more fully and exactly the relationship between self and circumstances required by this conception of freedom. But the description is not as helpful as it first appears to be. For the absence of constraints from the environment is not like the absence of mosquitoes or wolves or noxious fumes. Constraint does not designate any specific *thing* or *class of things* whose absence would ensure freedom. "Constraint," too, is a term that refers to a *relationship* between an individual and circumstances—a relationship that might most readily be defined as an absence of freedom, which is scarcely any great help. It only suggests that freedom and constraint are opposite relations between self and circumstances, that they are *contrary* relationships, since the absence of one is the presence of the other and vice versa. But that hardly sheds much light on the structure of either relationship. Recognition of this contrariety *might* lead toward a more precise and complete understanding of freedom if we could define constraint independently and in its own right. But we cannot simply define each contrary as the absence of the other, or we will be caught up in an endless interplay of negations. In order to describe the structure of freedom more specifically, we must find a more direct and positive way to explain how freedom differs from constraint.

And yet, there seems to be something that is already negative and

---

1. *Leviathan* (Cambridge: Cambridge University Press, 1904), pt. 2, chap. 21, p. 147.

inherently contrary about the notion of constraint. The very idea seems to carry opposition and negation within itself, as do the other terms summarized under this heading: "impediment," "obstruction," "bondage"— "opposition" itself. And since the absence of a negative suggests a positive result, perhaps we can reach a more positive description of freedom if we can locate this negative, contrary moment in constraint more exactly.

But the contrariness of constraint is not so easy to pin down. It cannot be discovered by any simple objective observation of the relationship between individual and circumstances. What is there that is inherently negative about a chained animal, for example, or a woman being raped, or a man in the grip of a homicidal rage? The animal may be gnawing or tugging vigorously on the chain, trying to break it; the woman may be struggling with all her strength to break away from her assailant; the enraged man may be attempting just as energetically to break his victim's skull. All three individuals are actively engaged with their surroundings. Just what is it that stamps these relationships as negative? Is it the fact that all three are engaged in destructive activity, attempting to alter their circumstances by *breaking* something? Surely not; for if their attempts succeed, they will no longer be constrained. The destruction of the environment by an agent is not at all what is typical of constraint. On the contrary, in all three of these cases, it would seem more apt to say that constraint consists in the fact that the world opposes the self—and to locate the negativity of constraint in that opposition between agent and environment. The trouble with that answer, however, is that wherever there is action there is *some* sort of opposition; we cannot identify constraint with any and *every* form of opposition between the self and its surroundings and define freedom as the absence of all such opposition. Whoever is satisfied with the way things are and has no quarrel with the status quo also has no motive or reason to act. In the absence of any and all opposition, self and world would merge.

And it isn't only the negative, contrary aspect of constraint that escapes us here. The three cases just cited are readily recognizable because they are standard examples of constraint. Apart from such conventional examples, how could mere observation of the relation between self and circumstances ever identify a case of constraint *as* such? Convention itself may prove constraining. In Hans Christian Andersen's fable about the emperor and the nightingale, the emperor of China seems as safely beyond coercion as a human being can ever be. The emperor occupies the highest pinnacle of human power, with subjects and courtiers to obey his every whim. But any child can see that the emperor is as much a captive of his imperial office as the nightingale is imprisoned by the cage at court, which is his "reward" for singing so beautifully for the emperor. The nightingale is granted the "liberty to walk out twice each day, and once in the night." But it always has

"twelve footmen with each one holding a ribbon . . . tied round its leg."
One soon sees that the emperor is as bound to his courtiers as the poor
nightingale is to its footmen, the prisoner of the very courtly etiquette upon
which his own power and efficacy depend. Andersen depicts both the
emperor and the nightingale as constrained by circumstances that others
would envy. Their predicament reminds us of how anyone can be entangled
by the conditions of his own power or trapped in the consequences of his
own success.

How, then, are we objectively to identify constraint and distinguish it
from freedom? Is it a purely conventional distinction, or a matter of merely
subjective judgment? Or is there some mysteriously unobservable ingredient that is the key to understanding the contrariness of constraint and the
contrast between freedom and constraint?

An example founded in a simpler set of conventions helps to illustrate
this problem and shows that all that is needed is a more adequate analysis
of the structure of constraint. Consider two players engaged in a game of
chess. Within the conveniently rule-governed world of the chess game, a
checkmate represents constraint rather aptly. But you cannot "see" a
checkmate merely by observing the postures and movements of the two
players, or by examining the spatial positions and relations of the pieces on
the board. The checkmate does not reside in the mere opposition between
the two players or their "men," or in their efforts to defeat one another, for
these are present throughout the game, and there would *be* no game
without them. But if we cannot see a checkmate merely by observing all this,
what more is needed in order to discern whether either player has the other
in checkmate? In the case of chess, this missing, unobservable ingredient is
quite obvious. In order to discover a checkmate, the observable situation on
the board must be referred to something that is *not* present or observable
because it is only *possible*. To find a checkmate, we have to consider what
moves are *possible* for each player: whether either can "take" the other's king
in the next move and, if so, whether the other can remove that king from
jeopardy, or whether every possible move would leave the king vulnerable.
It is just because a checkmate occurs when *no moves are possible* for one player
that checkmate provides such a fitting analogue of constraint, though we do
not insist that constraint always involves complete immobilization. Checkmate is an artificially simple model of constraint, of course, because the
possibilities are all governed by the rules of chess and chessmen can only be
moved about on a board. But the model serves very well to show that
neither constraint nor freedom can be understood as a two-termed relation
between the self and its circumstances, R(*sc*). In order to understand
constraint, we must refer beyond the objectively given situation and include
a relation to *possibilities*, which are *not* given. Constraint can only be

understood as a *three*-termed relation between self, circumstances, and possibility: $R(scp)$.[2] And as the example of checkmate clearly displays, constraint occurs when circumstances prevent the self from moving—or, to put it more generally so as not to confine ourselves to the limited activities of chessmen, when circumstances prevent the self from realizing any possibility.

This structure clearly displays the inherent contrariness, or negativity, of constraint: to constrain is to prevent or preclude the realization of possibilities. Does the contrariety between constraint and freedom mean that we can now define freedom in comparably simple terms? If freedom is the *absence* of constraint, then is the self free insofar as its circumstances do *not* prevent the realization of a possibility? Or, stated more positively, is the self free insofar as its circumstances *permit* the realization of a possibility?

We do say that a person is "free to realize" a particular possibility provided that circumstances do not prevent it. But this definition is clearly still too loose to be useful. It really does not provide for any clear contrariety between freedom and constraint, freedom and slavery, after all. For the self always realizes *some* possibility, regardless of circumstances. By this definition, then, the self would *always* be free, since circumstances always permit the realization of at least *one* possibility. At best, this conception only defines what might be called "abstract freedom," the freedom to realize whatever possibilities my circumstances happen to permit, however remote, indifferent, or unpalatable they may be. This freedom is abstract because it is a freedom I may enjoy even in relation to possibilities I've never thought about and would not seriously consider if I *did* think of them. Thus, circumstances may not prevent an unemployed mechanic in Wichita from reading Aristotle's *Metaphysics*, even though he cannot find a job. His "freedom" to read Aristotle while out of work is entirely abstract. Napoleon at St. Helena was *abstractly* free to live out his life in comfortable exile or to

2. Cf. this entire analysis with that of Gerald C. MacCallum Jr., "Negative and Positive Freedom," *Philosophical Review* 76 (1967): 312–34, which I discovered after completing this account. MacCallum, too, argues that the apparent diversity of conflicting conceptions of freedom can be dissipated by recognizing that freedom is a triadic relation "taking the form: 'x is (is not) free from y to do (not do, become, not become) z'; x ranges over agents, y ranges over such 'preventing conditions' as constraints, restrictions, interferences, and barriers, and z ranges over actions or conditions of character or circumstances" (314). MacCallum shows how this triadic schema undercuts the distinction between negative and positive freedom that Isaiah Berlin and others have used to identify different "freedoms" or conceptions of freedom. He argues that such distinctions have "encouraged the wrong sort of questions," and concludes that "it is both clumsy and misleading to try to sort out writers as adherents of this or that 'kind' or 'concept' of freedom. We would be far better off to insist that they all have the same concept of freedom as a triadic relation" (327). The concurrence between MacCallum's analysis and the program of the present chapter should be obvious.

escape to a life of obscure anonymity in the hinterlands of his native Corsica. But the contemplation of such alternatives was as foreign to Napoleon as the contemplation of Aristotle is to this mechanic. To tell the mechanic that he is "free" to read Aristotle or to remind Napoleon that he is "free" to enjoy St. Helena isn't likely to prove consoling. They are more likely to regard such reminders as a bad joke and to reply that conditions that permit only such options are still constraining. You might as well tell a drowning man that he is free to drink the water.

In fact, this definition of freedom is even compatible with constraint, since the self realizes *some* possibility even when constrained. The slave is always free to go on being a slave. The antithesis between freedom and constraint cannot be sustained, or even properly formulated on this basis. The same individual may be simultaneously free in relation to one possibility and constrained in relation to another. Indeed, by this definition, every individual must *always* be *both* free and constrained: free in relation to whatever possibilities his circumstances permit and constrained in relation to whatever possibilities they rule out. The contrariety between freedom and constraint is essential to the basic generative conception of freedom as self-realization. Yet there *need be no* contrariety between freedom and constraint if you pick different possibilities or sets of possibilities to construct the three-termed relation between self, circumstances, and possibility—or if you do not specify any particular possibility. That contrariety only arises in relation to some *specific* possibility, which conditions may either permit or preclude. (Or some *set* of possibilities. There's more than one way to skin a rabbit, which might therefore be regarded as standing for a whole *set* of possibilities. But the individual who is prevented from using one method is not therefore constrained from skinning a rabbit. What is important here is that the same specification of the possibility term of the relation be considered in both cases.)

Possibilities and Potentialities

But *which* possibility? And how is it to be selected? If we cannot answer these questions, then the difference between freedom and constraint will collapse— or will be left an entirely abstract and arbitrary issue, since any individual at any moment can be proved either constrained or free, and any circumstances will prove constraining or not depending upon which possibility you pick, so that it will be impossible to determine when and whether any individual is free until you determine which possibility is relevant. Of course, the other terms of the relation must also be specified. You cannot tell whether given circumstances are constraining without asking, "For whom?" Nor can you determine whether a particular individual is free or constrained in relation to a given possibility without specifying the circumstances.

Perhaps a fable will help to illustrate this nest of problems. Let us suppose, through one of those anachronisms permitted in fables, that Voltaire, the French liberal, and Epictetus, the Stoic sage, are traveling together in India. In a square in Calcutta, they come upon an old man crouching, cramped in an iron cage. "This is constraint most cruel indeed!" Voltaire exclaims. "You must have a very poor opinion of freedom," Epictetus replies scornfully, "if you think that a human being can be constrained by a mere cage of iron!" The two men fall to arguing over this, but break off their quarrel very shortly, upon agreeing that they cannot really be sure, without further inquiries, whether the old man is constrained or not. His immobility suggests that if he is not asleep or dead, he may be in a mystic trance. He may be a Hindu fakir who has consigned himself to this cage as a self-imposed ascetic discipline and may be quite content with his harsh circumstances. Our two philosophers agree that if that is the case, then he is not constrained by the cage. Whether the old man is constrained, then, depends upon the relation of his situation to what is *possible*—in particular, to the alternatives of either remaining in the cage or leaving.

"So we agree," Voltaire sums up, "that the cage alone is no proof of constraint. This gentleman is not constrained if he wishes to remain in the cage and has no desire to escape. But if he wishes to leave and cannot, then he *is* cruelly constrained."

"I agree to no such thing!" Epictetus replies. "That he is not constrained by the cage is quite true. But he is as constrained if he wishes to stay as he is if he wishes to leave. He is free only if he is indifferent to *both* alternatives alike. For it is exactly our desires and wishes that enslave and constrain us. Only the sage is able to become free—and he becomes free only through perfect indifference."

At that, Voltaire explodes in indignation. "That is the freedom of resignation, of 'Je m'en fou!'" he objects. "It is the liberty obtained by shrugging one's shoulders at life. Such a view of freedom only invites the public to tolerate tyranny!"

"And that is how we Stoics remained free even under Nero," Epictetus replies. "Only the slave of his own desires can be tyrannized."

Their heated debate resumes. And yet, the structure of constraint is the same on either of these views. The cage constrains the old man if and only if it prevents him from realizing some specific possibility. If the particular possibility in question is that of remaining in the cage, or if it is a possibility that renders the cage a matter of indifference, then there is no constraint involved.

How might this quarrel be resolved and the question whether the old man is constrained or free be settled once and for all? Evidently, it is necessary to specify just *which* possibility is to be considered in relation to this individual and these particular circumstances. Again, we find that *any* circumstances, even an iron cage, will prove constraining in relation to some possibilities but not in relation to others. And if freedom is the absence of constraint, then under given circumstances an individual will be free in relation to the latter possibilities but not in relation to the former. But this does not tell us whether the old man is free or constrained. How are we to consider *which* possibility to consider in his case—or in any given case?

The simplest, most obvious answer is that it depends upon what the individual *wants,* that constraint occurs where circumstances prevent the individual from realizing his or her wishes and desires, and that an individual is free when he or she is able to realize those same desires or wishes. This would help to explain why objective observation alone cannot ascertain whether an individual is constrained—why our two philosophers cannot settle whether the man in the cage is free or constrained. For insofar as a desire remains unrealized, it also remains merely *subjective* and inaccessible to objective observation. Constraint obviously occurs when a situation prevents the self from realizing its desires. Accordingly, the only way to ascertain whether the old man is constrained by his cage is simply to *ask him what he wants.*

Now, as it happens, the old man is indeed a fakir, an Oriental sage, who is eventually roused from profound meditations by the noisy argument between Voltaire and Epictetus. When their guide explains the dispute to him, he commends them for recognizing that the cage need not be a prison and that it is, rather, a means of self-discipline and concentration, as they suspected. "Some people lie on beds of nails," he explains. "Others swear by their mantras. I find the cage more apt. But constrained? No more than you are constrained by living on the earth. Only the man who is so foolish as to wish to *leave* the earth can find terrestrial life confining." "Eh, voilà!" exclaims Voltaire, thinking that this concurs with his side of the argument. But the old man very soon disabuses him and shows that he sides with Epictetus instead. "The cage is apt," he goes on, "because it symbolizes so well the way we are imprisoned by finite existence. But that is not the fault of finite things. It is our own desire for those things that enslaves us—our petty cares and concerns about finite events and persons. The sage attains liberty of the spirit by rising above all desires and finite concerns to a blissful state of perfect indifference. That is what I hope to express by meditating in a cage."

This reply shows that there is an embarrassing fault in the "simple and obvious" description of constraint as occurring when circumstances prevent the realization of desire, and in the corresponding attempt to define self-realization as the realization of desire. Based on that description, we would, by consulting the individual's wants and desires, solve the problem of specifying which possibility is to be realized. But this solution would scarcely be acceptable to the Stoic or to the Oriental sage. To adopt it would be inadvertently to take sides with one particular stage of the dialectic traversed in the last chapter: with the immediate view, which understands freedom as the ability to do whatever I happen to desire at the moment. But that would simply beg the question of *psychological* constraint, the question whether desires and wishes themselves may be the sources of coercion and constraint. What are we to say of the docile rape victim's desire to placate her attacker in hopes of saving her life, for example? There are those, too, who would insist that the rapist, in turn, is the victim of his own impulses, that he is constrained by psychic mechanisms over which he has no control. Fortunately, these issues need not be settled here, but nor should they be begged at the outset. And we need not agree with Stoicism or asceticism, but only have to recognize that if desire can *ever* be the source of coercion and constraint, then the distinction between freedom and constraint cannot be founded upon desire. For if it is desire that constrains, then freedom cannot be the realization of that desire, nor can constraint be defined as that which obstructs or prevents the realization of desire.[3]

We might try to save some version of the ordinary notion of freedom as "being able to do what I want," by retreating to a more neutral term such as "intention" and defining freedom as "the ability to realize my intentions,"

---

3. Indeed, as Robert Kane argues (*Free Will and Values* [Albany: State University of New York Press, 1985], 33–46), the absence of constraint is not a sufficient condition or definition of freedom—at least where constraint is defined as that which prevents me from doing what I want. For what if my very wants are covertly instilled in me by some external power—whether the creator of Skinner's *Walden II* or an omnipotent deity or merely the forces of nature? Such covert control would be "nonconstraining" insofar as it would not prevent me from doing what I want. Would I be free whenever circumstances allowed me to do as I please if "what I please" were subject to such covert nonconstraining control, Kane asks? Surely not! A control that operates *through* my wants would leave me even less free than one that operates *despite* them, which I can at least struggle to escape. Kane concludes that in order to be free, I must have "sole or ultimate dominion" over my own choices. If anything, such covert control would seem to be the subtlest, most irresistible form of coercion or compulsion, as Stoics and ascetics have always maintained. It therefore suggests that we revise the boundary between self and circumstance and redefine constraint so as to make room for *psychological* compulsion and constraint.

whether those be immediate desires or intentions grounded in moral scruples or religious beliefs. At first glance, that seems a simpler, more straightforward solution than this long, roundabout attempt to analyze freedom and constraint as relational structures. But that solution is deceptive just because of its neutrality, and it only serves to conceal the difficulty by casting the problem in more introspective, psychological terms. But disputes about the nature of freedom all too readily become entangled in an introspective melee of shifting and conflicting desires and intentions, only to lose sight of the fact that what is finally at stake is the self's relationship to possibilities. Stripped of all the subtleties of mutual qualification and conflict and of their overtones of intensity, anxiety, and discomfort, desires and intentions may be construed as positive evaluations or attitudes of the self toward possibilities. Introduction of such subjective terms might somewhat *narrow* the field of possibilities pertinent to freedom to those toward which the self is favorably disposed. But that would still leave a plurality of possibilities. Any one individual may harbor a host of desires, some faint, some strong, some practical, others quite fantastic. Any condition or state that I deem at all preferable to the one I currently enjoy or suffer is in some degree desired. If I were to stop to draw up the sum of my wishes, I would find myself with a very long list indeed. And although the ethical man may be able to cross off some of the more immediate and selfish of these, he will add on enough "oughts" at the other end to make up the loss. As for intentions, if the road to hell is paved with good ones, it is not because circumstances have prevented their realization, since no man is damned for that, but because they have been abandoned along the route. Is there anyone who does not keep a sizable store of such intentions on hand at all times, set aside or filed away in the course of other preoccupations? Desires and intentions might somewhat narrow the field, but they still point to a multitude of possibilities and would still leave the same basic problem of determining how any of these is to be singled out as that upon which freedom and constraint depend.

Yet if we cannot distinguish between freedom and constraint by appealing to what an individual *wants,* then how *are* we to settle upon which possibility to consider in determining whether an individual is free or constrained? At any given moment, of course, just which possibilities are relevant to me will depend largely upon my circumstances. (If I am in New York, I can ride the subway downtown, but that possibility is simply not relevant in New London or Topeka.) But we cannot leave it up to circumstances to determine which possibility is to be realized, because the realization of that possibility is *ruled out by circumstances* when I am constrained. When I am constrained, my circumstances prevent me from realizing one possibility and force me to realize some other possibility in its stead. (It is possible that my vacation flight to Acapulco will crash, or that I will be beaten and robbed on the way to the bank, or that a paralyzing blood clot will form in my brain while I am out jogging. But these are not possibilities that I am free to realize under favorable conditions. They are possibilities that circumstances may thrust upon me.) This role of constraining conditions, whereby they *impose* a possibility upon me, is *coercion* or *compulsion*. Insofar as circumstances single out what possibility I am to realize, I am *coerced* rather than free.

But if it is not the nature of circumstances that determines which possibility is to be realized, then that possibility must be founded in the nature of the self. And that possibility must somehow be inherent in the self *apart from* circumstances, since circumstances *may* prevent its realization. This would mean that the self is free when it realizes a possibility that is determined by its own nature and constrained when circumstances prevent it from doing so and compel it to realize some other possibility instead.

This account of the contrariety between freedom and constraint seems a fitting amplification of the basic, generative idea of freedom as self-realization, since the possibility to be realized is inherent in the nature of the self. It also has a number of other advantages to recommend it. First, this analysis helps to explain *why* this conception of freedom as self-realization generated a whole series of different and competing versions. For if it is the nature of the self that selects which possibilities freedom depends upon, then the concrete import of freedom will vary with differing conceptions of the self. Our earlier recognition that self-realization makes the nature of freedom a function of the nature of the self is therefore repeated and accommodated here. But this account also reflects the *conditional* character of self-realization and clarifies the three-termed relationship between self, circumstances, and possibility that is required in order to distinguish between freedom and constraint. For although the possibility to be realized is a function of the nature of the self, the actual realization of that possibility depends upon favorable conditions, upon the absence of coercion and constraint, which would compel the individual to realize some other possibility instead. Moreover, this account is especially attractive because it is in accord with a familiar and powerful tradition in Western thought: that classical philosophical tradition, stemming from Plato and Aristotle, which conceives of self-realization as the realization of one's natural potential. For a natural potentiality is, precisely, a possibility that is inherent in the very nature of an entity, but that may or may not be realized, depending upon whether appropriate conditions are present. Finally, this appeal to nature serves as a timely reminder to keep the whole natural order within view. Reflection upon human examples has tended to dominate this discussion, despite my earlier resolve not to confine my focus to the rather special case of the human species, but to consider whether freedom might be encountered elsewhere as well.

The description of freedom as the realization of natural potential *invites* the application of the concept to nonhuman examples and species, since human beings are certainly not the only beings who realize their natural potentialities under favorable conditions. The attempt to understand freedom in these terms should therefore help to extend the range of this inquiry and to place the problems of human freedom in a broader perspective, which may help us appreciate what is peculiar about the human condition.[4]

The obvious disadvantage of this approach, inseparable from these advantages, is that it leads directly back toward the impasse over the true nature of the self encountered at the beginning of this chapter. It is hardly great progress to have replaced the problem of how to decide which is the real self with the problem of how to decide which possibilities are to be accounted natural potentialities. The second problem is all too obviously inseparable from the first. But the definition of freedom as the realization of natural potentialities also presents other difficulties that may point to a way out of this impasse. A simple example will help to expose these difficulties. Let us apply this analysis of freedom to Thomas Hobbes's discussion of the freedom of water.[5] Hobbes says that water enjoys freedom or liberty insofar as it is permitted to spread out or flow, but not if it is contained by a vessel or dams or banks. Thus, water can flow *freely* down a

---

4. Christine Swanton adopts this strategy in *Freedom: A Coherence Theory* (Indianapolis: Hackett, 1992), though in a way that confines freedom to *human* agency. Drawing upon J. L. Austin's "A Plea for Excuses" (in *Philosophical Papers* [Oxford: Oxford University Press, 1961]), she conceives of freedom as "the absence of limitations in the practical activity of human beings" (33). Acknowledging that "[s]omething is a *limitation* relative to some end, goal, value or comparison class," she argues that "limitations related to the *freedom* of a given individual are relative to the potential of that individual in agency" (38). Swanton thereby incurs all the problems of defining individual potential that occupy the pages that follow. She tries to solve them by appealing to an ideal of self-realization: "In the richest sense of potential in agency, that potential is not just one component or aspect of flourishing qua agent: it is synonymous with that flourishing. A person realizes his potential if and only if he flourishes or is 'self-realized.' This conception of potential presupposes a value-based selection of capacities and propensities to be realized by the agent"(39–40). Obviously, her strategy would not work here, since it would only revive the problems of defining self-realization with which this chapter began. What counts as flourishing or self-realization will differ depending upon the definition of the "self." Swanton's own account of "potential in agency" is far too rich to capture in a footnote. But as the above citations may suggest, the potential in question is not defined simply by the original *nature* of the individual, but also by analysis of the *agency* of the self and by the values to be realized by that agency. Insofar as that is so, it does not lend itself to the present context.

5. *Leviathan,* pt. 2, chap. 21, p. 147.

slope or channel, for instance, provided that it does not meet with opposition or limitation in the form of a dam. Now, we can certainly analyze Hobbes's illustration in terms of the realization of inherent or natural potentialities and say that, in descending a river channel, water realizes an inherent potential thanks to the absence of constraining circumstances in the form of a dam.

The trouble is that if there *is* a dam, the water will realize an *equally* inherent and natural potentiality by rising to form a pond or lake. The absence of a dam prevents the realization of this potential just as much as the presence of a dam frustrates the water's potential for flowing down hill. Or consider water's natural potential for freezing, which may either frustrate or be frustrated by its potential for flowing, since frozen water will not flow and flowing water may not freeze.

The problem here is that the nature of water founds a variety of contrary potentialities. No one possibility or type of possibility among these is any more "natural" or "inherent" than any other. In order to sustain the antithesis between freedom and constraint, some principle of selection among these various and contrary potentialities is required, and there is no such principle inherent in the nature of the water. But, it may well be replied, that only means that to speak of "freedom" in describing water or other *inanimate* beings is to indulge in metaphor. In the realm of *animate,* living beings, however, the nature of the organism *does* seem to exercise such a selective function. Here, we can appeal to the *teleological,* or *goal-directed,* natures of all living things. The possibilities of growth, sustenance, and reproduction seem to be singled out as distinctively *natural* potentialities of the organisms. The mature plant is implicitly present in the seed, the chicken implicit in the fertilized egg. The whole evolution of the mature individual seems to be prescribed by the arrangement of nucleic acids in the single egg or seed. Any organism seems to have certain *specific* possibilities bound up in its very nature in a way that *other* possibilities are not. Surely, then, natural potential serves as a meaningful selective principle in the biological sphere, even if it doesn't work to extend it into the inorganic realm.

And yet, the same difficulties present themselves here as in the case of water. The nature of the acorn lends itself as well to nourishing a squirrel as to generating an oak tree. The egg *may* become a chicken, but it may also be broken or eaten or used in painting a fresco. The chromosomes that prescribe an organism's development may be consumed by bacteria or parasitized by a virus or reorganized by radiation. All of these contrary possibilities are founded in the "natures" of the organisms in question. What makes any one of them more natural than another? Does the acorn stop being an acorn if a squirrel eats it? Very well, but it must also stop being an acorn if it is to become an oak tree. In neither case does the possibility it realizes cause it not to *have been* an acorn, so its nature cannot *depend* upon its realizing the "right" possibility. Is the possibility of becoming an oak "more natural" in the sense of "more typically or frequently realized"? Hardly, else we would find ourselves in a world unendurably crowded with oak trees! Only a small fraction of the seed of any species ever reaches maturity, and the most typical fate of an acorn is probably to rot or to feed a rodent rather than to become an oak.

In the light of these reflections, what *are* we to make of the notion of natural potentialities? One possibility may be called more "natural" than another in the organic realm only because we identify the nature of the individual with a possibility that we regard as paradigmatic for the entire species. This paradigmatic possibility need not be realized in any one particular case, however, or even in the majority of cases. We single it out as paradigmatic, rather, because it is a *distinctive* possibility. The acorn's possibility of becoming an oak distinguishes it preeminently from everything else. Its other possibilities are each shared with a diversity of other things. Other nuts and seeds may nourish squirrels, whereas nothing but an acorn can generate an oak tree. And because this potentiality differentiates the acorn from everything else, it is well suited for use in defining the nature of the species, much as the distinctive mating call or flight pattern of a species of birds differentiates it from other species. To use traditional Aristotelian terms, the potentiality to become an oak is one of the "specific differentiae" of acorns. But whereas a paradigm suggests a norm or ideal, to single out such distinctive potentialities is not to say that it would be better or more ideal or even "more natural" if that potentiality were realized by every member of the species: if every acorn became an oak, every hen's egg a chicken. There is nothing lamentably wrong or unnatural about squirrels' eating acorns. And there would have been no evolution of life if every generation of individuals perfectly reproduced the specific types.

Nor is the paradigmatic possibility any more "inherent" in the constitution of the organism than all other possibilities. For notice that when we define the nature of a thing in terms of such a paradigmatic possibility, we also implicitly write a prescription for a favorable set of conditions that will permit—or even *cause*—the realization of that possibility. It is in warm, moist, fertile soil and temperate climate that an acorn may realize its potential to become an oak. But a contrary prescription would yield a contrary outcome. In a squirrel's stomach, an acorn will realize a different potentiality. Clearly, one cannot say that either of these possibilities is inherent in the nature of the acorn "prior to" or "apart from" circumstances. All such potentialities are "natural" in the sense that they are *consonant with* a given natural constitution. But although indeed founded in the nature or structure of acorns or water, such natural potentialities also presuppose certain necessary conditions, circumstances without which they could not be realized. And by specifying one or another set of necessary conditions, we can construe *everything* that can ever happen to *anything* as "the realization of a natural potentiality." And if freedom is the ability to realize one's natural potential, then everything will *always* be free.

Evidently, the antithesis between freedom and constraint cannot be sustained on this basis. The specific nature of an organism is the foundation for a *variety* of potentialities that may be realized under differing conditions. It does not single out any *one* possibility from all the others. It is not up to the acorn whether it generates an oak or feeds a squirrel, or a function of the nature of water to determine which of its various potentialities it will realize under given conditions. That depends upon the circumstances. But we cannot leave it to circumstances to determine which possibility to realize, for that is coercion. And if the determination of what possibility the self is to realize is left to circumstances, then circumstances will never *prevent* self-realization, and constraint is impossible. The definition of freedom as the realization of natural potentialities fails, then, because in allowing circumstances to determine what possibility the self is to realize, it confounds freedom with coercion and cannot yield a clear distinction between freedom and constraint. Some more precise principle of selection is required, and some more intimate bond between self and possibility than those provided by the nature of the species.

But perhaps all these difficulties arise just because we have only been dealing with the nature of the *species* rather than with the individual nature of the particular organism. After all, the *specific* nature includes only what is universal, what is shared by all the members of an entire species. It is therefore bound to be ambiguous and open-ended, since it must accommodate all the individual differences and idiosyncrasies of all the members of that species. For while every individual must share in the common nature of the species (by definition, else it would not be common), each individual does not share the total range of potentialities of the entire species. Some acorns are sterile; some individuals can do what others cannot. (Otherwise, there would be no horse races.) Each individual organism has a unique genetic heritage that determines its individual nature[6]—in the sense that what is natural is what is innate, inherited at birth. That is why there are family resemblances, but only twins generated from the same egg are identical. Studies of these exceptions, especially of identical twins reared

---

6. This does not hold, of course, for organisms reproduced by mitosis, or for monozygotic twins, triplets, etc. But such exceptions may only help support the point at issue, as suggested below.

separately, have found similarities of behavior, taste, and disposition so striking as strongly to suggest that the genetically inherited *individual* nature that identical twins share may provide a principle of selection that would unambiguously determine every individual's entire career. Is it that individual nature, then, that the self must be able to realize if it is free?

The idea that every individual has a unique nature or essence was central to the philosophy of Leibniz. Leibniz coined the term "monad" to refer to any genuinely and irreducibly individual being and argued that every monad has its own singular essential formula. He insisted that the entire career of each individual monad is already inherent in its essence potentially and that the realization of those potentialities is simply the explication or unfolding of the essence as a series of acts or perceptions. The temporal career of the individual is therefore rather like the playing of a phonograph record or tape cassette, or the projection of a reel of movie film. And if Leibniz's metaphysics strikes some contemporary readers as a seventeenth-century museum piece, they will find a contemporary variation of the same theme coming from the very opposite end of the philosophical spectrum in the suggestion of some existentialist authors that each individual has a personal fate or destiny and that his freedom consists in embracing or realizing that destiny.[7]

Have we finally discovered the foundation of freedom in an individual's nature or essence or destiny, then? Does this provide a principle for determining that possibility upon which the antithesis between freedom and constraint depends? The mention of destiny and fate causes some hesitation about whether to embrace this solution. A closer look at Leibniz justifies that hesitation. For the doctrine that the individual essence implicitly contains the individual's entire career leads Leibniz to treat it as a kind of inner fatality, to insist that the individual's career could not possibly be otherwise, that it cannot be altered in the slightest detail, else it would be the career of a different individual. Every act of the individual is a necessary realization of a unique essential formula and could not possibly be done otherwise. Nor could anything *happen* to alter the individual's career or

---

7. This theme appears in Nietzsche, Buber, and Jaspers. A passage from Buber's *I and Thou* illustrates the theme: "Fate and freedom are promised to each other. Fate is encountered only by him that actualizes freedom. That I discovered the deed that intends me, that, this movement of my freedom, reveals the mystery to me . . . this free human being encounters fate as the counter-image of his freedom. It is not his limit but his completion; freedom and fate embrace each other to form meaning; and given meaning, fate—with its eyes, hitherto severe, suddenly full of light, looks like grace itself" (Martin Buber, *I and Thou*, trans. Walter Kaufmann [New York: Scribners, 1970], 102). Cf. Jaspers's discussion of *amor fati* in *Philosophy*, trans. E. B. Ashton (Chicago: Chicago University Press, 1970), 2:191–93.

prevent the complete unfolding or realization of that essence.[8] But that means that every being realizes its natural potentialities *inevitably* and cannot be *prevented* from doing so—which means that constraint is quite impossible. The suggestion that to be free is to "love one's fate" or "embrace one's destiny" points toward a similar collapse of the antithesis between freedom and constraint. The contrariety between freedom and constraint— and therewith the *conditional* character of freedom as self-realization—can only be sustained in relation to a possibility that may *either* be realized *or* prevented and whose realization therefore *cannot* be fated, destined, or otherwise inevitable.

The son who inherits a hereditary disease from his father will scarcely see the onset of that disease as "liberating" simply because it is the realization of his own natural potential. He will not regard that possibility as his "own" simply because it is part of his genetic endowment—or because he has come by it naturally. His father and his father's chromosomes are just as circumstantial, just as external, as any other ingredient in his situation—if not more so, since some of his circumstances will be of his own making, the results of his own deeds. If he has inherited a terrible temper or a weakness for drink, then it is not perverse to "go against his nature" and attempt to overcome this heritage. It may be futile and foolish to regret my blue eyes or fair skin, but it is not foolish or futile to try to overcome the liabilities of that skin by using sunscreen. The same holds for any other natural disposition or potential. If my father and grandfather were suicidal manic-depressives who shot themselves in the end, why should I embrace their fate as my own? Surely, I have every reason to regard this inheritance as coercive and to seek to free myself from their fate by every means available.

The notion of a univocal individual nature, essence, or destiny exposes the underlying fault in the whole effort to conceive of free self-realization as the realization of one's natural potentiality. Under this conception, the individual is even less free than he would be under the traditional Hindu caste system—and for similar reasons. A social order that condemns the son to repeat the pattern of his father's life is constraining because that leaves the individual so little control over his own life. But a univocal individual nature or destiny would mean that not only the individual's social class and function but *all* his possibilities, his every action and feeling,

---

8. Therefore must Leibniz insist that the monads do not interact and that there must be a preestablished harmony among all these independently unfolding natures. All of these doctrines derive from his conviction that all truths are necessary truths because every true statement is analytically true, that in every true judgment the predicate is *contained* in the subject. Therefore, everything that can *ever* be truly said about me could have been said at the moment of my birth.

would be *innate,* genetically programmed, already settled by inheritance, "by nature" rather than by himself. If every detail of an individual's career is prescribed by nature and inheritance, there is no room left for self-control or self-realization, or for any meaningful distinction between freedom and constraint. Evidently, the source of that distinction must lie elsewhere.

❋ Part II ❋

Pure
Freedom

Part I has led from meanings to actions, from a confusing variety of uses of the word "freedom" to a recognition of how most of those meanings emerge from the confrontation between an agent who seeks to impose a purpose upon the world and a world that may not lend itself to that purpose. The agent must always reckon with circumstances that may prove constraining, and the meanings of freedom emerge from the confrontation between purposive agent and constraining circumstances. This contrast between freedom and constraint evokes the contrast between freedom and causal necessity encountered in the Introduction, which showed how the demand for causal explanations leads to the dismissal of freedom as an illusion. From the perspective of the agent, that same opposition appears as the contrast between freedom to act and the constraints thrown up by opposing circumstances. Indeed, from the standpoint of the agent, the extreme antithesis to freedom is not mere constraint but the *coercion* that occurs when the causal action of circumstance displaces the agent's own purposes.

But although the general form of the dialectic between freedom and coercion or constraint is easy enough to understand and has helped to illuminate the variety of meanings of freedom (since the meaning of freedom shifts with every relocation of the border between freedom and constraint), the exact location of that difference remains elusive. If we cannot anchor that distinction somewhere, then we have only displaced one ambiguity with another. Worse still, the contrast between freedom and coercion itself will prove vacuous, since any action may be described in either way, depending upon where one draws the distinction. At the end of Chapter 2, I tried to anchor the difference in the *nature* of the agent—and saw why that only leads back into the impasse between freedom and determinism and to the conclusion that freedom is a mere illusion. In Chapter 3, I demonstrate that the reality of freedom can only be vindicated by grounding it in the agent's *choice* rather than his nature. The negative conception of freedom as absence of constraint proves meaningless unless balanced by a positive freedom of choice, which displaces any inherited nature or determinate potential by the power of self-determination.

Thus, if freedom is to have anything more than an ambiguous verbal reality, it must be founded in a self-determining agent whose purposes are chosen rather than imposed by nature or circumstance. In the remainder of Part II, I shall try to extricate this fundamental freedom of self-determination from all such limiting conditions. That attempt will pose difficulties of another, rather surprising sort.

❊ 3 ❊

The Fundamental Freedom

> The music master praised the bird tremendously, and insisted that it was much better than the real nightingale, not only as regards the outside, with all the diamonds, but the inside too.
>
> "Because, you see, my ladies and gentlemen, and the emperor before all, in the real nightingale, you never know what you will hear. But in the artificial one, everything is decided before hand. So it is and must remain, it can't be otherwise."
>
> —Hans Christian Andersen, "The Emperor's Nightingale"

Introduction: The Necessity of Choice

It is not up to the acorn whether to become an oak or feed a squirrel. That, in a nutshell, is why the appeal to the nature of the self fails. The attempt to understand freedom as the self's realization of its natural potential founders because the specific nature of any entity is the basis for a whole spectrum of possibilities, wide enough to encompass whatever could possibly become of any member of the species. Since it is not up to the acorn whether it becomes an oak, or a function of the *nature* of water whether it flows or freezes, the selection of *which* possibility gets realized in any given case proves to be a function of circumstances rather than of the nature of the self. But if circumstances determine which possibility is to be realized, then those same circumstances will obviously never *prevent* that very possibility from being realized, and constraint is impossible. Or, one might just as well say that if circumstances determine which possibility is realized, then the individual is *coerced,* and it is *freedom* that is impossible.

I therefore asked whether the notion of freedom as the realization of natural potentialities could be preserved by making the unique individual nature of the organism responsible for determining which possibility is to be realized. But that solution also fails. It would require that an individual's entire career be inscribed in an original nature much as an entire song is built into the artificial nightingale of Andersen's fable, or as an entire symphony may be inscribed upon a compact disc. If every incident in my career were implicit in my essence as every note of the music is engraved in the record, then the possibilities I realize *would* be independent of circumstances. But if that were so, then there could be no constraint. For in that case, circumstances cannot prevent the realization of any of these potentialities, since the whole tune—or life—is settled from the outset. If we are to preserve the contrast between freedom and constraint, then circumstances *must* be able to interfere with the realization of those potentialities.

And of course, it is not up to the compact disc whether it will be bought and played, or what song or symphony it will play, any more than it is up to the acorn whether it will become an oak. CDs do not play themselves[1], and the music it plays is not determined by the disc, but by the die that stamped it, much as the genetic constitution of the individual bears the stamp of the parental chromosomes. The inherent nature of the individual is no less a product of circumstances because the determining events and conditions all lie in the past, at the moment of conception. One might just as well describe the rule of such a fixed, inflexible inherited nature as a form of coercion and constraint, which leaves no room for freedom. To be "as free as a compact disc" is not, after all, to be so very free.

Evidently, if freedom is the *absence* of coercion and constraint and if the possibility to be realized is to belong to the self *apart from* circumstances in any genuine sense, then the determination of what possibility to realize cannot be left to circumstance *or* to a nature that the individual has no part in determining but merely inherits from past circumstances. But if it is not up to circumstances to determine what possibility is to be realized, or to desire, or to the inherent nature of the self, then how *is* that possibility to be selected? Since the circumstances ultimately include everything else *but* the

---

1. One could design a closed-system cassette and deck with an internal power supply and cuing device, of course. At that point, one would be on the way toward designing one of Leibniz's windowless monads. The only way to guarantee that the realization of inherent potentialities will be entirely independent of circumstances is to adopt Leibniz's most controversial stratagem and deny any and all interaction between entities. But that makes constraint strictly impossible.

self, only one answer remains: *It must be up to the self to determine for itself which possibility to realize.* To put this answer in the simplest, most emphatic terms, the antithesis between freedom and constraint and the idea of freedom as self-realization can have no meaning unless the self can *decide* or *choose* for itself what possibility to realize.

If the self selects what possibility to realize, then the antithesis between freedom and constraint can be readily and simply formulated: to be free is to be able to realize that chosen possibility; to be constrained is to be prevented from doing so by circumstances. Indeed, the appeal to choice offers such a simple answer that it has probably long since occurred to the reader, who may well have wondered why I have taken such a long way round to arrive at this point. Haven't I taken a very long ramble around Robin Hood's barn only to arrive at the rather simple and obvious recognition that to be free is to be able to choose for oneself? Wouldn't it have been easy enough just to say that at the outset: Freedom consists in the realization of one's own decisions or choices? What is gained by all these reflections upon linguistics and genetics, upon functions, relations, relevance, natural potentiality, and the like, when the same result might have been reached by appealing to free choice or decision at the very beginning?

To justify the longer route, to appreciate how this path has led to a more comprehensive and fundamental grasp of the nature of freedom, one need only reconsider the ground already traversed. Granted, it would have been easy enough to present some doctrine of freedom of choice or decision at the very beginning of Chapter 2. But would that have led us beyond the corner of Oak Street and the dispute about free choice from which this entire inquiry began? A direct invocation of free choice would only have added to the series of conceptions of freedom compiled in Chapter 1—thereby aggravating the problem of the ambiguity of the meaning of freedom that provoked Chapter 2. Instead, I have traced the diversity of ideas of freedom encountered in Chapter 1 to a single generative idea of freedom as self-realization, from which all those competing conceptions can be derived by simply altering the definition of the nature of the self. That alone is a considerable gain, since it allows us to escape the conclusion that the meaning of freedom is arbitrary. However, while that helps to *explain* the ambiguity of freedom by tracing it to its source, it does not solve the problem, but only displaces the impasse from the nature of freedom to the nature of the self.

Confronted by this impasse blocking one avenue of inquiry about the meaning of freedom, I altered course and tried to lay bare the structure of freedom independently of disputes about the nature of the self, while still making the basic, generative idea of freedom as self-realization the point of departure and focus. Since the freedom of self-realization depends upon the absence of coercion and constraint, I have been able to use the contrariety between freedom and constraint to guide the inquiry. This led to the analysis of both freedom and constraint as three-termed relationships between self, circumstance, and possibility.[2] But not every possibility inserted into this relational structure—or even every *relevant* possibility— would yield an antithesis between freedom and constraint. Some special connection between self and possibility proved necessary in order to account for that contrariety.

There seems to be a glaringly obvious solution to this predicament: Surely, the relevant possibilities are those that the individual *wishes* to realize, the ones he *desires* or *intends* to act upon. Many philosophers have formulated the difference between freedom and constraint in just this way: To be constrained is to be prevented from doing as I want; to be free is to be able to do as I please. Unfortunately, this path leads straight back to square one, to the ordinary definition of freedom from which we began, and would plunge us back into the same dialectical progression that we seek to escape. We would have to contend with views, both Western and Asian, that see desire and want as significant obstacles to a freedom only attainable through Stoic indifference or the Buddhist extinction of desire.[3] The appeal to desire begs the question at issue among those different conceptions of freedom as self-realization by assuming one particular demarcation of the boundary between self and circumstance. I therefore turned to the

---

2. Gerald MacCallum deftly analyzes how different versions of freedom result from variously specifying any of the three terms of this triadic relation. But he also calls attention to the ways in which the specifications of the three terms are mutually interdependent, as I have shown. For example, the definition of constraining circumstances reflects how one conceives of the nature of the self and which possibilities one specifies as relevant. See Gerald C. MacCallum Jr., "Negative and Positive Freedom," *Philosophical Review* 76 (1967).

3. In *The Importance of What We Care About* (Cambridge: Cambridge University Press, 1988) Harry Frankfurt has argued that we have to reckon with the fact that our desires, themselves, become objects of our judgment, intention, and desires. I may wish to rid myself of some desires. I may also wish to harbor desires that I do not have—and even to experience desires that I would not wish to act upon. Frankfurt rightly emphasizes the importance of these "second-order desires" in human motivation. This suggests that we might solve our problem by defining freedom and constraint in terms of possibilities endorsed, or "seconded," by an individual's second-order desires. But Frankfurt recognizes that this answer will not suffice. For what if my second-order desires are the product of a racist upbringing that I now regard as an alien and pernicious influence and struggle to overcome? Faced with examples of this sort, which pose the threat of an infinite regress of higher-order desires, Frankfurt resorts to the notion of an act whereby the individual *identifies* himself with some of his second-order desires, "so that they are not merely desires that he happens to have or to find within himself, but desires that he adopts or puts himself behind. . . . Without such identification, the person is a passive bystander to his desires and to what he does, regardless of whether the causes of his desires and what he does are the work of another agent, of impersonal external forces or of processes within his own body" (53–54).

notion of a natural potentiality as a possibility inherent in the original nature of the individual. But that, too, has now proved inadequate.

The failure of these alternatives has led to the conclusion that the self must decide for itself which possibility to realize.[4] And although I might have begun with "free choice"—as indeed I did by questioning Domer Ringuette's choice to forsake his life in Chicopee for a career as a gambler in Las Vegas—that would not have eliminated the other candidates. Yet it was very important to consider them, because some advocates of determinism deny that there is any freedom of choice, but argue that freedom and determinism are quite compatible with one another. These "compatibilists," or "soft" determinists, try to reconcile freedom with determinism by defining freedom as self-realization and founding it in one of these alternatives instead. Champions of immediacy and spontaneity see freedom as the realization of natural impulses and desires and may regard deliberation and choice as repressive. Advocates of ethical and ascetic views are more likely to appeal to reason or to the essential nature and inherent potentialities of the self as grounds for treating immediate desires and impulses as circumstantial influences. Either one of these appeals may be employed to argue that there can be freedom *without* free choice and that freedom is therefore compatible with determinism. Simply to appeal to choice without considering these alternatives would have been to beg the questions posed by their arguments and dodge the whole issue whether there can be freedom *without* choice. By considering these appeals to desire and to natural potentialities independently of that issue and by showing that we cannot distinguish between freedom and constraint on these grounds, I have shown that the idea of freedom as self-realization is not self-sufficient—and thereby established the necessity of founding any and all of these conditional, relational forms of freedom upon choice. Instead of merely adding another definition of freedom to the list, then, I have

---

4. Frankfurt reaches much the same conclusion by a different path that converges with my own at this point. In "Three Concepts of Free Action" (in ibid.), Frankfurt confesses that he finds the notion of "identification" cited in the note above "a bit mystifying." His attempt to clarify it in "Identification and the External" (in ibid.) engages him in the dialectic of internal and external traversed in Chapter 2 above. That leads him just where it has led here: to the indispensable role of a self-defining choice whereby the individual decides for himself where to draw the line between internal and external or, as I have put it, between self and circumstance. And because "[d]ecisions, unlike desires and attitudes, do not seem to be susceptible both to internality and externality" (ibid., 68 n. 30), Frankfurt escapes the problem of an infinite regress of higher-and-higher-order desires described in note 3 above. He explores the self-defining, or self-constitutive, role of decision at greater length in "Identification and Wholeheartedness" (ibid., 159–76). For a more extensively elaborated analysis of the problem of infinite regress and its resolution through appeal to choice, see Robert Kane's *Free Will and Values* (Albany: State University of New York Press, 1985), especially the discussions of choice in chapters 5 and 8.

exposed the basic structure of freedom and constraint and demonstrated
that all conditional, relational forms of freedom depend upon free choice.

Thus, if either immediate freedom or ethical freedom is to have any
secure meaning, that must be discovered in and developed out of a more
fundamental kind of freedom. These relational freedoms, which are contingent upon circumstances, depend ultimately upon an original and
intrinsic freedom that is, by definition, independent of circumstances and
therefore must belong to the very being of the self *un*conditionally. None of
the views of freedom explored in Chapter 1 is adequate or self-sufficient
apart from this precondition.[5] All versions of self-realization, from that
which champions the most immediate or insistent desires to the most
extreme forms of ethical or religious asceticism, presuppose a being
capable of choice, of *determining for itself* which possibility to realize. We can
therefore describe this as the freedom of *self-determination,* to distinguish it
from these several versions of *self-realization.* And indeed, this is the third
major conception of freedom that Mortimer Adler and his associates
distinguish in *The Idea of Freedom.*[6]

5. Kant eventually and somewhat reluctantly reached this same conclusion, as John Silber
explains in "The Ethical Significance of Kant's *Religion*," his part of the introduction to the
Harper edition of Kant's *Religion Within the Limits of Reason Alone,* trans. T. M. Greene and Hoyt
Hudson (New York: Harper, 1960), lxxix-cxxiv. Kant originally argued for a version of ethical
freedom, identifying freedom with practical reason, that is, with autonomous, moral choice in
contrast with heteronomous action, action governed by the laws of nature instead of the moral
law. But in the *Critique of Practical Reason,* he recognized that the rational, autonomous will is
not really free unless it has also the power to *reject* the moral law and choose heteronomy
instead. (See esp. lxxiv-xciv of Silber's essay.)

More recently, Susan Wolf (in *Freedom Within Reason* [Oxford: Oxford University Press,
1990] and "Asymmetrical Freedom," *Journal of Philosophy* 77 [March 1980] : 151–66.) has
arrived at a similar result by an opposite route. On the one hand, Wolf identifies positive
freedom with choices determined by reasons that the agent perceives as valid, and argues that
responsibility for *moral* action is therefore compatible with "psychological determinism." But
she goes on to argue that we cannot reasonably blame anyone for evil deeds unless our
irrational choices are *un*determined. For if my *wicked* choice is psychologically determined,
that means that reason could not possibly have triumphed and prompted me to do what is
right. Both authors see that without the freedom to choose between autonomy and heteronomy, between good and evil, ethical "freedom" would boil down to an empty, honorific way
of describing the difference between two classes of psychological cause: rational and irrational.

6. Adler and his colleagues designate this third major class of conceptions of freedom "the
natural freedom of self-determination," where "natural" specifies a freedom shared by *all* men
independently of circumstance and of their acquiring any special virtue or wisdom. They list over
sixty philosophical proponents of this idea of freedom, ranging from Aristotle, Augustine, and
Aquinas through Rousseau, Kant, and Hegel to Bergson, Whitehead, and Sartre. After
exploring many specific differences among these very diverse thinkers, they formulate the
generic definition of this conception of freedom as follows: "To be free is to be able, by a power
inherent in human nature, to change one's own character creatively by deciding for oneself

This long excursion through immediate and ethical conceptions of freedom has led to the recognition that the source of freedom must lie in self-determination. Freedom as self-realization depends upon freedom as self-determination. Attempts to retain the superstructure of self-realization without this foundation are built upon sand. For, as I have shown, in the absence of self-determination, the function of determining the self's possibilities must be conceded to circumstances. This is precisely what occurs for the acorn. What possibilities the self realizes and, therefore, what becomes of it must then be ordained by the influences of its environment. But that is coercion. As for the essential nature of the self, if it is not conceived as an equally coercive personal fate, it will only serve to limit the available *range* of possibilities, not to select *which* among them is to be realized.

But in that case, what could be meant by the distinction between freedom and constraint? How can the stipulation that self-realization is conditional, that freedom depends upon favorable circumstances, be justified? The only possible answer would be that the self is free under the influence of some circumstances but constrained under the influence of other circumstances. The distinction between freedom and constraint would rest merely upon a distinction between two classes of circumstantial influence: between genetic influences and environmental influences, for example, or between nature and nurture, as we used to say.

But according to this hypothesis, the self cannot determine *which* of these two types of circumstance will influence it. Therefore, apart from choice, the self can have no possibilities of its *own*; it cannot "have its own way" if its way is picked out for it by circumstances, whether genetic or environmental. In the end, this means that the self can have no separate reality of its own either, since what it becomes will depend upon its inheritance or its surroundings.[7] Without choice, then, the self becomes nothing but an arena or point of converging, conflicting influences. And inasmuch as such alien forces sweep through this arena or hold sway there, there can be *no*

---

what one shall do or shall become" (Mortimer Adler, *The Idea of Freedom* [Garden City, N.Y.: Doubleday, 1958], 1:606). The reference to "human nature" in their definition is a little misleading, however, since they recognize that some of the authors they list do not see this ability as peculiar to *human* beings. This power to decide for oneself is not an example of the sort of natural potentiality discussed above, since the *nature* of the agent does *not* determine how or what he will decide to do, but only that he is able to choose for himself.

7. Cf. Michael Sandel's account of such a self as "a radically situated subject," so completely constituted by "my" attributes that "just *any* change in my situation, however slight, would change the person I am. But taken literally, and given that my situation changes in some respect at least with every passing moment, this would mean that my identity would blur indistinguishably into my situation" (*Liberalism and the Limits of Justice* [Cambridge: Cambridge University Press, 1982], 20–21).

well-founded distinction between internal and external. In the absence of the ability to determine itself, the individual might be regarded as resembling a relatively closed physical system. Such a system can be regarded *as if* it were a separate reality for certain specific scientific purposes. But the separation is a hypothetical artifice, since the system is really continuous with its context in the final analysis.[8]

The lesson is clear. If freedom is *not* founded in choice, then the meaning of freedom and the distinction between freedom and constraint will be arbitrary, since everything will depend upon how you choose to divide up circumstantial influences into constraining and nonconstraining, and upon how you choose to describe the limits of the relatively closed system that is the self. For freedom will no longer be a relation between self and circumstance, but a relation between circumstance and circumstance within a very limited region of reality whose borders depend upon your extraneous purposes. Without a foundation *in* choice, then, the meaning of freedom is *left* to choice; therefore we found that meaning arbitrary and ambiguous at the end of Chapter 1. The arbitrariness upon which our inquiry foundered, then, has its source in the instability of a freedom founded only upon a distinction between circumstances and a self that has no real "inside." This does not prove that there *is* freedom of choice, of course, but only that, if there is not, there are no free beings and no beings capable of satisfying the relational structure of self-realization. We must now consider what sort of being could possibly determine itself through freedom of choice.

Self-Determination and the Nature of the Self

What must the nature of the self be, if the self is to be free to choose? Doesn't this very question return us to the impasse about the nature of freedom from which this chapter began?

---

8. Cf. Thomas Nagel's account of how "the self which acts and is the object of moral judgment is threatened with dissolution by the absorption of its acts and impulses into the class of events": "[S]omething in the idea of agency is incompatible with actions being events, or people things. But as the external determinants of what someone has done are gradually exposed, in their effect on consequences, character and choice itself, it becomes gradually clear that actions are events and people things. Eventually, nothing remains which can be ascribed to the responsible self, and we are left with nothing but a portion of the larger sequence of events which can be deplored or celebrated, but not blamed or praised" ("Moral Luck," in *Mortal Questions* [Cambridge: Cambridge University Press, 1979], 37). Nagel sounds the same theme in the essays "The Objective Self" and "Freedom," in *The View From Nowhere* (Oxford: Oxford University Press, 1986).

On the contrary, by founding freedom upon choice, we actually escape that impasse, which arises from disagreements about the nature of the self. I began Chapter 2 by encountering the problem of how to decide among competing conceptions of the self. What I have demonstrated, however, is that it cannot be the *nature* of the self that decides which possibility to realize. Rather, the nature of the self must be such as to be *able to decide*, to choose among the possibilities at hand. The difference is radical and critical. If the nature of the self determines what it does, then there is no room for choice, since the selection is the product of the individual's innate constitution. But freedom and choice presuppose a being whose inherited nature does *not* predetermine how it responds to given circumstances, but instead allows the individual to choose among the alternative possibilities available in that situation.

If we are to allow any meaning to the idea of freedom as self-realization, however, it isn't enough to be able to choose among actions and ends that are *really* possible in a given situation. To limit the range of possibilities to *real* possibilities would be to revive the problems that beset abstract freedom. It would be like limiting Napoleon to the possibilities available within the confines of St. Helena—or Elba. But that leaves no room for constraint, or for the *conditional* character of self-realization. The problem here derives from the very logic of constraint. If the range of choice is confined to what is *really* possible, then it is limited to those alternatives that the circumstances *allow*. But then constraint is impossible, since the circumstances cannot *prevent* the realization of the very same possibilities they *allow*. To retain the contrast between freedom and constraint, then, we must provide for possibilities whose realization may be prevented by circumstances; that is, we must allow for possibilities that prove *unrealizable*—or possibilities that are not really possible after all. The very idea of constraint seems to rest upon a contradiction, then, by presupposing impossible possibilities. We can soften the contradiction somewhat by distinguishing between "abstract" and "concrete" possibilities, or between "possible in principle" and "possible in fact." But whatever the nomenclature, it is still true that the antithesis between freedom and constraint, the very notion of constraint itself, presupposes possibilities over and beyond those that the universe actually serves up as *real* or *realizable* possibilities. How are such impossible possibilities possible?

The answer, of course, is that an individual may entertain possibilities whether or not circumstances happen to permit their realization.

"I can call spirits from the vasty deep," boasts Owen Glendower to Hotspur in *Richard II*. To which Hotspur replies sarcastically, "Why so can I, or so can any man. / But will they come when you do call for them?"

Just as a spirit invoked need not appear, so a possibility envisioned need not be achievable, nor need it be any more real than Glendower's "spirits from the vasty deep." Only a being capable of envisioning and choosing such unrealizable possibilities can be constrained. The antithesis between freedom and constraint therefore assumes a being that is an original source of possibilities in the universe[9] and that can *choose* to realize possibilities even if they are incompatible with the limitations of circumstances—*or* the limits of the individual's natural potentialities. To be free is to be able to call up spirits from the vasty deep, whether or not they come when called.[10]

Of course, that alone is only a freedom of the self to determine its own possibilities, and to be free only within the realm of possibilities may seem to be only *fancy-free*. But it is just here that the freedom of self-realization takes over—and first takes on its true importance. For if a being is able to determine its own course in terms of possibilities and is also not constrained, that is, not prevented from realizing those possibilities, then it will be able to determine its own reality as well. Freedom as self-realization is therefore only an aspect of the freedom of a being that is at least *capable* of *fully* determining itself under favorable circumstances. Freedom may therefore be defined as self-determination, while self-realization can be recognized as a mere stage in the process of self-determination, a process that begins in the ability to entertain possibilities, proceeds to the choice of which possibility to realize, and reaches completion, in the absence of constraint, in the realization of that chosen possibility. In this light, freedom with regard to possibilities wears a less frivolous aspect. For in determining myself qua possibility, I am at least prospectively determining what I shall be.

The whole relationship of possibility to the nature of the self is transformed accordingly. If *circumstances* determine what is to become of me, then my possibilities are external to me, as I have already noted. Although their content must be partially founded upon my nature or my present reality, the force of external circumstance determines their realization. Each of them is only related to me as an accident. This may not be conspicuous in each single case, but it becomes quite obvious when I consider the total sum of my possibilities. For if circumstances determine

9. But not necessarily in the *cosmos,* understood as that which includes all reality. If possibilities are real independently of the universe, as some philosophers (such as Whitehead and Weiss) claim, then this originative function of the self is obviously more modest. However, metaphysical systems that include such an independent realm of possibilities usually limit it to that which is not self-contradictory. There is room to question whether the range of contents the self may posit as possible goals is limited by self-contradiction, since that would rule out the individual who attempts to eat his cake and have it too, among others.

10. Not that anything so exotic need be involved. The unrealizable possibility need not be the product of any great leap of imagination. It may seem to lie right beneath my feet, "to leap across this puddle instead of going around."

my entire career, it will appear as a series of possible accidents that compose my *fate.* Yet this fate is not really "mine" at all; it does not really belong to me. If anything, *I* belong to *it.* My fate is not secreted within my being, waiting to be spun out like the thread from a spider's gland. Fate is patently external, a shadow that falls ahead of me to darken my tracks in advance. And it is my surroundings that cast this shadow. Oedipus surely does not *realize* his fate as if it were his own intent; he is *overtaken* by it. Or rather, he falls prey to its concealed snares. Oedipus and his parents strive to outwit this ominous, lurking destiny. But it is that very striving which entangles them in the net of circumstances that, alone, could be the means of realizing their destiny. Herein lies the *irony* of fate.

The accidental encounter between Oedipus and his father epitomizes the nature of fate. For neither the vindictiveness nor the implacability sometimes associated with fate is essential to it. Nor is it essentially a matter of stern necessity, for fate has often been represented as capricious. On the contrary, what is essential to the notion of fate is its foreignness, the indifferent exteriority of possibilities to the person who is destined to realize them. That is what is so perfectly expressed by the fact that Oedipus commits both patricide and incest *by accident,* that he *unwittingly* plays into the hands of fate through his very efforts to *outwit* it.

By contrast, insofar as the self can determine what is to become of itself, these extrinsic, accidental possibilities are transformed into *alternatives* whose foundation and disposition is an *intrinsic* function of the self. What the self is to become thereby ceases to be a fate that haunts it or lies ambuscaded in its circumstances, for the self can foreshape its own career and reality. To be able to decide one's fate turns fate inside out, however—or outside in, as external accident becomes inner choice. There is all the difference in the world, then, between the ability to decide one's fate and *amor fati,* the notion that to be free is to *love* one's fate or to embrace one's destiny. That view counsels assent and acceptance of what is determined by circumstances. It recalls the Stoic doctrine that to be free is simply to conform one's will to the course of nature. Those who see freedom in these terms tend to see in fate some divine wisdom,[11] so that the love of fate converges with the love of God and the acceptance of divine providence. They recognize that the locus of free choice lies "within," and they would willingly abandon self-realization in order to fortify themselves within an impregnable, purely inner freedom, immune to constraint: the freedom to accept whatever vicissitudes God or "Nature"—or Nero—happens to serve up.

To be able to *decide* one's own fate, on the contrary, is to be able to realize

---

11. The obvious exception is Nietzsche.

possibilities of one's own choosing, able to determine oneself outwardly as well as inwardly. The phrase evokes the scene at the end of Plato's *Republic*, in the myth of Er, in which the souls about to be reborn are brought before the three fates who move the universe. But it is not God or the fates who decide their destinies. Instead, they are told to choose for themselves: "Souls that live for a day, now is the beginning of another cycle of mortal generation where birth is the beacon of death. No guardian genius shall cast lots for you, but you shall choose your own genius. Let him to whom the first lot falls first select a life to which he shall cleave of necessity. But virtue has no master over her, and each shall have more or less of her as he honors her or does her despite. The blame is his who chooses. God is blameless."[12]

The individual who chooses becomes responsible for his own future life, the myth seems to say. Presented with a choice between two different careers, two different lives, each individual determines himself—and is determined by himself. This relationship has extensive implications for the nature of the self that is able to determine itself. Choice bridges the gap between present and future, between reality and possibility. To the extent that the self is able to determine itself, its possible reality is clearly a function of its present act. But the present self cannot just unilaterally determine its future while remaining untouched, as a judge may walk away "scot-free," unaffected by the sentence he or she has imposed upon a convicted defendant. In the case of self-determination, there is a reciprocal influence of the future upon the present. Self-determination bridges the gap between present and possibility, and that bridge opens a two-way traffic. Choice allows the self to reach out beyond its present actuality and lay hold of possibility. But possibility is thus drawn into the bosom of the actuality of the individual, and that actuality is not left unaffected by thus embracing possibility. For once possibility gains entrance into the heart of actuality, it acts as a universal solvent that permeates every element of determinate structure and dissolves it into an ambiguous solution. Like a virus, which has no life of its own outside the cell, yet acquires life within the cell by appropriating the structure of the cell to itself, so possibility, which has no reality outside the self, appropriates the given structure of the self to its own vital requirements, turning everything actual and determinate into food for possibility. We must consider more carefully what this means, for this "infection" of the self by possibility has important consequences for understanding the nature of freedom.

In one sense, of course, all the determinate features and structures of the given makeup of the self remain unaltered by the influence of possibility. If

---

12. *Republic* 617d (trans. Paul Shorey [Cambridge, Mass.: Loeb Classical Library, 1930], with one or two changes).

anything, *they* determine what is possible, whereas mere possibility has no causal efficacy and cannot alter or "dissolve" what the individual actually *is*. The introduction of possibility due to freedom does not destroy any definite feature of the self. It is not those determinate characteristics that are dissolved by possibility, but the self. For the inclusion of possibility means that the self cannot be identified with what it already is by nature, at birth, or with whatever it has since become. By engaging the self in possibility, in choosing what it *will* be, self-determination dislodges the identity of the self from what it is, its given, determinate nature, and shifts it toward what it can become. Viewed in this light, from the perspective of choice, the already actual and definite nature, or the developed "personality structure," is only the proximate matter for possibility. Like someone about to remodel or redecorate an old house, the self sees this given structure not for what it is, but for what can be made of it. Every feature appears as something to be either preserved or eliminated—or modified in any of a variety of ways—and thereby loses its sharp definition in an indefinite halo of alternatives. In effect, the introduction of possibility into the nature of the self makes the nature of the self a possibility. Even the actuality of a free self cannot be identified with what it already is in fact, since to be free is to be already actually engaged in determining the form of that possibility, while the actual nature of the self is always already relegated to the status of the material out of which that possible nature must be fashioned. The self-determining self determines its *own* nature. Therefore, it *has* no nature except self-determination itself.[13]

We have finally arrived at the fundamental nature of freedom (since self-determination is the fundamental form of freedom upon which all others depend), only to discover that freedom denatures the self (since to be self-determining leaves the nature of the self still to be determined). But although this presents the self with ever new ambiguities, to be resolved only by choice, it presents *us* with a way of resolving and understanding the ambiguities of freedom that have perplexed this inquiry. I began Chapter 2 by surveying the array of differing conceptions of the nature of the self that

13. Existential philosophy has made much of this recognition. Indeed, the very "existentiality" of existentialism seems to center in the way in which the actual nature, or essence, of the free self is displaced by possibility and free choice. Heidegger's analysis of *Dasein*, that is, his very own existence, begins from the insistence that "[t]he 'essence' ('Wesen') of this entity lies in its 'to-be' (Zu-sein)." Heidegger goes on to explain that "[t]he essence of Dasein lies in its existence. Accordingly, those characteristics which can be exhibited in this entity are not properties present-at-hand . . . ; they are in each case possible ways for it to be, and no more than that" (*Being and Time,* trans. John Macquarrie and Edward Robinson [New York: Harper & Row, 1962], 67). Sartre renders the same theme by saying that in the case of human reality, "existence precedes essence," or that man is not what he is, but rather "has to be" what he is.

the preceding chapter had generated and whose very multiplicity seemed to foreclose any hope of finding a single, unambiguous meaning of freedom. For although I did manage to subsume all the meanings of freedom encountered in Chapter 1 under the heading of self-realization, the gain was more abstract and apparent than real, since that only displaced the locus of ambiguity from the nature of freedom to the nature of the self. The concrete import of freedom as self-realization still varied according to whether the self was understood to include the whole psychophysical complex of the individual, or only the psychic portion of this, or only the conscious portion of the psyche, and so on and so on.

At that point, we struck an impasse. For the idea of freedom seems to offer no principle of selection among these competing versions of the nature of the self, and hence no basis for deciding among the several conflicting interpretations of freedom as self-realization. But now both the source and solution of this impasse should be clear. It is up to the self to make this selection, to determine its own nature in deciding among the possibilities before it. The available options may not explicitly present themselves as alternative natures. But choices among specific concrete possibilities implicate more general decisions about the nature of the self. In deciding to adhere to truth and principle in the face of torture, exile, and death, the Stoic defines his nature as something distinct from his body, his home, even his life. In his determination to shun all worldly honors, offices, and options as temptation, the ascetic defines his whole mundane existence as accidental to his essential eternal nature, which "is not of this world." Similarly, in determining to follow instinct, impulse, or reason, I define my nature as instinctive, impulsive, or rational. Every choice is the choice of a self, as Plato tells us in explaining the myth of Er. For it is not only the souls about to be reborn who have to choose their lives. Their mythic choice stands for all choices, for every choice is the choice of a way of life, and the quality of the soul is determined by the kind of life one chooses.[14]

In relation to self-determination, then, *all* the conceptions of the nature of the self surveyed at the beginning of Chapter 2 are merely possible natures among which the self must choose, at least by implication. That does not mean that the self has no actual nature, however, for its actual nature is just to be self-determining, which means that whatever definite nature or character has been inherited or acquired is already only the material for further possibilities, the point of departure for further choices, if only the choice to "stand pat."

14. *Republic* 618b–619b.

To be free, then, is not only to be able to realize myself, but to be able to determine what sort of self to realize. That is only possible, however, insofar as the character of the self is not entirely defined by nature or nurture, but is open to choice. Consequently, we can say either that the nature of the free self is indeterminate or that its nature is self-determination. Both phrasings state the same conclusion: that freedom cannot simply be appended to an already constituted nature of the self, whether inherited or acquired, for the logic of self-determination is such that it completely deposes any *given* nature.

Consequently, "the self" shrinks to a sort of contentless, dimensionless point of decision, an undefined power of self-definition that excludes from itself every concrete determination. That is why we can strip off layer after layer of the actual concrete person and place them all on the side of circumstance, as we did in the course of the dialectic of Chapter 1. For from the standpoint of self-determination, all determinacy belongs together. In relation to freedom, *every* given determination is only food for possibility and is therefore circumstantial and ambiguous. On the other hand, *not everything* is possible under given circumstances, so that the intrinsic ambiguity and indeterminacy of the free self are not boundless, but limited by the determinacy of what is already given. This limiting role of determinate fact includes not only the presently constituted nature of the individual, but his whole environment as well. Yet Plato's myth reminds us that these two are not entirely independent, that the external conditions of a life appear differently depending upon one's character and habits of life, but that "the soul must needs change its character accordingly as it chooses one life or another."[15]

For the free self faced with choice, then, there is no essential difference between the two sorts of circumstances, no clearly marked border between internal and external. Every concrete determination may appear to be external and circumstantial, and any circumstance may appear as an essential "part" of the self, *if* the individual so chooses, as the ancient Stoics knew so well. If I identify with my house, my reputation, my nation or income or golf score, then whatever threatens *them* threatens *me,* and my own being is at stake in maintaining them. But if I regard any or all of these as indifferent, as the Stoics advised, then I can view them as mere external conditions whose alteration leaves me essentially unaffected.

The ambiguity that attached to freedom in my earlier inquiries is therefore inescapable. However, it is inescapable not because freedom itself is ambiguous, but because freedom renders the concrete nature of the

15. Ibid.

self ambiguous. That ambiguity infects our idea of freedom only insofar as freedom is conceived in terms of self-realization apart from self-determination. Once freedom is fully understood as self-determination, that ambiguity about the nature of the self can be recognized as a mere consequence of the fact that if the self is to be free at all, then the nature of the self must be freedom.

❋ 4 ❋

Absolute Freedom

The Idea of Absolute Freedom

Able to determine itself as a possibility, yet hemmed in at every turn by the limits of stubborn circumstance, the free self may well yearn for a better condition, for a reality more in keeping with its possibilities. The limitations at hand are only contingent, after all, and they appear to cheat the self of the full range of its freedom. Thus, a child may expect complete freedom as the natural result of growing up. The child's life is so full of fantasy and possibility that the determinate limits of actual circumstance may generally appear rather hazy and pliant. In his play at being a doctor or pilot or cowboy, he can almost always adapt his circumstances to the needs of his fancy. Two old cartons and a blanket will make a hospital bed or a spaceship; a pony can be conjured from a broomstick, scraps of cardboard, and string. Limitation appears to the child primarily in the form of the discipline and authority of parents and teachers, and as a consequence of "not being old enough to . . ." (It is only because his parents refuse to get him a horse, after all, that he must make do with a broomstick pony; *he* would never go to bed so early if *they* didn't make him; and so on.) The child therefore looks forward to adulthood as a time when all limitations will be left behind and he will enjoy boundless freedom to realize in fact all the possibilities he now realizes only in play.

Comparable reasoning may convince a naïve colonial people that only the accident of foreign oppression deprives them of total and unconditional freedom. They may therefore expect that independence will mean complete liberation, that with self-determination all limitations and constraints will disappear, that "come the revolution," everything will become possible.

The adult, the man of the world, may smile at such innocence. He, of course, knows better. Or does he? What of the peasant or shopkeeper who watches the king ride by and enviously tells himself that only an accident of birth separates him from the perfect freedom that he believes the king enjoys? And how many "men of the world" have believed that only a century of scientific progress separated humankind from the final conquest of the limitations and frustrations imposed by nature and history?

It is tempting to dismiss all such dreams of unqualified freedom as the products of an unreflective shortsightedness that sees only the limitations immediately at hand and fails to recognize that adulthood or national independence or progress can only promise the exchange of one set of limitations for another, which may well prove more confining than the old. Yet there is something more than such naïveté at work here. It is indeed myopic to hope for total liberation through the removal of any particular limitations. But strategies of ascetic renunciation and Stoic detachment avoid that error by regarding *all* determinate conditions with equal indifference. As such, theirs is a deeper and more systematic version of all these hopes for absolute freedom. Such hopes arise from that very same source of freedom discovered in the last chapter.

Freedom as the ability to do as I please, the freedom of self-realization, has proved to be a conditional, relative freedom, dependent not only upon favorable circumstances, but upon the more fundamental freedom of self-determination. In contrast with self-realization, this fundamental form of freedom seems to be both independent of external conditions and even incompatible with any intrinsic preconditions. Self-determination denatures the self, dislodging it from any given nature and setting it over against all determinacy, internal or external, leaving only the innermost germ of freedom, self-enclosed and densely impervious to the introduction of any conditions within itself. There might, indeed, be preconditions of freedom, capacities or characteristics without which no being could possibly deter-

mine itself. But even if reason or self-consciousness makes freedom possible, for example, it does not therefore follow that the free self must choose
to be rational or self-conscious instead of indulging irrational passions or
seeking oblivion in drink. The free self need not identify with any aspect of
its own being, even those upon which its own freedom depends. Any such
"inner" prerequisites of freedom may therefore be distinguished from the
self and opposed to it as external conditions. Kant argued that only a
rational being can possibly be autonomous or self-determining, for example. At first, this led him to identify freedom with rational, moral choice.
But eventually, he had to acknowledge that to be free is to be able also to
ignore the voice of reason, that the very dictates of its own reason that make
the self free nonetheless appear to the free self as a transcendent authority
to be either obeyed or denied.[1] Because the free self need not accept or
identify with those aspects of its own being upon which its freedom
depends, they may be distinguished from the self and opposed to it as
external conditions. Self-determination therefore seems to be intrinsically
unconditioned and, in that sense, absolute.

The unconditional nature of self-determination finds more familiar and
positive expression in the boundless range of this freedom in relation to
possibility. Since *all* determinate conditions and limitations are external,
they do not infect or determine the free self, which may therefore *always*
project itself beyond any limits. Indeed, the merest suggestion of a limit may
be enough to provoke an attempt to surpass it, as every parent knows. The
sundry absurdities catalogued in *The Guinness Book of World Records* offer
humorous testimony of this provocative power of the limit. Whatever the
circumstances, the free individual can always dream of a freedom transcending those limits, and may posit possibilities far beyond any that
can actually be realized. And there is nothing to prevent the self from
identifying itself with any possibility it dreams up, however extravagant or
harebrained. There can therefore be no definite limit upon the self's
determination of itself *as possible.*

But a freedom that is boundless only within the realm of possibility is
still a limited freedom—a freedom still unrealized. And although self-
determination may be *intrinsically* absolute and unconditioned, the self
still finds its freedom confined by *ex*trinsic circumstance. Although self-
determination may dislodge all conditions and limits from within the self,
they do not therefore vanish, but only reappear as external conditions.
Boundless in the realm of possibility, freedom still collides with the obdu-
rate limits of reality nevertheless, and that collision seems almost to cancel

---

1. See note 6 to Chapter 3 above.

that intrinsically boundless reality of freedom, banishing it to the child's realm of fantasy and make-believe. To the self that finds its capacity for self-determination obstructed and confined by the limits of stubborn circumstance, true and complete freedom may seem to be possible only in the absence of those limits. The free self's ability to generate its own possibilities and originate its own determinations seems to be undone, set at naught by the limits presented by the alien determinacy that confronts it. This determinacy is alien because it is not self-imposed, and the limitation it imposes upon the self may well seem a gratuitous, contingent encumbrance. Freedom *need* not be thus limited and conditioned, it would seem, since self-determination is unconditional and absolute in and of itself. It is as though a pure freedom, which is absolute in itself, is compromised and adulterated by the mere *presence* of external conditions, and the finite freedom that issues from that conjunction is only an impure, bastard version of freedom, a dwarfish distortion of its true nature. To grasp the pure essence of freedom, then, we would have to study it as it is *in itself,* apart from this accidental, extraneous conditioning.

But just what is the "impurity" thus imputed to finite freedom? It is the shadow that falls "between the intention and the act," the gap between the choice of a possibility and its realization. In effect, the "impurity" imposed upon self-determination by the resistance of external conditions is that very freedom of self-realization with which we began: the ability to do as I choose. Once we discovered that self-realization must be founded in self-determination, we also saw that self-realization may be regarded as a mere stage or moment within the process of self-determination.[2] But its presence as a distinct moment of self-determination is evidence that this *intrinsically* unconditional freedom is conditioned and limited after all, a reminder that, notwithstanding the power to determine itself, the self may be constrained and coerced by circumstances, that the attempted self-determination may issue in frustration and futility. So long as there is any such possibility of constraint, self-determination appears to be threatened, insecure, and partial. That is why freedom is so often described merely as the *absence* of such constraining limits. But to describe it so is to define freedom in terms of what it is *not,* in terms of coercion and constraint, and to distract attention from what freedom is in itself. Seen in this light, self-realization is not a necessary and completing moment of self-determination, but an index of incomplete and imperfect freedom, a symptom of compromise by the external, the conditioning, the determinate. Self-realization may therefore come to be regarded as an impurity that

2. See page 78 above.

debases the pristine essence of freedom, conceived as unlimited self-determination. But this suggests that the two modes of freedom are really antithetical rather than complementary, that one subverts the other.

What is at work in all these reflections—and in the systematic version of the visions of absolute freedom with which I began—is the logical response of self-determination to any determinacy that is not of its own making. Encountering extrinsic limitations upon the realization of its possibilities, the self posits and covets a pure and unqualified form of self-determination, a freedom that would *not* suffer under any such limitations. If the circumstances immediately at hand often get confounded with limitation in general, fostering naïve expectations that the disappearance of these particular limits will yield absolute and unconditioned freedom, that is quite understandable, for those expectations reflect the intrinsic thrust of freedom to surpass every limit and negate every condition that is not *self*-determined. Thus, finite freedom itself seems to project an absolute, infinite freedom as its own ideal and truth.

This idea of absolute freedom requires closer scrutiny. Are its pretensions to represent the essential truth of freedom justified? Or are they as illusory, in their way, as the child's naïve expectations? *Can* self-determination really be unconditioned extrinsically as well as intrinsically? Does the logic of self-determination call for the supreme self-sufficiency that this idea of absolute freedom implies?

These are highly speculative questions. Yet they have an important bearing upon the understanding of freedom. If the ideal of absolute freedom can stand and the pretensions ascribed to it above prove warranted, then the freedom described hitherto is only an imperfect semblance of true freedom. In that case, the effort to understand freedom should concentrate upon its absolute and perfect nature and recognize finite freedom as a mere approximation to that standard, or as its partial and defective avatar. Self-realization will then appear as a stain upon the purity of freedom rather than a legitimate and necessary moment of its nature. If so, it would seem to follow that finite freedom reflects the essential truth of freedom only in the determination of possibilities, while the whole problem of realization merely betrays the defectiveness of a freedom that is conditioned and finite. In human terms, that would mean that the essence of freedom resides entirely in subjective choice or decision and that the relation of this subjective act to objective realization is not only accidental and extraneous but, indeed, a symptom of the impurity or defectiveness of human freedom.

Absolute Freedom and the Finite Self

The idea of absolute freedom does not readily yield to direct questioning, however. Absolute freedom would be a power of self-determination utterly unlimited and unconditioned from without as well as from within. That much is evident from what has been said above. But the nature and implications of such a power are not easy to conceive. A more exact account of the requirements and ramifications of such an unconditioned freedom may be easier to reach indirectly, by considering what happens when this idea is made the ideal and goal of a finite self.

That absolute freedom *may* be taken as a goal by the finite self should not be surprising in light of the above discussion. If the very nature of finite freedom points to the idea of absolute freedom, then it is "only natural" for the finite self to set up this idea as an ideal to be realized. That seems all the more likely given the tendency to confuse the limitations immediately at hand with limitation in general. When "the boy becomes a man" and his expectations that adulthood will bring unlimited freedom are disappointed, he may very well continue to seek such a freedom rather than abandon a hope he has cherished so long. If the dawn of independence still leaves an oppressed colonial population burdened with the most galling of their former fetters, they may embark upon a *series* of revolutions aimed at acquiring the total freedom of which they feel cheated.

Individuals do sometimes set up absolute freedom as an ideal of life and a goal of action; any of a variety of examples in which this ideal is more or less operative will serve to illustrate what happens when individuals do so. There is one type of dilettante, for instance, who veers from one enthusiasm to another to another in a bootless attempt to be "the universal man" because he cannot bear to be any particular man, cannot bear the thought that any possibility might be closed to him. John Barth's portrait of Ebenezer Cooke in *The Sot-Weed Factor* depicts the type wittily. Ebenezer, whose childhood tutor turned all learning into imaginative play, is "sore bit by the muse's gadfly" during his second year at Cambridge, and he begins to neglect his serious studies. Barth's portrait is too apt to skip:

> As might be expected, the more this divine affliction got hold of him, the more his studies suffered. The sum of history became in his head no more than the stuff of metaphors. Of the philosophers of his era—Bacon, Hobbes, Descartes, Spinoza, Leibnitz, Locke—he learned little; of its scientists—Kepler, Galileo, Newton—less; of its theologians—Lord Herbert, Cudworth, More, Smith, Glanvill—nothing. But *Paradise Lost* he knew inside out; *Hudibras* upside down.

At the end of the third year, to his great distress, he failed a number of examinations and had to face the prospect of leaving the University. Yet what to do? He could not bear the thought of returning to St. Giles and telling his formidable father; he would have to absent himself quietly, disappear from sight, and seek his fortune in the world at large. But in what manner?

Here, in his difficulty with this question, the profoundest effects of Burlingame's amiable pedagogy become discernible: Ebenezer's imagination was excited by every person he met either in or out of books who could do with skill and understanding anything whatever; he was moved to ready admiration by expert falconers, scholars, masons, chimneysweeps, prostitutes, admirals, cutpurses, sailmakers, barmaids, apothecaries, and cannoneers alike.

Ah, God, he wrote in a letter to Anna about this time, *it were an easy Matter to choose a Calling, had one all Time to live in! I should be fifty Years a Barrister, fifty a Physician, fifty a Clergyman, fifty a Soldier! Aye, and fifty a Thief, and fifty a Judge! All Roads are fine Roads, beloved Sister, none more than another, so that with one Life to spend I am a Man bare-bumm'd at Taylors with Cash for but one pair of Breeches, or a Scholar at Bookstalls with Money for a single Book: to choose ten were no Trouble; to choose one, impossible! All Trades, all Crafts, all Professions are wondrous, but none is finer than the rest together. I cannot choose, sweet Anna: twixt Stools my Breech falleth to the Ground!*

He was, that is to say, temperamentally disinclined to no career, and what is worse (as were this not predicament enough), he seemed consistently no special sort of person: the variety of temperaments and characters that he observed at Cambridge and in literature was as enchanting to him as the variety of life-works, and as hard to choose from among. He admired equally the sanguine, the phlegmatic, the choleric, the melancholic, the splenetic, and the balanced man, the fool and the sage, the enthusiast and the stick-in-the-mud, the talkative and the taciturn, and, most dilemmal of all, the consistent and the inconsistent. Similarly, it seemed to him as fine a thing to be fat as to be lean, to be short as tall, homely as handsome. To complete his quandary—what is probably an effect of the foregoing—Ebenezer could be persuaded, at least notionally, by any philosophy of the world, even by any strongly held opinion, which was either poetically conceived or attractively stated, since he appeared to be emotionally predisposed in favor of none. It was as pretty a notion to him that the world was made of water, as Thales declared, as that it was air, *á la* Anaximines, or fire, *á la* Heraclitus, or all three and dirt to boot, as swore Empedocles; that all was matter, as Hobbes maintained, or that all was mind, as some of Locke's followers were avowing, seemed equally likely to our poet, and as for ethics, could he have been all three and not just one he'd have enjoyed dying once a saint, once a frightful sinner, and once lukewarm between the two.

The man (in short) . . . was dizzy with the beauty of the possible; dazzled, he threw up his hands at choice, and like ungainly flotsam rode half-content the tide of chance. Though the term was done he stayed on at Cambridge. For a week he simply languished in his rooms, reading distractedly and smoking pipe after pipe of tobacco, to which he'd become addicted. At length reading became impossible; smoking too great a bother: he prowled restlessly about the room. His head always felt about to ache, but never began to.

Finally one day he did not deign even to dress himself or eat, but sat immobile in the window seat in his nightshirt and stared at the activity in the street below, unable to choose a motion at all even when, some hours later, his untutored bladder suggested one.[3]

Ebenezer is paralyzed by his infatuation with possibilities. He can keep them *all* before him only if he realizes *none*. His predicament aptly illustrates what we have already learned: that a finite being can enjoy absolute freedom only within the realm of possibility. He embodies the ideal of limitless freedom—but only at the price of forgoing realization, which is the burden of finitude. His paralysis is therefore a comic expression of the "impurity" that self-realization betrays in finite freedom. But for that very reason, his example does not promise to lead us beyond what we have already learned about the misalliance between the finite self and the ideal of absolute freedom. If we are to gain any further insight into the meaning of absolute freedom, we must look at examples that involve a more active attempt to realize that ideal.

But what sort of activity should we turn to in search of an example of the realization of absolute freedom in action? Should we consider some version of the anarchistic "free spirit"—the Bohemian artist, or the hippie, beatnik, or "flower child" of more recent decades? In the career of such willfully eccentric iconoclasts, we might discern an effort to realize unlimited freedom by escaping the confines of conventional, "square" society and repudiating the limitations of any and all socially sanctioned manners, mores, and values. But although such examples might prove instructive, it would be too easy to object that the limits of convention are not the only

3. John Barth, *The Sot-Weed Factor* (New York: Grosset & Dunlap, 1966), 20–21.

limits, and that defiance of tradition may prove as oppressive as Victorian manners, much as "the tradition of the new" eventually proved a constraint to modern art.[4] An act that is to realize absolute freedom would have to overcome *all* limitations, not merely those of social convention. We might seek our example of such an act in the suicide of Kirillov in Dostoevsky's *The Possessed*. Kirillov sees that complete and unconditioned freedom can only be embodied in an unconditioned action that negates all conditions. He explains to G——v, the narrator:

> "Every one who wants the supreme freedom must dare to kill himself. He who dares to kill himself has found out the secret of the deception. There is no freedom beyond; that is all, and there is nothing beyond. He who dares kill himself is God. Now every one can do so that there shall be no God and shall be nothing. But no one has done it yet."
>
> "There have been millions of suicides."
>
> "But always not for that; always with terror and not for that object. Not to kill fear. He who kills himself only to kill fear will become a god at once."
>
> "He won't have time, perhaps," I observed.[5]

Kirillov argues that in order to achieve perfect freedom, a man must conquer the fear of death and transcend the merely vital desire to go on living, since the love of life makes him slave to all the conditions upon which life depends: "There will be full freedom," he says, "when it will be just the same to live or not to live. That's the goal for all."[6] The act of suicide is therefore the decisive proof of absolute freedom, the supreme assertion of self-will—provided that it is not motivated by despair or fear of suffering or any other finite cause. If it is done "without any cause at all, simply for self-will," it is an act in which the individual "rolls his life up into a ball," summoning all its conditions together and transcending them by one

4. Cf. Harold Rosenberg, *The Tradition of the New* (New York: McGraw Hill, 1965). Rosenberg's title calls attention to the tyrannical role that the worship of unprecedented novelty has played in modern culture. The convention that forbids convention or repetition is so confining that contemporary artists sometimes sigh in envy of primitive artists, who are free to exercise their creativity within a clearly defined formal tradition. For an analysis of modern art that parallels the argument of this chapter in striking ways, see Karsten Harries's discussion of "the meaning of modern art" in his book of that title (Evanston, Ill.: Northwestern University Press, 1968).

5. Fyodor Dostoevsky, *The Possessed*, trans. Constance Garnett (New York: Modern Library, 1963), 115–16.

6. Ibid., 114.

stroke, thereby establishing the absolute supremacy of his own will. That is why Kirillov expects to become God by killing himself.

But, "he won't have time, perhaps," G——v objects, an apt reminder that Kirillov's project is as mad as it is logical—and surely Dostoevsky intends to portray Kirillov as the madly logical outcome of the nihilism of his day. We can scarcely treat Kirillov as an adequate realization of absolute freedom, since he ceases to exist by the very act that is intended to realize that ideal.[7] Kirillov's tragic suicide displays the incongruity of finitude and freedom as exorbitantly as does Ebenezer Cooke's comic paralysis. Although we may learn something from each, neither of these extravagant fictions promises to provide a credible guide for reflection upon the nature and possibility of absolute freedom.

Fortunately, there is no need to rely upon such literary examples, since a provocative philosophical treatment of the pursuit of absolute freedom is available. Kirillov's suicide and Ebenezer's immobilizing indecision illustrate the same "logic" of absolute freedom that Hegel has described in *The Phenomenology of Spirit*. In the section entitled "Absolute Freedom and Terror," Hegel offers an incisive analysis of what happens when the finite self sets out to realize absolute freedom—and why that attempt proves suicidal. And the focus of Hegel's analysis is no extravagant fiction, but a major historic convulsion: the French Revolution. Writing in the shadow of the Napoleonic empire, which was the denouement of the revolution, Hegel asks why the revolutionary ambition to establish liberty, equality, and fraternity through the reign of the general will had aborted and led, instead, to a reign of terror that issued in military dictatorship and empire. He finds the answer in the idea of absolute freedom itself, arguing that the "rage and fury of senseless destruction" of the Reign of Terror was entailed by the attempt to realize that ideal. The force of his analysis is therefore not limited to the specific events of the French Revolution, which is why it lends itself to my purposes.[8] My concern is not with political history as such, but with the more systematic dimension of Hegel's account, with what it can tell us about the meaning and possibility of absolute freedom. We need not be

---

7. In fairness to Kirillov, it should be said that he does not regard this objection as cogent, because duration and temporality are not attributes of the absolute, or of the divinity he expects to become through his suicide. I attempt to do justice to this level of his reasoning later.

8. Hegel's analysis has a specific role in the development of the *Phenomenology* and is being appropriated for a somewhat different purpose here. Jean Hyppolite argues that Hegel intends the section as a critique, not of absolute freedom as such, but only of the attempt to realize that idea *immediately* in the form of the general will. See Jean Hyppolite, *Genesis and Structure of Hegel's Phenomenology of Spirit*, trans. Samuel Cherniak and John Heckman (Evanston, Ill.: Northwestern University Press, 1974), 453ff.

too concerned with the historical particulars of Hegel's analysis, then, or with whether it offers a complete and cogent explanation of those particular events. Many a subsequent revolution has traversed a similar course from liberal aspirations to terrorism and despotism. In *The Rebel*, Camus focuses attention upon this generic tendency of revolutions to terminate in terror:

> Freedom, "that terrible word inscribed on the chariot of the storm," is the motivating principle of all revolutions. Without it, justice seems inconceivable to the rebel's mind. There comes a time, however, when justice demands the suspension of freedom. Then terror, on a grand or small scale, makes its appearance to consummate the revolution. Every act of rebellion expresses a nostalgia for innocence and an appeal to the essence of being. But one day nostalgia takes up arms and assumes the responsibility of total guilt; in other words, adopts murder and violence.[9]

Hegel analyzes how the attempt to realize absolute freedom leads to a career of destruction. We can regard each destructive step in that process in a more positive light, however, by asking what requirement of absolute freedom that step attempts to fulfill. In other words, we can focus upon *why* the ideal of absolute freedom requires each stage in that career of destruction. What conditions, characteristics, or consequences of absolute freedom make this destruction necessary?

The career of absolute freedom begins with the proclamation of the reign of the general will—Rousseau's *volonté général*. According to Hegel, this general or universal will comes to be perceived as absolute through the spread of utilitarianism, the Enlightenment's doctrine that the value of any thing, act, or institution consists in its *usefulness* in promoting the general welfare. Once utility is accepted as the only source of value and legitimation, the existing social order can no longer be justified by appeal to inherent rightness, hereditary authority, or divine right. Its justification can only derive from its utility in serving the purposes of the community, purposes that depend upon the will of the people. The public therefore sees its own will as beyond any legitimate opposition, and hence as absolute, as the ultimate source of sovereignty—at least in principle. Yet in *fact*, the people still find themselves confined by an order they do not recognize as their own, ruled by a sovereign not of their own choosing, organized in a feudal hierarchy based upon inherited rank. In this *ancien régime* they

9. Albert Camus, *The Rebel*, trans. Anthony Bower (New York: Vintage Books, 1956), 105.

encounter a vestigial opposition, one that has no right to exist, which the public allowed to be imposed upon itself before the people recognized their own sovereignty. So long as this residual opposition remains, the general will is only *implicitly* absolute. In principle, the monarch only reigns "by consent of the governed," but that consent was never explicitly sought or granted. In order to realize itself, to become explicitly what it already is implicitly, the people must prove the supremacy of the universal will by brushing aside this remnant of opposition—thereby demonstrating that the old order *had* only existed by public sufferance all along. The annihilation of the old social order and the explicit realization of the universal will are therefore accomplished by the same step: individuals rise up, cast aside their traditional stations and duties to identify themselves with the work and will of the whole.[10]

Why is this step necessary? What more general lesson does it hold about absolute freedom, apart from the historical particulars? The old order must be abolished because now nothing is to be accounted valid or real except insofar as it is a product of the action of absolute freedom or universal will. From the standpoint of the individual, this means that his status within that order, his inherited rank and function, is not valid, and that his true reality depends upon identifying his will with the universal will: "In this absolute freedom all social groups or classes which are the spiritual spheres into which the whole is articulated are abolished; the individual consciousness that belonged to any such sphere, and willed and fulfilled itself in it, has put aside its limitation; its purpose is the general purpose, its language universal law, its work the universal work."[11]

The positive reason for this first destructive step, then, is that absolute freedom is irreconcilable with any antecedent, inherited order, indeed, with any structure that is not of its own making. Absolute freedom therefore cannot be attained through reform, which would merely modify the status quo. It must come about through a revolution, which annihilates that established order. The same logic guides the Bohemian "free spirit," who believes that complete freedom begins with a complete disregard of the established social conventions.

Stated in the most general terms, the point is that absolute freedom cannot coexist with any alien determinacy. Not only that, but whatever nature the self may inherit will appear alien and opposed to freedom just because it is *already* determined rather than the product of self-determination. If freedom is to be absolute, then no such alien determinacy can be tolerated—regardless of how freedom may be able to transform or

---

10. G.W.F. Hegel, *Hegel's Phenomenology of Spirit,* trans. A. V. Miller (Oxford: Oxford University Press, 1977), 357.

11. Ibid.

refashion what it finds already given. However pliable and yielding, any such status quo, or given determinacy, would nevertheless limit freedom. We may think of potter's clay as relatively formless and passive stuff that can be molded at will. Yet if we try to make of it what we will, we quickly discover that the nature of the clay imposes limitations after all. Its very plasticity frustrates our first attempts, and we soon learn that in order to succeed, we must accommodate our aims and acts to the nature of the clay and design our works in terms of its properties. Similarly, freedom must accommodate to any reality that is already determinate, however passive and yielding— and a freedom thus compromised is not absolute. If freedom is to be unlimited, then, it must either begin with nothing or annihilate any existing order before beginning to build anew.

But Hegel's second step is to show why absolute freedom cannot "build anew" either, why it cannot establish any new order to replace the old one that it has destroyed. It "lets nothing break loose to become a *free object* standing over against it. It follows from this that it cannot achieve anything positive, either universal works of language or of reality, either of laws and general institutions of *conscious* freedom, or of deeds and works of a freedom that *wills* them."[12]

The universal will finds itself at an embarrassing impasse, a predicament remarkably like the absurd paralysis of Ebenezer Cooke, who would gladly become everything, but therefore cannot decide to become anything. Absolute freedom sets out to produce works that are universal—but finds that it therefore cannot produce anything in particular, since anything it produces would be limited and would therefore qualify its absoluteness, confining freedom by the very particularity of its own achievement. Absolute freedom cannot produce any objective result because it cannot allow anything to become detached from itself and established as an independent reality. For such an independent object would constitute a limitation, an opposing reality that would compromise its absoluteness. Indeed, whereas the *old* order could simply be dismissed as invalid and brushed aside, freedom would have to recognize the *new* order as its own work and therefore have to acknowledge the legitimacy of these new, self-imposed limits.[13] Even though freedom could recognize its setting as the product of its own act, the mere independent, determinate existence of that setting would be an obstacle with which freedom would have to reckon. If freedom is to be unconditioned and unlimited, it cannot be faced with any independent setting or conditions, even if they *are* of its own making. It is not only an *already given* determinate setting that is incompatible with absolute

---

12. Ibid., 358.

13. Hegel analyses this predicament at greater length in an earlier section, "Individuality Which Takes Itself to Be Real in and for Itself," in ibid., 236–62.

freedom, then, but *any* external determinacy whatsoever. This conclusion deserves further emphasis: it means that *nothing whatsoever can coexist with absolute freedom.* If freedom is to be absolute, it must have to do *only* with itself and with nothing else.

And perhaps that is the solution. If absolute freedom cannot produce any object distinct from itself, why can't it *make something of itself,* nevertheless. After the overthrow of *l'ancien régime,* why couldn't the general will proceed to articulate itself into a new social order? This is the question Hegel considers next: why the revolutionary society failed to "make something of itself," why it did not organize itself into a stable new order to replace *l'ancien régime.* He answers that the universal will could not differentiate itself into "estates," or into functional organs such as executive, legislative, and judicial branches of government, because any such inner articulation would mean assigning the particular individual to a determinate social status or role. That would contradict his identification of himself with the universal will, however, reversing the very process of its formation.

In fact, the revolutionary mass does become articulated, of course. A government emerges and proceeds to act in the name of the universal will. But "[t]he government, which wills and executes its will from a single point, at the same time wills and executes a specific order and action. On the one hand, it excludes all other individuals from its act, and on the other it thereby constitutes itself a government that is a specific will, and so stands opposed to the universal will; consequently it is absolutely impossible for it to exhibit itself as anything but a *faction.* What is. called government is merely the *victorious* faction, and in the very fact of its being a faction lies the direct necessity of its overthrow."[14]

Successive governing factions condemn their predecessors and opponents as *only* factions and therefore "counterrevolutionary," only to be condemned and overthrown in turn. This pattern of revolutionary politics has been so often repeated since 1789 that it is now completely familiar to us. But what can it tell us about absolute freedom as such, apart from the particular context of the revolutionary process? What requirement of absolute freedom do these particulars illustrate?

The attempt to realize absolute freedom reaches this embarrassing impasse because absolute freedom can no more harbor any determinacy *within* itself than it can tolerate external determinacy. But whereas it cannot tolerate external determinacy because it is absolute, it cannot admit any *intrinsic* determinacy because it is *freedom,* since freedom is not compatible with any inner determinacy. I have already remarked how freedom dena-

14. Ibid., 360.

tures the finite self, displacing any inherent nature or determinate character—so that the free self can have no nature except freedom itself. In
relation to freedom, all such determinations are only limiting conditions—
and hence external, opposed to freedom. From the standpoint of self-
determination, *all* determinacy appears to be limiting. Absolute freedom
can therefore neither *have* nor *develop* a determinate structure of its own.
The logic of freedom entails that *any* determinacy is foreign to it and
appears as an extrinsic condition. But of course, as already demonstrated,
absolute freedom cannot coexist with any such extrinsic conditions, which
must therefore be destroyed if absolute freedom is to be realized.

The realization of absolute freedom thus proves utterly barren, a wholly
negative process whose only achievement is "the grisly harvest of the
guillotine." "The sole work and deed of universal freedom is therefore
death, a death too which has no inner significance or filling, for what is
negated is the empty point of the absolutely free self."[15]

The universal will has found its sole remaining object and opposition
within itself, Hegel explains, in the freedom of will of the single, particular
self, and it proceeds to fulfill itself in the only work available—the liquida-
tion of particular individuals. The senseless horror of the Reign of Terror is
epitomized by the fact that any individual might be executed on mere
suspicion of counterrevolutionary tendencies—hence, not for any prov-
ably guilty action, Hegel remarks, but simply because his private subjective
intention and freedom place him in opposition to the universal will *in
principle.* So understood, the Reign of Terror is exactly parallel to Kirillov's
suicide, since Kirillov insists that it is not those who kill themselves for any
reason who will attain perfect freedom, but only the one who kills himself
"without any cause at all, simply from self-will."

Since the universal will discovers this opposition in the individual wills of
which it is composed, we could regard this last, most destructive step of all
as another illustration of the abolition of intrinsic determinacy. Or, we
might interpret this step as the final concrete expression of the incompatibility of absolute freedom and the finite self. But the parallel with Kirillov
draws attention to another, even more important systematic lesson of the
Terror: its suicidal character. For *in destroying the single, particular self, the
universal will destroys its own foundation.* By destroying the individual in his
bare existence, the universal will turns upon the elementary condition of its
own existence, which it owes to the act whereby the individual will identifies
itself with the universal purpose. Historically, of course, the Reign of Terror
did prove to be revolutionary suicide, since it eventually brought on the

15. Ibid.

military dictatorship that spelled the death of the revolution's liberal
aspirations.

What does this last suicidal step tell us about absolute freedom as such,
apart from the circumstances of the revolution? It dramatizes the fact that
absolute freedom cannot depend upon any constitutive conditions, that
there can be no preconditions of its being. For any such preconditions
would stand as limitations that would prevent freedom from being absolute.
They would mean that its *being* was not the product of its own free act, but
a function of something other than freedom itself. Surely the barest and
least of limitations, from one point of view, it is the limitation involved in
not being the ground of one's own being. But that limit must be removed
in order adequately to conceive the idea of absolute freedom. A would-be
absolute freedom limited *only* in respect to the ground of its being would
doubtless destroy itself, like Kirillov, simply to prove its superiority over the
conditions of its own existence. That is why both Hegel and Dostoevsky
describe the quest for absolute freedom as self-destructive, because a
freedom that aspires to be unconditioned must end by destroying the
conditions of its own existence.

Only in the final stage is the fundamentally *negative* character of absolute
freedom fully revealed by the reign of terror, Hegel says. Yet this catastro-
phe is the apt culmination of a process in which the realization of absolute
freedom has manifested itself as a "rage and fury of destruction."

Should we conclude, then, that absolute freedom is inherently negative?
No, for all this negativity is the work of the *finite* self, of a freedom that is *not*
absolute, though it aims to become so. Each destructive step in the career
I have traced aims at the cancellation of a limit that stands as an obstacle to
the *realization* of absolute freedom. They are all, therefore, the acts of a
freedom that is still limited. Absolute freedom would only become real at
the *end* of this process, once all the destruction was over and all the limits
canceled. It could not be destructive or negative in itself, since there would
be nothing left to destroy or negate. Absolute freedom is not inherently
negative, then, but only so in relation to finitude and limitation.

And just as we cannot ascribe the negation and destructiveness of this
process to absolute freedom itself, neither can we judge the possibility of
absolute freedom by the fatal outcome of that process. Neither Hegel's
analysis nor my other examples of the pursuit of absolute freedom prove
anything about the possibility of absolute freedom as such. They only
exhibit the failure of finite individuals to realize the ideal of absolute
freedom.[16] The finite individual collides with the demands of absolute

---

16. It does not strictly prove that the finite self cannot possibly attain absolute freedom
either, but only that to do so is to cease to be finite. The suicidal strategies I have chosen as
examples may not exhaust the possibilities.

freedom and is destroyed. At most, this might show that absolute freedom is not possible *for the finite self.* But that would not prove that it is impossible in and of itself. Meanwhile, this survey of the wreckage of that collision provides a better conception of what is required of a freedom that *would* be absolute.

But *could* there be such a limitless freedom? Armed with a more adequate conception of absolute freedom, we can turn from the suicidal efforts of the finite self to become absolutely free and inquire, instead, about the possibility of absolute freedom in its own right.

Is Absolute Freedom Possible?

Is absolute freedom, as now understood in its full, rather awesome range, possible? At first glance, it seems simple enough to answer this question in the affirmative. For one can construct a simple "ontological argument" for the possibility of absolute freedom, after the manner of Saint Anselm's proof that the very concept of God implies that God exists. Absolute freedom is a freedom for which nothing is impossible. Any impossibility would, of course, betray a limitation, and absolute freedom must be unlimited. Accordingly, it cannot be impossible for such a freedom to *be*, since that would involve a limitation, which is contradictory to its concept. Surely, a freedom for which everything is possible can give itself *being*, which is the most rudimentary prerequisite of all other possibilities. Indeed, as just noted, the very concept of absolute freedom entails just such an act of self-creation, since the existence of absolute freedom cannot depend upon conditions outside itself but must be the product of its own free activity. Absolute freedom must therefore answer to Spinoza's definition of God as *ens causa sui*, "a being that causes itself."

But this argument that absolute freedom must be possible savors as much of Gilbert and Sullivan as of Saint Anselm's celebrated proof of the existence of God. It is a trifle too ingenious, and really begs the question at hand. For what we are actually asking when we inquire about the possibility of absolute freedom is whether it is possible for freedom to be absolute, whether any genuinely intelligible conception can be formed from the conjunction of these two terms. My exploration of what it would mean for freedom to be absolute has raised doubts about whether freedom could ever be entirely without limits. I was originally led into this inquiry because the logic of freedom itself seemed to point toward the idea of an unconditioned, unlimited freedom. But that was only because the fundamental freedom of self-determination proved to be *intrinsically* unconditioned. The very concept of freedom as *self*-determination excludes all conditions from *within* itself, since a being is *self*-determining only insofar as it is not *other*-determined. But that does not mean that freedom must be *absolutely* unlimited, or unconditioned extrinsically as well as intrinsically. If that were true, then the very idea of *finite* freedom would be self-contradictory, whereas I have only demonstrated that the idea of absolute freedom suggests that finite freedom may be an impure and defective form of freedom. It was because of *that* suggestion that I felt it necessary to deal with the question of the nature and possibility of absolute freedom.

What I am seeking to establish, then, is whether a freedom for which nothing is impossible is itself possible. Or, to put the matter in another way: since absolute freedom is a composite idea, are its component elements really compatible? The ontological argument given above simply *assumes* an affirmative answer to both these questions and constructs a proof of the possible being of such a freedom on the basis of the assumption. And of course, if we assume that freedom *can* be absolute, then we have already admitted that absolute freedom is possible—and such a freedom would have to be the ground of its own being. But the reasoning is clearly circular and fails to address the prior question whether freedom can be absolute. Can there be a freedom for which everything is possible, one that is utterly unconditioned, infinite, or without limit, and even *causa sui,* the cause of its own being?

Such a freedom would be divine. Whether we like it or not, to ask about the possibility of absolute freedom is to become entangled with theology. A freedom for which nothing is impossible implies an omnipotent being, which is a conventional definition of God. Therefore, to question the possibility of absolute freedom is, implicitly, to question the possibility of an omnipotent god—or at least to question the freedom of such a god. Because such a god might enjoy absolute freedom, it would be presumptuous hubris to conclude that absolute freedom is impossible merely because it is beyond the reach of a finite self. Regarded in this context, the suggestion that finite freedom might be only an impure or faulty version of a truer, more perfect freedom evokes the doctrine that man is only an imperfect and finite embodiment of the image of God. But although this theological dimension of the question must be acknowledged from the outset, we must beware of losing our way in a sea of theological controversies, as might easily happen here if I allow questions about God to displace questions about freedom in directing my reflections. My aim is to understand freedom, not God, and I must fix the direction of my inquiry accordingly, while keeping a weather eye peeled for the theological storms and shoals that may beset the course.

I cannot assume without further argument that an omnipotent deity would also be absolutely free, for example, since some theologians hold that God acts out of inner necessity rather than freedom, and regard free choice as a sign of human frailty and uncertainty of purpose. God always knows and does what is best out of his essential goodness, they argue, and could not possibly do otherwise. I need not consider whether this is sound theology—fortunately. Instead, I can begin with absolute freedom and ask whether and how the activities of *any* sort of god might satisfy its requirements, since that is the question that is germane to the problem of whether absolute freedom *is* possible. And it should be clear that if absolute freedom is possible, its characteristics are such as have often been ascribed to God, as is most obvious in the case of omnipotence. A further, less obvious example is *eternity*. For if an absolutely free being is possible, it must be, in and of itself, a completely atemporal or eternal being. Finite freedom is inescapably temporal because its limitations impose a discursive form upon its activity. It must seek out and adopt the means necessary to attain its ends, and it must pursue divergent aims or possibilities in a sequential order because it cannot accomplish them all at once. But such discursiveness has no place in absolute freedom, for there would be no opposition to involve it in such a piecemeal process. An absolutely free being would accomplish everything at once, *totum simul,* in a single stroke. Unimpeded by any limitation in either its conception or its execution of possibilities, absolute freedom would conceive and execute *all* possibilities in a single act, *in* which and *to* which there could be no before or after. Divine creation is sometimes so conceived, as a single act whereby God creates everything at once. Time is then explained as an illusion or appearance that characterizes our merely finite, discursive perspective but that does not belong to reality as it is in itself or as apprehended *totum simul,* all at once, in God's synoptic omniscience.

Of course, God might be eternal in his own right, yet still contemplate the temporal unfolding of his creation, thereby participating vicariously in time. Alfred North Whitehead proposed that although God's original creative act encompassed all *possibilities* at once in a single primordial evaluative ordering, a temporal process of realization of possibilities discursively, one by one, then ensues. According to Whitehead, then, God acquires a consequent, reflected temporality by appreciating the temporal actualization of the possibilities provided by that primordial act. Hans Jonas has suggested a similar view of God's relation to temporal creation. But whatever the *theological* merit of such proposals, it is clear that such a God would not be absolutely free. Whitehead's God is finite, as is Jonas's, and as is any God who is conceived as responding to the independent activity of his creatures. An absolutely free being would not only have to be timeless and eternal in itself, but could not even be related to a temporal realm outside itself so as to acquire such a reflected temporality. For any such external temporal realm would confront absolute freedom with an alien order to which it would somehow have to accommodate. The timeless moment of creation, in which absolute freedom realizes all possibilities would be located temporally as occurring before, during, or after this other sequence. But that would make it a finite act, since it would be bounded by others. Moreover, this locating and relativizing of its own single, synoptic act would be quite beyond the control of the freedom concerned, which would consequently be conditioned rather than absolute. Thus, Whitehead and Jonas describe God as passively suffering the effects of the independent activities that constitute the historical unfolding of creation.

But this argument overleaps itself and falls into contradiction, it might be objected. Granted, absolute freedom *could* accomplish everything at once and so exhaust all its possibilities in a single act. But to argue that it *must* do so is to fall into a contradiction by consigning absolute freedom to such an utterly timeless, inescapably eternal condition. This argument implies that absolute freedom is completely excluded from time. Its very eternity thus seems to become a limitation, which contradicts the idea of a freedom that can determine itself in every possible way. If it is to be absolute, then, freedom must be able to determine itself as temporal.

But to propose this objection is to incur the burden of explaining just *how* absolute freedom could either acquire or sustain the attribute of temporality. It might be supposed that an absolutely free being would simply generate its *own* time. Couldn't it simply "take its time" in realizing possibilities? Why crowd them all into a single act? Instead of expending all its possibilities in one act, it could bring them about sequentially so as to savor each in turn, just as God is depicted in Genesis as surveying his work with satisfaction after each day of creation.

But this account is deceptive—as confused as the account in Genesis, which tells of three "days" with their evenings and mornings "before" the creation of the sun. Although we may suppose, for the moment, that an infinitely free God might very well realize possibilities in some sort of ordered pattern, we must still ask what would make any such order *temporal,* just as we wonder what would make a morning or evening before the creation of the sun. For the entire order would have to be established in a single act of self-determination. To suppose that God might make a beginning without knowing the end and, indeed, the entire sequence from beginning to end is to suppose a limited God and a limited freedom. And if God determines the entire order in a single act, then there is nothing to mark either the act or the order as a temporal one. On the other hand, to suppose that the order might be decided upon all at once, yet *realized* sequentially would be to forget that the distinction between self-determination and self-realization is a distinction that is proper only to finite freedom.[17] It is a distinction that arises because the finite self has to maintain itself and work out its intentions within the resistant medium of an opposing reality. But there can be no such resistance or opposition to introduce a distinction between intention and action into the activity of absolute freedom. It traffics only with itself, and to determine itself *is* to realize itself. Therefore, although absolute freedom may be thought of as bringing possibilities into some sort of order in the act of determining itself, that order must be contained and realized within the timeless unity of that act.

To put the matter in another way, if God is really to be unlimited, and so to encompass within himself at once both the beginning and the end, alpha and omega, then any order within that compass can present no more than an illusion of temporality. Indeed, it is on just this basis that Asian religious thinkers have argued that time is illusory. When there are no real limits, there is no real temporality, for the reality of time supposes the opposition of a limiting reality with which the self has to struggle. Only this opposing reality can introduce a discursive process into self-determination. Without such opposition and the mediation it imposes, the entire order is absorbed within the immediate unity of the eternal act, wherein all the elements of that order are present together.

But couldn't absolute freedom supply itself with the requisite mediation by creating its own opposition? That would amount to Fichte's scenario, according to which the absolute ego posits the non-ego in opposition to itself. The same formula encountered above might be cited in support of this objection: for absolute freedom, nothing is impossible; it therefore cannot be impossible for absolute freedom to generate its own opposition. But here again, we will find that this formula simply slurs over the exigencies and implications of a freedom that would actually be absolute and the problems of what sort of *being* such a freedom must have if it is to exist at all.

This particular objection brings us face to face with the problem of divine creation, with all the problems that entails. In order to reduce the scope of the problem somewhat as it relates to the present inquiry, we must avail ourselves of a distinction that runs throughout theology, often to its own despair. We have to ask whether God is to be conceived as immanent in his own creation. To put this question in terms more appropriate to the present inquiry: Is this creation to be a genuinely independent reality, with a being outside of and apart from its creator? Or is it to remain in some way within

17. Cf. page 88 above.

the compass of the being of God—or absolute freedom—so that creation cannot ultimately be said to possess a separate reality of its own?

The second of these alternatives may be dismissed at once. For if creation remains ultimately *within* the being of God, then God encompasses both sides of the opposition. This alternative would not really alter the situation described above. The created order would remain within the unity of the single, timeless act of absolute freedom and could provide only a show or illusion of mediation and temporality. In the final analysis such a view of the relation of creation to creator denies that genuine creation occurs.

Thus, if absolute freedom is to attain temporal being through the mediation of its own creation, then that creation must be a truly distinct and independent reality. But how is absolute freedom to generate an opposing reality? We must remember that absolute freedom has *nothing* outside itself. The question at hand is whether it can create something to fill this void, when it has nothing to work with in forming its creation—no chaos or matter or Platonic "receptacle" upon which to impress its designs. Its creation must therefore be a creation out of nothing, or *ex nihilo,* and it is doubtful that creation *ex nihilo* makes any sense at all. To derive a universe out of nothing is about as intelligible as producing a rabbit out of an empty hat, and we would not chuckle at such tricks if we did not know that the magician cannot possibly get something from nothing. In the past, the paradox of producing something out of nothing has often been overcome by simply appealing to God's omnipotence or absolute freedom—for which everything is possible. But this appeal obviously cannot be allowed in the present context, where it is precisely the possibility and intelligibility of absolute freedom that are in question. We have, as yet, no assurance that the explanation of a creation *ex nihilo* through appeal to absolute freedom is anything more than the displacement of one paradox by another—or by the same paradox in a different version. In any case, we certainly cannot allow the use of the paradoxical notion of creation *ex nihilo* as the ground for the possibility of absolute freedom's attainment of a temporal existence without begging the question as transparently as did our "ontological" proof.[18]

18. Robert Neville has developed a conception of creation *ex nihilo* in a series of books beginning with *God the Creator* (Chicago: University of Chicago Press, 1968). Neville's theological reflections parallel those in the present chapter surprisingly often, though they lead him to very different conclusions. He insists, for example, that the act of creation must be eternal and that God cannot have any nature or determinate character apart from creation. To respond adequately to Neville's theory of creation would require a critique of the whole of his subtle and ambitious system, and no footnote could possibly accomplish that task. Suffice it to say that I do not find that his account of a timeless act of creation dispels the mystery inherent in conventional versions of creation *ex nihilo.* For it seems to be simply another way of describing

However, there remains the possibility that God could bring forth his creation out of *himself* rather than out of nothing. Perhaps absolute freedom could give birth to an independent reality by exfoliating or releasing a portion of its own being, as in the Neoplatonic notion of creation by emanation, or the overflow of the fullness of being of the One. This proposal may be entertained, provided only that we insist upon the strict and final separation of the created being once it has been exfoliated. Otherwise the creation will remain immanent in the creator in the final analysis, and there will be neither real opposition nor real mediation nor real temporality. In short, unless the umbilical cord is completely severed, the idea of the birth of an independent reality out of the being of God may only be another version of the idea of an immanent God, and we have already found that such a God cannot be both absolutely free and temporal.

With this proviso, let us suppose, for the moment, that absolute freedom *could* generate a genuine opposition to itself by letting go of its creation so as to give it a reality and being of its own. Just how this creation would really be "other" to the creator is almost as mysterious as the notion of producing something out of nothing, but that need not detain us here. For this "solution" only further demonstrates the impossibility of a freedom that would be both absolute and temporal. Granted, by producing a genuinely independent creation, absolute freedom would indeed open the way to a

---

the *contingency* of the determinacies in our actual cosmos. Contingent upon what? Upon *nothing,* Neville answers, since apart from the determinacy thus created, the creator is nothing. Nor can this "emergence" of determinations out of nothing be a genuine *becoming,* since creation is a timeless, eternal "act," or "making." (See *Eternity and Times Flow* [Albany: State University of New York Press, 1993), 156–57.) Neville's appropriation of "creation," "act," and "making" to describe an eternal ontological relationship between pure indeterminacy and contingent determinations is clearly metaphorical. Within Neville's system, that does not count as an objection, since he sees metaphor as a legitimate form of conception. An older theology would defend the role of analogical predication in speaking of God. Still, it is important to understand that Neville's doctrine of creation *ex nihilo* is a sort of bottom-up Neoplatonism, in which everything determinate wells up out of nothing instead of emanating from the One. Of course, Neville's "nothing" is no mere emptiness, but the "fertile void" of Buddhist and Vedantist metaphysics. Still, in both cases, the suggestion of a process is misleading and conceals the mystery of the derivation of the many out of the One, in the one case, and of how one can get determinacy out of the absolutely indeterminate, in the other case. When Neville writes of creation *ex nihilo,* he might as well be saying that Nirvana and Samsara are the same—and he invites this comparison himself. Since the particular determinations that characterize our cosmos are not necessary and cannot be *deduced* from nothing, Neville can characterize the creative act as perfectly free. Lacking his talent for viewing things *sub specie aeternitas,* I find that his metaphorical bridge gives way somewhere between eternity and activity, and I am left with the de facto contingency of our cosmos. To acknowledge that it might have been otherwise does not seem tantamount to accepting it as the product of a free act.

temporal existence for itself. But by the same act, it would also destroy itself as absolute freedom. The opposition it created would constitute a conditioning and limiting factor over against itself, so that by the act of creation, freedom would bring about its own finitude.[19] Indeed, this point merely reiterates Hegel's analysis, insofar as Hegel insists that absolute freedom "lets nothing break loose to become a *free* object standing over against it."[20]

The opposition between absolute freedom and time is only underscored by this excursion. As the attempt to realize absolute freedom proves suicidal for the finite self, so the attainment of temporality in this manner would be suicidal for absolute freedom. Absolute freedom can only attain temporality by sacrificing its absoluteness, as the passion of Christ so aptly symbolizes. Kirillov's suicide is an inverted image of Christ's passion, as Dostoevsky perhaps intended. Kirillov kills himself to become God. "But he won't have time, perhaps," as the narrator comments. The God who enters time in Christ consigns himself to suffering and death at the hands of his own most independent creation. A God who creates a free and independent other thereby makes himself finite and vulnerable. "But he won't have time, perhaps," to enjoy absolute freedom, after all. For the most that could be said of such an act of creation would be that absolute freedom had exhausted its being in a single act of self-destruction. Its omnipotence would be realized and annihilated in a single moment.

But even that is granting too much. Such a God would no more "have time" to be absolute than Kirillov will have time to be God. For by becoming part of a series that is in some part independent of itself—as "the beginning of the world" or "the beginning of time"—the act of creation loses its absolute status. It is retroactively defined and determined by the nature of the series that follows. Since this series is at least partially independent of the act of creation, and to that extent out of control of the creator, it qualifies and limits the freedom whence it arose. This leads us back to a view such as that of Whitehead or Jonas, according to which the fate of God

19. I think that the same would hold for Neville's God, though I have admitted above that I find his doctrine of creation *ex nihilo* mysterious. But if we accept his account of an eternal act of creating all determinacy, then God *becomes* finite by the very act whence determinacy is born of the fertile void. But since there can be no serious meaning for *becoming* in eternity, this act really stands for a relationship between actual determinacy and the absolutely indeterminate that renders the finitude of freedom inevitable. In some passages, Neville writes as though God *might* have created some other cosmos, one without time, for example. But insofar as that suggests the existence of determinate alternatives between which God might choose prior to the origin of *all* determinacy, it does not seem consistent with the rest of his view. But here again, I have to admit that I find Neville's retention of theistic metaphors more confusing than illuminating.

20. *Phenomenology*, 358. Cf. page 97 above.

depends upon the independent activities of his creations. Whatever the merits of this conception, it is clear that such a God is not absolutely free. Absolute freedom is as little compatible with a *posterior* order independent of itself as it is with an *ancien régime* or antecedent world. As an independent reality, the created order places its creator in a determinate setting, which qualifies and limits his freedom. Its posteriority may disguise the fact that it is a limit by allowing the original act of creation to appear to *have been* the act of an absolute freedom that had nothing outside itself *at that time*. But actually, the fact that the created reality is posterior to the free act of creation is only a temporal expression of the independence of the creation in opposition to its creator, and that independence is what is essential here, while posteriority is only its temporal dimension. The same would be true of a God who came to *destroy* the world and bring about the *end* of time, much as Hegel describes how absolute freedom destroys the fabric of society. A destroying God would not make himself absolutely free by destroying all opposition. Ontologically, the antecedent world would still remain outside his act as an evidence of his finitude, forever beyond his reach. And it would infect and qualify his very freedom, determining him as "the God who destroyed the world." Such a God may have no limits *afterward*. Just as the creating God had no limits *before*. But this very "before" and "after" are actually signposts pointing the direction in which limitation is to be found. By having a position in time—even as its beginning or end—God would violate the requirement that absolute freedom can have *no* determinate setting, whether of its own making or not.

Thus, I return to my original assertion that if absolute freedom is possible, it must be eternal, timeless. It follows that absolute freedom cannot possibly *exist*—if existence is taken in the usual, restricted sense of temporal or spatio-temporal being. This will scarcely seem a defect to the theologian, who recognizes that God must not be thought of as existing in the same way as sailing ships and sealing wax and cabbages and kings. Since to be in time is, after all, to be limited, it would be sophistry to argue that God's eternity is a limitation. According to a tradition as old as Parmenides in the West, perhaps far older in the Orient, temporal existence is a defect, a privation of the fullness of being. The eternality of absolute freedom should therefore be recognized as an aspect or corollary of its limitlessness rather than as a limitation.

Consequently, to show that absolute freedom cannot possibly *exist* is not to show that it is altogether impossible. It only proves that if absolute freedom *is* possible, it can only exist as a single, timeless act of self-determination in which all possibilities are realized at once. So far, then, I have not established *whether* absolute freedom is possible or not, though I have discovered what manner of being it must have if it *is* possible.

Proceeding on the working assumption that freedom might be absolute, I have developed a more adequate description of what the idea of absolute freedom implies. The question whether it is possible now must take the specific form of asking whether a being of this particular description is possible.

Thus far, I have assumed that absolute freedom can determine *itself,* even while I have attempted to prove that it cannot create a reality opposed to itself. But I never properly explored or criticized the idea of an *immanent* creation, one that would not be independent or separate from the being of its creator. I simply set that idea aside because it did not promise to contribute anything to the question whether absolute freedom can be temporal. To have dismissed it altogether would have been to dismiss the possibility of absolute freedom altogether, since we now understand that freedom is self-determination and we discovered earlier that, if freedom is to be absolutely unconditioned, self-determination must be *causa sui,* the cause or creator of itself by its own free act.

So far, I have taken it for granted that absolute freedom might somehow articulate or define itself so as to give itself a determinate form or character and have only argued that it would have to do so in an utterly timeless act that would exhaust all possibilities at once. But that unquestioned assumption must now be questioned more critically, for that is what it means, finally, to ask whether absolute freedom is possible.

How *could* absolute freedom acquire this inner determinacy—or create it for itself? I have spoken as though there were a plentiful store of determinate possibilities available to absolute freedom, a supply of "forms" that it could draw upon and even exhaust in its single, eternal act of self-determination. But where could these forms come from? Whence is absolute freedom to derive such a supply of determinate possibilities? It should be obvious that we cannot appeal to a timeless realm of Platonic forms to answer this question. Platonic forms are principles of *limitation,* and the existence of such a realm of forms over against freedom would suffice to limit it and prevent it from being absolute.

One theological tradition readily supplies the answer that God finds the forms of his possibilities within himself, in a set of "divine exemplars." Superficially, this does seem to avoid qualifying or conditioning God in any way, since he is limited only by himself. But upon closer inspection, it is clear that what this Augustinian answer really says is that the divine will is limited only by the divine intellect. Proponents of this solution saw no difficulty here, since the doctrine of the unity of God led them to deny any real distinction between divine intellect and divine will. But this doctrine cannot be reconciled with what we have learned about the nature of absolute freedom. Unifying of the divine will with a divine intellect containing the eternal exemplars would amount to introducing the forms of those exemplars *into* absolute freedom. But I have shown that absolute freedom *can have no determinacy within itself.* Indeed, the reasons for this characteristic of absolute freedom rule out the very possibility of the supposed unity of the will and intellect of God. Absolute freedom cannot harbor any intrinsic determinacy, because the very nature of freedom is such as to eject or repulse all intrinsic determinations. The freedom of the divine will would set it in opposition to the eternal exemplars for the same reasons that freedom displaces all natural determinations from the finite self. Freedom could not admit of any identity between itself and these given forms, which it must see as alien and external. Otherwise, the divine creation would not be self-determination, but self-explication, a mere unfolding of the determinate forms already inherent within itself—the opening of a flower or the hatching of a cosmic egg. But the notion of an *immanent* self-explication will not bear up under scrutiny, because we have ruled out the temporality required to give any meaning to images of unfolding, flowering, and hatching. If the eternal exemplars already belong to the eternal intellect of God, then there is no need or room for an eternal act whereby they would be realized. For we have seen that the distinction between conception and realization does not pertain to absolute freedom.

Seen in this perspective, there is no essential difference between the Augustinian tradition, which locates these possibilities in the mind of God, and the frankly Platonic tradition, which speaks of a realm of forms that is independent of God—or of the mythical *dēmiourgos* of Plato's *Timaeus,* who forges a temporal world according to patterns supplied by the realm of forms. Because there can be no determinacy *within* freedom, freedom *must* find the forms of its possibilities outside itself. In any case, forms contemplated by a divine intellect are as much *objective* as any object can be, regardless of how we "locate" them. Meanwhile, the whole notion of the mind as a place or container *inside* which objects or ideas may be found has been sharply attacked by recent philosophers of both analytic and phenomenological persuasions. Deep as their differences may be, Wittgenstein and Heidegger alike urge us to recognize that ordinary language and experience show that the mind is not a private place, but is "in-the-world," dependent upon the objects that engage its activities and concerns. Or, to put the point in the terms Husserl and Brentano borrowed from medieval philosophy, the very being of consciousness is "intentional." It is always a consciousness *of* something, always aimed at an object, whether mathematical, physical, or even fictional. If we accept this intentional account of consciousness, then the eternal exemplars may be the objects of divine thoughts or intentions, but cannot really be said to be "in" God. But a freedom that must contemplate and contend with an independent order of possibilities or realm of forms outside itself is not an absolute freedom. Even if it is only limited by the laws of logic, as William of Ockham held, God's freedom is still finite, for an absolutely free being can be subject to no law that it has not established itself. Indeed, even if we suppose that there is no intrinsic *order* to the possibilities that freedom confronts and no laws of logic restricting their realization, their very separate determinacy still constitutes a limitation upon the freedom that must, on this hypothesis, find its opportunity to be in and through just *those* determinate forms. Thus, even if God first establishes order in a realm of eternal objects, as Whitehead's God does, he is nonetheless limited by the determinacy of the possibilities presented to him, while it is only *through* them that he can attain actual being. Whitehead concedes the finitude of God accordingly.

This leads us to the ultimate paradox at the heart of the notion of absolute freedom: absolute freedom would be absolutely impotent! Or, to put the paradox in a different way, a being for which nothing is impossible is also a being for which nothing is possible! It is not only for finite freedom that the idea of absolute freedom is paralyzing, as in the case of Ebenezer Cooke, or suicidal, as Kirillov demonstrated. Absolute freedom would prove paralyzing or suicidal even for an infinite God, who could only choose between doing nothing and some definite deed that would vitiate his absolute freedom in its very doing. But in the first case, God would not be free, since he would fail to determine himself. And, in the second case, God would not be absolute, since his very exercise of freedom would render him finite and determinate.

Completely indeterminate in itself and with nothing outside itself, absolute freedom is the idea of a pure, infinite potentiality—with nothing to do. This is as impossible a conception as would be Aristotle's prime matter without any forms—to which it exactly corresponds, since Aristotle says that pure matter is just the indeterminate potentiality for form. Such a pure *potentiality*, which cannot become actual and is therefore impotent, is an unintelligible contradiction. Yet this is where the idea of absolute freedom leads us in the end.

❄5❄

A Critique of
Pure Freedom

The Illusion of Absolute Freedom

I have tried to characterize freedom in its purest, most complete form, unencumbered by burdensome limits and relationships, to isolate the inner nature of freedom from everything extraneous and accidental to it. The whole course of this inquiry could be described as an attempt to purge the essence of freedom of every adulteration and to grasp freedom as it is in itself, apart from all else. Beginning with immediate freedom, "the freedom to do as I please," I have stripped away layer after layer of apparently unessential adjuncts of freedom in order to get to this inner nature. This led, eventually, to the recognition that freedom must be founded in self-determination. Guided by that recognition, I searched still further in the direction of pure freedom by exploring the possibility of a freedom unqualified by external limitations and uncontaminated by the consequent inclusion of a moment of self-realization within itself. Thus, in the last chapter, I was seeking *absolute* freedom in *both* those senses of the term "absolute" that Kant so carefully distinguished. That is, in seeking after the possibility of *unlimited* freedom, I was also seeking after the nature of freedom *in itself.*

Looking back upon this progressive isolation of freedom from any determinate context, it is easy to see that the process has also progressively emptied the self of all determinate content as well. The self and freedom alike are refined away to nothing by this process. The self excludes any nature or defining characteristics and shrinks to a mere point, while its freedom shrivels to an impotent potentiality! Thus, the free self evaporates in the very process of the attempted distillation of the essence of freedom, and my inquiry finds itself without a subject.

This was the upshot of the last chapter. Clearly, it must prove a turning point, since it shows us the ultimate futility of the whole enterprise of isolating freedom and purifying it of all alien involvement and limitation. The establishment of the impossibility of absolute freedom proves both the impossibility of *unlimited* freedom and the impossibility of a *pure* freedom that would not be related *to* or affected *by* a reality outside itself. With that conclusion, we have hit bottom and must now turn away from the empty quest for a freedom pure and complete to consider the implications of its futility.

The impossibility of absolute freedom means that freedom is only possible as *finite* freedom. That means that freedom cannot *be* or be conceived apart from the limitations of an opposing reality, or in isolation from involvement in an external, determinate milieu. Only the determinate setting that such an independent reality opposes to freedom can offer a ground of actuality for freedom's potentiality or provide its possibilities with any shape and substance.

But although freedom must be finite and the idea of absolute freedom is an illusion, that illusion arises almost inevitably from the relation of finite freedom to itself. For in all its dealings with opposing conditions, freedom still refers through or beyond those conditions back to itself. Since its very being consists in determining *itself,* freedom is irretrievably self-ish. It is incapable of a selfless act, an act that does not ultimately recoil back upon itself. But this selfishness is not moral, but metaphysical or ontological. It does not mean that the free self cannot act generously, altruistically, or disinterestedly, but simply that in so doing, even in an act of utter self-sacrifice or self-abnegation, it inevitably also determines and *defines itself* as generous, disinterested, self-sacrificing, etc. Therefore, in all its relations with anything outside itself, freedom is always reflexively related beyond that other and back to itself. In a sense, then, freedom always has to do *finally* with itself and tends to foster the idea of a pure freedom that would have to do *only* with itself. That evokes the idea of absolute freedom, which simply drops out the intermediate content involving any relation to an *other* so as to leave the self-relatedness of freedom standing in the clear. But that clearing is empty, since nothing is left *but* the self-relatedness of freedom.

Moreover, the inescapably self-referential movement of finite freedom means that it sees itself beyond every horizon. For it projects its own possibility beyond every condition and every limitation. The mere recognition of any limitation *as* such may well provoke the free self to envision the possibility of surpassing that limit. Of course, merely to envision the possibility of transcending some limit or obstacle is not necessarily to be able to do so, or even to attempt to do so, or even to be able to envision any concrete program for realizing that possibility. Like some of the early science fiction accounts of interstellar flight, the possibility thus projected may be a largely fanciful one that does not seriously grapple with the nature or severity of the limitation to be surpassed. Indeed, this possibility may have no determinate shape at all, but simply be the indefinite possibility of being-beyond-this-limit—like the proverbial "other side of the mountain" or "seeing myself as others see me." (In H. G. Wells's *Voyage to the Moon,* the force of gravity is overcome by the use of "antigravity plates.") This ability of finite freedom to project itself beyond *any* limit easily passes over into projecting the possibility of a freedom beyond *all* limits, beyond determinacy and finitude itself, and is a second motive for the illusion of absolute freedom.

There are thus two sources of the illusion of absolute freedom built into the relation of a self-determining being to itself. The source of illusion in each of these ways of arriving at the notion of absolute freedom is easy enough to discern now that we understand why that goal is impossible. In the first case, in dropping away the determinate situation or context of freedom's self-reference in order to reach pure self-determination, the baby is thrown out with the bath water. For freedom is thereby deprived of the determinacy of its self-determination, which is the very substance of that self-reference. Without any definite situation or context to supply it with determinate alternatives, only an abstract self-relatedness remains, entirely too empty and indefinite to be self-*determination*. The reference back to self has no definite meaning apart from an initial movement of relation away from the self. Deprived of all determinate opposition, self-determination is placed in the comic predicament of a man trying to play leapfrog with himself.

Similarly, in generalizing from its ability to project itself beyond *any* limitation to the possibility of projecting of itself beyond *all* limitation, freedom precipitates itself beyond its sustaining medium. "The light dove, cleaving the air in her free flight, and feeling its resistance, might imagine that its flight would be still freer in empty space."[1] This image, which Kant evoked to depict the aspirations of pure reason, seems even more aptly to describe this source of the idea of pure freedom—and to reveal its error. The opposing reality that resists the efforts of freedom is also the necessary medium of its existence, without which those efforts would be as vacuous and futile as the beating of wings in a void. To recognize that those aspirations are illusory, that even God could not be absolutely free, is to "come back down to earth," to acknowledge that the only freedom that is possible is mundane and finite.[2]

Mundane Freedom

To be free, then, is to be finite—to be limited by an opposing realm with its own intrinsic determinacy and being, its own definite features and exigencies that oppose and limit freedom. Yet that limiting, resisting realm is, all the same, the necessary sustaining milieu of freedom, the indispensable ground of its opportunity to *be* at all. In short, freedom must necessarily be mundane; it must have a milieu, or *world,* in order to exist and can only be consistently conceived as confronting that world and coping with it.

The determinate world that the free self has to confront is *already there.* It cannot begin as a world of the self's own making or choosing, for such a creation *ex nihilo* is incompatible with freedom. And yet, freedom must also be conceived as already involved or entangled with that world. Freedom cannot stand back and choose whether to accept that world as a whole, or whether to plunge itself into it or hover indifferently outside. For freedom can define itself—and therefore can *be* itself as self-determining—only in and through the world that opposes it, without which it amounts to an

---

1. Immanuel Kant, *Critique of Pure Reason,* trans. Norman Kemp Smith (New York: St. Martin's Press, 1961), A-5, p. 47.

2. Cf. Sartre's argument that there can be no freedom without facticity (in *Being and Nothingness,* trans. Hazel Barnes [New York: Philosophical Library, 1956], 79–84 and 481 ff.) and Jaspers's critique of the ideal of absolute freedom (in *Philosophy,* trans. E. B. Ashton [Chicago: Chicago University Press, 1970], vol. 2, chap. 6). Robert Kane (in *Free Will and Values* [Albany: State University of New York Press, 1985]) reaches the same end by a rather different route, concluding that the outcome of moral choice "really is uncertain and tragedy is an ever present possibility. To think otherwise for libertarians is a form of *hubris* or pride. . . . It is to labor under the illusion that you can be free in an undetermined sense *and* have total rational control over your situation. The present theory . . . has tried to expose this as an illusion, by showing the connection between the libertarian view of freedom, on the one hand, and consequent finitude of free beings, on the other" (154).

empty and impotent self-relatedness. Freedom can exist only by finding its way in that world and by acting upon it.

Nor is this necessary entanglement in the world canceled or overcome by the fact that the free self always refers *beyond* the world and back to itself, which I have described as metaphysical selfishness and found to be one of the sources of the illusion of absolute freedom. Rather, this necessary involvement with a world is the necessary and complementary counterpart of the self's projection of itself beyond the world. Just as freedom cannot define itself *except* by coping with an independent world, it also cannot help *but* define itself by its dealing with that world, and that is why its relations with the world always recoil back upon itself. It cannot *otherwise* determine itself, but it cannot *avoid* determining itself.

To put the matter in another way, the self's reference back to itself, beyond whatever is given and determinate, is really a reference *forward* toward its own *possible* identity and being, which depend upon how it chooses to relate to the world. Implicit within this self-relation, then, is the fact that the nature and being of the free self are at stake in its relations with its determinate milieu. The *self*-relatedness of freedom therefore really indicates that the free self's relation to its *other* is of crucial, decisive importance to its own being and *not* merely accidental, as the idea of absolute freedom would imply by illegitimately abstracting this self-reference from any entanglement in a world. Freedom's reality lies *in* the world that opposes it, and therefore freedom cannot be conceived of *outside* that world except by an abstraction that belies the very conditions of its being. Consequently, we can say that it is inescapable that freedom must be in a world.

Phenomenologists have developed similar reflections, insisting upon the worldliness of human existence, thereby refusing the Cartesian dilemma of how a self-contained and self-subsistent consciousness can assure itself of its contact with any other being whatsoever. Even Husserl dwelt upon the relation to the *Lebenswelt,* or life-world, in his later works, while Heidegger replaced the Husserlian analysis of phenomena as appearances within a field of "transcendental consciousness" with an analysis of *Dasein,* or human existence as "being-in-the-world," shunning all reference to "consciousness." Sartre, who returns to the more Cartesian terminology of consciousness, nonetheless agrees that what is phenomenally concrete is always "man within the world" as a "synthetic totality" from which consciousness and the phenomenon are only abstractions.[3] Both Heidegger and Sartre describe the worldliness of the subject as a fundamental and inescapable fact of human existence. Yet both therefore also treat being-in-the-world as a

---

3. Cf. Sartre, *Being and Nothingness,* 3–4.

merely contingent *fact* disclosed by the analysis of the concrete phenomena of human experience. Heidegger finds that he has been "thrown" into the world in order to die there, and describes this "thrownness" (*Geworfenheit*) as one of the fundamental characteristics of man's very being. Sartre renders the same theme by dwelling upon the contingent "facticity" of human reality, a contingency that is one of his central preoccupations. These two existential phenomenologists thereby show that they have not entirely escaped the Cartesian dilemma after all, since it is the search for a *necessary* connection between consciousness and an independently existing world that provoked Descartes's meditations.

But I have not tied my own analysis of freedom to the human condition, or confined it to the facts of human experience, and have had to conclude, quite independently of any peculiarities of the *human* condition, that the existence of a world that limits and entangles any free being is *necessary* to that being's very existence. Being-in-the-world must therefore be recognized as a constituent necessity of the being of freedom and not just a phenomenologically certified, contingent truth about *Dasein* or human freedom alone.[4] Being-in-the-world is a necessary condition of *any* free existence because it follows directly from the impossibility of absolute freedom and is really only another way of saying that finitude is not merely accidental to freedom. For finitude would still appear to be accidental, a contingent imposition, if freedom and its world were simply set in external confrontation with one another. The assertion that freedom *must* be in a world summarizes and epitomizes the fact that finitude is a necessary characteristic of freedom, that there can be no freedom that is not finite.

But that does not mean that we have escaped contingency. For although it is necessary that freedom be in *some* particular world, it is *not* necessary that it find itself in whatever particular world it actually inhabits. To show that it is necessary that freedom be engaged in *some* world is not to show that it need be in *this* one rather than *that*. "World" is simply a convenient term for designating any determinate milieu capable of supporting freedom and providing a ground for its possibilities. It need not be our familiar world, or any similar world of space and time. For example, a finite deity might inhabit a world of pure possibilities, such as confronts Leibniz's God prior to creation,[5] or the similar realm of "eternal objects"

4. Sartre's "ontological argument" from the intentionality of consciousness to the existence of a transphenomenal being-in-itself provides a comparable necessary connection. See ibid., lx-lxii. But Sartre's being-in-itself is not a world, but a seamless, immutable unity reminiscent of Parmenides' monism.

5. I make somewhat casual use of Leibniz's theology for illustrative purposes in this chapter. I have depicted Leibniz's God as contemplating an independent realm of possibilities from

that Whitehead describes God as "ordering" in a primordial act of creation. Each supplies freedom with that source of determinate form which is necessary to its own activity. Thus, although finitude itself is not accidental to freedom, the particular *form* that finitude takes is contingent, since the world might be different, and Heidegger and Sartre are therefore right to stress the contingent facticity of the specifically *human* world. Indeed, a world that could *not* be different would leave no room for action or freedom. Even this contingency of the particular nature of the world is therefore a *necessary* contingency, for if the *particular* nature of the world were also necessary, then freedom could not *alter* that world without destroying its own foundation. But such a freedom could *do* nothing, would be unable to realize itself without destroying itself, and is consequently impossible.

The relation of freedom to its world therefore conjoins necessity and contingency, and this introduces a fundamental ambivalence into the being of freedom. On the one hand, it is in the world out of an inner necessity of its own nature, such that its very being is bound up with its world. On the other hand, any particular free self is in the specific world it *is* in by sheer accident. (That is, the particularity of its world is accidental in relation to its freedom. It may not be accidental in relation to the nature of that world, or accidental in any absolute sense.) Freedom cannot recognize itself in its world, because freedom has no inherent determinacy of its own that it might rediscover and recognize in the determinate features of its world. Again, that world *could* be different and *can* be different because, if no other world is possible, then all is necessity, which leaves no room for freedom. Consequently, the free self has no reason to feel that it *belongs* where it is. And yet, this is *the* particular world with which that self must "make do." It must at least begin by coping with this particular milieu and must define itself in so doing. There is another sense, then, in which this is its "very own world," a world that belongs to it and to which it belongs in turn. For although the particular form of that world is only contingently given and might be otherwise, it is nevertheless decisive for the free self, which can

---

which he freely chooses the best combination as the one to realize in creating the actual world. Although this is a convenient way of representing Leibniz's position and serves the purpose of providing a needed example in the present context, it is not strictly in accord with the texts. Leibniz does not accord the possibilities any being except as objects of the divine intellect. See, e.g., Gottfried Wilhelm von Leibniz, "On the Radical Origination of Things," in *Philosophical Papers and Letters,* trans. and ed. Leroy E. Loemker (Chicago: University of Chicago Press, 1956), 2:793. However, see my remarks upon the relation of this view to freedom, in Chapter 2, pages 70–71, above. Furthermore, the nature and status of the freedom of God's choice, in Leibniz's view, is beset with considerable problems. See J. F. Ross, "Did God Create the Only Possible World?" *Review of Metaphysics 16,* no. 1 (1962): 14–25.

only determine itself in the terms supplied by the world it *has*. Since this ambivalence in the situation of freedom is so important, let us pursue the matter somewhat further.

The world presents freedom with a realm that is determinate, which therefore has its own inescapable features, its own necessities. To this extent, freedom is bounded by, and subordinated to, necessity. Thus, even the realm of infinite possibilities that confronts Leibniz's God imposes its own exigencies. If the world God chooses to create is the best of all *possible* worlds, as Leibniz claims, that is because he could not create a better one, and if he could not create a better one, it is because of the exigencies governing his own world of infinite possibility. Each possibility has its own determinate nature or formula, which makes it compatible or compossible with certain other possibilities and incompatible with others. God's freedom is restricted to a choice among *com*possible groupings. Thus, God has no real alternative in creating the world he does—unless he were to choose to create less than he is capable of achieving. Origen argued on similar grounds that God is neither infinite nor free. He cannot be infinite, Origen argues, because he is limited by his own perfection, which means that he could not choose to create a less perfect world. But he is also not free, for he cannot do anything that he has not done, else he would be less than perfect. It is sometimes argued that Leibniz and Origen nevertheless do not describe God as limited by any opposing reality, but only by his own perfection. But in fact, it is to the limitations of possibility that Leibniz must appeal in order to argue that a world better than the one we know was simply beyond the realm of possibility. If the realm of possibility were not governed by logical principles such as the law of noncontradiction, then any set of possibilities would be compatible, and there would be no such limit to what is possible. Medieval debate about God's omnipotence therefore often came to focus upon whether God is limited by the law of noncontradiction.

When we descend to the more familiar plane of man's involvement with the natural world, this subordination of freedom to the exigencies of the world becomes still more acute. Compared with a God who only has to contend with the airy limits of logical possibility, man appears a very earthbound creature, caught in a web of material and causal necessities. The limitations of the laws of nature loom so large as to seem to threaten to overshadow or even eclipse any possibility of human freedom. But this appearance must be overcome by recognizing that the necessities imposed upon the self by the world are counterbalanced by the necessity of the world *to* freedom. For these necessities are inseparable from the determinacy of this world, and the resistance they oppose to freedom is, once again, the very medium that supports it. The laws of nature are the enabling conditions of action; discovery of those laws is at the foundation of an engineering technology that has allowed human beings to alter their world profoundly. Even in art, that least mundane, most godlike of human activities in which the earthbound creature turns creator, freedom depends upon its concrete limits for its support. Stravinsky provides us with a lucid account of this ambivalent relation of freedom to necessity in his *Poetics of Music*:

> What delivers me from the anguish into which an unrestricted freedom plunges me is the fact that I am always able to turn immediately to the concrete things that are here in question. I have no use for a theoretic freedom. Let me have something finite, definite—matter that can lend itself to my operation only insofar as it is commensurate with my possibilities. And such matter presents itself to me together with its limitations. I must in turn impose mine upon it. So here we are, whether we like it or not, in the realm of necessity. And yet, which of us has ever heard tell of art as other than a realm of freedom? This sort of heresy is uniformly widespread because it is imagined that art is outside the bounds of ordinary activity. Well, in art as in everything else, one can build only upon a resisting foundation: whatever constantly gives way to pressure constantly renders movement impossible. My freedom thus consists in my moving about within the narrow frame that I have assigned myself for each one of my undertakings.[6]

The free self derives its possibilities from the world and, indeed, from the very necessities of its world. These necessities are what make that world the "resisting foundation" that freedom requires. It is yesterday's necessities that disclose to me the possibilities of today, and my vision of possibility alters and grows in keeping with my grasp of necessity. The world itself, with its necessities, is the only thing that can give a content or shape to freedom's possibilities. There is nothing in the nature of freedom that would give the free self an independent access to any determinate possibilities *as such*, as pure possibilities apart from any world. But even if there were, even if intellectual intuition or pure reason or creative imagination afforded a vision of pure forms or ultramundane possibilities, the free self would still have to be guided by the exigencies of its world in discovering the relevance of those possibilities to its situation in the world and in attempting to realize those possibilities. But this supposition is absentminded, forgetful of the

---

6. Igor Stravinsky, *The Poetics of Music* (New York: Random House, 1960), 67-68.

fact that, for freedom, the "world" comprehends whatever determinacy freedom encounters. Any set of determinate possibilities it might envision would form a part of its world, so that the problem of relating these to actuality would be a problem of relating two determinate regions within the world.

Moreover, although the necessities of the world disclose possibility to the self, that can only happen insofar as the self *is* free. That is, it is only the nature of freedom that *makes* the world a ground for the disclosure of possibilities *for* the self *as* possible. Otherwise, the content of any possibility would simply be one more determinate element *within* the world. It is the self's ability to determine itself in and through its world that transforms the structure of necessity into a foundation of opportunity or possibility for the self. This may be most clearly recognized if we consider once more the relation of Leibniz's God to *his* world of infinite possibilities. Here, it would at first seem that since this world is made up of mere possibilities, their status *as* possibilities would be independent of God's freedom. However, upon closer inspection it is clear that apart from God, this world is not made up of possibilities at all, but is only a realm of determinate forms. It is only in relation to the freedom of God's act of creation that these acquire the status of possibilities. From the standpoint of God *prior* to creation, these would only have the status of a determinate milieu that offered a foundation for *his* possibility, which would be the possibility of creation. From that standpoint he would survey the infinite array of determinations with an eye to their compatible combinations—that is, to see what *possible worlds* could be created from them. But if God is *not* free, if he *must* choose the best possible world, then all lesser worlds are not possible at all, but impossible alternatives that God *could* create if he *were* free to produce evil and imperfection.

Thus, while it is only through the necessities of its world that possibilities can be disclosed to the self, it is only the freedom of the self that makes such a disclosure possible. In this process, the free self appropriates necessity to the service of its own possibility. It organizes and regards the world in terms of its own opportunities, and the naked necessities of the given world thereby become clothed with possibility. The necessities of the world are integrated into larger structures that involve possibilities, and these larger structures, though they include necessities within themselves, are not themselves necessary. Let us call these structures "opportunities" and "dangers," since that is how we usually think of them.[7] Since it is in terms of these

---

7. Psychologist J. J. Gibson coined the term "affordances" to suit structures of this sort, which are born of the conjunction between an organism and the physical or perceptual—or even social—properties of its environment: "The *affordances* of the environment are what it *offers* the animal, what it *provides* or *furnishes,* either for good or ill" (127). For a full account of

larger structures that freedom functions and appraises the world, freedom does not initially come into direct confrontation with necessity. For in relation to these structures of opportunity and danger, necessity becomes flexible and ambiguous—not that the given exigencies of the world cease to be rigid and unyielding in themselves, of course. But these necessities are qualified by the variety of opportunities they may subserve.[8] I cannot change the physics or geography of the earth, for example. Its mountains and oceans will not move to suit my will. Yet as I sit, surrounded by travel brochures, trying to decide upon vacation plans, those mountains and oceans are woven into my purposes and options, and their physical properties scarcely present *obstacles* to my choice between surfing and skiing. A simple, analytic necessity like "Fire burns" is the nucleus for a vast complex of myriad possibilities, and it is in terms of this complex array of possibilities that freedom is related to that simple necessity. Consequently, from the standpoint of freedom, every necessity is freighted with ambiguities, surrounded by a halo of multiple possibilities.

Freedom therefore does not encounter sheer necessity directly. Consequently, the exigencies of its world do not *exclude* freedom by their very nature, as one might expect. But these same reflections show that freedom is *dependent upon* those necessities, so that its horizons are *defined by* its world and the exigencies thereof. For these are the source of its opportunities, and they shape those structures in terms of which the free self orients itself toward its *own* prospects as well as toward its world. The features of the realm that opposes freedom define the horizons of its possible self-determination and spell out the particular terms of its finitude.

Thus, in one sense, man takes over his world to his own use and transforms it, converting neutral geographical facts into nations, and the natural landscape into property, into lawns and farms and cities. Still, by the same process, man becomes definite and determinate in terms of that world and its features. His dwelling, his nationality, his occupations are

---

his theory of affordance, see chap. 8 of his *Ecological Approach to Visual Perception* (Boston: Houghton Mifflin, 1979).

8. Gibson's chapter on affordances supplies ample examples. E.g.: "An elongated object of moderate size and weight affords wielding. If used to hit or strike, it is a *club* or *hammer*. If used by a chimpanzee behind bars to pull in a banana beyond its reach, it is a sort of *rake*. In either case, it is an extension of the arm. A rigid staff also affords leverage and in that use is a *lever*. A pointed elongated object affords piercing—if large it is a *spear*, if small, a *needle* or *awl*. . . . A graspable rigid object of moderate size and weight affords throwing. It may be a *missile* or only an object for play, a *ball*. . . . The fact that a stone is a missile does not imply that it cannot be other things as well. It can be a paperweight, a bookend, a hammer, or a pendulum bob. It can be piled on another rock to make a cairn or a stone wall. These affordances are all consistent with one another" (ibid., 133, 134).

defined by the world to such an extent that, in the end, his self is as much formed by that world as that world is formed by him.[9]

Finite Freedom and the Dialectic of Freedom

I have now established the general outline of the nature and extent to which freedom depends upon a reality that opposes and limits it. I have shown that such an already determinate context or world is necessary to freedom, but that the exact nature of that world is accidental. Freedom must, therefore, by its very nature, be situated in a world that is nonetheless, in its every detail, alien and accidental to the nature of freedom. Yet these alien details and exigencies constitute the specific terms of the finitude of any free self and prescribe the range of its possibilities. They therefore *belong* to the free self, and freedom belongs to them, notwithstanding the fundamental opposition between the two. Since the world is defined for the self in terms of the self's own opportunities, that world is the self's very *own*. Yet since all of its possibilities depend upon the exigencies of that world, the self's very freedom is lodged within that world.

It is not freedom itself that is threatened or excluded by the world and its exigencies, then, but only the ideal of *pure* freedom, or freedom in itself. The necessary, inextricable entanglement of freedom in its world is only the positive complement of the impossibility of such a pure, isolated freedom. I began the chapter by calling attention to the fact that the attempt to isolate the pure, inner essence of freedom was a process of stripping layer after layer away from the concrete substance of freedom. But the goal of this process has proved illusory, and therefore what was stripped away from freedom in the pursuit of that goal must be restored to it. We have to work our way back from the empty core of pure and absolute freedom, recovering what had been cast aside in the abortive endeavor to isolate freedom from everything alien to it. Since absolute freedom is a cul-de-sac, an extreme point of abstraction, we must turn about and undertake to recover the concreteness of freedom. But our excursion into this blind alley would

---

9. If the human condition seems too specific and controversial to illustrate the relation of freedom to its world, consider one of Whitehead's actual occasions. An actual occasion is unified and defined by the possibility that is its subjective aim. But that subjective aim is itself more or less limited and prescribed by the antecedent world that the actual occasion inherits. The relations between freedom and the world in this example are exactly those described here. Each actual occasion must integrate physical feelings deriving from the given, antecedent world with conceptual feelings or prehensions of possibilities informing its subjective aim.

prove of little profit if we sought to accomplish this recovery by returning straightforth to its very beginning in the dialectic of immediate freedom. Instead, we must recognize that the *source* of that dialectic lies directly before us, in our present understanding of the necessary finitude of freedom. Only that recognition will enable us to restore those concrete aspects of freedom that the immediate view embraced, without becoming involved once again in the futile dialectic to which that view led us before.

That which is independent, external, and opposed to freedom has proved to be necessary to its very being. This is the ultimate source of the dialectic of freedom. In a sense, freedom itself *is* inescapably dialectical because it requires its opposite in order to be. Therefore, all attempts to conceive or understand freedom in an undialectical manner must end in failure. We must avoid two undialectical extremes. On the one hand, in order to understand freedom, we have to try to grasp it, *not* as it is *in itself,* pure and absolute, but as it is *in situ,* in all the complexity of its entanglement with an opposing reality. But, on the other hand, we must not let freedom melt into that opposing reality altogether, so that it becomes wholly a function of external factors. That was shown to be the flaw in the conception of freedom as self-realization, in all its immediate and ethical variations, all of which made freedom a function of circumstance. Freedom can be defined neither wholly as a function of the self nor wholly as a function of circumstances. Because each of these extremes fails to apprehend and preserve the intrinsically dialectical character of freedom, each is caught up by a dialectic from without and carried along to a point at which freedom simply vanishes.

Rather ironically, both of these extremes define freedom in terms of the absence of opposition. But whereas the idea of freedom as self-realization tries to work out this antidialectical definition in terms of relations *within* the world by seeking to distinguish between "internal" and "external' circumstances and influences, the other extreme, the idea of absolute freedom, tries to accomplish the same result by abstracting freedom *from* the world altogether. Each therefore lacks what the other has, and has what the other lacks. As was shown in Chapter 3, self-realization lacks a self-determining being, which it needs to provide a foundation and center of reference for its distinctions among intramundane relations and influences. As was shown in Chapter 4, absolute freedom lacks a determinate world, which it needs to provide substance and content for its pure self-determining being. This one-sidedness leaves each of these conceptions of freedom vulnerable to a dialectic that seems to catch it from behind yet only forces each to dissociate itself thoroughly and consistently from its opposing complement. Once each is forced by this insistence to an extreme point of self-consistency, it becomes evident that freedom has disappeared in the process. In the first case, it evaporates into an arbitrary distinction among relations within the world, and in the second case, it disappears into the absurdity of an impotent potentiality.

Only by accepting and even embracing the inherent dialectic of freedom can we find a basis for a positive account of freedom that will not be subverted by that dialectic. For each of these undialectical conceptions of freedom leads, in its own way, to the denial of the possibility of a constructive metaphysics of freedom. Not only does freedom evaporate in both instances, but even if it did not, the attempt to gain a positive understanding of freedom would strike insurmountable obstacles. In the first instance, where freedom is made wholly a function of the world, inquiry would be brought to a halt by the dispute between immediate and ethical conceptions of freedom. It could proceed no further because, as already noted, there would be no basis in principle for choosing between these two opposing extremes—or among the several versions of either.[10] Hence, the sole lesson of an inquiry into the nature of freedom based upon *this* undialectical conception would have to be that there is *no* real basis for a systematic, constructive account of freedom. That was the impasse that threatened this inquiry at the end of Chapter 1.

If, on the other hand, we were to try to articulate a clear understanding of freedom on the basis of pure or absolute freedom, we would run afoul of quite the opposite difficulty. In the former case we arrive at a parting of the ways with no justification for following either; in this case we come to a simple dead end. For even if an absolute freedom were possible, it would be impossible to describe it in any positive way. No description of its nature, conditions, structure, or relations would be possible, for the simple reason that it could *have* none of these. It could only be approached or indicated *negatively,* as it was in the preceding chapter, through a series of denials reminiscent of the *via negativa* of medieval theology. Once we completed this process of delineating what freedom is *not,* inquiry would simply have to come to an end in the confession of inability to say anything positive about freedom.

In any case, both of these one-sided alternatives have proved incapable of accounting for the nature and being of freedom. Each tries to understand freedom as the *absence* of opposition, albeit the conception of opposition is different in each case, whereas we have been forced to recognize that, quite to the contrary, opposition is necessary to freedom. And in contrast to both these alternatives, an acceptance of the inherently dialectical character of freedom does leave the way open for further inquiry into the nature and

---

10. Cf. pages 47–48 above.

meaning of freedom. Indeed, this necessary finitude of freedom is the very basis for the possibility of a positive and systematic account of what it must be. For whereas absolute freedom, or pure self-determination, would altogether escape positive conception, a self-determination that is involved in a determinate opposing reality does not. Finitude imposes definite and describable conditions upon freedom. The necessary relationship of freedom to its world entails certain exigencies whose most general characteristics can form the basis for a positive understanding. That is, it should be possible to analyze the most general, inescapable conditions bound up with freedom's relation to the world. And since this relation to an opposing world is itself necessary to the very being of freedom, whatever belongs necessarily to that relationship will be a categorical necessity of the being of freedom. Such an analysis can therefore reveal the fundamental logic of freedom. Or, since that presses the term "logic" beyond its technical meaning, perhaps it would be more accurate to acknowledge that what is envisioned is an account of the *being* of freedom by speaking, instead, of an ontology of freedom, if *ontology* is simply understood as the study of the irreducible, inescapable features and conditions of the being of what is.

This prospectus must guide any attempt to recover the concrete reality and complexity of freedom. Instead of simply returning to immediacy in an attempt to recapture the concrete elements that have been stripped away, we must work our way back in a systematic progression whereby every factor we recover is justified and bound into our structure by showing that it is necessary to the very existence of freedom in relation to an opposing world.

❋ Part III ❋

Freedom
Within
Limits

The attempt to ground freedom in an unconditioned power of self-determination proves to be as vacuous as the attempt to define it by the absence of constraining circumstances. But that failure is instructive. By demonstrating the necessary finitude of freedom, this line of inquiry discloses the source of the dialectic that has vexed the effort to understand freedom from the very outset. The attempt to conceive of freedom as distinct from all that limits and opposes it has only revealed how intimately it depends upon a limiting world; the dialectic that seemed to bedevil this inquiry has been traced to the inherently dialectical character of freedom. We can now turn our negative results to positive account by trying to understand how a necessarily finite freedom can exist in dialectical interplay with its world. We can descend from the heights of theology and abstract conceptual analysis and attempt to understand how freedom *can* inhabit a world and how the world can *limit* freedom without precluding it entirely.

But that means that we must undo the abstract notions of both freedom and world that we have concocted in an attempt to purify our conceptions of each. We have opposed a world that is entirely determinate to a freedom determined only by itself, unscathed by any alien causes. Having conceived the two by mutual opposition, we cannot simply throw them together. How will such a freedom find any place in such a world? Can a world that includes a free agent still be described as entirely determinate? We now turn to the constructive task of understanding how freedom can be finite.

Chapter 6 considers how free agency can gain a foothold within a world that is already determinate—how freedom can be limited and even defined by such a world without losing its character as self-determination. That consideration involves a study of the necessary *embodiment* of freedom and leads to a fresh appreciation of the notion of freedom as self-realization. Freedom can only exist if it can realize itself in particular actions that alter the world. But the very actions that realize freedom also limit and determine freedom. Indeed, its reality *as* self-determination is embodied in those very limitations that it has brought upon itself. In Chapter 7, I investigate how freedom limits itself by the very act of determining itself, which leads to a fresh appreciation of those ethical views that insist only those actions or choices that accord with the true nature of the self are genuinely free.

Thus, by the time I have finished considering how freedom can be embodied in mundane existence and how it defines itself through its own activity, I will have built up a fuller, more positive account of freedom that will enable us to reconcile the competing conceptions of freedom encountered in Part I. With the conceptual disputes thus clarified and resolved, we can return to the questions about human freedom from which we began. In Chapter 8, I ask how well this richer, more synoptic conception accords with human experience.

❧6❧

Incarnation

Freedom Requires a Body

The last chapter demonstrated that the existence of freedom presupposes a world, where "world" should be understood in a very general sense—as an independent, determinate reality that opposes and limits the free self, while serving as the ground of its opportunities. It dealt with some of the problems of the relation of freedom to its world, albeit in a very schematic fashion. Yet in all of this, I never really raised the problem of *how* it is possible for freedom to be in a world. It is one thing to consider freedom on the one hand and an independent world on the other hand and to insist that freedom requires such an opposing reality. But it is quite another to place freedom *within* a reality that, by definition, opposes it. Or, to put the matter slightly differently, it is not enough to point out that freedom requires such an opposing reality and then simply to place the two alongside one another. Such a procedure would only yield a relation of juxtaposition—a juxtaposition that would only hold for *us* as observers, moreover, and not for the free self. To discover that freedom must have a world only poses a new problem that is not solved by the sheer coexistence of self and world. We still have to explain how freedom can come into contact or relation with its world *for itself,* so as to enable it to have access to the forms or determinations that the world provides.

In short, we have still to account for the "in" of freedom's being in the world. Modern phenomenology has addressed this question with admirable vigor and subtlety. Husserl's analysis of the "life-world" and, especially, Heidegger's analysis of "being-in" (*Insein*) in *Being and Time* describe the experience of being in the midst of a world. Heidegger argues quite persuasively that phenomenology must substitute the analysis of "being-in" for the conventional modern philosophical preoccupation with "the problem of knowledge," which has asked how information and objects can be gotten from "the external world" *into* the mind—or how the knowing subject can get "outside" the mind to verify whether its ideas are true to the "external objects" they purport to represent. Heidegger invites us to recognize that this whole problem, which has so occupied modern philosophy since Descartes, is artificial, that we do not have to begin from an "inner," "subjective" domain of representations, or "mental objects," because that is not what we *have* at the beginning. In fact, what we have in the first place (*zuerst und zumeist*) is an experience of being already "out there," in the midst of a surrounding world.

It would be convenient if we could simply appropriate Heidegger's analysis of "being-in" to meet our present need. Unfortunately, Heidegger's analysis is no more helpful at this particular juncture than is the sheer juxtaposition of freedom and world, which Heidegger, too, rejects. For although Heidegger's *Dasein* is a free being, to which being-in-the-world belongs as a fundamental constitutive moment, nevertheless his account of the being-in part of this structure does not explain, and is not intended to explain, how this being-in is possible. Here, as elsewhere, the difference in methodology between the phenomenological approach and my own procedure prevents me from using the products of Heidegger's analysis *directly.* Founded upon a phenomenological description that discovers *Dasein,* or his own self, *already* in the world, Heidegger's account provides an ontological analysis of the resultant structure. But that does not explain how it is *possible* for freedom to be in the world. We cannot answer that question by invoking care (*Sorge*) or concern (*Besorgen*) or mood (*Befindlichkeit, Stimmung*), because these refer to the nature of relations that freedom has to a world that it is in already. Accordingly, that world is not fully independent of *Dasein* or opposed to *Dasein.* The very "worldhood" of the world is entangled in the self's understanding and projects. To invoke Heidegger's answers here would be to beg the question.[1]

How, then, is the free self to be set within its world? A free self can have no intrinsic determinacy except that which it gives itself. And it cannot give itself determinacy except in and through a world. How can such a being intelligibly be within a *world* that is already determinate? We cannot just *assume* that the self is in such a world simply because we have shown that it cannot otherwise exist at all. That would beg the very question that is disputed by determinists, who deny that there is any place or room for freedom in the world just because—and insofar as—the world is already determined through and through. And they raise a troubling, fundamental problem that cannot be dodged. The determinacy that is definitive of the world and the indeterminacy of the free self do seem to exclude one another so utterly that no thought experiment can successfully bring them together without ignoring the distinctive characteristics of each.[2]

The solution to this problem necessitates further modification and qualification of our previous thinking about freedom. To be free, as self-determining, is to be active. So long as we were in quest of a pure freedom of self-determination, we could pursue the idea of a *pure* agency or potentiality or spontaneity. But we have had to abandon the ideal of pure

1. Heidegger stays with the concrete phenomenon of the being of *Dasein,* so that, although *Dasein* is a free being, he never separates that freedom from the concrete context of its worldly involvements. In contrast, I *have* separated and isolated freedom from any limiting context, only to discover that the strategy proved self-destructive. I have therefore undertaken a deliberate self-conscious reconstruction of that concrete context. Consequently, although the structures I reach in the end may *parallel* those described by Heidegger and other phenomenologists, my procedure demands that I account for their possibility and for the necessity of their belonging to freedom before I avail myself of them.

2. Richard Double urges that "[a]ny libertarian theory needs to suggest some vehicle by which indeterminacy enters into human choices, given the initially plausible assumption that human decisions are the result of deterministic events in the same way that other macroscopic events are" (*The Non-Reality of Free Will* [Oxford: Oxford University Press, 1991], 192). We cannot adopt Double's "plausible assumption" without foreclosing questions about freedom in natural processes that still remain open here. Many philosophers, from Kant to Robert Kane, set up the problem of the existence of freedom in the context of the assumption that determinism holds throughout nature—or at least macroscopic nature. Having done so, they can only maintain the reality of freedom by either resorting to the ingression of some *super*natural agency or by relying upon microscopic, quantum indeterminacy. In order to avoid this prejudicial construction of the issue, I have not taken a deterministic theory of nature for granted and have held open the question of the possible *range* of freedom. However, even if we do not assume that human choices are natural events or that natural events are entirely determined, we still have to cope with the basic problem of how the indeterminacy of freedom can enter into an already determinate world. That problem will arise even if all natural events include a moment of free decision, as Whitehead maintains.

freedom because freedom needs a realm of determinacy that opposes and limits it. I have dwelt upon this requirement at some length—yet have not articulated its most important consequence: that to admit that a realm of determinacy is indispensable to freedom requires that we abandon not only the unconditionedness of pure freedom but also the idea of pure agency or spontaneity. Freedom cannot merely be alongside of, or copresent with, its world, because the reason freedom must *have* a world, in the first place, is that the self must have *access to* the determinacy of the world so as to be able to determine itself. But this access to the world cannot be conceived in terms of *pure agency* whereby freedom would act *upon* the world without being acted upon *by* the world in turn. If the self is to have access to the world, then the world must have access to the self; for the self to *enter into* the world, in this sense, means that the world must gain entrance to the self. In order for the self to have access to the determinacy of the world, it must *receive* that determinacy into itself in some fashion. The being of freedom therefore requires some sort of *receptivity,* and to be receptive to the determinations of the world is to be in some manner and measure determined *by* that world. But that entails that freedom must have a *passive* moment, which is incompatible with the ideal of sheer spontaneity or pure agency.[3]

Moreover, this passivity or receptivity cannot be conceived as a mere *adjunct* of freedom, or as a constituent of the self that is separable from its freedom. The very freedom of the self requires, *as part of its being,* a passive nature whereby it makes contact with the world—or which *is* its contact with the world. But this reception of the determinacy of the world *by* the self amounts to the same thing as the determination *of* the self by the world. *Thus, in order to determine itself, the self must be determined by the world as well.* Without that passive receptivity to the world, the self could not enjoy the sort of access to the world that is necessary to freedom.

To say that freedom must have this receptive dimension is to say that the free self must have a "body"—or that embodiment is one of the necessary conditions of freedom. That should help to alleviate the abstract character of this argument by suggesting a familiar example. But the familiarity of the term and of the obvious example of the human or animal body must not be allowed to foreclose questions about the range of freedom. "Body" is used here in a very broad sense, which is metaphysically neutral. The body required to make freedom possible need not be a physical organism, for example. Initially, "body" should simply be understood as the moment of

---

3. That is why Aristotle, who conceived of God as pure activity, concluded that God cannot be thinking about the world, can indeed have no relation to the world, since that would involve a moment of passivity that is incompatible with pure agency. See *Metaphysics* XII, 7 and 9.

passive receptivity that is necessary to the existence of a free self. That may seem a rather odd and unorthodox way to think of the body, but it is necessary to preserve the neutrality of my inquiry—and this rather minimal conception of the body is not without important philosophical antecedents. According to Aristotle, for example, the bodily or material principle is that which is acted *upon* by formal, final, and efficient causes, which is to say that it is never active itself, but only the passive recipient of activity exerted upon it by other causes. That association of the body with passivity reflects the commonsense conception of matter as essentially inert, as moving only insofar as it is pushed from without. Leibniz and Whitehead both attacked the materialist metaphysics associated with Newtonian physics precisely because it conceives the elements of the physical universe as essentially passive material particles, "vacuous actualities," as Whitehead called them. Yet each of these anti-Newtonian physicist-philosophers preserved a role for such a passive, bodily aspect of their active elementary beings. Whitehead conceived the universe as an ongoing process whose elements are events or "actual occasions" rather than passive material particles. But each actual occasion grows out of a "physical pole" whereby it "prehends," or takes account, of the antecedent world that it inherits from prior events. Leibniz's monads are *immaterial* force points, or atoms of agency; yet each has a passive aspect insofar as it reflects the status of all the other monads that constitute the world. This primitive passive aspect of the monad is what Leibniz calls its body or matter in the primary sense.[4] It is in this minimal, metaphysical sense that I use the term "body" initially in saying that freedom requires a body. This requirement simply means that in order to be free, the self must have a passive aspect whereby or wherein it is determined by its world. This is the primary significance of the body here. This functional definition of the body could be specified in a number of ways. It might include anything from the familiar human body to the physical pole of a Whiteheadian actual occasion to the *intellect* of a finite God engaged in contemplating a world of pure forms.

The Body Belongs to the World

However, while the free self must *have* a body that is receptive to the world, that body must also belong to the world—and for the very reason that

4. See Leibniz's letter to De Volder, June 20, 1703, in *Philosophical Papers and Letters*, trans. and ed. Leroy E. Loemker (Chicago: University of Chicago Press, 1956), 3:859–66. Cf. also paragraphs 49–52 of *The Monadology*.

necessitated its introduction as a precondition of freedom. Freedom requires a body that will receive the determinations of the world, and the body will therefore belong to the world at least in the sense that it is determined *by* the world. The reality that opposes the self has a legitimate claim upon the body insofar as the very receptive function of the body places it under the influence of that independent reality. The being of the body is necessarily intermediate between the two realities. As the receptivity of the self, it is also receptive *to* the world.

In order to serve this intermediate function, the body must be homogeneous or continuous *with* the world. Otherwise the relation between body and world would constitute a mere juxtaposition of two incommensurable or incompatible realities—the very problem that the introduction of the body is supposed to meet, and yet another factor would have to mediate between the two. The body must therefore be "of a piece with" the world in order to receive its determinations. This homogeneity, or continuity of being, between body and world is a second dimension of the body's belonging *to* the world.

The self must therefore have a body that is appropriate to the specific nature of its world. If that world is a completely determinate, particularized physical cosmos, then the body must be a completely determinate, particular physical body, the sort of body to which we are accustomed. But if we would liberate our reflections on freedom from the limitations of the human condition, then we should bear in mind some nonhuman examples. We might well reflect upon how the dolphin's body and receptive capacities suit it for its watery world, for instance. Or we might consider examples such as Plato's mythic *dēmiourgos,* a divine artisan who begins by contemplating a realm of universal and eternal forms, or Leibniz's God, who confronts an array of possible worlds and chooses to create the best of them, or Whitehead's God, whose primordial act is to order a realm of "eternal objects." If the world of the free self is such a realm of relatively indeterminate universal forms or possibilities or eternal objects, the sort of body required to place the self in contact with such a world will be of a character very different from the one familiar to us. For in that case, a receptivity will be demanded that is similarly pure, universal, and relatively indeterminate. In short, the body required to mediate between the self and a realm of pure forms is the pure form of body. In terms of the present stage of this inquiry, that must mean a pure passivity and receptivity that does not interpose any intrinsic determinacy of its own between the self and those pure forms or possibilities. The body required to place a self in contact with a world of forms must therefore be what would traditionally be called a purely intellectual intuition. So, a physical body is required for the physical world, an intellectual body for an intelligible intellectual world.[5] Because the receptive function of the body requires its conformity with the world it is to receive, then, it is altogether appropriate that God's "body" in relation to a realm of pure ideas should take the form that was traditionally described as a pure or divine intellect.

Thus, the body required by the free self must belong to the world for two reasons: first, because its very receptivity means that it is determined by the world; second, because its conformity, homogeneity, and continuity with the world virtually make it a *part of* that world. This cannot be without extensive consequences for the free self. Insofar as the body is, on the one hand, a necessary moment of the self and, on the other hand, must belong *in* and *to* the world, it follows that the *self* must also belong in and to the world.

This is precisely the result I set out to obtain, however. I set out to discover how freedom can be *within* its world in some manner that would not amount to a mere juxtaposition or mutually exclusive contiguity—like oil drops suspended in water. Freedom can only gain access to its world by being receptive, and I have appropriated the familiar term "body" to designate this passive, receptive aspect of freedom. But it now appears that that same receptive function means that the body must also belong to the world. And since the body is a necessary aspect of freedom, it follows that the self, too, must belong to that world. So, the first consequence to the free self of the body's belonging to the world is exactly the one that I sought to begin with. However, this advantage entails corresponding liabilities—it imposes significant limiting conditions upon freedom.

First of all, having a body will *locate* or *situate* the self within its world. Insofar as the world and the body are fully and concretely determinate, that will mean a completely determinate location. In other words, the self is given a definite *locus* within or with respect to its world by virtue of the fact that its body belongs *to* the world. Like the body, the "location" at issue here must be understood as an ontological location that is prior to and more basic than mere spatiotemporal location, for it includes (and, indeed, is defined in terms of) the *entire* network of determinate relationships that obtain between the body and the rest of the world to which it belongs. Spatiotemporal location can only be an abstraction from this more fun-

---

5. This is a rather difficult point to exemplify, but an illustration of sorts can be drawn from Whitehead's cosmology. It is a striking and necessary feature of that cosmology that the normal order of physical and mental poles of an actual occasion is reversed in the case of God. For, since God is the very first actual entity, before the creation of the world he does not yet inhabit an actual, physical world. Instead, he faces a realm of abstract possibilities that can only be experienced through pure conceptual feelings. The "physical" pole in the case of God must await the coming to be of the actual, physical world.

damental ontological location. The entire network of definite relations between the body and the world compose an ontological locus, which establishes the free self in a definite *point of view* upon the world. That is, the self is related to the world in terms of, or through, the whole network of definite relations between its body and the rest of the world. Indeed, we could even say that the body *is* the point of view—or at least that the point of view *is* the body as it is *for* the free self. For the very continuity of the body *with* the world makes the distinction between the body and the *rest* of the world rather problematic. And since the body is defined, in this primary ontological sense, as the passivity of the self in relation to the world, there would seem to be no reason not to define the body as coextensive with the totality of determinate relations imposed upon the self by virtue of its passivity. The point of view is simply the determinacy that the self acquires by being in the world as regarded from the standpoint *of* the self—or, rather, regarded as establishing a standpoint *for* the self. Stated in more familiar terms, my body places me in the world—and my body establishes the place from which I can view the world.

In any case, to say that the self must have a body that places freedom in the world in this way precludes the possibility that freedom could be in the world in an indeterminate, free-floating, or all-pervasive manner—like the ubiquitous, omniscient God of some traditional theology, who is everywhere and nowhere. Such a perspective, or lack of perspective, might be appropriate to the divine apprehension of an array of pure forms or possibilities, but it is alien to a world of definite actualities. The self that is in a fully determinate world by virtue of a fully determinate body cannot enjoy the "absolute" point of view of a pure and universal receptivity that God might enjoy vis-à-vis a world of ideas.[6] Even if human beings can also contemplate the eternal world of pure forms, we cannot escape into it, but must remain caught in the sensible world of space and time as well. At best, as Aristotle said, we can only enjoy briefly and sporadically the contemplative point of view that God enjoys eternally.[7]

Vulnerability

The way the body locates the self within the world may seem as much an advantage as a limitation—an innocent implication of the recognition that

---

6. See the section "Mundane Freedom," in Chapter 5 above.
7. *Metaphysics* XII, vii, 9.

in order to have access to its world, freedom must have a body that belongs to that world. Other implications of embodiment in the world are more obviously liabilities and limitations to freedom, however. Insofar as the body is determinable by the world and is, nonetheless, a moment of the self, the self will also be determinable by the world. The preceding argument has at several points hinted at this consequence of the body's belonging to the world. But it deserves to be appreciated in all of its ramifications. It is actually a simple tautological necessity that the self cannot enjoy the benefits of receptivity without being exposed to external determination. For receptivity simply *is* one form of external determination of the self. But that means that the self can no longer be adequately understood merely as a self-determining being. Implicit in its finitude, in its being-in-an-independent-world, is the fact that it *must* be determined by its *other* as well as by itself. Having a body not only puts the self in contact with the world, it also *exposes* the self *to* the world. As noted before, the self cannot gain access to the world without the world gaining access to the self, which means that the way is open for the world to invade and overthrow the self in its freedom. Once the self is situated *in* the world, its freedom, as self-determination, is threatened *by* the world. The line between receptivity and vulnerability is inherently vague. We could speak, here, of the light that blinds or the sound that deafens, since these are cases in which the human body is threatened by the very media upon which its receptive organs depend. But the threat in these cases is really primarily to the body as such rather than to the self in its freedom. The fusion of receptivity and vulnerability in human experience would be better illustrated by the psychically traumatic experience. For in that case, the body functions precisely as the organ of receptivity and is itself left unscathed, and yet the self is profoundly determined, indeed, scarred in its inwardness in spite of its freedom.

However, the extreme threat of determination by the world to which the body exposes the self is *death,* that complete and final assertion of the world's suzerainty over the body. Since freedom requires a body that is determinable by the world, this possibility is inherent in the necessary conditions of freedom. Moreover, since the freedom of the self does require the body, it would seem that once the world completely takes over the body in death, freedom is deprived of a necessary condition of its being and is thereby destroyed. The mortality of the self as freedom does not necessarily follow from the vulnerability of the body, however.[8] For I have only shown

8. Whitehead's God is *vulnerable,* but not mortal, for example. In his "consequent nature," Whitehead's God is vulnerable to determination by the ongoing creative process, but not *entirely* determined thereby. Indeed, one might doubt whether it makes any sense to consider whether a pure intellect confronting a world of eternal objects or timeless forms could be

that the body is necessary in order to give freedom access to the determinacy of the world. Having had this contact with the world, the self might conceivably pursue a career of self-determination after death on the basis of content that has been acquired and accumulated in and through the body before death. In that case, old age would be an overture to immortality, at least to the extent that it is characteristic of old age to "live in the past," to be more preoccupied with dwelling upon the content of a recollected world than with the world that is currently at hand. This condition suggests the possibility that the self *may* continue its active existence even after the body has been entirely claimed by the world and all concurrent contact with the world has been severed. Of course, this possibility depends upon the supposition that the body, which has been defined solely in terms of receptivity, is *not* also required for the *retention* of the received content.

Traumatization is the extreme possibility corollary to the body's function as receptivity. Death is the extreme possibility corollary to the body's status as belonging to the world. And having a body imposes a third condition upon the being of freedom: It necessitates that the self occupy a *point of view*. This locating function of the body introduces its own form of vulnerability into the self's situation. That the self should have *some* point of view is a minimal corollary of its having a body that belongs to the world. But where the world and body are fully determinate, that point of view must be a particular point of view. Now, insofar as the body can be determined *by* the world, the self is vulnerable because its particular point of view may also be determined by the world. The *self* can therefore be "pushed around" and confined insofar as the body can. The obvious extreme possibility corresponding to this form of vulnerability would be complete paralysis—where the individual cannot move about in the world, but must depend upon others to push him around in order to change his point of view. But it is important to remember that the "point of view" imposed by the body is not merely spatial, but comprises the totality of determinate relations between the body and the world. Consequently, the self's point of view may be confined or transfixed by the world in many ways that are not merely spatial in character.

But doesn't this vulnerability to which bodily existence exposes the self place its very freedom in question?

It does indeed. In fact, it raises two distinct sets of problems. First, how can the self be free *at all* if it is bodily determined by the world? After all,

---

mortal. But contemplative philosophical traditions sometimes speak of a "death" or annihilation of the self that occurs when the knower is completely overcome by the eternal object of contemplation, which suggests a model for thinking about the complete determination of a purely intellectual subject by its object.

even the victim of paralysis satisfies this current account of the necessary conditions of freedom—to a fault. The paralytic is certainly situated in the world by his body. Yet the world has so completely determined his body as apparently to leave him without the slightest residue of freedom, no opportunity at all to determine himself. Hasn't such a self got into the world at the price of its freedom? To answer this question we must turn our attention to the relationship between freedom and time. But even if that enables us to resolve this first problem, a second issue remains: How can the self sustain *both* its freedom and its bodily existence together? Addressing that problem requires that we enlarge upon our conception of the body. Finally, the resolutions of these two problems must be taken in conjunction if we are to attain complete accounts both of the body and of the self's relation to its world through the body as conditions of the being of freedom.

Freedom and Time

In the course of the preceding chapters, I have frequently introduced themes that suggest a connection between freedom and temporality. An intimate connection between freedom and time has been implicit through-out much of this discussion and has manifested itself at numerous points. But only now am I in a position to illuminate the fundamental and necessary relationship of freedom to time. Here again, the dialectical nature of freedom as both requiring and conditioned by a world enables me to present, in a systematic and explicit fashion, relations that were only implicit in my earlier discussion.

Now that the conditions of bodily existence have been shown to be necessary conditions of freedom as being in a world, I can also show that freedom must be temporal—just as and because it must be corporal. In order to demonstrate this connection, we have only to regard the self as body and ask how it can also be free. As body, as passive receptivity to the determinations of the world, the self is determined *by* the world. Nothing could illustrate that more emphatically than the predicament of a man totally paralyzed by spinal injury. Insofar as it is passively determined by the world, the self is *not free,* not determined by itself. But it is also, so far, not necessarily temporal. The self's determination by the world does not necessarily imply a temporal relation between the two. To be in the world as a body doesn't necessarily entail any temporal priority of world to self or self to world. True, I have spoken of the possibilities of trauma, death, and paralysis in language that suggests time, but that was because I was *presuming* that the bodily self was also free, and therefore temporal. These possibilities are ways in which the self might be completely determined by the world, which determination is a logical possibility coeval with the corporeal existence of the self. But that possibility might obtain from the very outset. That is, the self might be so entirely determined by the way its body belongs to the world that there would be no freedom of the self—and hence no *self* in the sense I have been using.

And that is just the perspective in which I now propose to view the matter. The self is regarded as a body in the world, determined by the world. Therefore, it is as if it were dead. For considered from this perspective, the self does not exist as freedom at all, but only as completely under the suzerainty of the world.

Obviously, if the self is to be free at all, it must go beyond this being in the world as a being determined by the world. If it is to determine *itself*, a movement is required, a modification of this relationship, a *novel* determination over and beyond the totality of determinations imposed upon it as a body receptive to the world. Thus, if freedom is to *be* at all, it must be as an act that adds a fresh determination to an already determinate world. The world in question might even be static and changeless and the body's relation to it equally so, but if there is to be any freedom whatsoever, then a movement *beyond* this established order is required. The act in question may be only the appreciative act of acceptance of the world as it is, but that itself is an innovation, an addition to the established order. It may be objected that the world would be left unaltered by such an act. Very well, but if so, then the *cosmos* has been altered by the introduction of acceptance and appreciation as a novel reality alongside the world.

Freedom can therefore only *be* as an advance beyond the given order of a world, and freedom is therefore necessarily *temporal.* To restate this point in somewhat different form, freedom must not only be in the world, but must also transcend its being in the world insofar as that being-in consists in passive receptivity. In order to be free, the self must go beyond the world in which it finds itself and beyond its own being in that world as a receptive body, and must thereby leave them both *behind.* The world—and the body as part of the world—must therefore be surpassed by freedom, and they must consequently acquire the status of being *antecedent* or *prior* to the being of freedom. The being of freedom centers in the act of self-determination whereby the self moves beyond any determinacy imposed upon it by the world—toward its own self-established determinacy. Therefore, the world and body appear as the *past.* That does not mean that the world ceases to exist, or that it is annihilated by the being of freedom, but only that the nature of freedom propels it beyond the world toward a determinacy that is its own attainment.

This self-wrought determinacy *toward which* freedom thrusts and quests in order to be constitutes the temporal dimension of futurity. Freedom *must* therefore generate its very own futurity. Its future cannot be one that is necessitated or determined *by* the world. Such a future would belong to the world as one region bound to others by perfectly determinate relationships—and would therefore be indistinguishable from the past.[9] Nor can the free self have a self-subsistent future that lies in waiting for the self. For such a self-subsistent, intrinsically determinate future would still only constitute another region within the total determinate milieu that is the world of the free self. As belonging to the world, such "futures" must be relegated, with the world, to the status of being past.

Thus, although the world might have its *own* future, independent of freedom, that future is not the future for freedom. Or, to put the matter otherwise, if that future coincided exhaustively with the self's future, then the self would not be free, since its entire career would be determined by the world. The future for freedom lies in a determinacy that the self has to attain through its own self-creative act, an act wherein the *being* of freedom is realized.

The future is therefore immanent in the being of freedom as the determinacy that has yet to be attained, whereas freedom relegates to the past that determinacy of the world which is immanent in the self as body. We could say that the *present* of freedom consists in the movement between the two, but this could easily be misleading. For this future and past are not just given as fixed termini between which the self moves. It is the act of self-determination itself that establishes and separates them in the very process of traversing that separation. It would therefore be better to say that the present consists in this act, which establishes past and future in constituting freedom. Such a present is no mere meeting point between past and future. It *is* only insofar as it holds the two apart by constituting the difference between them. But it constitutes this difference only because the act of self-determination is the attainment of the future on the ground of the given world. In Chapter 5, I showed that freedom could only be by deriving its own determinacy from an already determinate world. It is the process of this derivation itself that constitutes the *present* dimension of the temporality of freedom.

The basic connection between freedom and time now stands clear.

---

9. Knowledge of the future and knowledge of the past are therefore isomorphic for the strict determinist. Prediction involves essentially the same inferential processes as retrodiction, and both future and past are "implicit" in the present.

Freedom is not temporal because it is "in" time or because it is in a world that happens to be temporal, so that it participates in time by the same token that, as body, it is determined by the world. Quite the contrary, freedom is necessarily temporal precisely because it must determine itself *independently* of the world. Freedom is not *in* time, and *therefore* temporal; it *is* temporally. Its being is such as to require temporality of itself.

Thus, the insistence upon the temporality of freedom does not really conflict with Kant, as would appear superficially to be the case. Kant's insistence that the freedom of the self must be conceived as lying outside of time really corroborates, rather than contradicts, our observations here. For this claim of Kant's stems from his identification of time with the order of the received world. Insofar as time is thus identified with "nature" or the world as received by the self, then clearly, by the above reasoning, freedom must *indeed* transcend time in transcending its world. But it is exactly in this very transcending, this movement beyond the given world, that the *intrinsically* and inescapably temporal character of freedom lies. As part of the order of nature, or as a form of receptivity, time is to be ascribed to the world and the body that freedom must transcend in coming to be. But for freedom thus to transcend world time cannot mean that it is "timeless," but only that it generates a time of its own by determining itself. Consequently, if time is understood to be coextensive with change and becoming and perishing, then Kant's identification of time with the order of nature is unjustifiable. Indeed, it is belied by Kant's own accounts of moral process in his ethical writings, where, for instance, he speaks of the agent's gradual development toward holiness.

For present purposes, it is sufficient to show that freedom is necessarily temporal. This same ontological connection between freedom and time, along with the description of the temporality of freedom as poised between an antecedent world and its own possibility, has received considerable attention in recent metaphysics. It is developed in varying contexts by Heidegger, Sartre, Whitehead, and Weiss, for example. Indeed, these thinkers suggest that the connection is even more intimate than I have been able to demonstrate here. I have only shown that the being of freedom necessarily involves time, whereas each of these four thinkers suggests that the converse is also true, that the being of time necessarily presupposes freedom. I will find occasion later to consider why that might be so,[10] but arguments to that claim would be out of place here. They require careful reflection upon the nature of time, which would distract attention from the deliberations at hand.

---

10. See the section "Freedom, Time, and Dialectic," in Chapter 9 below.

These thinkers have also provided more detailed discussions of the dimensions of the temporality of freedom than are given above. I have only attempted to indicate the connections between these dimensions and freedom's situation as *in* the world yet facing *beyond* the world toward its own possible being. The present context neither calls for nor *allows* a more extensive treatment of these dimensions. The further development of this topic must be accomplished in the context of a renewal of this inquiry into the conditions of freedom's existence in the world as body. Just as I have had to embark upon this brief discussion of temporality because the discussion of body could not proceed further without it, so now I must return to a discussion of body in order to proceed further in understanding the temporality of freedom.

The Body Belongs to the Self

Freedom requires a body in order to have access to the determinacy of the world. But, as we now see, this body also gives the world access to the self. As *mere* receptivity, as continuity with the world, and as location within the world, the body is a necessary mediating moment that allows the self to be in the world. Considered only in this one respect, the body would appear solely as answering to the requirements of freedom. But reflection upon these very aspects of the body has shown that each of them actually involves the exposure of the self to alien determination. Thus, although the body is *introduced* solely in order to satisfy the requirements of freedom, the exigencies of bodily existence seem to compromise the status of freedom rather seriously. If the self could enjoy the benefits of receptivity *without* incurring those attendant liabilities, then perhaps freedom might be an *immanent* process of self-determination, one that occurs entirely *within* the self. That is, the self might derive *from* the world the determinate content it needs in order to determine itself without ever acting *upon* the world in turn.

The idea of a wholly immanent freedom is the ideal of the Stoic sage. The ancient Stoics sought to attain a perfect and invulnerable freedom by *disowning* the body, along with everything else that does not properly belong to the self. Epictetus repeatedly argues that freedom is forfeited as soon and as long as the individual attaches himself to anything that is not properly his own—and that includes anything that it is not finally within his power to control, including all worldly goods, other persons, and even his own body. By recognizing everything beyond control as alien and indifferent and by giving up the desire to control anything but himself, the Stoic sage attains a freedom to determine his own will and judgment that is invulnerable because it is entirely immanent. Here is a freedom one might enjoy even despite complete paralysis. The Stoic may insist that the paralytic need no more be imprisoned in his body than the Indian fakir of my parable in Chapter 2 was imprisoned by his cage.

But that suggests that there is a catch, as indeed there is. For it is well known that the perfect and invulnerable freedom the Stoic sage purchases by complete detachment from the world turns out to be the freedom to bow to destiny and accept his fate, to accept determination by the world. This central ironic paradox of Stoic thought proclaims how radically the ideal of a merely immanent self-determination is undercut by the conditions that are inherent in the passive, bodily being of the self. Simply to *disown* the body and the world is to deny conditions that are essential to freedom, in that freedom depends upon the receptivity of the body to place it in contact with a world, without which it cannot exist. The self cannot enjoy the benefits of the body as an opening into the world without incurring its attendant liabilities and vulnerabilities. For even at the level of sheer receptivity, the determination *of* the self *by* the world challenges and counterbalances any exclusively inner self-determination. Any process of self-determination that is purely immanent and heedless of the self's exposure to the world through the body is therefore condemned to the status of mere fantasy. That becomes quite obvious in the case of paralysis or in the face of the more extreme forms of vulnerability to which the body exposes the self. But we need not rely upon such extreme examples as paralysis. Any merely immanent flight of freedom will eventually reach the end of its tether and be brought to earth by the world's grip upon the body, which holds despite that inner movement. (I emerge from my anticipatory reveries to discover that I have ridden beyond my station and therefore missed the crucial appointment upon which I had staked my future.) The complete separation of these two strands into sheer fatality and pure fantasy—or determination of the self by the world and by itself—constitutes a profound schism within the self.

The self can avoid this schism only by integrating its body into its determination of itself. The passivity and receptivity of the self—indeed, its very being in the world—must be included within its self-determination. Because being a body in the world is a condition of its freedom, its freedom is conditioned by its being a body in the world. In effect, the self is placed in competition with the world for the ultimate determination of itself. If its determination of itself is to be more than partial, more than fantasy or mere acceptance of fate, and if it is to cope with its own vulnerability, then its determination of itself must go beyond its own inner being to determine the body and the world. Because freedom must be in a world and can only be in the world as body, the self can only maintain itself as free by acting in and upon the world. Self-determination cannot survive as a purely immanent process whereby the self fashions itself inwardly, in sublime Stoic withdrawal from the world. Freedom cannot simply determine itself in terms of forms provided to it *by the world. It must act upon the world* if it is even to hold its own against the threat of being overwhelmed by the world.

At this point the discussion has completed a circle. For, at the beginning of the chapter, I observed that in order to be in the world at all, freedom had to have its passive moment and consequently could no longer be conceived as pure activity or spontaneity. Now it turns out, however, that freedom cannot be in the world in a merely passive or receptive way, but that the self must be in the world actively as well. This discovery, in turn, means that the activity of self-determination cannot be a merely *reflexive*, inner activity of the self upon itself. The free self is necessarily concerned with the world.

Moreover, since the self must act in order to maintain its freedom in face of the influence of the world upon the body as passive receptivity, then clearly the mediate status of the body takes on still more decisive importance. First of all, since the body is the meeting ground between inner and outer determinations, or, at least, is the route by which the self is exposed to outer influences, the self must maintain itself as freedom by maintaining final control over the body. The body is therefore, in one sense, the primary field of action. This fact adds a whole new dimension to the ontological status of the body.

What does it mean to say that the body is the primary field of action? It means that the body must be passive or determinable in relation to the self as well as in relation to the world. And whereas the passivity of the self vis-à-vis the world constitutes its receptivity, this same passivity becomes an *organ* of *activity* in relation to the self. For through determining the body, the self not only *can* but *must* act in and upon the world. This is necessarily the case because, it must be remembered, the body belongs to the world, is a part of the world. Consequently, in determining the body in any way, the self *ipso facto* acts upon the world. But of course, if the self *must* act upon the world in this limited respect, then by the same token it *can* act in the world at large. That is, the fact that the body belongs to the world means that the self is in a position to make changes in the world, to meet and vanquish external influences and to make provisions against its own vulnerability. The paralyzed victim of a stroke is helpless in relation to his world *because* he is unable even to move his own body. Utterly paralyzed, he is nothing but a *patient* in the literal sense, having lost the very basis of all agency: the command of his own body. He can still think, which is activity of a sort, to be sure, but of an entirely immanent sort. His freedom is radically curtailed because his body is entirely reduced to its receptive role, to being part of the world, a passive object to be moved about by other agents. But just because paralysis is so exceptional, this plight reminds us that embodiment does not *necessarily* entail such complete passivity. And the pathetic extremity of this condition is a forceful reminder of the error of the Stoics, who would disown the body, abandon it entirely to the world, and try to lodge freedom entirely in the inwardness of the mind, will, or spirit.

In sum, freedom requires a body because it requires a world, and in one sense the body is only the concretization of freedom's being *in* its world. On the other hand, insofar as the body belongs to the world, one might also say that the body is the being of the world *in* the free self. For by having a body, the self not only gains access to the world, it also becomes continuous with the world and exposed *to* the world. Consequently, the self cannot fully determine itself unless it determines the world as well. On the other hand, since the body belongs to the world yet also belongs to the self, there is always at least one item in the world whose relations to the rest of the world are dependent upon freedom. Thus, the self is placed in the position of determining the world in determining itself as a body and of determining itself in determining the world *through* the body. Obviously, this discovery radically qualifies the import of freedom as *self*-determination. Whereas the previous section showed that the self must transcend the world in order to determine itself, it is now clear that *self*-determination must transcend the self, in turn, to impinge upon the world.

Consequently, the intrinsic temporality of the self has now to be considered in relation to the body in a new light. As receptivity to the world, the body is relegated to the past by the intrinsic temporality of freedom, since the self is free only by going beyond determination by the world. But since the body is an organ of activity as well as of receptivity, we have to reconsider the relation of the body to the temporal structure of freedom.

The Body and Possibility

The body must be determinate. I have already pointed out that the body must be appropriate to its world—that whereas a world of abstract forms would require a body of similar nature, a fully determinate world, in either the physical or metaphysical sense, would require a fully determinate body. In any case, the very status of the body as receptive to determinations from both the world and the self means that, even it if were intrinsically wholly passive and indeterminate—like the *apeiron* of Anaximander or Aristotle's prime matter—the body would nonetheless have a determinacy acquired from without. But since freedom is temporal, the body must not only *receive* determinations, it must also *retain* them, and this points to the need for an intrinsic determinacy of the body. For if the body were *sheer* passivity and indeterminacy, subsequent determinations would simply replace and obliterate those that had preceded them. Like wax, stamped and then melted, the self could no longer have any currently available data that had previously been received from the world, but only the determinations of the immediate world. This would undermine the self's ability to derive its possibilities from its world if, as suggested before, the opportunities of today are derived from yesterday's necessities. And a similar problem would be posed with respect to the determinations of the body by the self. In a purely passive body, these would simply be obliterated by the continued impact of the world upon the body. The vulnerability of the body would be heightened to such a degree as to make the reality of freedom extremely doubtful. No, a freedom that is temporal requires a body that is retentive as well as receptive, a body that has its own enduring, determinate structure.

Finally, the utter vulnerability of a wholly passive and indeterminate body would be seconded by an utter incapacity to act in the world. To hammer a nail with a sponge is a hopeless enough task, but to act upon the world through an entirely passive and receptive body would be far more so. If the body is to be an organ of activity as well as receptivity, then the body must have a structure and determinacy of its own that can be brought to bear upon the world.

Since the self must act because of the body and must act through the body, and since the body must have its own determinate character, the features of the body become a center of reference and a criterion of relevance for the self's outlook upon the world and upon possibility. Conversely, regarded in this relation to what can be done and what can happen, the determinate features of the body acquire a halo of possibility for the self and thereby cease to be simple properties. This corresponds to the way in which the necessities of the world are invested with possibility, which I discussed in the last chapter. This infusion of possibilities into determinate reality represents the qualification of both body and world by the intrinsic temporality of freedom. Freedom is always beyond both the body and the world, reaching toward its *own* possibility, or futurity. But inasmuch as freedom must be active, these possibilities must ultimately come to a focus in the body. For the determinate features of the body are the necessary basis for the self's action in the world. Every act upon the world must be initiated through the body, so that the relevance of possibilities must finally be gauged by reference to the given, determinate structure of the body. Granted that in the human world the range of what is possible has been vastly enlarged by the development of technical apparatuses, yet these only form a part of a transformed world, and in any case, the most intricate of mechanisms still has its handle or pedal, button or eyepiece, to indicate its connection with the features of the human body.

The specific features of the body all serve to define what sort of activity is possible for the self. The dolphin's fins and lack of an opposable thumb shapes its horizon of opportunities as definitively as does our possession of the latter and lack of the former. The very passivity of the body vis-à-vis the world is also a crucial basis for the self's possibility because it is the means whereby the self has access to any determinate possibility at all. Indeed, as we shall see later, even this passivity finally becomes, or *is*, a form of activity. Freedom therefore finds in the bodily structure not an *is* but a *can*, not *attributes* but *capacities*.

This role of the body in defining what is possible means that the *locating* function of the body not only places the self in a definite situation within the world, but also, indirectly, prescribes its perspective on possibilities as a result. Or, we might say that the point of view in which the body locates the self is *pro*spectival as well as *per*spectival. As receptivity, the body locates the self within the world because the body *belongs* to the determinate world and *its* location in the world is a function of the determinate relationships between its own properties and the rest of the world. But the combined requirements of temporality and activity transform the *locus* of the body into a *prospectus* of the free self. As temporal, the self transcends the body's locus in the world toward its own possibility. But as having to act, the self must envision that possibility of itself in terms of action in the world. Thus, the temporality and corporeality of freedom must be fused in the point of view of the self as a prospectus as well as locus. This prospectus will bring the halo of possibilities surrounding the body into partial focus. What the self can do through its body *in general* includes a broader range of possibilities than what it can do in any *particular* situation.[11]

However, the determinate character of the body is not only the foundation for a variety of *faculties* or *capacities* of the self. It also defines the form

11. Cf. Paul Ricoeur's discussion of the body as "anchoring" the self in the world (*Oneself as Another,* trans. Kathleen Blamey [Chicago: University of Chicago Press, 1992]): "[H]ow can human action constitute an event in the world, the latter taken as the sum of all that occurs, and at the same time designate its author in a self-referential manner, if the latter does not belong to the world in a mode in which the self is constitutive of the very sense of this belonging[?] One's own body is the very place—in the strong sense of the term—of this belonging, thanks to which the self can place its mark on those events that are its actions" (319). Cf. also 54–55.

of the vulnerability of the self, how the self is open to determination, perhaps even destruction, by the world. The specific structure of the body therefore discloses possible *threats* as well as possible *acts*, and these must be integrated into the prospectus of the self too. It is not only the tools and instruments of activity that mirror the structure of the human body by their handles, pedals, and the like, but also the instruments of torture, which are designed to seize and manipulate the body as well as to be manipulated by the torturer. Since the body is an element within the world, there will be determinate conditions for the survival or maintenance of its own structure. In short, the body will have its own conditions of existence as the body *of* the self. And since the body is a condition of the being of freedom, these will be indirect conditions of the existence of freedom. These *needs* of the body will therefore have a certain priority in relation to the freedom of the self, which depends upon the body. These basic needs of the body must be somehow provided for within the framework of any program of possible activity—unless it is a very special program in which freedom intends or risks its own destruction, either directly or incidentally. That is, unless either suicide or self-sacrifice is involved, the self must introduce provisions for the maintenance of its body in any action it purposes. The mountaineer must bring to the assault upon Everest not only ice ax, pitons, crampons, rope, and the other equipment necessary to deal with the mountain, but sufficient food, clothing, oxygen, and the like to meet his minimal bodily needs while he is at it. Consequently, the bodily needs introduce a sort of basic substructure or rhythm into the career of self-determination. The self can improvise upon this basis with considerable latitude, but cannot depart from it altogether without either incurring disaster or, at the very least, being brought up short by the exigencies of bodily existence.

When the body is regarded as belonging to the world, the bodily needs appear simply *as* the objective exigencies of bodily existence. It is under this rubric that I have introduced them here. But this is not the way in which they will appear *for* the self primarily. We have to consider more carefully the status of these needs when regarded subjectively, recognizing that the body belongs to the self as well as to the world. From this standpoint, the needs of the body do not appear as mere exigencies, at least in the first instance. As freedom, the self will apprehend these needs primarily *in terms of* the possibilities to which they point. They will therefore announce themselves in terms of the appeal, urgency, or ominousness of certain possibilities that are closely bound up with the conditions of the existence of the body in the world. That is, they will appear in the form of appetites and aversions, desires and fears, and so on. In short, from the prospectival standpoint of the self, the exigencies of bodily existence will have the character of "passions of the soul." As Descartes saw, the *passivity* of the body in relation to the world naturally gives rise to the *passions* of the self.[12] The latter are simply the inner and possibility-oriented aspect of the exigencies of bodily existence.

It is important not to misinterpret this corporeal foundation of the passions. They are not merely *imposed* upon the self by the body so as to be suffered passively by the self. It is only because temporality conjoins bodily existence with possibility that the passions arise as such. This is reflected even in Descartes's general theory of the passions. Although he does take as his principle of classification of the passions the diverse ways in which "our senses can be moved by their objects,"[13] and despite the physiological details of his treatment of the passions, he does not regard the passions as merely corporeal in their basis. He sees the passions as bound up with the possibilities of the self as a union of soul and body: "Beyond that, I remark that the objects that move the senses do not excite diverse passions in us because of all the diversities that are in them, *but only because of the diverse ways in which they can harm or profit us.*"[14]

The passions thus involve the functioning of the body as a criterion of the relevance of immediate possibility. In this function—and hence through the passions—the body is *present*, whereas as a receptivity determined by the world the body is made past by the temporality of freedom.

On this basis it is easy to see that the passions arising from the body's relation to the world will not be limited to those that are directly and indispensably bound up with the necessities of the protection and survival of the body. Because the body *is* the center of reference for the self's relation of possibility to settled actuality, the immediate possibilities of the body will naturally occupy the foreground of the self's perspective on possibility. Since the range of these possibilities will exceed the mere requirements of the survival of the body, the range of passions may far exceed those appetites that announce the body's survival needs. Indeed, the experience of the body's temporality means that the *presence* of every determination of the body will involve *some* emotional tone by virtue of its relation to possibility or futurity. As Whitehead puts it, "All physical experience is accompanied by an appetite for or against its continuance."[15]

12. *Les passions de l'âme*, in *Oeuvres de Descartes* (Paris: J. Vrin, 1967), vol. 11, article 52.
13. Ibid.
14. Ibid.; translation and emphasis mine. Descartes's passage reads, "Je remarque, outre cela que les objets qui meuvent les sens n'excitent pas en nouz diverses passions à raison de toutes les diversités qui sont en eux, mais seulement à raison des diverses façons qu'ils nous peuvent nuire ou profiter."
15. *Process and Reality*, 48.

Moreover, even though the self may look beyond these immediate bodily possibilities to more remote possibilities, it cannot finally overlook this proximate, bodily region of its prospective. As I have noted, those bodily possibilities that are bound up with the inevitable needs of the body will force themselves upon the self regardless of its concerns with more remote possibilities. And, when the self does seek to realize more remote opportunities, it must also concern itself with the region of immediate physical possibility in order to carry through the active implementation of the distant possibility. Whoever sets out to climb Mount Everest must not gaze steadfastly at the pinnacle, but had better watch his step.

However, this very interplay of proximate and distant possibilities also means that the passions that accompany bodily existence are never simple and unambiguous. For the needs and wants of the body are always presented against a horizon of other possibilities. As I have noted, the basal rhythm or framework of bodily needs leaves considerable room for improvisation. Correspondingly, the whole proximate region of corporeal possibilities is qualified by the more distant possibilities with which it is continuous. On account of planning to climb Everest *next* spring, I go into training *now*, changing my diet and bodily regime.

Freedom is corporeal *and* temporal. Each dimension qualifies the other. The free self is related to the body in terms of possibility and to possibility in terms of the body. The body is not ingredient in the present of freedom primarily *as* body. It is present as capacity and as passion—corresponding to its active and passive dimensions. And, on the other hand, possibility is not primordially present as mere detached possibility. Instead, freedom must apprehend possibility in terms of the body because the determinacy of the body—in itself and in relation to the world of which it is a part— defines the prospective point of view of the self. The immediate present of the free self is therefore founded in *feelings* that refer at once both to a body, which, as such, is past, and to a possibility, which, as such, is future. In Whitehead's terms: "In the phraseology of physics, this primitive experience is 'vector feeling,' that is to say, feeling from a beyond which is determinate and pointing to a beyond which is to be determined. But the feeling is subjectively rooted in the immediacy of the present occasion: It is what the occasion feels for itself, as derived from the past and as merging into the future."[16]

16. Ibid., 274.

The Ambiguity of the Body

As this inquiry has explored the dimensions of bodily existence, the clarity of the initial conception of the body has dissipated. Some attempt to recover from this diffusion is called for, if only to exhibit clearly why that initial clarity cannot be recovered.

The body was initially introduced simply as a receptive, passive aspect of the self vis-à-vis its world. But this determinability by the world implies that the body must belong to the world and, consequently, that freedom is vulnerable. These conditions of bodily existence led us to recognize the necessary temporality of freedom, in the first place, and the necessity that freedom act in the world, in the second place. As a result of these further requirements, the body is placed in a status of threefold intermediacy. In the first place, the body is intermediate between the self and its world inasmuch as it belongs to and is subject to the determinations of both. This status reflects and is reflected by the second side of the status of the body as intermediate between passivity and activity. As both organ of receptivity and organ of activity, the body presents two faces both to the self and to the world. Finally, both these sides of the ontological status of the body are reflected in its temporal status. As passive and as belonging to the world, the body belongs, with the world, to the past dimension of freedom's temporality. But as active and as belonging to the self, the body is present as conditioning and conditioned by futurity. The *present* status of body is therefore *also* an intermediate one—between established actuality and possibility.

As a result of all this, bodily existence is shot through with ambiguities and loses all semblance of simple determinacy. However simple and determinate the body *might* be in itself, or considered solely as part of the world, as the body of a free self it becomes so ambivalent and indeterminate as to be extremely difficult to pin down unequivocally. Considered in these terms, the clear conception of body with which we began, or *any* attempt to gain an unambiguous conception of the inherent determinacy of the body, either by itself or as a portion of the world, is revealed as a patent abstraction.[17]

This ambiguity of the body is very aptly expressed in English idiom by the fact that we speak of a person as "having" a body and speak of our own

---

17. Maurice Merleau-Ponty has explored this theme of the ambiguity of the body at length in both *The Structure of Behavior* (Boston: Beacon Press, 1963) and *The Phenomenology of Perception* (London: Routledge & Kegan Paul, 1962). See also Hegel's discussions of physiognomy and phrenology in *Hegel's Phenomenology of Spirit*, trans. A. V. Miller (Oxford: Oxford University Press, 1977), chap. 5, 185–210.

bodies as "ours" and "owned"—as if the body were an intimate piece of property, a bit of the world that a self "possesses." This use of possessives to refer to the body reflects a recognition that the body is part of the world, like a razor or a toothbrush, from which I can distinguish myself yet which is "personal" and *proper to me* and not merely a neutral, alien object. But the person is invested in his body, as he is in his home, and the body is possessed by the person as a house may be "possessed" by a ghost. And indeed, in other cases we do *not* distinguish between the self and the body. We say, "I have cut *myself*," or "He hit *me* right in the eye," or "I threw *myself* against the door to hold it shut." Phrases such as these express a recognition that what happens to the body happens to the self. They correspond quite aptly to the conditions of freedom. Since freedom cannot exist *without* a body, to be free is to *be* a body, to be incarnate. Yet the body cannot be entirely identical with the free self, since the self needs the body in order to place it in the world, and to satisfy that requirement, the body must also be a part of the world.

Every attempt to resolve this ambiguity by allocating the body to one side or the other results in a misleading abstraction. For example, the passive receptivity of the body is an abstractly isolatable aspect of its being that was, in my order of inquiry, logically prior to its function as the active organ of freedom—which is another isolatable aspect of its being. But the separation of the two is an abstraction. In *fact*, these two functions of the body are concomitant and suffuse one another. Thus, for example, "seeing" and "hearing" indicate receptive functions of the human body in their most passive aspect. But what are we to say of "watching" and "listening"? Are these active or passive functions of the self? Clearly, they are both. And for that matter, can seeing and hearing really be considered *wholly* passive?[18] Thus, even the passive, receptive function of the body is suffused with activity.

On the other hand, it may well be asked whether there is any activity in which the body does not also function as passive. Eating is a prime example of this ambiguity: my working upon the world is its working on me! (Alas.) Every act of the body would seem to include a corresponding exposure to determination *by* the world, and hence the passivity of the body. What is the status of my body in smoking or in swimming or in sexual intercourse? Is it functioning actively or passively? These may be peculiarly ambivalent examples because they are activities engaged in for the sake of the physical experience they cause. But even in hammering a nail, the body is at once active and passive. In the concrete career of the being of freedom, the body

---

18. "Prehensions" whereby Whitehead's actual occasions take account of the world offer another example. Are they either wholly active or wholly passive? Certainly, they are neither one nor the other, but both.

plays an ambiguous and fluctuating role. Its status varies along a continuum between passivity and activity, but never wholly occupies either extreme exclusively.

The temporal status of the body gives rise to another set of ambiguities. On the one hand, the body's actual properties and locus define the conditions of relevance for possibilities and thereby determine the prospective of the self. But, on the other hand, possibility so claims the body from the standpoint of freedom that the self is related to the actual features and locus of its body primarily in terms of possibilities they may serve or to which they may subject the self. Again, the status of the body is indeterminate and fluctuating because of this ambiguity. On occasion, the body may provide the prime and authoritative direction to a life, as in the case of a handicapped person or a serious bodybuilder, who knows just what exercises to use to sculpt each contour of his body for aesthetic effect. Analogous aspirations fill the exercise rooms of city "health spas" and suburban "figure salons." But most serious athletes and weekend joggers, golfers, and tennis players are animated by other concerns. For them, it is the serviceability of the healthy body for activity that is important. And for those purposes, it is not the determinacy of the body as such that is important, but its relation to possibility. The determinacy of the body will appear more bound up with sheer possibility insofar as it is serviceable for actions. Myopia, for example, may tend to be regarded merely as a handicap, a limiting actuality. Yet it would scarcely seem so to the blind. In fact, it is a kind of vision, a capability. (My most myopic friend cannot recognize a face at five yards—but can read fine print or do needlepoint without glasses.) A given bodily determination will thus appear closer to one or the other of these two poles depending upon the perspective or prospective from which it is regarded.

Asceticism ascribes the human body to the world; sensualism claims it for the self. But the ascetic would never mortify the body if it were really only another item *in* the world, and the sensualist would not claim the body if it were utterly isolated *from* the world. In fact, the attitudes of both depend upon the intermediate status of the body as belonging to *both* self and world. It is really that contact with the world which the body *is* that asceticism wishes to negate and sensualism to affirm. Here again, the intermediate function of the body renders ambiguity inescapable.

The lesson in all these ambiguities is that whatever *inherent* reality and determinacy the body may possess *in itself* are animated by its mediating role and diffused into almost endless ambiguities. Doubtless it *does* have at its core a determinate nature of its own, as I have indicated, *if* considered apart from this status between freedom and world, passion and action, fact and possibility. But to consider it so is an extreme abstraction. Its intermediate status completely eclipses the intrinsic nature of the body, so that every feature thereof is infected with ambiguities. If these ambiguities are to be resolved at all, it cannot be by the body itself; they can only be resolved in and by the self's specific determination of itself.

All of this has a familiar ring. In effect, the relation of freedom and body is a very special instance of the relation of freedom and world as it was described in Chapter 5. It is a very *special* case—indeed quite unique— because it is *in* the body that freedom and world actually meet. Since the body belongs to *both,* the whole relationship between freedom and world focuses in the body. Moreover, precisely because it mediates between the two, its *own* reality tends to be eclipsed and so thoroughly subordinated to the relation of self to world that the body does not obtrude itself as separate. Consequently, major points touched upon in discussing the relation of freedom to the world find their parallels here. Because it is in the world, the body, like the world, has its own necessities, or exigencies. (The exact nature of bodily needs will depend upon the exact nature of the body and its world, of course. They would not be the same for a dolphin as for a human being—and would differ still more drastically for Plato's *dēmiourgos.*) And, again as in the case of the world, these necessities are the basis for the self's derivation of its own possibilities. (The dolphin could no more project an ascent of Everest than we can imagine what it would be like to enjoy a dolphin's horizon of opportunities and perils.) And the result is that the body is inescapably and fundamentally ambiguous, just as the world was seen to be. Indeed, *because* of its mediating status, the body is caught up in a far wider range of ambiguities than was the case with the world.

Action and Self-Realization

But if the freedom of the self renders its body ambiguous, there is also an important sense in which embodiment renders the self ambiguous. The word "self" has been used here as a conveniently vague term to designate any being that is free, so that "self" and "freedom" have been used as virtually synonymous.[19] But since the self must be incarnate, or embodied, in order to be free, it cannot be *entirely* free or exclusively *self*-determined. For if freedom must have a body in order to be receptive to the world, then the free self must also be vulnerable to determination by the world and must even participate in the determinate character of the world through the nature of its own body.[20] The self is not wholly or univocally identifiable

19. This usage seemed to be justified by the argument that the free self can have no nature *except* freedom itself. See pages 81–84 above.

20. See pages 137–43 above.

with freedom, then, but must be conceived as caught between freedom and the world, between self-determination and determination by the world. But to be determined by the world rather than self-determining is, precisely, *not* to be free but to be constrained by alien circumstances or coerced by external causes. This means that the embodied self is poised between freedom and unfreedom, or between freedom and determinism. Insofar as the body is passive, receptive, and vulnerable, then, the self is *not* a free being—even though freedom is impossible *without* such an exposure to the world. To maintain itself *as* free, notwithstanding this necessary moment of passivity, the embodied self must *act* in and upon the world. There is therefore another sense in which the free self can no longer be conceived as purely *self*-determining, since it must determine the *world* as well as itself, or else it will find itself shaped and moved by circumstances and causes beyond itself. This, in sum, is the brunt of the argument of the opening of this chapter.

This is all thoroughly familiar terrain. If the self can only sustain its freedom through action, then it must actualize, or *realize,* itself in the world. Thus, we encounter anew the ordinary, immediate conception of freedom as the ability to do as I want, to realize my own personal aims, desires, and intentions in the world rather than be constrained by my circumstances or coerced by external causes.

But what if my desires and intentions are themselves only the product of constraining circumstances? How am I to distinguish those intentions that are really "my own" from those that are only determined by external causes? Questions such as these plunged us into a dialectic of competing definitions of freedom and led, finally, to the recognition that the distinction between freedom and constraint is vacuous unless it is founded in the contrast between self-determination and determination by the world, and that the ordinary, popular understanding of freedom as self-realization presupposes a more fundamental freedom of self-determination. Further reflection even raised the question whether self-realization is a *necessary* form of freedom or only a symptom of the impurity and imperfection of finite freedom, the product of deficiencies that would not afflict freedom in its most complete and perfect form. A perfectly free being would not *have* to struggle to realize its purposes in an opposing, resistant world, I suggested, nor would it be vulnerable to constraint or coercion by that world. For such a perfect freedom, to *conceive* a purpose would be to *realize* it, so that the exercise of freedom would be a wholly inner, reflexive action of the self in determining itself.

That ideal of a limitless, absolute freedom proved to be an illusion, however. Freedom cannot possibly exist without a world that limits it and that may even constrain or coerce the embodied self. For such a finite freedom, to conceive a purpose is *not* to realize it, and the exercise of freedom cannot consist simply in an inner reflexive act whereby the self merely determines *itself.* The self that determines only itself and not the world has not even fully determined itself, because that leaves the embodied self to be determined by the world. At first, this difference between conception and realization, and the fact that the conception alone does not fully determine the self, may seem a liability, a necessary but lamentable consequence of the finitude of freedom.[21] Certainly, it means that finite freedom is liable to failure, since it is not always possible to translate inner intentions into actions in the world. But this distinction between conception and realization also means that the self does not realize a possibility simply by conceiving or entertaining it. Consequently, the finite self may entertain possibilities and even inwardly identify with one or another of them in a purely tentative way, in fantasy, without thereby committing itself to realize them and even without ever seriously *intending* to act on any of them. That murderous look does *not* kill, and I am not a murderer for having harbored the wish behind the look. As W. E. Hocking points out, the *absence* of this distinction between conception and act would be a dubious boon. "It belongs to our kind of selfhood to contemplate action for a time before we do it. Certain philosophers have thought that with God contemplation and action are identical. For us this would be a destructive advantage. It is part of our nature to contemplate many foolish and criminal deeds; it is part of our moral being to do this. But it is also part of our moral being that contemplation of a crime is not a crime."[22]

Indeed, if contemplation and action were identical, then there could be no freedom at all, and the problem of realizing intentions through action is therefore a necessary moment of freedom. For without it, there could be no room for any choice. If there were no difference between contemplation and action, there would be no transition from possibility to actuality. To entertain a possibility would *be* to act, and to contemplate a set of alternatives would be to realize them *all* alike. A god for whom conception and action were identical could not choose to create the best of all possible worlds, or even choose to create any *one* universe rather than another, since to *contemplate* the alternatives would be to *create* them *all.* To create *freely,*

---

21. Kant described the archetypal intellect in just these terms—in contrast with "our" finite mind, which depends upon sensuous intuition. But Kant also saw that there would be no distinction between actuality and possibility for such a mind—and where there is no transition from possibility to actuality, there can be no "action" or "realization," but only a timeless identity of thought and being.

22. W. E. Hocking, *The Self, Its Body, and Freedom* (New Haven: Yale University Press, 1928), 81.

God must be able to entertain the alternative possible worlds first and *then* choose which of them to create. Otherwise, God's creative act would be as involuntary as that of the cosmic dreamer of some Asian myths. And similarly for us: If one contemplated possibility simply displaced another, to be supplanted by yet another in turn, and if *all* of them were realized merely by being conceived, then the career of the self would be exactly like our dreams, in which images simply follow one another adventitiously, without our direction or choice, and all alike have the force of reality for the dreamer. It would not even be possible to order, control, or edit this dream sequence, since that, again, would presuppose an opportunity to entertain the alternatives before realizing any of them. The difference between contemplation and action is necessary to freedom, then, because without it there would be no choice. For choice depends upon the ability to envision alternative possibilities *without* thereby realizing them and determining oneself in so doing.

It might still be objected that the whole problem of realizing any of these alternatives is extraneous to freedom. Surely, it might be argued, the locus of freedom lies in the *choice* among alternatives. Doesn't the self actually determine *itself* in the inner act of choice, quite independently of whether the world permits the realization of the chosen alternative? Wasn't Immanuel Kant correct to insist that the true measure of a man's character is the inner quality of his will, whether or not he succeeds in translating that will into action? Is the man who risks his life to save another any less admirable if he fails—and perhaps even loses his own life in the effort? Has he not determined *himself* in deciding to attempt the rescue, regardless of success or failure in the world? Surely his personal merit does not depend upon the external result. The Stoics insisted that a man finds true freedom only in *self*-control, only by recognizing that he *cannot* control the world, but only his own inner being.

This objection invokes the idea of a purely immanent act of self-determination that would be completed in the act of choice. The "catch" in this idea was revealed by the Stoics, who purchased their inner freedom at the price of indifference to everything external and an "acceptance of nature" that is difficult to distinguish from resignation to fate.

It is true that the act of choosing is the essential exercise of freedom, the primary locus of self-determination. But without the prospect and problem of realization, choice could have no meaning. I have already noted that choice presupposes an opportunity merely to conceive or entertain alternative possibilities *without* thereby realizing them and determining oneself. But there could also be no choice if there were not a subsequent phase of action, of *realizing* an alternative in the world. A *choice* among possibilities would have no serious point or any real meaning if it were not a determination to *realize* one alternative rather than another. The menu in the window of a closed and abandoned restaurant does not present me with any real choice. Since there is no meal to be had, it is simply a list of dishes and prices. Choice effects the transition from the mere *contemplation* of possibilities to the *intention* to realize one of them. Without the prospect of realizing any of the alternatives, there is simply no occasion to *make* a choice, nor is it any comfort, to the man who has *failed* to realize his intentions, to insist that he has nonetheless succeeded in determining *himself*, since it is the decision that determines character and not the result. The dead hero is nonetheless dead for being a hero. In an obvious sense, he has been determined by the world rather than by his own choice. We may certainly admire his good intentions. But do we show any real respect for those intentions if we say that the result doesn't matter? What would remain of his intention if the result had not mattered to *him*? Severed from any concern about the result, all that remains of the intention is a daydream, a mere act of fancy, and the most that remains of the *choice* apart from any ability to realize it is a mere *wish* or *hope* that one possibility might come to pass rather than another.

If wishes and daydreams were enough to determine the self, then we would all be heroes. Indeed, like James Thurber's Walter Mitty, we would all be heroes many times over. But it is only through action, which embodies choice in the world, that the self's determination of itself acquires any substance or stability. In his inner, "secret life," Walter Mitty "becomes," successively, a naval air commander, a great surgeon, the world's greatest pistol shot, an army bomber pilot, and a man facing a firing squad. He performs heroically in each of these capacities. Yet none of them seems to leave any mark upon him. The inner life is as ineffectual as it is ephemeral. In *Lord Jim,* Joseph Conrad describes the young Jim, with "all his inner being carried on, projected headlong into the fanciful realm of recklessly heroic aspirations": "Ever since he had been 'so high' — 'quite a little chap,' he had been preparing himself for all the difficulties that can beset one on land and water. He confessed proudly to this kind of foresight. He had been elaborating dangers and defenses, expecting the worst, rehearsing his best. He must have led a most exalted existence. Can you fancy it? A succession of adventures, so much glory, such a victorious progress! and the deep sense of sagacity crowning every day of his inner life."[23]

Yet all these preparations and inner rehearsals, all the days of that inner life, do not have the effect of making Jim a hero. When the heroic opportunity for which he has yearned finally presents itself, Jim finds that he has jumped into the *Patna*'s lifeboat with the cowards he so despises! If self-determination *were* entirely an inner affair, it would be as mercurial as

23. Conrad, *Lord Jim* (New York: Modern Library, 1931), 83, 95.

fantasy and far too evanescent to determine the self effectively. As in Walter Mitty's case, one moment's reverie would simply give way to another, to be replaced by yet a third. In what sense would the self be *determined* by such a career? The self restricted to a purely interior freedom would be rather like an artist deprived of any material medium such as paint or clay or marble or bronze in which to realize his ideas. Imagine the despair of a sculptor compelled to cast his works in mercury rather than bronze. Surely, that would be the sculptor's version of the plight of Sisyphus. Or imagine the plight of a brilliant photographer afflicted by the curse of always discovering, in the midst of developing his film, that he has no chemical to *fix* the images on the film. That would be a photographer's nightmare indeed! Yet such would be the plight of a free self if there were no possibility of realizing chosen purposes in an independent world.

The analogy is by no means extravagant. It aptly renders a rather common experience. Everyone is familiar with those agonies of vacillation in which a choice is made, then unmade, then made or revised again . . . and again, without ever issuing in action. I sometimes wonder that the local travel agent will still do business with me after so many canceled reservations and alterations of vacation plans. This is sometimes called "indecision," but the problem is not really a *lack* of decision but an excess of decisions, each of which fades away before it is ever "fixed" by action. But once I am *on* the plane for Paris, my vacillation about canceling the flight reservation and the trip is at an end. Even if I now decide to take the first available flight back to New York, that is very different from deciding not to go to Paris at all. Once the decision is *realized* in the world, the self's determinations of itself acquire a stability and objectivity that may be regretted in cases of folly or crime, but that nonetheless provide an opportunity for a cumulative development of the self that the merely subjective exercise of freedom could never supply. If I cut off my right hand or make recompense for a wrong, I effectively change *myself* and my situation and even my possibilities in ways that have a genuine efficacy that remorse or regret cannot supply. For when the self acts upon the world, its choice becomes embodied in the world. The effect of the action upon the world externalizes the choice and gives it an objective, independent being in the form of an altered world *with* which and *in* which the agent must live, and which has to be reckoned with in future choices and plans. Indeed, even *forbearance*, or the *refusal* to act or change the world, is a choice to accept the status quo or the anticipated future—and that choice is embodied in the further course of the world because of my inaction. The finite self determines itself as much by forbearance as by action, as much by what it chooses to leave alone as by what it attempts to change. Even the action that *fails* to realize its intended purpose still embodies a choice just as *much*, though not *as well*, as the action that succeeds.

All this should make it quite evident that the freedom of self-realization, or the ability to realize a purpose in action is not an incidental, extraneous adjunct to a freedom of self-determination that is already consummated in an inner act of choice, regardless of the success or failure of the intended action. Reflection has shown that a "perfect" freedom for which conception and realization would be identical is impossible because that would allow no *room* for choice, and that a purely reflexive, inner freedom of choice is a vacuous notion because, without the prospect of action, there would be no *occasion* for choice. Self-realization is not merely the index of the imperfection of finite freedom, then, but must be understood to be a *necessary* moment of freedom, one to which choice refers for its meaning and which is necessary to complete self-determination. In Chapter 3, I established that the freedom of self-realization is not intelligible by itself, that it must be founded in self-determination. It is evident now that self-determination is not intelligible by itself either, that it would be meaningless without the prospect and problem of self-realization.

This is not to deny that the choice or decision is the primary and indispensable locus of freedom. The self that *chooses* freely is thus far *"really"* free, even if the choice is never successfully realized in action. But the self that chooses is an *embodied* self, and its body is a part of the world. And the choice that is never realized in action remains a disembodied subjective intention, which leaves the *embodied* self determined by the world. Indeed, action has proved to be essential to freedom precisely because freedom cannot exist without a body and because the embodied self is caught between active self-determination and passive determination by the world.

However, this moment of realization in the world has profound and extensive implications for the very being of freedom. These must now be considered.

※7※

The Conditions of Free Existence

Self-Determination and the Determinacy of the Self

The actuality of freedom is the exercise of self-determination, the determination of the self by itself. In the very act of determining itself, the self gives rise to a distinction within itself. It invests itself with *determinacy*. Of course, in a way it is already determinate from the outset, insofar as its body situates it in a determinate world. But that determinacy attaches to the self from without—and hence insofar as it is *not* free—whereas the determinacy acquired by determining itself belongs to the self just because it is free, since it is acquired by its own free agency. For any free agent must confront limiting determinations that result from its own free acts—both in the world and in itself. And that is what creates a distinction within the self as free self. Chapter 3 showed that the free self can have no other nature or intrinsic character than freedom itself. But in being free, the self gives itself determinate characteristics that it possesses in and through its freedom. It thereby brings determinacy within itself and *does* have an intrinsic character that belongs to the self as a free self rather than merely as a finite self. The distinction that thereby arises is that between the self as *producing* determinations and the self as determinate *product* of its own acts. It must be stressed that these are both aspects of the very freedom of the self. Freedom cannot be identified entirely with the determining self, since, without a self it has determined, it could only be *potentially* free, at most. The actuality of freedom is only realized in and through the self-determined self.

But the distinction that thus arises within freedom cannot be adequately described by invoking the familiar distinction between actuality and potentiality. The determining self is not just potentially free—and the determined self the actuality of freedom. For the reality of freedom resides in the choice or act that determines the self, not in the result, though only the result testifies to the reality of the act. An artist is only a painter if there are paintings produced. But the process of applying the paint is the actuality of painting, not merely its potentiality. It is in determining himself that an individual is actually exercising his freedom. But that act would not *be* real if the self remained unaffected by it, as formless as a blank canvas. Evidently, we must find some other way to understand the distinction that arises within freedom through its own exercise.

The distinction arises because the actual process of self-determination *internalizes* the dialectic of freedom. At the end of Chapter 5, I located the source of the whole previous dialectic of freedom in the necessary finitude of freedom, the fact that it can only exist in an already determinate world. But that means that freedom requires its very opposite in order to be, and that is what stamps freedom as an inherently dialectical concept. In Chapters 5 and 6, I described that dialectical character of freedom in terms of the *world* that finitude implies and the *body* required to place the free self within its world. But all of that only provides the necessary preconditions of freedom, conditions that would have to be satisfied to make it *possible* for any entity to determine itself. The determinacy of the body and world still belong "outside" of the freedom of the self and prior to its exercise, even though indispensable thereto.

But the act of self-determination brings determinacy—and therewith this dialectic—within the self. To put the matter otherwise, whereas the freedom of the self has appeared as only one pole of an inseparable dialectical opposition, in actuality, both of those poles must fall within freedom, or within the free self. For, having determined itself, the self is now both determinate and free. It is tempting, at this point, to try to resolve this inner dialectic by dissolving the self and sundering it into two selves—a determining self and a determined self, one self that decides and acts freely and another self that passively absorbs the results of those free activities. Then the passively determined self can be relegated to the side of the circumstances that limit and oppose the active, determining self, which alone deserves to be described as free. The determined self is thereby allocated to the realm of circumstances, to the world over against freedom. The distinction within freedom can thus be resolved back into the opposition between freedom and world.

But although it may sometimes be rhetorically convenient to speak of a determining self and a determined self (and I have done so myself in opening this chapter), that division is paradoxical and self-defeating if taken literally, since freedom as self-determination can only be genuinely effective and actual if the self that is determined through freedom is the same as the free and determining self. It is futile to allocate the determined self to the world in order to preserve pure and unconditioned freedom for the active, determining self. For the determinate world defines the very situation, opportunities, and options of the self that chooses and acts.

Insofar as an agent determines his body and his world, then, he also determines himself. To deny that the determining and determined selves are the same is to deny this active, reciprocal connection between them. Yet that connection *is* precisely the act of self-determination, without which neither self would be free. And indeed, if the self that determines is *not* the same as the self that is determined, it follows that *neither* of the selves thus distinguished and opposed is free. For in that case, the determining self does not in fact determine *itself*, but something else instead, an other self. And the determined self is not determined *by* itself either, but from without, and is therefore also not a free self. If freedom is genuine *self*-determination, then clearly the determining self must be the same self as the determined self and vice versa. To abstract the free, determining self from the very determinate limitations it has produced in itself through its own free agency is to deny the reality of freedom altogether.

What tempts us down this misleading path, I believe, is the illusory ideal of a pure and unlimited, absolute freedom that so readily and regularly befuddles inquiry into this subject. Here, as everywhere, that idea only renders freedom unintelligible by dissolving its inherent dialectical tensions. That temptation is especially seductive at this particular juncture, and indeed, the classic notion of "free will" might be interpreted as the result of succumbing to this temptation to split the self in two and to abstract freedom from its own acts. In that case, the active or decisive moment of freedom is separated off and hypostatized as a "will" that always determines and *is* never itself determined. Although this doctrine is often ascribed to "libertarians" by opponents, it is difficult to find anyone who advocates it in such a simple form. But Jean-Paul Sartre has provided a more modern and subtle example of this bifurcation of the self. Sartre sunders the being of the self into a being-*for*-itself, which is wholly active, and a being-*in*-itself, which he lumps together with the being of the past and of objects or things in the world. All the accomplishments of the active "for-itself" are automatically transferred to the world, to being-in-itself, so that the for-itself gets nothing for its efforts. If Sartre ends by concluding that "man is a useless passion,"[1] that is because he identifies human consciousness with being-for-itself, which is a power of self-determination that is unable to determine itself—a genuine force in the world, but impotent and futile as regards itself.[2]

The temptation to split the free self in two must be resisted, then, because it only yields two selves that are *not* free. Yet the temptation also has a legitimate basis, and it does direct attention to the fact that the very act of self-determination gives rise to a distinction within the free self. And if it is important to avoid hypostatizing that distinction by dividing the self in two, it is also important not to lose sight of this distinction, which expresses the internalization of the dialectic of freedom. The distinction has to be expressed, yet in such a way as to preserve the identity of the free self.

At first glance, this distinction may just seem to be another version of the difference between freedom of choice and freedom of action—or the ability to realize my chosen purposes in the external world—so that all that need be said is that in realizing *one* chosen purpose, an agent either limits further choices or creates obstacles to realizing them. But in fact, the equivocation lurking in that "either/or" points to a flaw in this formulation. The difference between an inner, subjective freedom of choice and an outer, objective freedom of action doesn't adequately express this distinction in the self. For if the realization of one choice limits future *choices* by determining what options will be available, then the freedom that is affected is not simply freedom as self-realization, or freedom of action, but freedom of choice as well, or freedom as self-determination. And indeed, at the end of the last chapter, I showed that these two forms of freedom are interdependent, that self-realization must be founded in self-determination and self-determination is only completed in self-realization. The self that chooses *is determined* through action—not only as body and as in the world,

---

1. *Being and Nothingness*, trans. Hazel Barnes (New York: Philosophical Library, 1956), 615.

2. Sartre keeps the dialectic *outside of* freedom in this way, but can only do so through a sort of bad faith that interprets freedom in terms of transcendence alone, to use his own terms. Freedom is rooted in the negativity of being-for-itself, which gives rise to a dialectic of which it always remains an impervious and unaffected pole, so that the dialectic is always between being-for-itself and being-in-itself, which is an equally undialectical pole. And *that* is surely nondialectical—to describe a dialectic of freedom whose terms are unaffected by the dialectic in which they are involved.

but also as choosing. It is not enough to consider how freedom may be
abridged by the way in which actions modify the agent's situation and the
options it offers. We must also consider how choices and actions affect the
way the agent chooses, how freedom is affected by its own exercise. If I have
smoked a cigarette with my breakfast coffee every morning of my adult life,
it is futile, idle, and evasive to tell myself that my choice this morning is as
free as it was on the very first day—or that I can stop tomorrow as easily as
I started twenty years ago. Nor is this just because my body has grown
accustomed to regular infusions of nicotine. All those years of smoking have
infected my very ability to choose. Through all those intervening choices, I
have made myself into a "confirmed smoker." To choose to quit now would
be to choose to embark upon a prolonged struggle with the self I have made
myself, which tends to reach for a cigarette at the first sign of an inner
conflict. But that is the very self that must carry on the campaign to quit
smoking! In principle, I may be free to stop at any time by simply choosing
not to have a cigarette when the occasion arises. But that possibility has
remained unrealized for years. If I do succeed in "kicking the habit,"
moreover, it will not be through a series of actions that modify my world, but
through a series of *inactions* or *refusals* that modify my self.

The distinction that arises through self-determination cannot be identified with the distinction between freedom of choice and freedom of action,
then, because it is not merely the ability to realize my choices in action that
is affected by the exercise of freedom, but the choices that are available, and
even *how* the individual typically chooses. This is simply to say that the free
individual actually succeeds in *determining* himself, and that he determines
himself *as* free, as chooser, so that his very freedom itself is qualified and
modified by his choices and actions and even by his inactions.

What the act of self-determination does is to generate a basic difference
between the *being* and the *existence* of freedom. The *being* of freedom is
simply the act or process of self-determination. The self *is* free in and as
determining itself, and the being of freedom consists in, and is complete
in, the self's determination of itself. And inasmuch as the nature of the free
self is freedom itself, that nature is completely actual in the act of self-
determination simply *as such*. Therefore, in one sense, one could say that
freedom is fully described as the act of self-determination, regardless of the
content of the choice and regardless of the specific character of the
determinacy that the self gives itself through its own act.

However, the very reality of this act of self-determination is such that *by* it
the self acquires a determinacy that belongs to it in and through its own
freedom, in contrast to the determinacy that attaches to it from without
because it is bodily situated in the world. Once freedom is actually exer-

cised, therefore, the nature of the free self is *not* merely freedom itself, but freedom as individually defined by its own act. It is for this reason that the existence of freedom may be distinguished from the being of freedom, though it must be remembered that this distinction arises *through* its being. Freedom *exists* as qualified freedom, as determined freedom, though it is determined and qualified by itself. Indeed, the distinction might be further specified in these terms: The being of freedom is also qualified, but qualified from without as finite, as limited by its world, whereas the existence of freedom is qualified from within, as limited by its own act. This reemphasizes the way in which the dialectic of freedom is absorbed within freedom by the actual process of self-determination.

Therefore, the distinction within freedom that arises through the exercise of freedom can be described as a difference between ontological freedom and existential freedom. Obviously, this implies a corresponding distinction with respect to the self. The being of the self is freedom itself. Or, *ontologically*, the free self *is* self-determination. But the existence of the free self consists in a determinate career in the world, a career composed of concrete, particular choices and actions. Existential freedom, then, is always freedom within the context of such a career, a self-determined self-determining, a freedom qualified by the exercise of freedom.

This distinction differs from a mere distinction between potentiality and actuality. Ontological freedom is not merely a potential that is actualized in existential freedom. Rather, ontological freedom is actual in the exercise of self-determination, whereby the self becomes intrinsically determinate, so that existential freedom *is* only by virtue of the actuality of ontological freedom. Moreover, as we shall see presently, ontological freedom may also be actualized in a mode of existence that is *not* free. Apart from the act of self-determination and the self-imposed determinacy that it establishes, ontological and existential freedoms are both only potential. But through that act, both *may* become actual.[3]

---

3. This distinction would also seem to differ from Aristotle's distinction between first and second actualities in *De anima*. For Aristotle compares first actuality to the possession of knowledge and second actuality to its exercise. But the actuality of ontological freedom *is* the exercise of self-determination, and existential freedom can arise only *through* that exercise. Moreover, the actuality of ontological freedom is bound up with the reality of the existential determinacy of the self in a way in which the possession of knowledge is not bound up with its exercise. The relation between the two is rather more like that between knowing (in the sense of learning) and the possession of knowledge. Insofar as knowing is actual, knowledge is possessed, and the actuality of the knowing is inseparable from the knowledge thus acquired. Any further acquisition of knowledge is thereby qualified as a knowing that knows. Similarly, existential freedom involves a further actualization of ontological freedom, but one in which freedom is already self-qualified as self-determined.

Existential Freedom and the World

I have said above that the being of freedom, the act of self-determination, introduces determinacy within the free self and, in so doing, generates existential freedom while also internalizing the dialectic of freedom. Now, the determinacy that qualifies freedom from without, and is a necessary condition of the being of freedom, is the *world* of the free self. (And in this sense, the world includes any psychological determinacy that is innate or the result of illness or accident.) Consequently, to say that the exercise of ontological freedom introduces determinacy into the free self *as* free is, in effect, to say that through the being of freedom the world is brought within the free self. For the world is the source of that determinacy in terms of which the self determines itself, and the dialectic that is therewith interiorized is that between self and world. Of course, a single act of self-determination does not incorporate the world in its entirety, but only some very limited and determinate aspect or portion thereof. If a bachelor finally marries his mistress, for example, it might seem that he has only determined himself by altering his relationship to her—that at most he has decided to accept her as a part of his life, or to define himself by his relationship with her. Yet the self cannot determine itself vis-à-vis some portion of the world without at least implicitly assuming a determinate stance with respect to the rest of the world. Therefore, in a very important sense, the self "takes on the whole world" in determining itself, and the world *is* brought within freedom by the act of freedom. (The bachelor who marries has not just redefined himself vis-à-vis his bride; he has adopted a very different social identity that carries with it an institutional status and set of legal commitments that transform his horizons and his place within the social world.)

Moreover, precisely the *particularity* of the self's adoption of the world is of great importance here. In discussing the necessity of the world to freedom in Chapter 5, I noted that though it is necessary that the self be in *a* world, the particular character of that world is contingent. I pointed out, however, that the self is not in a position to accept or reject the particular world in which it finds itself *as a whole*. It must determine itself precisely in terms of the determinate particularity of the given world. We can now regard this point from a different perspective. As a condition of the possibility of freedom, the determinate world is only necessary *as such* while the exact shape its determinacy takes is completely external, accidental, and contingent to the free self. But by the act of self-determination, the self adopts the world into itself *in its particular, given form* and not simply as satisfying the *general* condition that the free self requires a realm of determinacy. The self determines itself in terms of *this* particular world, and it is therefore *this* world that is taken into the self through the actuality of its freedom, and not merely worldliness in general. Thus, though the given shape of the world is accidental and external to ontological freedom, it is *integral* to existential freedom.

But if ontological freedom incorporates the world into the self in the act that establishes existential freedom, existential freedom, conversely, incorporates freedom into the world. Of course, the free self is and must be in the world, as I have argued, as a precondition of its being. But my point here is quite different. It is that the existential career of freedom enters into the constitution of the world. In determining itself, the self contributes to the total configuration of its world. This is most clearly the case inasmuch as the self's determination of itself involves action through the body in and upon the world in such a way as to *transform* the world. The bulldozer operator and the assassin of a world leader afford dramatic examples. But the self also constitutes the world and determines itself even when it refuses or fails to act. Such inaction involves an acquiescence to the state or course of the world, and therefore might be regarded as a negative contribution to the configuration of the world. Moreover, the refusal to act cannot help but determine the status of one item within the world—the body—and therefore also enters *positively* into the constitution of the world. To decide to "let things be" or to "stay put" is as much a contribution to the state of the world as the initiation of a change. Similarly, in Whitehead's cosmology, an actual occasion contributes objective data to the constitution of the subsequent world whether its contribution involves the ingression of novelty into that world or the mere reiteration of a pattern inherited from an antecedent occasion in a personal order of occasions.

Thus, while the world enters into the constitution of the free self *qua* free through the process of self-determination, the self also enters into the constitution of the world through that process and therefore *qua* freedom and not just insofar as its body also belongs to that world. The free self may be said to build itself into the structure of the world, so to speak, and to do so in, through, and *as* existential freedom. As already noted at the end of the last chapter, this gives freedom a substantiality and fixity that it would not have if self-determination were, or could be, a merely immanent process within the self.

What is most important about this for present purposes is that the stability or concrete individuality thus attained by the self is not canceled out by its freedom. That stability and fixity belongs as an integral moment within its existential freedom. The self cannot fall back on its ontological freedom so as to accomplish a *redintegratio in statum pristinum,* a return to a pristine freedom unaffected by its own act. For its qualified existential freedom is precisely the reality of its ontological freedom. That is, such a return to a pristine state would presuppose that the self had *not* in fact determined itself in the first place, and therefore would presuppose the unreality of its ontological freedom.[4] Existential freedom involves an interpenetration of the determinacy of the free self and its world such that it is perfectly clear that freedom cannot be thought of as canceling, suspending, or negating the worldly individuality of the self. The self must lie in the bed it makes for itself—or else *undo* what it has done.

Freedom in Contradiction with Itself

The barrier of opposition between the free self and its world is thus finally broken or dissolved by the activity of freedom itself. This dialectic is now interior, is *within* the freedom of the self, while the actuality of the self's freedom is constitutive of the world. As such an internally qualified freedom, the free self harbors within itself the tension between freedom and world. Now, this dialectical tension might be resolved—or, rather, quelled or stifled—by a complete assimilation to either of these poles. That is, the self could destroy this inner tension if it could identify itself completely either with the world *or* with itself as freedom. And, indeed, these alternative ways of quelling the dialectic must be recognized as possibilities *for* the self's determination of itself. Since the self defines itself through its freedom, these alternatives may be regarded as two extreme forms of self-definition. On the one hand, the self may define its own existence as wholly worldly in character, may so surrender itself to the world as to become a mere item within the world, thereby qualifying its own freedom as canceled. On the other hand, the self may withdraw into itself in such a way as to make its determination *of* itself vis-à-vis the world a wholly negative one of rejection.

Surrender and withdrawal are not specific alternatives, of course, but are generic *types* of possibilities that the self may realize through the particular way it determines itself, without necessarily recognizing these generic options *as such*. Similarly, to say that it is possible for the self to dissolve the inner tension between self and world by determining itself in either of these ways is not necessarily to say that if it does so, it does so *for the sake* of quelling

---

4. This is not to say that the self may not use its existential freedom in such a way as to disown its own act and so contradict the conditions of its own being. But this is precisely a case of that discrepancy and contradiction between existential and ontological freedom toward which I am now moving.

that dialectical tension as such. These general results may be implicit in the self's specific determination of its existence whether or not they are intended.

But insofar as the self determines itself in such a way as to realize either of these general alternatives, and thus dissolves the opposition between itself and the world, it also voids or destroys its own existential freedom. Again, this may not be intended, but only an indirect or implicit consequence of a specific decision. Nevertheless, the loss of existential freedom is a direct consequence of these generic alternatives. On the one hand, for the self to determine itself as wholly worldly, as a mere item or part within the world, is for it to surrender itself to determination *by* the world. The full force of this alternative will best be recognized if we keep in mind that this is no mere immanent movement within the self, but an act wherein the world and the self constitute one another reciprocally and that therefore has a fixity and substantiality that cannot be annulled merely by evoking the ontological freedom of that same self. On the other hand, insofar as the self withdraws into itself and rejects the world, it forgoes not only action, but all determinacy except that which attaches to it negatively by virtue of its act of rejection.[5]

Insofar as the self determines itself in either of these ways, it suspends its own existential freedom. But the tension or opposition between self and world thus excluded is replaced by one that arises within the distinction between the existential and the ontological levels of freedom. For the self will have exercised its ontological freedom in such a way as to determine itself as existentially unfree. Consequently, the *distinction* between ontological and existential will take the form of an *opposition*. Indeed, the existence of the self will be in contradiction with its being.

The self that rejects the world and withdraws into itself does not cease to *be* in the world through this determination of itself. The existential withdrawal does not *cancel* its ontological condition in contradicting it. Therefore the tension between these two levels is not overcome but is, indeed, generated by the act of self-determination, which thus dissolves the inner

5. This may, of course, be the *goal* of that withdrawal, as when the self seeks inner oblivion or that undifferentiated state of Nirvana or *chit* consciousness which is the goal of meditation in Buddhism and other Indian religions. But it may only be a consequence of an attempted positive assertion of freedom. In this connection, see Hegel's analysis of Stoicism, in *Hegel's Phenomenology of Spirit,* trans. A. V. Miller (Oxford: Oxford University Press, 1977), 119–22. See also the "Diapsalmata" in vol. 1 of Kierkegaard's *Either/Or,* where the aesthete has evidently attempted to attain a form of complete autonomy by devoting himself to the enjoyment of his own inner states, thus *freeing* himself from dependence upon the object of desire. But in so doing, he has brought himself to the brink of a condition of inaction and complete inner apathy.

dialectic between self and world. Nor does a self cancel its ontological freedom through this sort of withdrawal, for as a determination of itself, this withdrawn condition *is* an actualization of its ontological freedom. But this means that the existential condition of withdrawal *is* the reality of the ontological freedom of the self, so that the actuality of ontological freedom is involved in the reality of that condition. Apart from the existential reality of the condition of withdrawal, ontological freedom *would be* and *is* mere potentiality. Thus, the being of the self as freedom *is* in and through the existential determination that contradicts it.

Conversely, the self that identifies itself with its world does not cease to *be* ontologically distinct from the world in which it exists and to whose "mercies" it has surrendered itself. The most obvious form of this alternative is for the self to identify itself with its own body as an item within the world. But clearly, the self does not become ontologically identical with the passivity of its body by this act of determining itself as corporeal. On the contrary, by that very act it actualizes its ontological freedom and thereby distinguishes its being from the world to which it surrenders itself. Here again, the ontological freedom of the self is realized in the very existential condition that contradicts it.

Though already stated twice, this last point is important enough to merit further examination and emphasis. It constitutes the answer to an objection that naturally suggests itself at this juncture. Superficially, it would seem that insofar as the existence of the self is unfree in any real or effective sense, this would represent not only a contradiction, but also a cancellation of its ontological freedom. Though it might be conceded that the ontological freedom of the self had been exercised in determining the self as existentially unfree, the objection contemplated would contend that this freedom was destroyed by that exercise and that there is therefore no opposition between being and existence involved in the existential condition of unfreedom.

But this objection arises from a failure to grasp the nature of the distinction that freedom generates between the ontological and the existential. For the contradictory relation between the two is, after all, only a specific determinate form of that distinction. What the objection overlooks is the fact that the actuality of ontological freedom is at stake in the reality of the existential determinacy brought about through its exercise. In a sense, the actuality of ontological freedom *depends upon* the reality of that condition. If the self determined itself in such a way that the determinacy it gave itself were not fully real or effective, then the reality and effectiveness of its ontological freedom would clearly be equally questionable. Only insofar as the self really qualifies its freedom through its freedom is the being of its freedom actual. Conversely, then, far from being canceled in the existential unfreedom it has brought about, the ontological freedom of the self will have its reality in and through the reality of that unfree condition, so that its actuality is involved in its own contradiction. But once again, this is only a special case of the fundamental relation between the ontological and existential moments of freedom. Even where it amounts to a condition of unfreedom, the existential determinacy of the self can no more cancel its ontological freedom than the latter cancels the reality of its existential condition. To allow either would involve an implicit denial of the reality of the self's determination of itself.

I have said above that apart from the existential condition of unfreedom—wherein it has its actuality in this case—the ontological freedom of the self remains a mere potentiality. And indeed, mere potentiality is all that it *does* remain apart from that unfree condition. That is, so long as, and insofar as, the actual ontological freedom of the self is bound up in an unfree existential determination, that ontological freedom can only *be* outside that contradiction as a potentiality or possibility. Of course, the presence of this potentiality need not appear to the self in such an abstract form as the term "ontological freedom" suggests. Instead, it presents itself in and through that whole set of alternatives to the self's unfree condition that remain possibilities *for* the self despite its unfree existential condition. These imply that the potentiality of ontological freedom remains present because these alternatives *can* still be possibilities *for* the self only insofar as that potentiality *does* persist notwithstanding the actualization of the being of freedom in the contradictory condition of unfreedom. And it may well be that it is precisely or primarily in the persistence of these alternatives as possibilities that the self apprehends the tension of inner contradiction. That is, the contradiction between the being and existence of freedom may appear to the self in the guise of a contradiction between its unfree condition and the persistence of options that can only *be* possibilities for the self because the self *is* ontologically free. If I were really hopelessly addicted or enslaved to the habit of smoking cigarettes, I would not have to wrestle daily with the possibility of quitting. But that option remains, hovering on my horizon, to challenge and accuse me.

We see now how the tension between self and world that may be banished by choosing an undialectical mode of existing results in an opposition between the being and existence of the self. The self becomes unfree through its freedom and is thus brought to a condition of self-contradiction. That condition has been variously described by different authors—as self-contradiction, alienation, self-estrangement, despair, or inauthenticity. The term used to describe it is of no great importance. It *is* important, however, to recognize that this condition is *not* a necessary moment of freedom. The preceding discussion gives no reason to suppose that freedom inevitably places itself in contradiction with itself. That possibility is inherent in the nature of freedom. But it by no means follows from the nature of freedom that it *must* realize this possibility. Contradiction is only *one* way in which the ontological-existential distinction may be specifically determined. Indeed, it is only a generic possibility that may be realized in two quite contrary *types* of self-determination, each of which may assume a variety of concrete forms. Nonetheless, this general capacity of freedom to generate a distinction within itself, and a distinction that may even take the form of a contradiction, presents a new set of problems.

The Categories of Freedom

At the end of Chapter 5, I noted that the dialectical necessity of the world to freedom opens the way to an "ontology" of freedom, a positive account of the necessary and inescapable conditions of being free. That is the challenge and task that I have since undertaken—to discover what conditions and problems are entailed by the indispensable relation of freedom to its world. In Chapter 6, I established one such condition of the possibility of freedom: the self must have a body. In the preceding sections of this chapter, I have gone on to show that the actuality of self-determination opens a distinction within freedom between being and existence and that the relation of self and world is taken up within freedom in the process. Now it is clear that the self may determine its existence in such a way as to deny one or the other of these two poles and thereby falsify its being in its existence.

But if freedom can thus falsify or subvert itself, what are the conditions necessary to its self-consistency? That is the question that the above discussion obviously raises for this study of freedom. It is a problem that could only be raised against the background of the possibility of self-contradiction, or the subversion of freedom by its own exercise. I have therefore explored that possibility first. As a distinctive mode of freedom, this contradiction belongs properly within a complete account of freedom, in any case. But the exhibition of this possibility has provided only an account of *un*free existence, of the ways in which freedom can *be* without existing *as* freedom. I have still to discover the conditions of the possibility of freedom's *existence*, and therefore of its self-consistency.

Indeed, I *must* now pursue this inquiry into the necessary conditions of freedom on this level of the conditions of existential freedom. The distinction between ontological and existential freedom is a necessary concomitant of the exercise of freedom. And, since there can be no freedom apart from its existential determination, my account of the necessary conditions of freedom could not possibly be complete without an examination of its existential level. Moreover, this inquiry *must* now proceed at this level because freedom places the relation between self and world on this level by its own exercise, and my program for establishing the necessary conditions of freedom is tied to that relationship. On the other hand, I cannot undertake a detailed analysis of these categories within the context of this discussion, but must content myself with a more schematic indication of their nature. A thorough analysis would seriously distort the proportions of the present inquiry and must be postponed to some other occasion.

The conditions of existential freedom will also be conditions of the self-consistency of freedom, and these, in turn, will be conditions of the unity or consistency of the free self. Now, one might easily dispatch the problem of discovering these conditions with a negative solution: by merely resorting to the above discussion of the ways in which freedom may contradict itself. We *could* simply say that existential freedom will be assured if both withdrawal from the world and surrender to the world are avoided. But we cannot rest with such a merely negative account. Instead, we must seek to lay bare the positive, generic, constitutive conditions of the self-consistency of freedom. These might be termed the "categories" of freedom, or the "categorical conditions" of free existence, with apologies to Kant—though I will have occasion to elaborate on how they differ from Kant's categories.

The negative solution derived from my previous discussion can still be of some use, however. A more positive and suggestive formulation of this solution would contend that the self can only sustain its ontological freedom in its existence insofar as it determines itself so as both to preserve and to assert the dialectic of freedom and world. This indicates that the conditions in question will hinge upon the relation to itself and to its world that freedom establishes by determining itself.

On the one hand, we must examine how the already determinate world enters into the self-constitution of the free self. We have already seen that the being of the free self depends upon the being of such an opposing determinate milieu. This milieu, or world, is the ultimate ground or source of the self's determinacy. But if the determinate existential state of the self depended *solely* and *simply* upon that of its world, it would be determined by the world, and there would be no meaning to the idea of freedom as self-determination. Now, as we have seen, the self can bring about such a relation of direct dependency through a surrendering self-determination, in which case the being of freedom is actualized, but in such a way as to subvert its existence. The positive task is to establish the conditions of a mode of self-determination whereby the ontological dependency is pre-served without thus precluding existential freedom.

On the other hand, we have to consider the relation of the self to itself as a self-determined being. As we have seen, there are not two distinct selves involved here, one that determines and one that is determined. The two are identical, and yet it is possible for the existing self to be in contradiction with its own being. Indeed, this may even come about through a self-determination wherein the self identifies with itself as pure freedom, and thereby withdraws from the world. The positive task in this case is to discover how the self can preserve its identity in its existence despite and within a determination of itself in terms of its world. This means we must inquire into the relation of the self to its *own* self-imposed determinacy. The ontological identity of the self is assured, but its existential identity depends upon itself and is therefore problematic.

Clearly, the two relations just discussed are not independent of one another. Each refers to the other, as even this brief introductory discussion shows. If the categorical conditions of existential freedom are to be met with, then the self's relation to itself will be a function of its relation to its world and vice versa. Therein lies the persistence of the dialectic of freedom—and that dialectic must be preserved if existential freedom is to be assured. The two relations may be separated in reflection and may lead to two distinct categories of freedom, but the interdependence of the two should be reflected throughout.

The categorical conditions of existential freedom based upon the self's relation to its world and to itself will hold for *any* free self. This is because any free self must *both* give itself a determinate identity *and* adopt its world within itself in the course of determining itself. These relations should therefore lead to categorical conditions in the broadest sense. However, we must not overlook the possibility that the self may find itself confronted with other free selves as well as with a determinate world. The two relations introduced here only provide for the case of an isolated self. We must also recognize the hypothetical case in which there are a plurality of selves in relation to one another. However, as this *is* only a hypothetical case and not a necessary condition of freedom, it will suffice for the moment to deal in detail only with the other two relationships, both of which are necessary to freedom.[6]

We must therefore consider the categorical conditions of freedom in respect to the way in which the self determines its relation to itself, to its world, and, possibly, to other free selves. These three relations bear an obvious resemblance to Kant's categories of relation and have been intro-

---

6. I return to this question of relations among free individuals in Chapter 12.

duced in such a way as to help to exhibit this analogy. The self's relation to itself, upon which depends the existential identity of the self, corresponds to Kant's category of *substance*. The relation of the determinate existential state of the self to the world, upon which it depends for the ultimate ground of its determinacy, corresponds to the category of *causation*. The reciprocal relations between free selves correspond to Kant's category of *community*. I call attention to this analogy here because it will be useful to explore the difference between these categories of freedom and Kant's categories of relation. We needn't accept Kant's theory of knowledge to benefit from this contrast. Indeed, the comparison will open the way to a fresh perspective on Kant's relational categories.

Kant argued that substance, causation, and community are necessary to the very possibility of any and all objective knowledge. The categories of freedom obviously cannot enjoy any such status of a priori necessity. They cannot be categorical conditions of the possibility of freedom in any absolute sense, because they all presuppose the *being* of freedom. They will only be necessary conditions of the *existence* of freedom, and the very search for such conditions derives from a recognition that existential freedom *need not follow* from the being of freedom, that the ontological freedom of the self may issue in an existential condition of unfreedom. Therefore, though necessary to existential freedom and, hence, to the self-consistency of the free self, these categories will nonetheless have only a contingent and problematic status. Their fulfillment will depend upon the self, which *may* determine itself in such a way as to deny the conditions of a free existence. Therefore, each category will have a deficient mode or modes corresponding to the possible modes of unfree existence and self-contradiction.

This difference between the categories of freedom and Kant's relational categories means that the free self is not a substance, that its determinate states are not simply causally related to the world, and that relations among free selves differ from those of a community of substances. In the case of freedom, all these relations are rendered indeterminate and problematic by their dependence upon the ontological freedom of the self. These categories are therefore violable, and each has its deficient modes, whereas Kant's categories of objective knowledge admit of no such exceptions, since any exceptions would vitiate their a priori necessity.

Yet this difference of status between the two sets of categories does not involve as strong a contrast as these remarks might suggest. We have to bear in mind that we are dealing here with categories of *relation* and must recall the specific character of these categories in Kant's treatment. Kant treats the categories of relation as "analogies of experience," and he strongly emphasizes the fact that they are only analogies and, indeed, analogies of a rather special and *problematic* sort:

In philosophy, analogies signify something very different from what they represent in mathematics. In the latter they are formulas which express the equality of two quantitative relations, and are always *constitutive*. But in philosophy the analogy is not the equality of two *quantitative* but of two *qualitative* relations; and from three given members we can obtain a priori knowledge only of the relation to a fourth, not the fourth member itself. The relation yields, however, a rule for seeking the fourth member in experience, and a mark whereby it can be detected. An analogy of experience is, therefore, only a rule according to which a unity may arise from perception. It does not tell us how mere perception or empirical intuition in general itself comes about. It is not a principle constitutive of objects, that is, of appearances, but only *regulative*.[7]

Thus, though they do carry *a priori* necessity, the categories of relation do not allow us to infer *a priori* either the existence of the "fourth term" or its determinate features.[8] Consequently, the categories of relation are, in one sense, both problematic and indeterminate in character. They provide "only a rule according to which a unity of experience *shall* arise from perception."[9] Indeed, the problematic character Kant ascribes to the analogies in the first critique is even further enlarged upon by the introduction of teleological judgment in the third critique.

Kant's categories of relation therefore *share* in some respects in that indeterminate, problematic character previously ascribed to the categories of freedom. So, the two sets of categories are less dissimilar than might have been thought. At this point we may well ask where the real difference lies and what is the fundamental relation between the two sets of categories. In order to answer these questions, we have to recognize the relation between their respective fields of application—namely, between objective knowledge and freedom.

Kant's relational categories are rules governing the constitution of objective—that is to say, *known*—reality. However, by the same token, they are rules for the self's constitution of *itself* as a knower. They do not involve the self's free legislation to the contents of the given manifold, however. That is, they are not rules imposed upon known reality by a self that is autonomous in relation to knowledge. If they do have the a priori necessity

7. Immanuel Kant, *Critique of Pure Reason*, trans. Norman Kemp Smith (New York: St. Martin's Press, 1961), B222.

8. Ibid., B220–21.

9. Kemp Smith's translation, above, reads "may arise" where the original has *entspringen soll.* I have restored and italicized the original "shall" for purposes of emphasis.

that Kant claimed for them, it is because they are necessary conditions of the possibility of knowledge, and the self is *bound* by these conditions antecedently with respect to that possibility. Kant's categories thus define a certain mode of the self's constitution of itself and a certain mode of the self's relation to the world. Insofar as I *am* a knower and am to relate to my world in the cognitive mode, I must satisfy these categories as conditions of the possibility of objective knowledge.

Now, let us reflect more carefully upon this cognitive mode as a mode of self-determination. How is cognition related to self-determination in general, and what is the role of the apriority of the categories here? It is important to note that the necessity of these categories of objective knowledge is not a peculiar or unparalleled feature of this particular, cognitive option. *Any* specific, determinate mode of self-determination—and therefore of relation of the self to the world—would presumably depend upon a similar set of fundamental and necessary conditions that must be fulfilled if that particular mode of self-determination is to be realized at all. We could presumably seek out categories of cooking, for example, or of sexuality or warfare. But this is really only to say that the very specificity of such a mode implies a set of definitive preconditions for that mode. And in fact this is the case with existential freedom as well as with cognition.

But the question that immediately suggests itself at this point is, Does the self have any alternative about whether it will enter into a cognitive relation to the world, whether it will constitute itself as a knower? It is through this question that the peculiar status of this cognitive mode in relation to self-determination can become apparent. I argued in the last chapter that the free self must have a receptive moment whereby it can gain access to the determinacy of its world. Objective knowledge of the sort that is in question here is a special mode of determination of this receptivity of the self. Now, ontologically understood, the receptivity of the self is an aspect of the body. But it must be remembered that the function of the body *qua* receptivity is .to place the self in contact with its world, so that the content of that receptivity includes, along with whatever may belong to the body as such or as an entity belonging *to* the world, some apprehension of the world itself under the conditions of a point of view.

Since the world *is* the source of determinacy for the self, the self has no alternative to apprehending the world except, perhaps, that of total withdrawal—and this occurs only in *relation to* the world. But this does not mean that it has no alternative to objective knowledge of the world. For, as I pointed out in Chapter 5, the self initially apprehends the world in terms of larger structures involving possibilities for itself, which I designated "opportunities and dangers." Insofar as the self apprehends the world in these terms, its mode of relation to the world is opportunistic, or what would traditionally be called *practical,* rather than theoretical or cognitive in character. Such a practical apprehension of the world will always include a cognitive moment. However, this practical, opportunistic grasp of the situation is "subjective," rather than "objective," inasmuch as it is organized in terms of the self's own possibility for determining itself.

But the self may simply choose to explore its world, to identify its own possibility with the opportunity to inspect the given features of its world, to grasp the determinate world in its determinateness. If so, then the element of personal possibility ingredient in the practical structure will be directed back toward the element of given determinacy so as to posit the reduction of the total structure to the *given* factor within it as a subjective aim. This is the specifically cognitive mode of self-determination. This cognitive opportunity, then, is like any other opportunity in having its basis in an apprehension of the world and its terminus in a possibility for the self. But in this case the possibility is, once again, the apprehension of the world. Is this not, finally, the foundation of the unity of apperception and of its status as the essential condition of the cognitive mode, in relation to which Kant deduces the necessity of the categories of knowledge? In cognition, the self puts itself at stake in the apprehension of the world. For apperception is simply the turning back of the self *toward* the contents of its own receptivity *from* an orientation toward its own possibility.

The unity of the self that is thus required by the very nature of the cognitive project, or of the self *as knowing,* is surely not similarly assured a priori to the self *as free,* and the categories of freedom must therefore have a very different status. Insofar as the self views the world in terms of alternative opportunities, such a unity is only a possibility and is by no means assured. For in that case, each alternative possibility is the principle or nucleus of organization for a *separate* constellation of given material. Even if these alternative structures should contain the same data, the organization will differ with the possibilities in question. Therefore, in this case there will be no unity of the self's apprehension of the world except as a possibility to be attained by a choice of *one* alternative rather than others. In the preceding chapter I characterized this apprehension of the world in terms of possibilities as a matter of passions and feelings. My present point can therefore be stated in very conventional terms by saying that there is no *a priori* assured unity of the self insofar as it apprehends the world in terms of such passions and feelings except insofar as it attains that unity by a choice that selects one option to the exclusion of others. And even then, the excluded alternatives may continue to beckon or threaten, to be a source of misgivings or regrets that interfere with the "single-minded" unity of resolute choice.

In contrast, the cognitive opportunity aims at apprehending the "objective," *given* structure of the world. Now, for the self to grasp the world in its givenness is for the self to relate to it, not as a realm of opportunities for itself, but as an independently determinate realm in its own right. For this is what the world *is* for the self if considered apart from the self's own possibilities. That is, it is *as* such a realm of independent determinacy that the self requires the world in the first place. This is what is involved in apprehending the world "objectively," in its *Gegenständlichkeit*, its independence of the self. In order to attain such an objective apprehension, the self must distinguish itself and its personal possibilities from the world and must hold these apart from the world. Objective cognition is, therefore, a process whereby the self distinguishes what does *not* depend upon itself from what *does* so depend.

Herein lies the fundamental relationship between the two sets of categories. What is at stake with respect to the categories of freedom is precisely that relation of the self to itself and to its world which *depends* upon the self, whereas the possibility of objective knowledge involves precisely the apprehension of these relations insofar as they do *not* depend upon the freedom of the self. Therefore, though each set of categories has its indeterminate and problematic aspect, the resolution of this problematic is differently determined in the two cases. In the case of the categories of freedom, this resolution is to be determined by the self. In the case of the categories of knowledge, this resolution must depend upon the *world* as apprehended through the contents of receptivity.

Herein also lies the key to the status of *a priori* necessity of the cognitive categories of relation. I recognize that Kant deduces this necessity from the necessity of the unity of apperception. This is quite appropriate when these categories are approached from the standpoint of an analysis of knowledge. But they are here approached from the standpoint of freedom and the status of cognition as a mode of freedom wherein the self sets out to apprehend the world as independent of itself. In this case, their *a priori* necessity may be seen as following from the very character of this mode. For the world is to be grasped here as a realm of complete and independent determinacy. The requirement that its determinacy be independent requires in turn that the relations in question be determined *a priori* (since otherwise their determinacy would be conditioned by the merely subjective conditions of their apprehension and, hence, dependent upon the self). The requirement that the determinacy of the cognized world be *complete* requires, further, that these relations have the status of *necessity* in the sense that there must be no moment of indeterminacy involved in their connection. Thus, the peculiar status of the cognitive categories of relation follows directly from the goal of the cognitive program, which is the apprehension of the objective world, that is, of the world as a realm of independent determinacy. In adopting this goal, the self does indeed determine itself, but in such a way as to hold its freedom in suspense in order to appropriate its finitude.[10]

As we have seen in Chapter 5, the self's envisionment of its own possibilities depends upon its appreciation of the exigencies of its world. Consequently, the broader and more differentiated the latter, the greater will be the range of possibilities evident to the self. Herein lies the great advantage and obvious motivation for the adoption of this possibility of objective knowledge. However, there seems to be no reason to conclude that the ability to envision and adopt this opportunity is a necessary condition of freedom. Animals presumably have no alternative to a "subjective," practical view of the world, entirely biased by their sense organs, their individual associations, and by the opportunities and threats the world presents. But the inability of a cat or chimpanzee to adopt an impersonal, objective perspective seems no reason, of itself, to doubt that animals can choose freely between the alternatives available to them, between fight and flight, for example. A dispassionate, theoretical apprehension of the environment would scarcely make such choices any easier.

But although objective knowledge is not a *necessary* precondition of freedom, freedom *is* a necessary precondition of the very possibility of objective knowledge. Objective cognition is not an original or "natural" perspective or way of relating to the world, as is evident from brief reflection upon animal experience. The animal does not just have a limited, though objective, knowledge of its world. Though speculations about what it is like

10. Thomas Nagel develops the contrast between these two points of view in *The View from Nowhere* (Oxford: Oxford University Press, 1986). In chapter 7, "Freedom," he examines how that contrast illuminates the debate about freedom and determinism that concerns us here. Nagel insists that these two points of view cannot be reconciled. He thereby leaves his readers in roughly the same predicament that Kant bequeathed to his successors: confronted by two incompatible conceptions of themselves. Since he rejects the appeal to a transcendent, noumenal self that Kant offered as a resolution, Nagel aggravates that predicament into a complete *impasse*. But where is Nagel himself standing when he reaches this conclusion? The trouble is that he attempts to derive the experience of autonomy from the demand for objectivity—and therefore finds it unintelligible, for reasons I consider shortly. Yet he recognizes that objective knowledge assumes an autonomous intellect, so that neither point of view is coherent in the end and he leaves us "in the abyss, where the pursuit of objectivity undermines itself and everything else." No such impasse arises if we begin with freedom and recognize objectivity as a specific form of self-determination—a project that presupposes freedom and then derives the demand for objectivity from freedom's attempt to chart the contours of its own finitude, to discover the already determinate conditions upon which it depends. Thus, by the end of his chapter on freedom, Nagel reenters the standpoint of the agent, from which he is able to offer a richer, more positive account of this interplay between limited objectivity and limited autonomy, one that is more in keeping with my own account.

to be a bat or a dolphin are notoriously risky, it seems entirely safe to suppose that animal experience is profoundly practical, entirely shaped by the animal's interests, desires, and fears. If objective knowledge is a human possibility, it cannot be taken for granted, as though we begin with a pure, disinterested apprehension of facts that then becomes "distorted" by self-interest. On the contrary, objective knowledge is a very special option or ideal that can only be adopted by choosing to set aside all subjective, practical interests and submit to impersonal standards of truth and so govern my actions as to obtain a grasp of the world as it is independently of my agency. The individual's motives for adopting that peculiar possibility may be entirely practical and self-interested. But the whole enterprise only makes sense if we have some *choice* regarding what to believe—that is, if the knower is free to govern the course of his own inquiry. If he has no control over his beliefs, if his opinions are only the psychological *effects* of mundane causes, he cannot transcend those causal processes or abstract from their influences so as to obtain an understanding of the world that is unadulterated by personal interests and influences. So although there may be free choice in the absence of objective knowledge, there can be no objective knowledge in the absence of free choice, if the subject's relation to the world is entirely a product of causation. Epictetus locates the central core and inviolable power of freedom in this cognitive choice, this ability to suspend belief or to give or withhold assent to a proposition, whereas Descartes founds the very possibility of knowledge upon the ability to suspend judgment, to refuse to assent to any belief for which he does not find compelling evidence. This difference between causation and choice merits closer examination.

Choice

Against the background of this general comparison of the categories of freedom with those of objective knowledge, we can begin to derive some indication of the particular natures of the categories of freedom through a more specific comparison with the corresponding cognitive categories. In the case of cognition, the relation of an entity to its world is determined through the category of causation. Since, as I have noted, the nature of the cognitive categories requires that these relations depend upon the world, causation asserts that the determination of an entity depends upon its world.

In the case of freedom, the relation between a self and its world must depend, instead, upon the self. The relation between the two is determined by the self's choice of opportunity rather than by the world. The category of freedom that corresponds to causation, then, is choice. But whereas causation is merely a relation of an entity to its world, choice involves the self's determination of itself and therefore also involves a relation of the self to itself.

But it isn't enough to recognize that choice is the category of the relation between self and world that corresponds to causation and to indicate how it differs from causation. We must also try to distinguish between the positive and deficient modes of each category of freedom. For unlike the categories of knowledge, the categories of freedom are not necessary a priori. They need not be fulfilled. Each has deficient modes, in which the freedom of the self is subverted in its existence. These deficient modes must be distinguished from the forms of these categories whereby existential freedom is maintained.

I have suggested that the self may destroy its freedom in its existence in two opposing ways: through either a surrender to the world or a withdrawal from the world. How are these modes of unfree existence related to the category of choice? I have shown previously that in determining itself, the self identifies itself with one of a number of alternative possibilities whose determinate content derives from the world. It is primarily through this choice of an alternative that the world enters into the constitution of the self, and it is in its efforts to realize that possibility that the self enters into the constitution of the world. In surrender to the world, the self chooses a possibility whose realization depends upon the world rather than upon itself. In so doing, it identifies itself with that possibility and thereby places the determination of its own identity at the disposal of the world. Therein lies its abdication, or loss of freedom. In more extreme forms of surrender, the self may simply identify itself with the possibility of being a mere item within the world whose career depends upon the world. But wherever the self commits its being to a possibility that depends entirely upon the world, it places itself in a relation to the world that is passive in principle, however much it may struggle to *cooperate* in the realization of that possibility. If the realization of the possibility is *finally* dependent upon the world, then the cooperative efforts of the self are all too like those of a bowler to influence the ball in midcourse through "body English."

What the self must choose to sustain its own freedom, then, is not some worldly goal but *itself* and what depends only upon itself. That suggests that the self can retain freedom in its existence only by renouncing all worldly aims and concerns. This strategy for preserving one's freedom has often been championed by ascetics, and it was a pervasive theme of Roman Stoicism. But such a rejection of the world simply plunges the self into withdrawal, the other defective mode of choice. In this case, the self chooses itself as independent of the world and beyond worldly concerns. It treats its relationship to the world as a matter of mere accident.

The motives of such a withdrawal need not take the reflective form in which they are advanced by the stoic or ascetic. The self that finds its worldly hopes disappointed and frustrated may simply recoil from the world and withdraw upon itself for the sake of security and safety. Such would seem to be the case with those pathological forms of withdrawal in which the existential freedom of the self is annulled far more terribly and effectively than any ascetic or stoic withdrawal could ever exhibit.

In any form of withdrawal, the self seeks its identity apart from the world. But since the self *requires* the world as a source of determinacy and ground of possibility, such a negative determination of its relation to the world is a sterile starvation that loses freedom in impotence. If the answer to the loss of freedom by the choice of surrender is the self's choice of itself, that cannot mean the choice of withdrawal. And, indeed, in choosing withdrawal, the self does not really choose *itself*. It chooses what Kierkegaard calls the "infinite self," by identifying entirely with its power to refuse any and every finite goal, every "entangling alliance" with the world that might compromise its sublime indifference. But it refuses to choose itself as finite by abdicating its power to choose one alternative over another or to pursue any definite career or course of action.

Both of these deficient modes of choice *are* choices, but they are self-negating choices. That is, they are choices whereby the self vitiates its ability to choose. In the one case, it does so by placing its destiny, the "realization" of itself (that is, of that possibility with which it has identified itself) at the disposal of the world. In the other case, it vitiates its ability to choose by placing itself outside the range of finitude wherein, alone, there can be any question of choice. These are choices whereby the self escapes choice, then. Or at least they are choices that obviate choice, whether *in order* to escape it or not. The only choice still available in such a case is the choice that cancels this prior, deficient choice—that is, the choice, in the one case, of abandoning the worldly aim and seeking its identity elsewhere and, in the other, of abandoning the position of indifference or independence of the world.

The basic deficiency in these two modes of choice consists in the fact that each only partially expresses the nature of choice itself. I remarked earlier that choice is a relation of self to world, like causation, but that it differs from causation in being also a relation of the self to itself. Surrender expresses only the former of these, withdrawal only the latter. But such a one-sided choice is destructive to choice itself. In the case of surrender, the self determines its relation to the world as a *causal* relation and places itself in the status of the dependent effect. In the case of withdrawal, it cuts itself off from opportunity—and therewith from the possibility of having alternatives among which to choose.

Evidently, the categorical form of choice, the choice whereby freedom is maintained in existence, must be a choice that avoids both of these undialectical, one-sided extremes. Such a choice will reflect something of each deficient mode, yet without losing itself in the one-sidedness of either. It must have the reflexivity of withdrawal, yet not be a mere empty recoil of the self upon itself. This means it must embrace the finitude of worldly existence, yet without losing its identity in the world. These conditions can only be met by a choice whereby the self accepts the world into the constitution of itself, yet on terms prescribed by the self to itself.

If the self is to lead a free existence, it must determine itself through the choice of a possibility whose realization involves the world without depending upon the world. The possibility chosen must consequently be reflexive; that is, it must be a choice of a possible self though not of the pure, worldless self. In effect, the self must determine the *form* or character of its own existence. The categorical form of choice is the choice of character, which is to be the second category of freedom. But what this involves can at least be presaged here. We might almost say that the self has to choose the *style* of its existence and of its relations with the world. The realization of this form in concrete existence requires and involves the world. Yet it does not *depend* upon the world as does the realization of a worldly goal. Rather, it depends upon the self to realize or embody this form in every worldly context. What is at stake, however, is not the attainment of a foolish consistency. Foolish consistency is a form of partial withdrawal that limits the openness of the self to its world. (It is therefore justly represented so frequently in literature as self-destructive by virtue of its narrowness.) Instead of this, the self is challenged to *discover* the concrete reality of its character in every situation, much as the artist is challenged to discover and define his style in each successive creation. Such a challenge can only sharpen the self's sensitivity to the subtleties and possibilities of its situation in the world.

Character

The category of character and its relation to choice will emerge more clearly through comparison with the corresponding cognitive category of substance and its relation to causation. The category of substance requires that the identity of every entity be assured as given or determined a priori. On this assumption, all alteration and every alterable determination is *accidental:* that is, has its ground outside the entity in question. This alone rules out self-determination. It implies that causation is not and *cannot* be a relation between consecutive states or moments of a single entity, but *must* be a relationship *between* substances instead. In effect, these categories stipulate that "entity" shall be defined by self-identity and that all differences, even between states of a single entity, shall be produced by relations among entities.

The result is that in the case of the cognitive categories of relation, the identity of the substantial entity is prior, whereas causation, as a function of relations *among* such entities, is secondary, presupposing the *givenness* of substances. The case is altogether different with the categories of freedom. In this case, the identity of the self is not given or assured. It is precisely that which has to be determined *by* the self. Consequently, choice must be prior to character. Character presupposes choice and must be viewed as resultant from relationships between choices. Correspondingly, the states of the self are *not* accidental to it, but are constitutive of the very identity of the self. Freedom requires that the ground of alteration of states of the self lie, not outside the self in other entities, but *in* the self as self-determining. These last two statements are really equivalent, of course. That is, if the states and alterations of states of the self are grounded in the self rather than in an other, then those states are not accidental.[11]

The self constitutes its character through its choices, then, so that the ways in which the self determines its relations to the world are decisive for its identity, rather than merely accidental. But, conversely, the character thus constituted is decisive for the self's further choice, just as prior choice

---

11. Cf. Paul Ricoeur's extended reflections on the polarity of *ipse* and *idem* in *Oneself as Another* (Chicago: University of Chicago Press, 1992), where *ipse* represents self-constancy in contrast to the mere permanence of *idem.* See especially 119–22, where Ricoeur summarizes the development of his own conception of character since the publication of *The Voluntary and the Involuntary* in 1966. He had originally conceived of character as an "absolutely involuntary" innate core of permanent identity. In subsequent works, he recognized that this did not do justice to the *temporality* of character. He now understands it as the "core of lasting dispositions by which a person is recognized" and as "the limit point at which the problematic of *ipse* becomes indiscernible from that of *idem,* and where one is inclined not to distinguish them from one another" (121). The analysis of dispositions that follows focuses upon the roles of habit and "identifications" that require a certain fidelity to self, both of which depend upon the self's exercise of freedom in particular choices, and concludes, "This proves that one cannot think the *idem* of the person through without considering the *ipse,* even when one entirely covers over the other. Thus are incorporated into the traits of character the aspects of evaluative preference which define the moral aspect of character" (122).

is decisive for character. The self, even the existentially free self, is not free to determine itself afresh at every turn. Subsequent choices issue from a self that has been qualified and defined existentially by its earlier choices. A freedom of choice that would always be completely open would not succeed in determining itself. To suppose that the free self does not thus acquire a character that severely limits its further choices not only conflicts with human psychology as we know it today (which means that to hold this would require that we abandon the possibility that man is free), it also contradicts the nature of freedom itself because it implies that the self has not really determined *itself* by its prior choice.

But this means that the self always constitutes its own character through its choices in one way or another, even by the deficient forms of choice. Every choice contributes something to the definition of character. Yet character is not to be conceived as finally established through a single choice. It is, rather, as I have said, the cumulative product of relations among choices. Therefore, although the choice of character is the categorical form of choice, the deficient modes of choice are also constitutive of some form of character. We must therefore seek to discover deficient modes of character from which the categorical form of character can be distinguished, much as we had to distinguish categorical and deficient forms of choice. And since character is not the product of a single choice, a single choice of surrender or withdrawal does not establish the character of the self as similarly deficient. A single worldly goal is either realized or not and the self is then faced with choice once again. Similarly, ascetic emphasis upon the strict self-discipline required to withstand the constant temptations of worldly opportunity testifies to the fact that withdrawal is not established once and for all by a single choice.

Since a single choice of surrender or withdrawal does not constitute the surrendered or withdrawn character, we cannot indicate the deficient modes of character simply by referring again to what has been said above about the deficient modes of choice. In order to appreciate the nature of these deficient modes of character, we have to ask about the *continuity* of existence that results from the repetition of such choices.

Continuity, however, is precisely what the character of the self that consistently surrenders itself to worldly ends is liable to lack. For the surrendered character's choices do not depend upon itself, but upon the world. That is, the previous choice, since it is not a choice of self and of continuity of character, is not regarded by the self as constitutive or decisive for further choice. The subsequent choice is simply based upon the opportunities available to the self at that moment of decision. The result of this opportunism is a fragmentary character without unity or continuity. Or, it would be better to say that whatever continuity the surrendered character may have is accidental, as is the character itself, since it depends upon the world rather than the self.

There is an exception to this fragmentation and dispersion of the surrendered character, though it also has overtones of withdrawal. This is to be found in the case of the monomaniac, the individual who unswervingly pursues a single worldly aim—an *"idée fixe."* This has overtones of withdrawal because the monomaniac confines himself to a perspective and relation to the world constituted by his prior choice of the *idée fixe* and is indifferent or oblivious to all other worldly conditions and opportunities. The fixation might therefore be described as a sort of synthesis of surrender and withdrawal. But the self that has surrendered itself to such a fixation is in all the tighter bondage to the world upon which the realization of the *idée fixe* depends. The "foolish consistency" of which I spoke earlier is a milder cousin of this character type.

These mixed forms presage what is to be expected in the withdrawn character. In this case, a sort of consistency of character *is* attained, but at the price of sacrificing freedom. Since it is a consistency based upon exclusion, it is a narrow, empty consistency. Insofar as the self has actually constituted its character as thus consistent in withdrawal, it is so dominated by that consistency as to be closed off from the world and from novel opportunity. The loss of existential freedom is perhaps nowhere so graphic as in the pathological forms of the withdrawn character.[12]

The defect in the unfree modes of character is easy enough to recognize. They subvert the nature of character itself by making it into a matter of either substance or accident. I have already remarked that the surrendered character is *accidental* inasmuch as it is dependent upon the world. This fits perfectly with the fact that the choice of surrender turns the self's relation to the world into the relation of an effect to its cause. But because there is no assured core of substantial identity in this case, the accidental here becomes essential, or constitutive of the identity of the self, so that its character becomes "essentially accidental," and the result is the fragmented character. Conversely, in the case of withdrawal, the self attains the identity

---

12. Cf. Ludwig Binswanger's analysis of psychosis as a synthesis of withdrawal and self-surrender in "Introduction to *Schizophrenie*," in *Being in the World*, trans. Jacob Needleman (New York: Basic Books, 1963), 249–65. Binswanger concludes that the significance of psychosis in general is to be interpreted as "a resignation that takes the form of a retreat from Dasein's own decision, the complete renunciation of Dasein's own ability to decide and, with this, the complete *self*-surrender to the power of others" (263). In the passage that follows, Binswanger indicates that the surrender "to the power of others" is only one form of surrender. The psychotic's surrender may also be to "alien forces," whether real or imagined.

of substance by a refusal to constitute itself through its relations with the world. But the identity it maintains in this fashion is bare and barren, for only the world could give it content and opportunity.

As the deficient modes of character involve its perversion, the categorical form of character consists in its integrity. And, indeed, it is common enough to describe "*true* character" in terms of integrity. But this has a special meaning in the present context. In discussing the nature of character initially, I noted that choice is decisively constitutive of character—but that character is also decisive for further choice. It is these relations that must be sustained if the integrity of character is not to be subverted. This requires that the self accept the decisiveness of its prior choice for its present choice. Only by accepting the prior choice as constitutive of itself and choosing itself *as* thus constituted does the self really choose *itself* and attain a consistency that is not just negative. The novel choice thus appropriates, or "owns up to," what the prior choices have made of the individual—even when those choices have proved disastrous or futile. That need not mean foolishly persisting in a project even after it is recognized as folly. But it does mean refusing to *dis*own my decisions simply because their consequences are unpalatable, or because circumstances now make another option more expedient, or because I now recognize another alternative to be more rational or moral or attractive. That is what is we expect of a "man of integrity": that he will stand by his choices even when he rues them and has decided to change. But integrity of character requires consistent *choice* as well as consistency *of* choice. That is, it does not allow of an escape from the demands and possibilities of the present situation—from the present demand *for* choice—by a mere appeal to prior choice. Only in this way is consistency prevented from destroying freedom, as it does in the case of fixation or of foolish consistency.

The categorical form of character thus proves to be the character founded upon the decisiveness of choice, just as the categorical form of choice proves to be the choice of character. The categorical form of character described above answers precisely to the character that the categorial form of choice required. It is a form of character that is not dependent *upon* the world yet is not closed off *from* the world.

This interdependence of the categories of existential freedom should not be surprising, for at the outset of my explanation I observed that if the categorical conditions of existential freedom are to be met with, then the self's relation to itself will be a function of its relation to its world and vice versa. Therein lies the persistence of the dialectic of freedom—and that dialectic must be preserved if existential freedom is to be assured. The two relations may be separated in reflection and may lead to two distinct categories of freedom, but the interdependence of the two should be reflected throughout.[13]

Conclusion

Seen in relation to the preceding chapters, much of the development of this chapter is familiar. I have distinguished the conditions of existential freedom from the conditions of unfree existence. I have dealt throughout with two modes of self-determination whereby the self may determine its existence as unfree and thereby come into contradiction with itself as ontologically free. As I pointed out in introducing them, each of these modes quells the internal dialectic of existential freedom by determining the self in terms of one of its two poles to the exclusion of the other.

But none of this is *altogether* new. For these two ways in which the self may stifle the inner dialectic of existential freedom, these two ways in which the self may define its own existence as unfree, correspond to the two chief types of undialectical definition of freedom developed in the first three chapters of this inquiry: the ordinary conception of freedom as the absence of external constraints and obstacles to doing as I please, and the ethical conception of freedom as the realization of the "true" self.[14] In my critical review of those two views at the end of Chapter 5, I pointed out that the first attempted to define freedom solely in terms of the world, while the other attempted to do so solely in terms of the self. At that time, I was considering these only as alternative *theoretical* definitions of freedom. In this chapter I have confronted them again as alternative *existential* determinations of the free self through itself.

We can now appreciate the full meaning of my insistence, early in this chapter, that the dialectic of freedom is interiorized by the actuality of freedom itself, for we now find that the dialectic of the first part of this inquiry reappears *within* the structure of freedom. Through its ontological freedom the self can define itself in ways that correspond to the earlier theoretical formulations of the nature of freedom.

But the similarity does not end there. The burden of the first three chapters was to show that neither of these undialectical alternatives is adequate to provide for the possibility of a free *being*. Or, as I put it at that point, freedom disappears once either of these alternative definitions is

13. Page 180 above.
14. See pages 36–37 above for the most concise account of these two conceptions.

consistently followed out. In the one case, it disappears into the world. In the other case, it disappears into an impotent potentiality of the pure, absolute self. I concluded that freedom could not *be* at all without the dialectical opposition between self and world. However, I remarked that the result of such an undialectical definition of freedom was that that definition was assailed by dialectic as though from without. The dialectic excluded from the definition only reasserted itself elsewhere.[15]

The same results hold for the *existence* of freedom, as shown in this chapter. Insofar as the self determines itself in such a way as to exclude the dialectic of freedom and world, it subverts its freedom by either submerging it in the world or by vitiating it in the sterility of withdrawal. But the dialectical opposition thus excluded from the existence of the self simply reappears in the form of the contradiction between the ontological freedom of the self and its unfree existence. Conversely, this contradiction within the self can only be avoided if the self sustains the dialectical interdependence of self and world in the determination of itself whereby, alone, it actualizes its ontological freedom. The categories of freedom are therefore conditions of the preservation, at the existential level, of precisely those conditions of the *being* of freedom that we earlier discovered at the basis of the inadequacy of every undialectical theory of the nature of freedom.

This strikes still another familiar chord. To present such categories of existential freedom is, of course, to admit that freedom *exists* as free only if it determines itself in accordance with such conditions. Since these conditions prove also to be such as to accord with the nature of the being of the self as freedom, their admission virtually amounts to the reintroduction of the fundamental contention of the ethical view of freedom. For the essence of the ethical view could be restated ontologically as the insistence that the self is free only insofar as it exists in accordance with conditions appropriate to the nature of its being.[16]

Thus, the basic structure of ethical freedom reappears as a necessary moment in the total structure of self-determination. What is valid in the idea of ethical freedom is that the self is not in accord with itself and is not existentially free except under special conditions whose fulfillment depends upon the self. The "ethical" status of those conditions has not been established and is not within the scope of this chapter. For the moment, it is more appropriate to reflect upon how the reappearance of this form of

15. See Chapter 5, pages 125–27, above.
16. Cf. Adler's generic formula for this type of view: "To be free is to be able, through acquired virtue or wisdom, to will or live as one ought in accordance with moral law or an ideal befitting human nature" (*The Idea of Freedom* [Garden City, N.Y.: Doubleday, 1958], 1:606).

freedom fills out the course of these inquiries into the nature of freedom.

At the end of the last chapter I had similarly to reinstate the freedom of self-realization as a necessary dimension of self-determination. However, the self-realization reintroduced there was merely a matter of the self's ability to realize its intentions in the world, and it therefore corresponded to the loose, immediate definition of freedom with which I began. The ontology of self-determination has, therefore, forced us to rediscover *both* of the other forms of freedom considered in the first part of this inquiry.

Indeed, it should now be quite evident that these other two forms of freedom merely express the dialectical logic of the being of freedom. Each arises from the dependence of freedom upon one of the two poles of that dialectic of free self and world. It is because freedom can only exist in a world that the freedom of self-realization is a necessary dimension of self-determination, whereas ethical freedom is founded in the relation of the free self to itself as a being that determines itself. This is the foundation and justification for those theories that define freedom either as self-realization or as moral action or choice. Without a basis in self-determination, the claims of these views prove to be arbitrary, as shown in Chapter 2. Neither the freedom of self-realization nor ethical freedom can *be* as a separate form of freedom that is not founded in self-determination. But, on the other hand, it is now clear that self-determination cannot *be* without requiring these other two forms of freedom as dimensions of its being.

All three definitions of freedom are therefore founded in the ontology of freedom, but no one of them alone adequately expresses its nature. Each is correct, but partial, and requires the other two to be complete. Therefore, each has led to the other two. My initial examination of the ordinary, immediate notion of freedom as self-realization led to the ethical view, while the partiality of both of these led to self-determination. Careful analysis of the exigencies of self-determination has now led back to the basic claims of the immediate and ethical views. The necessities of the nature of freedom require all three forms of freedom, yet will allow none to stand alone.

Freedom thus has its own logic in the dialectic of its being, a logic that will force anyone who attends carefully to its nature to recognize all of these dimensions, even if he begins as a champion of only one of them against the others.

❋ 8 ❋

Freedom, Determinism, and Human Experience

Man is born free; yet everywhere he is in chains.
—Jean-Jacques Rousseau, *The Social Contract*

Of Human Freedom

Are human beings free? If we are born free, are we inherently and always free—even in chains? Or are we only sometimes free, in the absence of chains, or under some other special moral or political conditions? If we *are* free, are we the only free beings? Does freedom distinguish *Homo sapiens* from every other species—indeed, from everything else in the universe? Or can we also discover freedom elsewhere? These questions concern us personally and motivate much of our interest in the subject of freedom. I want to know whether I am entirely determined by external causes or free to choose for myself, whether I am inherently free—or only free under special conditions. If freedom does depend upon such conditions, I want to know what they are. And I want to know whether I and my species are set off from all the rest of nature by being free, whether we are surrounded by a universe that is entirely determined by necessary causal processes with the sole possible exception of human action.

These are the questions that launched this inquiry. We can now approach them with a clearer grasp of what is at stake in asking whether any action or event, human or otherwise, is free. For we now have a far more developed and articulated understanding of the meaning of freedom and of the conditions that must be met if freedom is to be meaningfully invoked to describe or explain any act or event. Our inquiry into the meaning of freedom has been hypothetical, treating freedom only as a possibility and attempting to establish the minimal and necessary conditions of that possibility so as to be able to ask whether any being—human or beast or god—fulfills those requirements. I have dealt only with the most general and fundamental requirements of freedom, in order to avoid introducing distinctions or conditions that may be peculiar to the human species, since that would prejudice questions about whether other animals are free and whether freedom may even be found at the level of physical events, as some authors maintain.[1]

My analysis of freedom is still not complete in every detail, but it is sufficiently clear and articulated to allow us to return to the problem of human freedom. Having found that the idea of an unlimited and absolute freedom is an illusory abstraction, we have explored the necessary characteristics of that finite, embodied freedom, active in a resistant world, which has proved to be the only form in which freedom can conceivably exist. To return now to the question of human freedom is to ask, Does this hypothetical account of what it is to be free apply to the human condition as we experience it?

---

1. Philosophical discussions of freedom all too often frame the issues in terms that rule out the question of freedom in nature from the very outset. Discussions of freedom inspired by an interest in moral responsibility typically ignore the question whether animals are free, since we do not regard animals as morally responsible agents. Galen Strawson does periodically refer to animals. But while he acknowledges that dogs can choose and might even be said to be free in some sense, Strawson rather cavalierly preempts the term "freedom" for distinctively *human* choice—indeed, for those human choices that are fully self-conscious of themselves *as* free. Strawson offers purely stipulative reasons for describing only human choices as free, and while these may make sense in the context of his book, his stipulative identification of freedom with "fully responsible" action or choice prejudices the metaphysical questions at stake in the present inquiry. Indeed, I think Strawson's identification of freedom with full responsibility seriously skews his own inquiry. For he defines full responsibility in such a way as to require *absolute* or *unconditioned* self-determination. But then, discovering, as we have, that absolute freedom is impossible, he concludes that freedom as self-determination is also impossible — and is left to a long, rather tortuous analysis of the incongruity between the human *experience* of finite freedom and the impossibility of an infinite freedom that would be an absolute *causa sui.*

At this point, that question may almost appear rhetorical. For in the course of dealing with the relations of a finite freedom to itself, its world, and its body, we descend from the abstract notion of an absolute, limitless freedom to a description of freedom that may seem all too obviously applicable to human experience. For we have learned that freedom is possible only for the very sort of beings that *we* are ourselves: finite, embodied, and struggling with a determinate and recalcitrant world, just the kind of situation in which human beings find themselves.

However, it is not our finitude that is in question, but our freedom. We still have to ask whether, within this familiar set of limitations, human beings are really able to *determine themselves*. And that boils down to asking whether we can choose between two or more possible alternatives. A being is unfree insofar as whatever it is and does is imposed upon it by external *causes,* whereas a being is free insofar as whatever it is and does is the product of its own *choices* among alternative possibilities. Freedom therefore depends finally upon two rather simple capacities: the capacity to envision alternative possibilities and the ability to choose between them.

The human ability to entertain alternative possibilities is surely not in question. We scarcely need to review the varieties of human fiction, fantasy, imagination, and invention in order to pile up evidence that human beings can look beyond whatever is actual and already settled and envision possibilities. Quite obviously, human experience is not confined to the actual world, to awareness of what is already determined. We traffic as much in possibility as in actuality, as all our desires and aversions, hopes and disappointments, and fears and plans clearly attest.

All that remains to ask, then, is whether human beings are able to *choose* among the alternative possibilities they entertain.

We certainly *experience* ourselves as choosing among those alternatives. Insofar as we do, our experience fully conforms to the most basic requirements of freedom, and that leads us to employ the idea of freedom in describing and interpreting human activity. That simple experience of choosing among alternatives is therefore sometimes described as "the experience of freedom" and even cited as sufficient evidence that we are free. Of course, at this point I need not invoke that single point of contact between the concept of freedom and our own experience, for I have developed a more complex and articulated account of the necessary conditions of freedom and its relation to its world and its body—and that whole account seems to be entirely consistent with our general experience of the human condition. Thus, whether or not there are any *other* free beings in the universe, the understanding of freedom that has been worked out in preceding chapters can at least be applied to our own experience and seems capable of rendering a coherent interpretation of human existence.

But to recognize that the account of freedom I have developed fits our experience of the human condition is certainly not to *prove* conclusively that we are free. It only shows that that hypothetical conceptual structure is consonant with human experience, that it provides a consistent framework for understanding and interpreting our experience. But to show that human existence *may be* understood and interpreted in terms of the hypothesis that we are free is not to prove that it *must* be so understood and interpreted. For we cannot ignore the competing hypothesis that human actions are so completely determined by prior events as to make free, *self*-determining choice quite impossible. Determinism *also* claims to provide a consistent and accurate framework for understanding and interpreting human experience—and its advocates insist that it offers the only *scientific* theory of man and nature. To prove conclusively that human beings are free, one would have to show that this alternative, deterministic interpretation of the human condition is false.

But how could such a conclusive proof be attained? We are not dealing here with mathematically formulated hypotheses of a strictly scientific sort, such as would lend themselves to rigorous experimental verification. Nor does experimental verification of any hypothesis yield conclusive proof that it is the *only* theory capable of explaining the evidence in question, or that all alternative hypotheses are false. Moreover, the very nature of the deterministic hypothesis appears to make a conclusive proof of its falsity virtually impossible. Normally, one would try to prove that a scientific hypothesis is false by showing that some prediction based upon the hypothesis is not supported by empirical observations made under controlled experimental conditions. But one could never prove the deterministic hypothesis false in this way, because at most, one could only show that some *particular* causal hypothesis or purported "law" of human behavior is false. But that would not refute determinism, since it only invites the determinist to reply that there must be some *other* law that would succeed where this one failed. In order to disprove the deterministic hypothesis conclusively, then, one would have to prove that there are cases of human choice or action that could not be explained or predicted by any *conceivable* law, even ones that are as yet undiscovered or unformulated. That is obviously an impossible undertaking.

But while this suggests that we cannot prove conclusively, once and for all, that we are free, it should also remind us that the same is true of almost all theoretical hypotheses. If conclusive proof means disproving every possible competing hypothesis, then even the most rigorously formulated and empirically confirmed hypotheses of mathematical physics cannot be proved conclusively. However, if the question cannot be resolved at this level of generality, perhaps it will yield to a more modest and detailed scrutiny, one that focuses more sharply upon the difference between these two competing interpretations of the human condition. Instead of asking about the general applicability of the two theories to human experience, let us consider more exactly just where these two hypotheses differ in their interpretation of experience.

The exact point of difference is not hard to find. It rests upon the understanding of choice. Our experience of choosing between alternative possibilities seems to offer the most obvious and essential evidence of human freedom. But advocates of determinism either dismiss that experience as illusory or acknowledge the reality of choice but deny that choices are ever free. Although it may *seem to* an individual that he has chosen one possibility over another, equally possible alternative, they argue that his selection is really inevitable. In fact, he *could not possibly* have chosen any other alternative.[2] Some *other* person might have taken the other option under the same circumstances, and the individual himself might have elected it under *different* circumstances or antecedent conditions. But it is only in that rather abstract sense that a different choice was "possible." Given the causal conditions operative at the time, however, his choice was actually necessary and inevitable.

This is familiar terrain. We are back at the corner of Oak Street and the dispute over whether Domer Ringuette left Chicopee "of his own free will." Domer Ringuette believes that he acted freely—never more so than on this particular occasion. He claims that it was through that very decision to abandon his daily rat race that he genuinely *realized* his freedom. "I made up my mind to be free, and so I became free," he told the *Times* reporter. Yet we could easily imagine how a skeptical psychologist would attack that claim and argue that Ringuette's subjective experience of free choice was an illusion. Finding that Domer's circumstances were sufficient to determine his act, this skeptic would insist that even his experience of *having* a choice was illusory. For if the action was causally determined, only one course of action was ever possible in the first place, and there was no real option. Given the circumstances and his unhappy state of mind, Domer Ringuette couldn't possibly have remained in Chicopee another hour. Indeed, the same psychological skeptic maintained that the experience of choice is *always* illusory, a deception produced by our ignorance of the causes of our

---

2. This is simply the general thesis of determinism as applied to choice: "Determinism is the general philosophical thesis which states that for everything that ever happens there are conditions such that, given them, nothing else could happen" (Richard Taylor, "Determinism," in *The Encyclopedia of Philosophy* [New York: Macmillan, 1967], 359).

actions. If we knew those causes, we would see that there is never any genuine option, that the apparent alternative is never really possible.[3]

This is a very strong claim that treats a common human experience as illusory. Even if we grant that we may *sometimes* be mistaken in supposing we can choose either of two alternatives and that the experience of choice is therefore *sometimes* illusory, why should we suppose that we are *always* mistaken or deceived in such cases—that the experience is *always* an illusion? What is the basis of this claim?

I surveyed the grounds of the deterministic hypothesis in the Preface and Introduction. But since I have analyzed the idea of freedom at such length in the meanwhile, it is only fair to review and elaborate upon the case for determinism at this point and consider whether it can summon sufficient arguments for dismissing the experience of choice as an illusion instead of interpreting it as evidence that we are free.

Modern proponents of determinism associate it with a scientific view of the universe and may even claim the authority of science in support of their theory. But that is not because determinism has ever been scientifically proved. Indeed, I noted in the Introduction that it would be almost as difficult to *verify* the deterministic hypothesis as it would be to *falsify* it. A scientific proof of determinism would require the development of the human sciences to the point at which they could supply a comprehensive

---

3. Daniel Dennett dubs this "actualism," following A. J. Ayer, and quickly dismisses it as claiming that only what actually happens is possible. Dennett is eager to distinguish determinism from both "actualism" and "fatalism." But what form of determinism remains if we do dismiss both and admit a multiplicity of real possibilities? Over and above what is logically or physically possible, Dennett defends the importance of "epistemic" possibilities—what seems possible to someone insofar as it is consistent with what he already knows. He argues that "the notion that is relied upon, not only in personal planning and deliberation, but also in science, is a concept of possibility—and with it, of course, interdefined concepts of impossibility and necessity—that are, contrary to first appearances, fundamentally epistemic" (*Elbow Room* [Cambridge, Mass.: MIT Press, 1984], 148). But where does that leave us? Does this mean that the necessity claimed by determinism is also purely epistemic? How are we to assess the ingredient of epistemic possibilities in the constitution of the real once we acknowledge their role in human deliberation and decision? Unfortunately, the chapter dealing with these issues is one of the sketchiest sections in *Elbow Room,* as Dennett acknowledges in a closing parenthesis. Here, as in *Brainstorms,* I find that Dennett's reluctance to come to grips with metaphysical issues, his retreat to a merely epistemic "stance," leaves pivotal issues unresolved. Suffice it to say that the critique of determinism that follows here doesn't seem to apply to Dennett's version, whatever that might be, since I take it that determinism *does* imply that nothing else could happen than what actually *does* happen. In dismissing actualism, Dennett abjures determinism as I understand it. Chapter 9 below shows that I am in complete sympathy with Dennett's more general project of attempting to reconcile freedom with a naturalistic account of human agency. However, I am not at all sure how far our versions of naturalism agree.

set of laws sufficient to allow for the prediction and explanation of *all* human behavior. Moreover, these laws would have to be of the strict deductive form characteristic of classical Newtonian physics rather than the probabilistic, statistical laws characteristic of contemporary physics and behavioral science. For laws that only state probabilities would not entitle the determinist to his claim that an agent could not possibly have chosen or acted differently.[4] Now, these demanding conditions of proof have never been met, or even approximated. Actually, the deterministic theory and its denial of human freedom don't really rest upon empirical scientific proofs, but upon purely rational arguments, arguments that antedate the beginnings of modern science but that have to do with the very possibility of *any* rational or scientific understanding of man or nature. We must examine these purely rational motives of determinism more carefully.

Determinism argues that to suppose that man is free would be to concede that human choices are unintelligible, inexplicable, and unpredictable. For to understand or explain any occurrence fully, whether it be a natural event or a human action, one must be able to cite sufficient reasons for its happening. And to cite sufficient reasons is to give an adequate causal account of the event by discovering those antecedent events and causal laws that rendered its occurrence *necessary*. Since knowledge of these laws and causal antecedents would also enable one to *predict* the occurrence of the event in question, the requirements of adequate understanding and explanation are also the conditions of complete predictability.[5] Even if we do not *now* know the laws or all the relevant causal factors needed to provide such an explanation of a human act, we must assume that they exist, though still undiscovered. For to suppose otherwise would be gratuitously to suppose that the action is inexplicable and unpredictable *in principle*. To ascribe the act to "free choice" is simply to disguise our ignorance, rather like ascribing natural events to "chance" or "fate."

4. See pages 13–14 and note 13 to the Introduction.

5. For a clear contemporary presentation of this classic case for determinism, see Ted Honderich's *How Free Are You?* (Oxford: Oxford University Press, 1993), esp. chaps. 1 and 6. Honderich presents the same arguments at far greater length in *A Theory of Determinism* (Oxford: Oxford University Press, 1988), also chaps. 1 and 6, and far more succinctly in "One Determinism," his own contribution to his anthology, *Essays on Freedom of Action* (London: Routledge Kegan & Paul, 1973). Honderich's own argument for determinism doesn't stop with the classic argument summarized here. He does go on to appeal to empirical evidence drawn from neurophysiology and develops a theory about the relation between mind and brain to bolster the case for determinism. I cannot do justice to that theory here—and fortunately, I need not. For Honderich cannot prove that the brain is a deterministic physical system on purely *empirical* grounds. The classical a priori argument about explanation and causation remains essential to his case, as I believe he would acknowledge, and I think he would endorse the vigor with which I have set it forth here.

These are weighty arguments, and they deserve the most serious consideration. I could not dispose of them at the outset of my inquiry, before a more exact examination of the meaning of freedom. But now that I have provided a clearer conception of freedom, I am in a better position to assess these serious charges. Would the hypothesis that human beings are free imply that their actions must be unintelligible, inexplicable, and unpredictable?

Freedom and the Predictability of Human Actions

Let us first consider the charge of unpredictability, for in addition to the *a priori* argument cited above, it also carries considerable empirical weight, though not of a strictly scientific sort. After all, even though we may not be able to give impeccably rigorous scientific explanations of people's actions, human deeds are scarcely unpredictable. We are seldom greatly surprised by the actions of the persons we know best—and even when they do surprise us, we often can say afterwards, "I really should have expected that!" Our expectations and predictions concerning other human beings may not be precise or elegantly scientific, and they may often be disappointed; but if they did not more usually prove pretty accurate, we would live in constant uncertainty and insecurity. Social existence, the stability of political and economic institutions, the success of the astute entrepreneur, the whole humdrum, everyday process of human interaction—all depend upon a broad range of reliable predictability in human behavior. If human beings are free agents and if freedom of choice entails that human actions are strictly unpredictable, then it follows that these commonsense, everyday predictions would not be possible, leaving us in a dire practical impasse.

But is all this actually a necessary consequence of supposing that we are able to choose freely? Is the charge of unpredictability a valid one in light of the understanding of freedom that I have presented here?

There is this much truth in the charge. The idea of freedom entails a moment of indeterminacy in the choices of a free agent, and that does mean that *complete predictability* is impossible in principle. But this moment of indeterminacy is not at all the same as *complete indeterminism*. Examination of the necessary conditions of freedom has brought to light extensive and significant limitations upon this indeterminacy factor, limits that are entailed by the concept of freedom. The trouble is that the deterministic argument tends to treat every free choice as though it were made by a totally undetermined and indeterminate self, a disembodied self with no definite character and no situation in the world. It is not hard to see that this assumption stems from the deceptive notion of an absolute and utterly unconditioned freedom. The persuasive force of determinism depends largely upon casting the debate about freedom into the extreme alternatives of complete determinism and the complete indeterminism of a freedom that would be absolute. *But I have shown that absolute freedom is impossible—and therefore have concluded that complete indeterminism is as incompatible with freedom as is complete determinism.* The self cannot be free without being partially determined by the actual world and by its body, upon which its access to the world and action in the world depend. But to be thus *partially* determined is really only to be *conditioned* or *influenced* by the world, which is very different from a strict causal necessity that would leave no room for freedom.[6]

Consequently, although freedom does entail a margin of unpredictability, freedom and predictability are not opposites of one another. There is a temptation to suppose that the two stand in an inverse ratio to one another, so that the most free individuals would therefore be the least predictable. But this is by no means the case. An individual might exercise his freedom by adopting a strict regimen or resolutely pursuing a clearly defined goal or policy, thereby rendering his career all the more predictable, but no less free. One thinks of the rigid schedule Kant set himself in his latter years in order to complete his major works before he died. Kant is said to have adhered to his schedule so scrupulously and predictably that his neighbors could set their clocks by noting when he passed on his regular constitutionals. Any writer who has tried to stick to such a rigorous schedule of work knows very well how much self-control and self-discipline such "predictable" behavior demands.

Such examples serve as a reminder that the reality of freedom consists in the self's determination *of itself.* Only a newborn infant, fresh from the womb, would even approximate the condition of a completely indeterminate self. If human beings are free, then it does follow that at the moment of birth, an individual's future career of choices and actions is unpredictable both in fact and in principle. Even in this case, of course, one might hazard some shrewd forecasts about the infant's future career based upon

---

6. Cf. Robert Kane's argument to this same conclusion in *Free Will and Values* (Albany: State University of New York Press, 1985). Kane concludes, in a similar vein, "If you are going to reconcile the common intuitions that one controls one's free choices *and* that they are not determined, then you are going to have to talk about partial control. You cannot have it both ways" (155). (But whoever thought he had more? To insist upon total control would be to demand absolute freedom or none at all.) Cf. also Kane's "Two Kinds of Incompatibilism," in *Agents, Causes, and Events: Essays on Indeterminism and Free Will,* ed. Timothy O'Connor (Oxford: Oxford University Press, 1995), 140.

its genetic heritage and the historical and social circumstances of the parents. But precise and certain predictions would be impossible in principle. Not even an omniscient God could write the infant's biography in advance. However, *except* in this limiting case of the newborn infant, we have to think of human freedom in terms of the concrete individual, whose freedom is not merely conditioned by his body and by worldly circumstances but who has already determined himself through the prior exercise of freedom, whose character is already formed to a greater or lesser extent. For it must be emphasized that if the idea of freedom as self-determination is to mean anything at all, then the individual must actually and effectively *determine* himself through his choices. He cannot confront each decision as an undetermined power of choice, as though each choice were the very first of the series. Freedom entails the development of a character, such that the free individual will tend to make characteristic choices. The choices of a free individual whose character is already formed will therefore not be entirely unpredictable. Anyone who knows another person well, who is familiar with how he has chosen in the past and who sufficiently understands how he views the circumstances in which he is to choose again, will be able to form a fairly accurate notion of what possibilities he will tend to envision under those circumstances and how he will probably choose among them.

Since this describes the level of predictability that we actually achieve regarding our fellow human beings, there is no contradiction between supposing that people are free and acknowledging the type of ordinary, commonsense predictability about one another that is so important to practical life. Psychology aims at a more precise and rigorous form of prediction through the employment of scientific methods and controls. But even the most refined and rigorous psychological methods do not raise the level of predictability of human behavior beyond *probability* to strict *necessity*.

Freedom does not rule out the degree of predictability that we can actually attain in human affairs, then. It only conflicts with the deterministic ideal of an absolute predictability that would allow us to say that, in each case, the individual could not possibly choose any other alternative than the one he actually does choose. Indeed, in *some* instances, freedom does not even preclude something that approaches such complete predictability. On the one hand, circumstances may be such as to leave an individual little or no alternative, or no attractive and viable alternatives save one. (If the choice is between sure death by drowning and stepping into a safe lifeboat on a calm sea, we can be almost certain of the outcome.) On the other hand, the very exercise of freedom may be such as to cancel itself. A free individual may determine himself in ways that are destructive of his own freedom. Even if he is originally free, an individual may develop such a rigid character or submit himself so thoroughly to external influences as to make his choices and behavior almost completely predictable. Yet, even in these cases, freedom is not consonant with perfect predictability. Where circumstances actually allow of only one alternative, we have to contend with the familiar human capacity to envision and pursue alternatives that are not actually realizable, to attempt the impossible rather than settle for what is possible but unpalatable or out of character. The woman who believes that her baby is still in the cabin below may refuse to abandon ship even if the deck is already awash. In the case where existential freedom has been subverted or destroyed, we have to contend with the possibility that the individual just *may* take this particular occasion to turn against the grain, to try to reshape character and career.

The argument about freedom and predictability is thus restricted to a rather limited issue. The idea of freedom does entail an element of indeterminacy and a consequent margin of unpredictability in the choices and career of any free agent. To suppose that human beings are free is to admit that they are not *completely* predictable, even in principle. But this falls far short of warranting the argument that freedom presupposes an absolute indeterminism that would entail *complete unpredictability* of choice and action. As for the sorts of successful prediction that we actually can and do make, they are consistent with either hypothesis. The determinist can attribute the limited range of human predictability to our partial ignorance of the laws and causes of behavior. The proponent of human freedom can concede that the more we know of individuals and circumstances, the better we will be able to anticipate one another's actions—*without* conceding that we can never really choose between two clear alternatives. The difference is over whether there is some *margin* of unpredictability that cannot, in principle, be eliminated. It is a disagreement due to the conceptual requirements of the two hypotheses and will almost certainly never be resolved empirically. An empirical resolution could only occur through the combination of a perfectly complete and deductive science of human events and an almost omniscient grasp of actual causal circumstances, both of which would be required to achieve absolute predictability in human affairs. Such a combination is scarcely more than a behaviorist's dream.

But if this difference between the two hypotheses cannot be empirically resolved, that does not mean that we are simply left confronting an impasse regarding whether man is free. Rather, it shows that the charge of unpredictability is not enough to prove that the experience of choosing between alternative possibilities is an illusion. True, the determinist can still claim that the very appearance of an option is a deception due to our ignorance, that, if we knew enough, we would see that one purported alternative is really impossible because the individual will necessarily choose the other. But this is only an embarrassed attempt to reconcile the deterministic hypothesis with an experience that seems to invite the use of the concept of freedom—and to do so by appealing to knowledge that is not actually available! What the determinist cannot do is support his claim on the grounds that to understand choice as an exercise of freedom would be to concede that it is utterly unpredictable. For human freedom *is* consistent with *limited* predictability, the sort of predictability that is actually attainable in human affairs.

Freedom and Explanation

However, the issue of predictability is not the only one that determinism raises against describing human choices as free. The charge of unpredictability is itself only a corollary of a more basic objection: that to suppose human beings are free is to regard human actions as unintelligible and inexplicable because, to explain or understand any event, one must be able to give a complete account of the causes that made its occurrence necessary. To attribute a man's actions to "free choice" is not to explain them, but to gloss over a lack of understanding with empty words that explain nothing. The problem is to explain *why* the individual acted as he did. To refer the overt action back to an antecedent covert act of choosing only postpones the problem without solving it. One cannot explain why a man left his wife by saying that he did it "because he chose to do so." One must then go on to ask *why* he made that choice. And to explain either the act or the choice is to discover the causes from which it necessarily followed. To fall short of that, to stop at a point at which it can still be said that he might have chosen some other alternative, is simply to fail to explain why he chose *this* alternative rather than that one.[7] Does our present understanding of

7. For vigorous contemporary presentations of this classic argument, see Thomas Nagel, *The View from Nowhere* (Oxford: Oxford University Press, 1986) and Galen Strawson's "Libertarianism, Action, and Self-Determination," chap. 2 of *Freedom and Belief* (Oxford: Oxford University Press, 1986). Nagel and Strawson do not present this as an argument *for* determinism, but as an argument that holds against "autonomy" or self-determination whether one accepts or rejects determinism on other grounds. They therefore concentrate upon the demand for a complete explanation independent of any other features or implications of determinism. Accordingly, both couch the argument in terms of the demand for sufficient explanatory *reasons,* very broadly conceived, rather than in terms of causation. But both assume that the reasons that inform a choice cannot render it intelligible unless they rule out all other alternatives—that is, unless the reasons themselves are so "decisive" as to leave

freedom lend any support to these charges? If we believe we are free, do we also have to abandon all hope of understanding or explaining actions?

If we accept the deterministic account of the nature of explanation, then the argument against freedom is inescapable. The sort of explanation that this view requires *can* only be satisfied if every human act or decision is completely determined by efficient causes—that is, by antecedent conditions and events that leave nothing to chance, or to choice. Since freedom must be founded in *self*-determination, the very *idea* of freedom is in conflict with the requirements of this theory of explanation. Evidently, we must examine this ideal of explanation more carefully.

The problems that confront us here have long been of special concern to philosophers of history because historical knowledge is especially concerned with the explanation of human actions.[8] The deterministic criteria of causal explanation would require that the historian who undertakes to understand or explain any historical action or event must be able to cite antecedent events and conditions from which the action in question follows as a necessary result according to known causal laws. But this creates an embarrassment. The earnest working historian can only groan in despair or sputter in exasperation at these requirements. He knows very well that historians never provide the sort of explanations that determinism demands. "We can't even supply that kind of causal analysis in the biography of a single individual," he may protest. "And when it comes to the decision of a council of ministers or the vote of a legislative body, or a battle—or any event involving large numbers of persons—such explanations are beyond hope." But if historians never supply such explanations—and it appears unlikely that they ever *will* be able to supply them—it seems to follow that human history is unintelligible, that no one ever has understood or explained anything that has happened in human history, nor will anyone ever be likely to do so. Thus, although it charges that human freedom would imply that human actions are inexplicable, determinism itself seems

---

nothing to choice. They thereby embrace exactly the theory of explanation that I challenge in what follows. For specific critiques of Nagel and Strawson that parallel my own critique of this general argumentative strategy, see Honderich, *A Theory of Determinism*, 177–80, and Timothy O'Connor, "Agent Causation," in *Agents, Causes, and Events*. In chapter 4 of *Free Will and Values*, Robert Kane explores this argument and criticizes several strategies for responding to it, before developing his own subtle defense of free will in part 2 of the book. Kane presents both sides of the argument with meticulous critical rigor. In so doing, I think he tends to concede too much to his opponents and accepts the model of intelligibility that informs the argument for determinism rather uncritically, though he does lay the basis for challenging that model in a critique of Leibniz (91).

8. For a vivid presentation of this argument, see Tolstoy's celebrated statement of the case for historical determinism in part 2 of the epilogue to *War and Peace*.

to lead to exactly the same conclusion by a different path. The determinist may still maintain that human actions can, *in principle*, be explained. But he must insist that they never really *are* completely explained, since the available explanations never satisfy his standards.

That is, just as we must distinguish between predictability in principle and the levels of predictability that we can actually achieve, so we must distinguish here between the sorts of explanation of human acts that are actually given or attainable and what would, in principle, constitute a *complete* explanation. Determinism can readily grant that historians go a long way toward explaining events and actions, while still insisting that those explanations remain *incomplete* insofar as they fall short of showing how historical events or actions can be deduced from their antecedents according to causal laws. Thus, the determinist may concede, or even insist upon, the inadequacy of all *existing* explanations of human actions in order to insist that they are nonetheless intelligible and explainable *in principle* in accordance with the *ideal* of a complete causal analysis that would show them to be inevitable. At least this ideal of explanation imposes a demand for further inquiry in search of more adequate explanations, whereas to introduce the notion of freedom would simply be a sop to our ignorance, a license to the historian to lapse into smug satisfaction with incomplete explanations.

This is not the end of the dispute, however, because many historians and philosophers of history insist that this deterministic position dismisses existing historical explanations as incomplete only because it measures them against an alien and inappropriate standard. They argue that historians do not give truncated or partial deterministic explanations, but explanations of some other, distinctively historical type, which does not approximate, or even attempt to satisfy, the deterministic ideal model of causal analysis.[9]

I shall return to this controversy later. For present purposes, this brief account is sufficient to highlight certain points that pertain to the issue at hand. First, it draws attention to the extreme demands and implications of the deterministic theory of explanation. Determinism charges that the theory that human beings are free would entail that human actions are

---

9. On the distinctive character of causation in history and the social sciences, see Alasdair MacIntyre, "A Mistake About Causality in the Social Sciences," in *Philosophy, Politics, and Society: Second Series,* ed. P. Laslett and W. G. Runciman (Oxford: Basil Blackwell, 1964). For especially clear statements of the distinctive character of historical explanations, see Louis O. Mink, "The Autonomy of Historical Understanding," in *Historical Understanding* (Ithaca: Cornell University Press, 1987), 61–88, and the "Epilegomena" to R. G. Collingwood's *Idea of History* (Oxford: Oxford University Press, 1956), esp. "Human Nature and Human History" and "Historical Evidence."

inexplicable, but it bases this charge upon standards of explanation that imply that human actions never are and never have been fully explained. Even if we were to turn from history to psychology, we would not find examples of the kind of explanations that determinism demands—except, perhaps, in the more physiological branches of psychology that deal with reflexes and autonomous bodily processes rather than with intentional actions. Freud embraced psychic determinism, as is well known. But psychoanalytic explanations do not show that actions can be *deduced* from antecedent conditions and events as their necessary consequences. In fact, they are more like the genetic explanations commonly employed by historians than those of classical physics.[10] Second, the controversy about the nature and adequacy of historical explanations has led to serious questions whether the deterministic ideal of explanation is appropriate to understanding human actions. With those two points in mind, let us return to the question of the intelligibility of free actions or choices.

It would be easy to seize upon the "incompleteness" of existing explanations as a "proof" that we are free. But the determinist would rightly respond that, far from "proving" that human beings are free, this argument would only confirm the link between the invocation of freedom and the lack of any real explanation, and would thereby demonstrate that freedom is a vacuous term invoked to cover our ignorance. *The lack of a complete causal explanation can never serve as a proof of the existence of freedom.* However, it is fitting to point out that freedom is just as consistent with the kind of *incomplete* causal explanations of human acts that are actually attainable as is determinism. Advocates of determinism all too readily equate freedom with complete *in*determinism, with a complete *absence* of causes. To their own ideal of complete determinism, they oppose an undialectical conception of absolute freedom. But I have shown that this idea of absolute freedom is a will-o'-the-wisp, that freedom is possible only for a self that is partially determined by a world and by a body that limits its possibilities and that even renders the self vulnerable to *total* determination by the world. A free self cannot have an infinite range of choice, but only a set of opportunities limited by its world and its bodily capacities.

Thus, the very possibility of freedom depends upon *partial* determinism or *partial* causes. Of course, in one very strict sense, one cannot really speak

10. Cf. W. B. Gallie's contrast between the deductive model of causal explanation and the use of genetic explanations in history and in evolutionary theory, in "Explanations and History in the Genetic Sciences," *Mind* 64, no. 254 (1955): 160–80; reprinted in Patrick Gardiner, *Theories of History* (Glencoe, Ill.: Free Press, 1959), 386–402. For a more complete development of his view, see Gallie's *Philosophy and the Historical Understanding* (New York: Schocken Books, 1964).

of "partial determinism" or "partial causes." If the "cause" of an event is defined as "that from which the event follows necessarily according to a rule or law," then the cause must be the *complete* or *sufficient* cause, which may well involve a vast complex of contributory events and conditions, no one of which alone is sufficient to necessitate the effect in question. But in this strict use of the term, there is also no sense in the determinist speaking of an incomplete causal explanation, since *no* causal explanation will be attained until we can deduce the effect as the necessary consequence of antecedent conditions. However, insofar as we commonly speak of the *several* contributing causes of an event, we can also speak of partial causes and incomplete causal explanations. But in this looser sense, we may also speak of the "causes" of a free choice, not as conditions that made the outcome of the choice necessary, but as determinate conditions that either made it necessary *to* choose or made certain options possible or impossible, or made the selection of a certain option probable. Freedom of choice and action does not rule out such limiting conditions. Indeed, it could not exist without them. By the same token, the existence of such "causes" does not rule out freedom of choice and action.

Consequently, even within the framework of the deterministic theory of explanation, it cannot be argued that freedom would render human action *wholly* inexplicable and unintelligible. So far as determinism is prepared to accept existing historical and psychological explanations of human actions as partial or incomplete explanations, it must also admit that freedom allows for the partial explanation of human action and does not license the abandonment of causal inquiry in human affairs. It also follows that *one cannot point to existing, incomplete causal explanations as proof of the deterministic hypothesis, any more than one can point to their incompleteness as proof of freedom.* Incomplete or partial causal explanations are as much required by freedom as they are consistent with determinism.

However, this recognition still leaves the heart of the deterministic argument unscathed. We are still left with incomplete explanations. The determinist can rightly point out that an action that has been partially explained remains partially *un*explained and that whereas determinism demands that the explanation be completed, freedom would entail that it can never, in principle, be completed. There is no reason why the determinist should not *grant* that freedom is consonant with incomplete explanations and partial determinism. But that does not alter the central issue of principle. For it remains the case that insofar as freedom is introduced, the causal explanation *cannot* be completed. Therefore, to whatever degree actions are supposed to be free, to that same extent they must be supposed to be inexplicable. Thus, freedom still entails that human actions are unintelligible and inexplicable. An absolute freedom would imply that they are totally inexplicable; a finite freedom implies that they are *partially* inexplicable and unintelligible. The issue of principle is the same in either case.

This last argument brings us to the fundamental incompatibility between the hypotheses of freedom and determinism. The idea of freedom as *self*-determination is opposed in principle to the *complete* determination of every choice by external causes. That much is incontestable. It follows that human freedom would indeed entail that it is impossible in principle to achieve the kind of complete causal analysis of human action demanded by the deterministic ideal of explanation and understanding.

But must we accept that ideal? It is certainly not beyond question, as is indicated by the example of those historians and philosophers who have raised questions about its appropriateness as a standard of historical understanding and explanation. They dispute the claim that all historical explanations are partial, incomplete approximations to the deterministic ideal, and argue that there are other forms of explanation and understanding that are applicable to human actions. It would require a very long digression to recapitulate all the arguments that have been developed in the course of this controversy about historical explanation.[11] It will be better to examine this issue independently so as to focus more directly on the problem of the intelligibility of free choice.

Causal Explanation and Human Understanding

Must *all* understanding and explanation aim at the deterministic ideal of a complete causal analysis? When we speak of the "deep understanding" between two friends, or of two men "reaching an understanding," do we mean that each is capable of providing a causal analysis of the other's action? If I ask someone to explain to me why he acted as he did, am I really requesting that he demonstrate that his action was the necessary consequence of antecedent events? Our ordinary employment of the terms "explanation" and "understanding" in human affairs scarcely seems to support the claim that the deterministic ideal embodies the single and exclusive standard of intelligibility or explanation. Of course, everyday discourse cannot supply a *refutation* of that claim. The determinist may very

---

11. The literature on this controversy is extensive, especially in discussions of the status and method of historical explanation. A fair selection may be found in Patrick Gardiner's *Theories of History* (Glencoe, Ill.: Free Press, 1959) or in William H. Dray's *Philosophical Analysis and History* (New York: Harper & Row, 1966).

well respond that ordinary usage is quite naturally satisfied to demand only the sorts of incomplete explanation that are ordinarily attainable, but that the standard implicit in those demands is still the deterministic ideal. However, ordinary discourse isn't just content to settle for partial deterministic explanations. Upon closer examination, common usage also suggests that there are other forms of explanation and understanding. When one man says to another, "Ahh, now I understand you!" it is probably the *meaning* of the other's words or actions to which he refers rather than their causes. When I ask a friend to explain her actions, I am more likely to be inquiring about her *purposes* than about the *causes* of the acts. In general, the understanding and explanation of human actions may have to do not only with efficient causes, but also with the meanings, purposes and intentions, and personality of the agent.[12]

This brings us to the very nub of the controversy. Determinism ultimately rests upon the principle of sufficient reason, rightly insisting that to explain anything is to be able to supply sufficient reasons why it should be just so and not otherwise. But determinism goes on to insist that sufficient *reason* must be interpreted to refer to *efficient causes* that are sufficient to render an occurrence necessary. To insist upon such sufficient causes is not to deny the other forms of understanding mentioned above. The determinist can acknowledge all of them, even insist upon their importance, while still insisting that explanation and understanding are never *complete* unless they supply a sufficient *cause*. Once the meaning or purpose of the act is clear, he may argue, we still have the task of explaining why the agent adopted that meaning or purpose rather than some other, and we can only explain *that* through a causal inquiry.[13]

---

12. Indeed, the difference between these two forms of intelligibility has been a central topic of inquiry in modern philosophy of history and the social sciences, beginning with Weber and Dilthey and running through Jaspers and Collingwood to Gadamer, Ricoeur, and Charles Taylor, among others. See also Robert Kane's defense of "teleological intelligibility" in "Two Kinds of Incompatibilism" and Harry Frankfurt's account of decision as "making up one's mind" in section 6 of his "Identification and Wholeheartedness" (in *The Importance of What We Care About* [Cambridge: Cambridge University Press, 1988]), two accounts that do not stem from that "hermeneutic" tradition. It is therefore all the more striking that both Kane and Frankfurt call attention to the *circularity* of the kind of rational decisions that they describe, since the circularity of hermeneutic understanding has been a central motif for thinkers concerned with the nature of explanation and understanding in "the human sciences."

13. Cf. Nagel, *The View from Nowhere*, 115–17, where Nagel considers and rejects the resort to "intentional explanations" on just these grounds. Of course, this argument begs the question by assuming that an intelligible explanation of human action must be such as to rule out all other alternatives—and thus leave nothing to choice. But Nagel recognizes that this reflects an objective point of view that projects an incoherent ideal of absolute freedom:

In the final analysis, then, the case for determinism rests entirely upon the equation of sufficient reason with a necessitating efficient cause. If we accept that equation, the deterministic rejection of freedom as tantamount to unintelligibility follows unavoidably. But that equation is scarcely a self-evident or incontestable truth. It could enjoy such an unimpeachable status only if "reason" and "cause" were completely synonymous, which is not the case. For there is another, quite common and legitimate meaning of "reason" that is entirely consistent with freedom.

When we search for "sufficient reasons" in circumstances where a practical decision is at issue, as happens in the deliberations of a policy-making body or a court of law, we are not inquiring after efficient causes. We are, rather, asking for reasons sufficient to *justify* or warrant the decision. And to discover such reasons is to explain the decision, not in the sense of showing that it is *necessary* or could not have been otherwise (since human beings do not always adopt the most rational and just course or policy), but in the sense of discovering that it *is*, indeed, justified or warranted by those reasons. Moreover, even when we are not ourselves satisfied that the reasons justify the decision, even where we think the reasons for the choice were abominable or the reasoning process illogical, we may *still* find that the reasons given are sufficient to explain the decision. That is, we may find it quite understandable that *this* individual decided as he did for *these* reasons.

The determinist may object that he can readily include the reasoning process among the efficient causes of the decision. But that is beside the point, which is that there are two entirely different senses of "sufficient reason" involved here, as even the determinist must admit. For even if we find that the reasoning informing an agent's decision is logically impec-

---

[F]or to be really free, we would have to act from a standpoint completely outside ourselves, choosing everything about ourselves, including all our principles of choice—creating ourselves from nothing, so to speak.

This is self-contradictory: in order to do anything, we must already be something. . . . Here, as elsewhere, the objective standpoint creates an appetite which it shows to be insatiable. (118)

For, as Kierkegaard put it, we must begin *with* the beginning, since we cannot begin "*in* the beginning." And in what follows, Nagel describes freedom as a dialectic of detachment and engagement that exhibits obvious parallels with Kierkegaard's account of freedom, or "spirit," in *The Sickness Unto Death* and elsewhere. By the end of chapter 7, Nagel's critique of "autonomy" turns out to be a critique of absolute freedom in favor of the sort of finite freedom that I have shown to be the only coherent conception of freedom. But Nagel's insistence upon the irreconcilability of the objective and subjective points of view seems to me to jeopardize that outcome. See my comments on this in note 10 to Chapter 7 above.

cable and that the reasons are sufficient to warrant the decision, that is by no means the same as to say that those reasons constitute an adequate *efficient cause* of the decision. Unfortunately, the *causal* efficacy of reasons is *not* a direct function of their *validity*.[14] If the most rational course were also causally compelling, human beings would presumably behave much more rationally than they do. Since that is not the case, the determinist's ideal of explanation will require that he seek out efficient causes to explain *why* the agent reasoned logically, assuming that the agent did, why he entertained *these* considerations and premises and not others and, finally, why he chose to follow the more rational course in the end rather than some other.

On the other hand, if we suppose that human agents are free, then in trying to understand their actions and decisions, we do not seek an explanation that would prove that the choice could not possibly have been otherwise. We are, rather, seeking the *grounds* for the decision in the sense of the reasons and purposes that led the agent to select one alternative

---

14. The thesis that explanations in terms of the agent's reasons and motives are to be understood as versions of causal explanation has been vigorously argued by Carl Hempel in "Rational Action," in *Proceedings and Addresses of the American Philosophical Association* (Yellow Springs, Ohio: Antioch Press, 1962) and by Donald Davidson in "Actions, Reasons, and Causes," originally published in the *Journal of Philosophy* in 1963 and republished with other essays by Davidson in *Essays on Actions and Events* (Oxford: Oxford University Press, 1980). But both of these essays have been subjected to searching criticism by Davidson himself in later essays. For his sympathetic but telling critique of Hempel, see "Hempel on Explaining Action," essay 14 in *Essays on Actions and Events*. Davidson also subjects his own original argument to a barrage of criticisms and qualifications in the series of later essays that follow it in *Essays on Actions and Events*. (He summarizes these revisions and qualifications in his introduction to that volume.) In particular, the essay "Psychology as Philosophy" argues that a rigorously scientific psychology is impossible just because an appeal to reasons, beliefs, desires, etc., introduces ingredients of meaning and interpretation that require understanding of a very different order from nomological explanations in the natural sciences. In effect, he rediscovers the basis of the distinction between the methods of the humanities and those of the natural sciences as Dilthey had formulated it.

In the end, Davidson still seems to believe that actions explained and understood on the basis of motives, reasons, and intentions are also explainable by appeal to causal laws under some other description. But it is hard to decide how much substance is left to that thesis by the end of the book, or even whether Davidson's doctrine of the causal role of reasons and motives is deterministic. In some passages, Davidson suggests that his conception of causation is nondeterministic. In others, his argument seems to assume determinism, as Myles Brand suggests in "Particulars, Events, and Actions," in *Action Theory*, ed. Myles Brand and Douglas Walton (Dordrecht: D. Reidel, 1976), 137. For example, Davidson's argument in "Mental Events" assumes the "Principle of the Nomological Character of Causality": "[W]here there is causality there must be a law: events related as cause and effect fall under strict deterministic laws" (*Essays on Actions and Events*, 208). But then he adds in a footnote that "the stipulation that the laws be deterministic is stronger than required by the argument and will be relaxed" (208n).

rather than another.[15] And to find those grounds is to explain the decision. We may abhor the agent's purposes; we may find his reasoning fallacious and his premises unfounded in his actual circumstances. But if we can understand how an individual who embraced *those* purposes and reasoned in *that* fashion could have chosen the alternative that he actually adopted, then we can understand the decision.

However, since the explanation of the grounds of the choice falls short of showing that the outcome was necessary, there must be some additional factor that accounts for the action, since someone might have entertained the same reasons and with the same intentions, yet not gone on to act in the same way. That additional factor is the decision itself, which adopts *this* option for *these* reasons and forgoes other possible alternatives in so doing. This is just the point upon which determinism fixes its attention and will claim that the invocation of free choice is simply a way of papering over our ignorance of the true causes of the outcome. But determinism here risks begging the question by simply assuming that such causes *must* exist, whereas the point was to *prove* that they must exist by showing that actions cannot otherwise be explained. Again, the fundamental and indispensable assumption of such a proof is that all intelligible explanation rests upon the concept of a necessitating efficient cause.[16]

The advocate of freedom may simply reject that assumption, however, and insist that free choice is an equally intelligible category of explanation. Of course, it is true that it is never a complete or self-sufficient explanation of an action to say, "She did it because she chose to do it." One must ask about the reasons and purposes informing the decision and even about the

---

15. The reasons for choosing one alternative need not entail reasons for *rejecting* the other — except for the moment. The unchosen alternative is not therefore *rejected;* the road not taken may only be postponed — although, as Robert Frost's poem deftly allows, I may never come this way again:

> Oh, I kept the first for another day!
> Yet knowing how way leads onto way,
> I doubted if I should ever come back.

16. Except in the case of Leibniz, whose determinism is based upon *formal* causation, since everything that will ever happen to a monad is implicit in the formula of its essence. But Leibniz is scarcely an exception to the main point at issue here, since he, too, identifies explanation with deduction. Indeed, his rather peculiar doctrine of formal causation derives from his belief that all true statements are analytically true because the predicate of any true statement about a subject must inhere in the subject. This leads, in turn, to the doctrine that no entity can have any contingent or accidental properties and, thence, to his conception of a universe of "windowless" monads that do not interact with one another. In such a universe, there can be no efficient causation in any recognizable sense. The critique of the standard, efficient-cause version of determinism applies to Leibniz's version "in spades."

causal factors that partially determined or conditioned the agent. One may even need to pass beyond the immediate conditions of the decision in search of *their* conditions. One may ask about the larger purposes that explain the immediate purpose at hand. One may ask about the more basic assumptions in order to explain the reasons directly informing the decision. One may examine the agent's biography in search of an explanation of her character, and this search in turn will lead back to prior events and decisions that have shaped her character. Free choice is not a self-sufficient category of explanation, then. *But neither is efficient causation.* We are led into the same kind of regressive series of explanation in causal inquiry as in the case of choice. To show that an event follows necessarily from certain antecedent conditions according to some law is not to show that either those prior conditions or that law is necessary. One may go on to ask about the conditions of those conditions or seek to find some more fundamental law from which the one in question may be derived. Thus, if the use of the concept of free choice does not supply an absolute and final explanation of an action, nor does the use of the category of causation.

The Intelligibility of Free Choice

Are we therefore to be left confronting a dogmatic conflict between two explanatory categories? Let us examine the grounds of this conflict more carefully to see if there is any way of avoiding a sheer impasse. Determinism has a reason for denying that free choice is an intelligible explanatory concept. That reason may be stated roughly as follows: To invoke the concept of freedom of choice in explaining any action is to admit, and even insist, that the act *does not necessarily follow* from any set of antecedents, from any premises known to be true. This sounds very close to the tautological assertion that every act *must* be necessary because otherwise some act would not be necessary, and that *would* amount to a merely dogmatic confrontation with the concept of freedom, which implies that at least *some* acts must *not* be necessary. But in its best formulations, the deterministic argument is not simply a dogmatic insistence upon necessity. On the contrary, it is founded in still more fundamental claims about the requirements of explanation. The determinist might state these claims in the following way: To provide a rational explanation of any event is to show that it can be rationally deduced from premises that are independently known to be true. But to establish this is to establish that the occurrence of the event is *necessary,* since otherwise no such deduction would be possible. But the very notion of freedom rules out such necessity and therefore makes rational explanation impossible.

This is the final source of the deterministic argument against freedom. It rests upon an identification of the conditions of intelligible explanation with the conditions of deductive proof. *Determinism's fundamental ideal of intelligibility is that of deductive rational argument, whose paradigms are the systems of pure mathematics and logic, and it is this ideal of intelligibility that leads determinism to insist that no explanation that does not show an event to be necessary can be complete.*[17]

It is certainly true that freedom cannot be reconciled with *this* definition of intelligibility. In that sense, and only in that sense, it is legitimate to say that freedom would render actions inexplicable and unintelligible. But is this not a rather narrow conception of intelligibility?[18] After all, how much *can* we understand—of ourselves or of external nature—on the basis of pure deductive reasoning alone? Very little! Much of our understanding must draw upon our experience and relate eventually back to that experience. This is quite obviously true of simple empirical concepts such as "green" or "sour," but also holds for most concepts that are important to understanding other persons, such as "envy," "hope," "contempt," and "desire"—even "procrastination" and "indecision." Of course, experience is not a complete or self-sufficient source of understanding. We must employ concepts that allow us to organize and interpret experience in a coherent way if that experience is to be intelligible, just as we must draw

17. Of course, there are forms of fatalism that do not appeal to the paradigms of mathematics and deductive logic but conceive of the course of events as ruled by a divine providence or fate that is mysterious and inscrutable. But determinisms rooted in such conceptions cannot reject freedom on behalf of clear causal explanation or intelligibility. They are all too close to the sort of appeal to chance or blind luck that scientifically minded determinists find even more unacceptable than freedom.

18. Robert Nozick poses the same question in "Choice and Indeterminism" (in *Philosophical Explanations* [Cambridge, Mass.: Harvard University Press, 1981]). After summarizing the "currently fashionable" (as of 1981) view of psychological explanation as requiring that any choice would have to be Turing-machine computable (hence, logically deducible), Nozick concedes that any choice that could be understood in this sense would not be free. But then, he asks: "Does the fact that we cannot, in this sense, understand what a free choice is, indicate some defect in the notion of a free choice or rather is the defect in the view that this mode of understanding is the sole mode? Is the result, that we cannot understand what a free choice is, an *artifact* of this method of understanding?" (303). This essay also appears in Timothy O'Connor's anthology, *Agents, Causes, and Events,* where essays by Thomas Nagel, Carl Ginet, and Roderick Chisholm also warn against uncritically assuming this as the sole mode of explanation. Indeed, as Nozick suggests, to assume this model of explanation is really to beg the question that is at issue here from the very outset.

upon experience to provide content and recognition of those same concepts if *they* are to be fully intelligible.

The preceding inquiry has shown that it is possible to conceive of freedom in a way that is consistent with human experience and that offers an internally coherent conceptual framework for interpreting that experience. That is, it offers a way of understanding our experience and of explaining human actions *without* representing them as necessary, inevitable, and deducible from antecedent conditions. Whether this manner of understanding human actions is finally intelligible does depend upon whether *choice* is an intelligible explanatory concept. But if we can understand what it means to say that an individual chose to adopt one of two alternative possibilities rather than the other, then we can understand the use of choice as an explanatory concept. And human experience furnishes all that is required to make this understanding possible. For the experience of making such choices is a very common one, which supplies adequate empirical grounds for recognizing the meaning of the concept of choice when it is employed in an explanation. Of course, it can never be a sufficient or complete explanation of an act to merely say that the agent *chose* so to act. For as I have shown, the act of choice can never be an exercise of absolute freedom, but only of a finite freedom that is subject to causal influences and conditioned by the individual's character, his purposes, his grasp of his situation, the reasons that he recognizes as relevant and cogent, etc. All of these factors may be pertinent and important to explaining the alternatives envisioned and the resultant choice. All that the concept of freedom requires is that we be able to understand that *part* of the explanation of the individual's act is that he chose *this* option over other alternatives that were also available under those conditions. And, again, our own experience of making such choices is sufficient to allow us to understand this.

"But determinism insists that the experience of choice is illusory," it may be objected. "Determinists argue that to suppose that the choice is free is an error due to our ignorance of the real causes." True, this is where we began. And determinism is right to insist that the experience of choice is no *proof* of human freedom. But the above objection will not hold up. To defend its deductive ideal of explanation, determinism cannot revive the claim that the experience of choice is illusory. For it is precisely that theory of explanation that was supposed to provide the proof that the experience of choice is illusory! I began by asking the determinist, "Why *must* this experience be dismissed as illusory? Why *can't* people choose among the possibilities they envision?" The answer was that this would make human action inexplicable and unintelligible. This answer has now been traced to its source in the assumption that all explanation must conform to the model of deductive proof, and *that* assumption cannot, in turn, be defended on grounds that the experience of choice is illusory, for that is what was to be proved in the first place.

However, if the whole controversy rested upon this one point, we would still be left with a quandary about the experience of choice and the intelligibility of free choice as an explanatory category. And indeed, much of the controversy over freedom and determinism has revolved endlessly about this single, pivotal point, with neither side able to dislodge the other, because the arguments on each side are themselves circular. The determinist argues either that the experience of choice is illusory or that the concept of a free choice is unintelligible. But that charge of unintelligibility is founded upon the supposed exclusive validity of the deductive model of explanation, which *presupposes* that the concept of a free choice is unintelligible and that the experience of choosing is illusory. The determinist's opponent argues that the concept of freedom must be employed in order to understand and interpret the experience of choice, but appeals to that experience of choice in order to supply content and empirical validity for the concept of freedom. Clearly, so long as both sides focus upon this one point of contention, there can be no escape from the deadlock between them.

Freedom, Determinism, and Time

Once again, we have returned to the dilemma from which we began, the old question about whether human beings are free. But the terms of that dilemma have changed in the interim. We no longer need circle futilely about the question of free choice. If the whole case for human freedom rested entirely upon the connection between the idea of freedom and the experience of choice, we would still be left in a stalemate between freedom and determinism. But this is not the case. For we have discovered that the idea of freedom involves *a whole complex of concepts* and not simply the concept of free choice.

And the same holds on the side of experience. It is not merely the experience of making choices that is at issue in this dispute, but virtually the whole of human experience. Along with the experience of choosing, there is also involved the experience of facing a future that is open and pluripotent, that has yet to be brought to a state of determinacy not only by my own choices and those of other persons but by the further course of natural events. According to determinism, this experience of an open future is *also* simply an illusion due to our ignorance. Everything that is yet to happen will occur of necessity, whether because of an extramundane fatality, supernatural destiny, divine providence—or entirely through the operation of natural causes. A perfect scientist, or a computer, supplied with a complete set of data and all the laws of nature would recognize that there is actually only *one* possible future course of events. The future is no more uncertain or undetermined than the past or the present. It is only our lack of knowledge that makes it *seem* to be open and unsettled. But this means that our experience of the difference between the past, present, and future is entirely askew. For our experience of the unknown *future* is qualitatively different from our experience of the unknown *past,* while both differ from our experience of the present. We experience time as a process of becoming and perishing, where what has not yet become differs fundamentally and ontologically from what has already perished, and both are different in principle from what *now* exists.

Thus, it is not only our experience of choice but the profoundly *temporal* character of *all* human experience that conflicts with the deterministic ideal of explanation and intelligibility. In the classical mechanistic metaphysics that was associated with Newtonian physics, this clash between determinism and our experience of temporal processes was obscured by the role of *motion*. For, although the particles that compose the universe do not change, according to that view, and although the laws of nature also do not change, those laws are the laws of the motion of particles, and all change was seen as reducible to such motion. But since the particles themselves were not supposed to act or change and could not *initiate* any movement, motion itself had to be taken as a brute given, so that the final source or principle of motion and change was an enigma that either remained unexplained or was "explained" by resorting to a supernatural or divine cause. Thus, the real problem of the intelligibility of time remained obscure.

For the real problem is that the fundamental assumptions and underlying logic of the deterministic hypothesis are such as to vitiate the reality of time as we experience it, and render the temporality of human experience illusory. This is not to say that most determinists would flatly and directly deny that time is real. Rather, like the classical mechanist, they take the process of becoming and change to be something that is merely *given* and that has to be explained, but without clearly recognizing that their standards of explanation require that it be *explained away* by showing that the future that is yet to come is every bit as settled and determined as the past that has already been. To explain my present decision would be to show that it is no more "open" than those I have already made a week ago. The decision I am about to make is already a "foregone conclusion," as deducible from its causes as the ones I made twenty years ago.

Process and change must be explained away because the deterministic ideal identifies complete explanation with deductive reason and efficient causation, and this identification leads determinists to regard the causal relationship as a *deductive, logical* relation. But logical relations are *atemporal,* which places the temporal sequence involved in causation in a very problematic status. The result is that strict determinism conceives of the universe as a set of systematic complexes that are called "states of the universe," any one of which may be deduced from any other because all are interrelated by connections that are logically deductive and necessary.

Of course, these states of the universe are *supposed* to form a temporal sequence. But the temporal character of this sequence is an enigma. For to say that the states of the universe are "necessarily connected" in the *logical* sense is to say that, given the existence of any one, it is *impossible* that the others do not also exist, for that is the logical definition of necessity. What is necessary could not possibly *not* exist.[19] That means that if one moment exists, all the rest *must* also exist.[20]

But that is in direct contradiction with time as we experience it. For it is characteristic of a temporal sequence that the existence of any one state or moment in the series entails *the nonexistence of all the others*. Indeed, that is the simplest and clearest way to draw the contrast between time and space. Points, or regions in space, can coexist, whereas moments or periods of time cannot. Chicago and Paris can both exist at once, whereas the nineteenth and twentieth centuries cannot, nor can Monday and Wednesday, or any two points in time. The moments of time form a *series* such that only one moment exists "at a time," which means that each moment excludes all the others.

Insofar as determinism insists that causal relations are deductive, necessary connections between events, it entails that what we *experience* as a temporal sequence is not really temporal, that the appearance of temporal

---

19. Modal logic defines necessity as $\sim\!\diamond\!\sim$, denial possibility denial, or "impossible that not."

20. Cf. Paul Weiss's discussion of the relation between deductive necessity and actual temporal production, in *Modes of Being* (Carbondale, Ill.: Southern Illinois University Press, 1954), 40-45. Robert Neville elaborates on the same point in chapter 6 of *The Cosmology of Freedom* (New Haven: Yale University Press, 1974), 150–54. Neville concludes that "the determinist thesis, if stated with the universality of the claim that an event is totally determined by antecedents, contradicts the thesis that there is real change in present moments. Our very experience of the present, in contrast to the past and future, is sufficient to allow us to reject it. Furthermore, the determinist thesis gains its initial plausibility only by interpreting the experience of causation; since change is incompatible with determinism, the determinist thesis loses its initial plausibility" (153–54).

succession in the states of the universe is an illusion of our experience. It is as though the series of states of the universe were laid out side by side, like the states of the union, and we were traveling through them. But then our *traveling* supplies the temporality, the experience of novelty and succession, and *it* is not accounted for by this hypothesis. The deterministic identification between a causal sequence and a logical sequence results in the conception of the universe as a system of *being* that excludes all *becoming*.

This result is not peculiar to determinism. Any thinker who identifies explanation with deductive proof or who sees deductive reason as the final criterion of reality or as the standard of genuine knowledge will be pushed toward a similar conclusion. The history of Western thought provides numerous examples, beginning with Parmenides, whose rigorous logic led him to conclude that true reality is a unity of being that admits of no motion or change and that the experience of time pertains only to appearance, to "the way of seeming," which is a route of error and illusion rather than of truth. Similarly, it was the ideal of mathematical reason, as much as anything, that led Plato to identify truth and being with timeless forms and to consign the world of "becoming" to the status of mere appearance. A series of subsequent Western thinkers, from Leibniz in the seventeenth century to Jean-Paul Sartre in the twentieth, have reiterated this Platonic conclusion that being itself is atemporal, that becoming and time belong only to the order of phenomena, the world of appearances. Kant's *Critique of Pure Reason* was a penetrating critique of this long tradition, attacking it precisely because it reads the demands of deductive reason into the nature of being itself. Kant clearly recognized, for example, that the deterministic ideal of causal necessity is the result of construing the experience of temporal succession in the terms of a logical, deductive sequence, but that deductive reason alone is atemporal and cannot account for temporal succession.[21] And yet, even Kant still insists that we must understand nature deterministically and still regards time as a mere *phenomenon* that is due to the limitations of man's sensible intuition.

Why does the ideal of deductive reason lead so unfailingly to the conclusion that time is not ultimately real? The answer is bound up with the very foundations of deductive logic. Deductive logic is founded upon the principles of identity and noncontradiction, to use the terms of traditional logic. Modern formal logic states this point in a slightly different way by insisting that deduction derives its necessity from the fact that all deductive proofs are tautological. That is, they establish that the conclusion of the proof does not state anything that was not already stated in the premises. It

---

21. Cf. "The Schematism of the Pure Concepts of Reflection," in *Critique of Pure Reason*, trans. Norman Kemp Smith (New York: St. Martin's Press, 1961), 180–87.

is therefore self-contradictory to assert the premises but deny the conclusion. This is sometimes expressed by saying that the conclusion of a
deductive proof "does not say anything new" or that the conclusion possesses "only a psychological novelty." That is, the conclusion only *appears*
novel to us, whereas in reality it has been implicit in the premises all along.
It is scarcely surprising, then, that the deductive ideal leads its adherents to
relegate time to the status of appearances, that is, to regard the process of
becoming as "merely psychological" rather than ultimately real. Determinism, in particular, regards the relation of an effect to its causal conditions as
though it were the relation of the conclusion of a deductive proof to its
premises.[22] But this would mean that the effect must already be implicit in
the complete cause and that there is consequently no real novelty involved
in the transition from cause to effect. Application of the deductive model to
the series of states of the universe or moments of time rules out real
temporal succession because the assumption that the sequence is deductive
means that to assert the existence of one moment or state and deny that of
the others would be self-contradictory. If the moments of time or series of
states of the universe form a deductive series, then each member of the
series must already be implicit in its predecessors, and there can only be a
"psychological" or "apparent" novelty in passing from one to the next.

But, of course, one does not *dispose* of the problem of time simply by
relegating it to the world of appearance or sense experience. Whether or
not we accept it as "real," the temporality of the sensible world still needs to
be explained—and such views can only explain time by appealing to some
ultimate principle that is irrational by their own standards. Thus, by using
the myth of the *dēmiourgos,* who creates a "moving image of eternity,"[23] Plato
disguises the problem of introducing time into his cosmology. But since the
dēmiourgos is only a myth and not a serious explanatory principle, the real
source of becoming and time must lie elsewhere, and in the final analysis,
Plato must resort either to "irrational necessity" (*ananke*) or to the completely formless and indeterminate "receptacle." Aristotle invokes a similarly indeterminate and irrational principle that he calls "prime matter,"
which he posits as the substratum for all substantial change. In classical
mechanics, it is the existence of motion that is simply accepted as an

---

22. An exception must be made for Hume and his ilk. Hume argues that there is "as much
necessity" in human affairs as there is in physical processes. But the brunt of Hume's own
analysis of causality is a demonstration that there are no necessary connections of a logical,
deductive sort in the realm of temporal events. In the end, he leaves us with probabilities, not
necessity. See pages 13–14 and notes 14 and 15 to the Introduction. Similarly, one would have to
make an exception of "methodological" determinists like Ernest Nagel, since they only regard
determinism as a sort of regulative ideal for scientific inquiry, not as a theory about real events.

23. *Timaeus* 38d.

inexplicable "given" that is *intelligible* only through a knowledge of timeless laws. Kant "explains" time only by ascribing it to the limitations of human sensible experience, which can only entertain discursively, one by one, what an absolute intellect might grasp all together in a single timeless intuition.

It is easy to see why these views have to resort to maneuvers of this sort in order to come to terms with temporal process. For if reason, intelligibility, and explanation are all defined in terms of deductive logic and if deductive relationships are atemporal, that means that the source of becoming and time has been excluded at the outset from the domain of what is intelligible and explainable. These thinkers can "explain" time only by violating their own rules of explanation. Yet even in so doing, they prove themselves consistent with their own principles, for their conception of reason compels each of these thinkers to appeal to an "irrational" principle in order to cope with temporal processes.

The charges of irrationalism and indeterminism that deterministic thinkers employ in attacking freedom thus recoil upon determinism itself. Determinism does not *escape* these charges by insisting upon a necessary connection between cause and effect. On the contrary, just because it represents the causal relation as a deductive relationship, determinism must appeal to an indeterminate or irrational principle in order to account for the fact that the causal relation itself involves temporal succession. If the standard of deductive reason *is* accepted as absolute, then freedom, determinism, and time must *all* be irrational. *Might it not be wiser to seek some less static and confining conception of rationality?*

❊ Part IV ❊

The
Liberation
of Nature

Of course, ants are different. They have a wonderful everlasting piece of engineering on which to work—the anthill.

The worthy ants began with their anthill and will most likely end with it, which is greatly to the credit of their single-mindedness and perseverance. But man is frivolous and unaccountable and perhaps, like a chess player, he enjoys the achieving rather than the goal itself.

—Fyodor Dostoevsky, *Notes from the Underground*

So speaks Dostoevsky's underground man. Observing the world from his mouse hole beneath the floor, he is scarcely a respectable authority. Yet his aphorism effectively summarizes the current predicament of this inquiry. Conceiving nature in the image of the mathematical reason of the engineer, he sees it as doomed to end as it began. He can therefore only make room for human originality and historical novelty by invoking a frivolous irrationality that renders human action "unaccountable." Yet the image of the chess player suggests the alternative option of a reason that serves and begets choice rather than confining it to single-minded perseverance, a self-imposed pattern that opens the way to an endlessly unpredictable play of opposing purposes that nevertheless depends upon the ability of each player both to understand and to anticipate the other's play.

In Part IV, I challenge the jurisdiction of the mathematical, deductive model of reason and the conception of nature modeled upon it—and show that we can abandon that ideal without resorting to a frivolous and unaccountable caprice. Chapter 9 argues that deductive reason is not the only alternative. A dialectical model of reasoning can accommodate the facts of temporal experience and the explanation of actions as freely chosen. Yet the most ambitious versions of historical determinism have depended upon a dialectical conception of reason. Closer reflection upon the difference between dialectical and deductive logic shows that although dialectical reason meets the demands of historical explanation, it does not warrant the claims of historical inevitability to be found in the works of Hegel and Marx. Sartre offers a clearer account of the relationship between freedom, time, and dialectic. But Sartre's account raises bewildering questions about the place of human freedom within nature so long as nature is conceived as "governed" by principles of deductive reason.

Chapter 10 shows that the preemption of freedom as an exclusively human privilege and the relegation of all nature to mechanical necessity together constitute an unwarranted prejudice, a fatal error that lies at the very root of modern Western thought, rendering both man and nature equally unintelligible. We can free ourselves of that prejudice by discovering freedom elsewhere in nature. Perhaps we can acknowledge the freedom of animals without portraying them as either engineers or chess players.

❊9❊

For a Different Reason

Freedom, Time, and Dialectic

Time is not simply one object that we experience alongside others. It is so pervasive a characteristic of our experience that everything we are and everything we do is inseparably entangled with temporality. Therefore, any conception of man and the world that cannot account for the experience of time also cannot render an adequate, intelligible explanation of the human condition. The deterministic hypothesis that all human actions are causally necessitated fails to meet this requirement. But when we turn to the hypothesis that human beings are free agents, the prospect of reaching an understanding of time is far more hopeful. For whereas determinism and the ideal of deductive reason leave time unexplained or consign it to a limbo between reality and unreality, I have demonstrated that freedom *must* be temporal. I examined the notion of a freedom that would be timeless and eternal in Chapter 4, where I showed that an absolute or limitless freedom would *have* to be atemporal or eternal. However, I also argued there that such an unlimited freedom, for which everything would be possible, is itself impossible, that the ideal of an absolute or infinite freedom is an illusion. Such a freedom would indeed be a pure principle of indeterminacy, without any opposing world or source of determinate forms in terms of which to determine itself. Completely without *opposition,* it would also be completely without *opportunities.* I therefore concluded that absolute freedom is unintelligible.[1] Insofar as it attacks the intelligibility of such a complete indeterminism, the case for determinism is entirely correct.

But freedom cannot be identified with pure indeterminism. Since absolute freedom is impossible, the only form of freedom that *is* possible is a finite, limited freedom. Freedom can only exist in an *already* determinate setting or world that provides definite opportunities for self-determination but that also *opposes* and *limits* freedom. And, as shown in Chapter 4, such a finite freedom *can only be conceived as temporal* because that independent, already determinate world is surpassed and thrust into the past *by* the act of self-determination, even if it is only a decision to accept the world as it is.[2]

Thus, the very being of freedom *is* a process of becoming. And while freedom does introduce a moment of indeterminacy into its world, that is not because it smuggles in an unintelligible ultimate "principle of indeterminacy" but because the very concept of self-determination implies the existence of a future that is open insofar as it has still to be determined.

These considerations also led to the recognition in Chapter 5 that the concept of freedom is *dialectical.*[3] For the very idea of freedom as self-determination places it in opposition to whatever is necessary and already determined. And yet, freedom cannot exist without the opposition of an already determinate world that imposes its own necessities and limits the possibilities of self-determination. Freedom can only exist in this dialectical tension between necessity and possibility, and it is therefore inherently and inescapably temporal. There can be no freedom *either* where everything is necessary *or* where everything is possible. The conceptual limits of freedom are, on the one hand, the empty tautology that is the foundation of logical necessity and, on the other hand, the empty ideal of limitless possibility. The former is at the root of complete determinism, while the latter would

---

1. Cf. page 112 above: "Completely indeterminate in itself and with nothing outside itself, absolute freedom is the idea of a pure, infinite potentiality—with nothing to do. . . . Such a pure *potentiality,* which cannot become actual and is therefore impotent, is an unintelligible contradiction."

2. Cf. the section "The Categories of Freedom," in Chapter 7 above.

3. Cf. esp. the section "Finite Freedom and the Dialectic of Freedom," in Chapter 5 above.

define a complete indeterminism. The dialectic of freedom is poised between these two empty and undialectical ideals.

This is the key to understanding the long, stubborn dispute over freedom and determinism. The entire dispute is the product of an undialectical understanding that splits the dialectic of freedom into its opposing moments and pits them against one another in an external controversy. The controversy itself tends to force the two sides farther apart, pushing them toward one or the other of these two undialectical poles: toward a necessity that admits of no alternatives or toward a freedom that admits of no limitations. The dispute is ever and again revived and perpetuated because its opposing sides are the sundered moments of the dialectical tension of opposites that is inherent in the concept of freedom. Thus, the very dialectic that animates the restless temporality of freedom here issues in the interminability of a dispute whose sides can never be reconciled.

Neither side can be entirely blamed for the perpetuation of the dispute. Each has rational motives, and each has an important basis in experience. The very logic of deductive reason motivates the insistence upon necessity that is the final source of the deterministic hypothesis. On the other side, the very dialectic that opposes freedom to an already determinate world and projects it beyond every particular limitation generates the ideal of an absolute freedom that would be beyond *all* limitations. The deterministic thesis has its experiential basis in the obstinate reality of the past, which admits of no alternatives, because it is already determined and unalterable. The ideal of a completely indeterminate and unlimited freedom reflects the experience of the future as a still undefined horizon of possibilities because it is still within the reach of agents who have yet to decide what they will do.

But this entire dispute between freedom and determinism turns upon a false dilemma. To grasp the dialectic of freedom fully is to see that *both* are required and that neither can stand alone. *Complete* freedom and *complete* determinism are alike incomplete and untenable. The one reaches out toward a pure futurity that is forever just out of reach. The other attempts to ensconce itself in the security of a pure past, which is already only a memory. Neither does justice to the fullness of experience or to the reality of the present, in which past and future meet and qualify one another.

But the interpenetration of past and future in present experience *does* receive an apt conceptual expression in a correct understanding of freedom. For an adequate conception of freedom must encompass both necessity and possibility, determinacy and indeterminacy, past and future, and must yoke them together in a dialectical tension wherein each of these one-sided terms is qualified and complemented by the opposition of the other. For, again, the very existence of a free being depends upon an opposing world that determines and limits it, but which also supplies a field of action and a source of opportunities that are necessary to the exercise of freedom. Therefore, freedom actually presupposes and depends upon a *partial* or *incomplete* determinism, which not only pertains to the world insofar as that world must be already determinate, but which also infects freedom itself, since freedom cannot be *in* the world without being limited and partially defined and determined *by* that world. Conversely, the presence of a free being inevitably infects the determinacy of the world with a moment of indeterminacy, since a self-determining being opens up within that world an uncertain future that depends upon choice. On the other hand, a determinism that is incomplete leaves a margin of indeterminacy that would be inscrutable if it were *not* complemented by a free decision, which closes the gap between what is already determinate and what is still indeterminate, between past and future.

The solution to the controversy over freedom and determinism is therefore to reject the dilemma upon which it turns, to recognize that the entire dispute is the result of turning the dialectic of freedom inside out, so that the tension of opposites that is essential to freedom appears, instead, as an external collision of opposing theses. The *opposition* between freedom and determinism is not to be entirely discarded, for that opposition is an indispensable and inescapable condition of freedom. What must be rejected is only the *contradiction* that arises from an exclusive insistence upon either *complete* determinism or *complete,* unlimited freedom.

The ideals of complete necessity and limitless freedom are both products of human reason, which is able to isolate, abstract, and complete in thought what we never encounter in such a pure, unqualified, or complete form in the richness of actual experience. Nor can experience be reconstructed by any mere combination or sum of these purified thought distillations. Indeed, there is no conceivable way in which a pure necessity or complete determinism *could* be combined with a pure spontaneity or complete indeterminacy, for the concepts are so framed as to be mutually exclusive. But there is no such difficulty in understanding the interplay of a partial determinism and a limited freedom. And if we are to account for the temporality of experience *or* come to terms with what we can actually hope to achieve through the exercise of freedom, then we must give up yearning for explanations that will exhibit the complete necessity of human events—*or* for either a political order or a personal transcendence that would raise us beyond all limitations to a condition of perfect freedom. Instead, we must recognize that actual experience and a full understanding of freedom can only offer a determinism that is merely partial and a freedom that is only finite. A philosophy that introduces the idea of freedom into its conception of the universe therefore has no need to deny the reality of time.

The positivist, or "scientifically" oriented, thinker is likely to balk at such a "metaphysical" reason for abandoning determinism and adopting the concept of freedom. But the whole controversy about freedom and determinism is not primarily a scientific issue: it never has been and never will be. It originated as a religious or theological issue and remains primarily an issue of metaphysics and epistemology. The controversy is rooted in questions concerning the nature of reason and explanation, the status of deductive logic, the reality of time, and the ultimate nature of being. These issues are clearly "meta" physical or "meta" scientific in the sense that they have to do with ultimate problems of constructing an intelligible account of the whole of things. And I have shown that the standard of intelligibility that leads determinism to reject freedom also entails rejecting all available explanations of human behavior as inadequate—and that it places determinism in a position where it cannot supply an intelligible account of time.

But in showing that freedom avoids this particular embarrassment because it is inherently temporal, have I really shown that either freedom or time is intelligible? Have I answered the determinist's argument that to allow freedom a role in human affairs is to undermine the very possibility of explaining or understanding them? Or have I merely shown that freedom is consistent with the temporality of human experience, whereas determinism is not? After all, it is one thing to show that determinism is untenable because it cannot supply an account of time that satisfies its own standards of rationality—and quite another thing to show that the idea of freedom is rationally intelligible. And it is no real help to be able to say that freedom is consistent with time, or even that freedom "explains" time, if the idea of freedom is itself unintelligible or irrational in the end. Indeed, this is a proof that cuts both ways. For have I not simply succeeded in showing that *both* freedom and time are irrational, since *neither* can be reconciled with the demands of deductive logic?

This objection confronts us, once again, with the question whether the logic of deductive proof is the final and exclusive standard of what is rational and intelligible. Evidently, I have not fully answered that question. In order to do so, I must examine the relation between freedom, time, and dialectic. I can best advance that inquiry by reflecting upon the views of Hegel, Marx, and Sartre, three philosophies in which those themes are quite intimately conjoined. A critical discussion of their works will help to elaborate a different conception of reason, one that can accommodate both freedom and time to a form of intelligibility more harmonious with the historical character of our experience.

Historical Determinism and Dialectic

Hegel was the first philosopher to exploit the connection between freedom and time clearly and systematically. Hegel conceived of the universe as a *process,* as the actualization of "spirit," or mind. He defined spirit as freedom, while he identified time with the self-realization of spirit.[4] And although his system culminates in an absolute knowledge that is nonetheless able to *transcend* time, according to Hegel, this is not accomplished through a deductive, rationalistic abolition of time, but is possible only because mind, or spirit, is able to *recognize* the temporal process as its own free activity of self-realization.

But how is Hegel's emphasis upon freedom and time to be reconciled with his celebrated "historical determinism," which has so profoundly influenced modern history through its Marxist mutation? Indeed, hasn't my whole discussion of determinism simply overlooked these important versions of the doctrine? Hegel and Marx are usually cited as the greatest proponents of *historical* determinism because, unlike those forms of determinism that derive from mathematical physics and the other natural sciences, they place the processes of human history at the very center of their philosophies.[5] In their views, we seem to encounter a form of determinism that doesn't just rudely impose the claims of deductive logic and scientific explanation upon human experience but takes human temporality and historicity quite seriously. Is the case against determinism incomplete? If determinism excludes both time and freedom, then how can Hegel both embrace determinism and allow for either time or freedom?

The answer, which is sometimes obscured in Hegel's writings, is that Hegel's "determinism," like his logic, is *dialectical* rather than mathematical or deductive, and that Hegel occasionally either forgot this difference or misrepresented its significance. Hegel's arguments and historical analyses are often criticized on the grounds that they are not rigorous deductions. But the dialectic is not supposed to be a deductive logic in the sense of a formal or mathematical logic. Hegel himself insisted upon this difference quite emphatically, contrasting dialectic with "the logic of the understanding" characteristic of mathematical thought, which he criticizes as a lifeless,

---

4. *Hegel's Phenomenology of Spirit,* trans. A. V. Miller (Oxford: Oxford University Press, 1977), 487ff.

5. The most celebrated attack upon Marx and Hegel as historical determinists is to be found in Karl Popper's *Poverty of Historicism,* which furthers criticisms advanced in *The Open Society and Its Enemies.* Popper's interpretation of Hegel has been often and justly criticized — most notably by Walter Kaufman, "The Hegel Myth and Its Method," in *From Shakespeare to Existentialism* (Boston: Beacon Press, 1959), 88–119.

petrified, abstract logic that loses touch with both the actual process of thinking in the subject and the real process of becoming in the object.[6] Thus, when Hegel speaks of historical or dialectical "necessity," it cannot be the necessity of mathematical reasoning or deductive proof that he means. Nor is it a necessity that contradicts freedom.

Unfortunately, Hegel only obscures this difference by writing as though the dialectic were a higher form of deduction embodying some superior form of necessity, while Marx tends to bury the difference entirely under asseverations about the "scientific" and "materialistic" character of his version of the dialectic. This is singularly unfortunate because it leads them both to claim a species of necessity and rigor for their historical analyses that they do not actually possess and that really belongs to another type of reason altogether. In so doing, they not only misrepresent dialectic, but obscure the real value of their historical insights by deflecting attention to a set of pretensions that they cannot vindicate and that only serve to evoke legitimate suspicion and criticism. The result is that the relationship between dialectic, time, and freedom is lost from view along with the difference between dialectic and deductive logic.

Whereas deductive logic is founded upon identity or tautology and therefore precludes real novelty or development, dialectic develops from one stage to another through negation, through opposition and contradiction. For dialectic is a logic of disputation and controversy rather than a logic of proof and demonstration. "Dialectic" is the term Plato used to characterize the logic of philosophical dialogue, where inquiry advances through the confrontation and interplay of opposing opinions and theories. It remained a logic of controversy even for Kant, although Kant mistook the classical meaning of the term and understood dialectic to be an illusory logic of futile and irresolvable disputes rather than a logic of positive and fruitful inquiry. Yet Kant nonetheless insisted that dialectic is not merely an accidental product of opposing opinions or fallacious inference, but is rooted in the very nature of human reason itself. Hegel carried this insight a step further by *identifying* reason and dialectic and restored the classical view of dialectic as a positive process of development. He still understood it as a logic of opposing theses. But it is also a logic of reconciliation and synthesis. The inner tensions or contradictions of one stage motivate the transition to its opposite, or antithesis, and these opposing theses are reconciled in the synthesis. The process of opposition and reconciliation springs from the very nature of reason itself, according to Hegel, and this allows him to propound a conception of reason that is

6. Cf. *Phenomenology*, 100–105, 329–31.

dynamic and developmental, as each new synthesis gives rise to a new antithesis, which calls for a new reconciliation in turn.[7] Consequently, Hegel can see reality as "rational" or "logical" without denying the reality of time and becoming.

However, this logic of dialectical development does not carry deductive necessity, for a very simple reason, which has been succinctly stated by F.S.C. Northrop. "From the negation of a present thesis one does not get one specific antithesis, but at least a finite and probably an infinite number of antitheses. And from a specific antithesis standing over against its prior thesis there are at least several theories which might provide a synthesis."[8] Now, the dialectician may rightly object that the antithesis is not just *any* logically contrary thesis, but a determinate negation *of* the original thesis.[9] However, while this might narrow the range of alternative antitheses, it does not eliminate all alternatives save one. Hegel sometimes writes as though the antithesis were already "contained" in the thesis implicitly (*an sich*), but such terminology is misleading insofar as it suggests a return to the logic of tautology, where the conclusion is, indeed, "implicit" or "contained" in the premise. But that would mean that there is no actual opposition between thesis and antithesis and no advance from one to the other or from their opposition to the synthesis. What Hegel probably means is, rather, that the contradiction within the thesis becomes explicit in the opposition of the antithesis. But this cannot be a *deductive* transition. For although the discovery that a thesis is self-contradictory does logically imply the denial of that thesis, it does not imply any *specific* opposing thesis.

Again, it is well to recall that dialectic is a logic of discourse and disputation. The development of a Socratic dialogue cannot be predicted, as if it unfolded like a mathematical proof. We cannot assimilate serious, productive discourse and argument to the rationality of deduction. But the objections that one party raises to the claims of another may be perfectly rational, however unpredictable. And if the argument ends in agreement, that agreement may be the culmination of a process of reasoning, even

---

7. In fact, this convenient schema of "thesis, antithesis, synthesis" is more characteristic of Fichte or Marx than of Hegel, who almost never employs these terms and who criticizes those who would reduce the dialectic to any such abstract schema. The schema provides a conveniently brief way of talking *about* dialectic, but one must remember that the brevity is purchased at the price of abstraction. See Gustav Mueller, "The Hegel Legend of 'Thesis, Antithesis, Synthesis,'" *Journal of the History of Ideas* 19, no. 3 (1958): 411–14. For a fuller account of Hegel's dialectic, see Alexander Kojeve, "The Dialectic of the Real and the Phenomenological Method in Hegel," chapter 7 in *Introduction to the Reading of Hegel* (New York: Basic Books, 1969).

8. *The Meeting of East and West* (New York: Macmillan, 1946), 246.

9. Cf. Kojeve, "Dialectic of the Real," 203.

though it has developed through opposition and controversy rather than as the deduction of a theorem from premises *in which it was already implicitly "contained."* The same may be said for a diplomat's response to the policies of a foreign power or of a general's response to the disposition of enemy troops on his left flank. Would they be *more rational* if they were predictable—or deducible by straightforward logical procedures?

In fact, the very deficiency of dialectic as a logic of deductive proof is actually a singular advantage for other purposes. Neither Hegel nor Marx thought of dialectic as an abstract or formal method of proof. As has often been remarked, Hegel's *Logic* is really a treatise on ontology or metaphysics, and both he and Marx understood the dialectic as a *description* of the inherent rationale of real processes rather than as a method of deduction. And it is precisely because the dialectic is *deficient* for deductive purposes that it is *able* to express the nature of temporal processes. The very fact that it is a logic of *negation,* which Northrop singles out as the source of its deductive inadequacy, is what enables it to express temporal *succession.* As I have already shown, a purely deductive logic cannot accommodate temporal succession, because to say that the moments of time are deductively related is to say that the existence of any one entails the existence of all the others, which conflicts with the very nature of succession. Because dialectic is a logic of opposition, because the transition from one stage to the next is not embraced within a tautological identity but involves a *negation* of one stage by the next, the dialectic can express the fact that the existence of one moment of time implies the *non*existence of the others, which is essential to understanding or representing the successiveness of time.

Or, again, the fact that dialectic is a logic of negation, rather than of strict deductive implication, is what enables it to allow for genuine novelty, for a coming into being of what did not exist before. I cannot fully anticipate what objections my opponent in a debate will raise to my arguments. She may even surprise *herself* by producing novel arguments in response to mine. Nor could Napoleon anticipate exactly what strategies Wellington would adopt at Waterloo—or be sure how he might respond to them in the midst of battle. The battle itself may be full of surprises that place it far beyond anyone's powers of deduction or prediction, yet still be the intelligible product of two rational master strategists. We have seen that the attempt to force temporal relations into the framework of deductive proof rules out genuine novelty by requiring us to suppose that each moment is already implicit in its predecessor. By contrast, the transition from one stage of the dialectic to another provides for a real becoming. For the negation of a stage is not a mere *nothing,* but a reality in its own right that is genuinely *other than* what had existed before—and hence a novelty. Again, the synthesis is not just an additive sum of thesis and antithesis, but a novel development in its own right, a new thesis.

Moreover, the dialectic does not just describe the *separativeness* of time, the exclusiveness of the moments of time that is essential to succession and novelty. If that were the only aspect of time that it could express, it would leave time shattered into discrete atomic moments that would simply be *opposed to* one another. It would not express the continuity of time, for it would describe temporal exclusion but not temporal *connection*. It could represent single alterations from A to not-A but not *processes,* single changes but not *developments.* But dialectic is not simply a logic of oppositions. It is also a logic of reconciliation, a logic of *cumulative* development. As Hegel himself stressed quite emphatically, even the relation of antithesis to thesis is not a relation of sheer contradiction or opposition. The antithesis comes into being through an overcoming and surpassing of the thesis. And since the antithesis only arises through this negation of the thesis and is motivated by tensions or contradictions within the thesis, it is not a completely independent and self-sufficient opposite, but an "other" that is rooted in and conditioned by the thesis it opposes. Thus, in an important sense, the thesis is preserved even in the antithesis, as the precondition of its being. Each new stage of a productive argument reflects the previous stage, to which it stands as an objection or reply. Or, if a more historical illustration is wanted, even a revolutionary government that claims to be a radically novel historical development (else it would not *be* revolutionary) will reflect the old order it has overthrown by its very efforts to establish a new social order that will rectify the injustices that motivated rebellion.

But the cumulative nature of dialectic is still more evident in its *synthetic* character. Dialectic is not simply a logic of antithetical oppositions, but a logic of syntheses that surpass and integrate those antitheses. Thus, it doesn't just describe a sequence in which one state supplants another, but a development in which each stage preserves its antecedents within itself. That is, each successive moment or stage of a dialectical sequence "contains" its predecessors as suppressed or transcended moments. Each new stage is not a substantial or self-sufficient being, but the result of the cumulative process, and is unintelligible apart from the process of which it is the product. And, because it is a logic of cumulative development, dialectic expresses not only the *continuity* of time, but also its irreversibility, whereas deductive logic would deny this *directional* character of temporal processes. This is a crucial difference between the two logics and must be examined more carefully.

As we have already seen, if the moments of time or the successive states of the universe are thought to be deductively related, then every moment is implicit in every other. There is therefore no difference in principle between the relation of present to future and the relation of present to past, or between prediction and retrodiction. According to classical mechanism, for example, an actual *reversal* of time is entirely possible, since all that would be required would be a reversal of the motion of the particles that constitute the universe. On these terms, irreversibility, like novelty, must be regarded as a merely psychological phenomenon. Indeed, insofar as the conception of time as a deductive "sequence" provides for any semblance of direction at all, it does so in a manner that is just the opposite of dialectic. On the deductive model, the stages of a process might be said to follow one another in the way that the conclusion of a proof "follows from" its premises by implication. All of the stages of the process or all of the moments of time must therefore be implicit in the very first stage or moment in the series, and this means that the entire process is predictable at the outset.

For dialectic, on the contrary, the successive stages cannot be *deduced* from the first stage, but because the development is cumulative, they *are* all implicit in the very *last* stage or moment. The result of this difference is that whereas dialectic can supply a *retrospective* or *reconstructive* form of explanation,[10] it cannot legitimately lay claim to any historical "necessity" or inevitability and cannot serve as a reliable basis for making exact predictions. That is, one can look *back* at a process of development and see how each stage arises dialectically either as a determinate negation of the antecedent stage or as a synthesis of antecedent oppositions. But one can never show that the development was *necessary*. Nor can one ever predict what the *next* stage will be, because there is always more than one alternative antithesis or synthesis possible at each stage. Once that next stage of the process has actually come into being, *then* a dialectical account can be given and may be quite illuminating. But it can only show how the various stages of the process were necessary preconditions of the outcome. That is, it might show that the result would not have come about *without* them but not that those conditions were *sufficient* to make that result necessary. It cannot show that the result is necessary, because it cannot prove that no alternative antitheses or syntheses were possible. Thus, Marxism is always able to explain, after the fact, why its predictions have failed and why something else has happened instead. But the very attempt to base such predictions upon the dialectic shows a misunderstanding of its logic, which leaves the future open and uncertain, though conditioned by the past out of which it arises.

Hegel and Marx were mistaken, then, if and insofar as they attempted to found deterministic theories of history upon dialectical analyses of histori-

10. Cf. ibid., 169–95, 202–6.

cal processes.[11] It should now be quite clear why the dialectic does *not* warrant determinism or contradict freedom, as the deductive ideal of explanation *does*. Dialectic is neither deductive nor predictive, because there is always room for alternative antitheses and syntheses. Wellington *might* have adopted other tactics in response to the disposition of Napoleon's troops. The United States might very well have concluded that Berlin was indefensible in the face of the Soviet blockade, or that American interests in southeast Asia did not warrant becoming embroiled in a land war in Vietnam. Most situations, like most assertions, admit of more than one reasonable response. This means that the logic of dialectic always allows for choice, that the outcome of a process is never entirely determined by antecedent conditions. Since the nature of the thesis does not determine the exact nature of the antithesis or synthesis, dialectic provides a form of rational explanation that is consistent with freedom.

But the link between dialectic and freedom goes much further than this merely formal compatibility between the two. I have already shown that the very concept of freedom is dialectical, since freedom requires its opposite in order to be. That is, the very exercise of self-determination engages the self in an independent and already determinate world that it must *negate* in determining itself. I have also shown how this dialectic of the very *being* of freedom gives rise to a dialectic of competing definitions of freedom.[12] I have now to show that dialectic itself presupposes or depends upon freedom, that the very intelligibility of those formal characteristics of dialectic that make it a logic of temporal process depends upon the existence of a being that is free.

In the first place, *it is only by introducing the idea of freedom that it is possible to overcome the explanatory gaps left by the dialectic.* It is all very well to note that

---

11. Whether Hegel ever actually *intended* to embrace historical determinism is itself a matter of debate. Hegel was quite aware that the dialectic is a logic of freedom. Its "necessity" is that which is inherent in the development of the "notion," or "concept," and that concept is the idea of freedom. History, as Hegel understands it, is the evolution of human freedom to self-conscious realization and embodiment in actual social and political institutions. His refusal to engage in historical predictions is further evidence that he did not intend to advance a deterministic theory in the usual sense of the term. Hegel does speak of historical or dialectical "necessity," but when he does so, it should be remembered that Hegel's conception of necessity is not that of deductive logic, but one that includes a moment of *contingency* within itself. (See Dieter Henrich, "Hegels Theorie über den Zufall," *Kantstudien* 50 [1958–59]: 131–48.) Nonetheless, in some passages Hegel does seem to be claiming some form of historical inevitability, and one could even argue that he *must* make such claims for systematic reasons. This is far too large a topic to pursue here, however, so I have dealt with Hegel's "alleged" historical determinism because he has been conventionally interpreted as advancing one of the major deterministic doctrines of history.

12. Cf. the section "Finite Freedom and the Dialectic of Freedom," in Chapter 5 above.

dialectical logic can express temporality because it is nondeductive, because the negation of a thesis can yield alternative antitheses. But if that were *all* that could be said, then we would still be left without any explanation of why *this* particular antithesis was realized rather than some other alternative. Introduction of the concept of freedom makes it possible to fill these gaps by explaining the selection of a particular alternative *as an act of choice.* Otherwise, we are left with a moment of pure indeterminacy ingredient in the dialectic—and in that case, dialectic would "solve" the problem of time, just as do the theories founded upon deductive logic, only by smuggling in an inexplicable principle of indeterminacy.

But the connection between dialectic and freedom goes still deeper. For it is not simply the choice among alternative antitheses that presupposes freedom, but the very possibility of alternative antitheses and the whole dynamism of dialectical development. For dialectic is not itself a "force" that produces change, but only a description of the pattern of development. It presupposes a *being* that is dialectical and that actually produces the development. The transition from thesis to antithesis does not come about by itself, but presupposes a being that *can* negate the thesis, that opposes itself to the *given* reality of the world as it *already exists* and transcends it toward an *other* that *does not yet* exist. The negation of the already extant reality cannot come about *ex nihilo,* cannot be the product of a sheer nothingness, or of the mere "passage of time." It must be the act of a being that already exists, but that is neither entirely determined or defined by *what is* nor even identical with its *own* given nature. But this exactly describes the dynamics of freedom, which, by definition, cannot be entirely determined by its world, since it is *self*-determination, and which must even oppose itself to its own *given* being, since whatever is simply given is not the product of self-determination.

The relation between dialectic, freedom, and time is now evident. Dialectic is not a logic of *proof,* but a logic that is capable of describing temporal processes and is able to do so just *because* it is not deductive. And it is for just this same reason that it can serve as a logic of freedom, whereas a deductive logic would exclude freedom as well as time. Moreover, a dialectical logic presupposes a being that is inherently dialectical. In fact, the very being of freedom has proved to be dialectical. *Hence, only the concept of a free choice can complete the logic of dialectic, and only the activity of a self-determining being can furnish the moving force of a real dialectical development.*

All of this was evident to Hegel. For Hegel not only identifies mind, or spirit, with both freedom and time, he also identifies it with that negativity which is the moving force of dialectical development. Modern existentialism has taken up this theme in Hegel's thought and developed it far more lucidly and consistently than Hegel himself, who only muddied the issues by reverting to the language of determinism and necessity and by belittling the role of choice in freedom. Existential philosophy was born out of Kierkegaard's insistence upon the opposition between the dialectic of temporal *existence* and a logical *necessity* that allows no place for the process of becoming or the uncertainties of freedom.[13] The relation between freedom and the dialectic of temporal existence has been further emphasized and explicated by Heidegger and by Sartre, whose treatment of the topic is especially lucid. Indeed, a brief examination of Sartre's view provides a useful way of drawing together the several strands of this discussion.

Freedom and Time in Sartre's Ontology

Sartre's philosophy illustrates *both* of the themes that have occupied the inquiry above: both the link between deductive reason and an atemporal conception of being and the link between time, dialectic, and freedom. I have already cited Sartre as a contemporary representative of the philosophical tradition that holds that, in and by itself, being is timeless and unchanging. Sartre describes being-in-itself in terms that recall Parmenides. Being-in-itself "is what it is." It is defined by the principle of identity or tautology, which is fundamental to deductive logic. Like Parmenides, Sartre therefore concludes that being-in-itself must be a cohesive, massive unity, without gaps or cracks or "interstices" of nonbeing, and that it therefore does not admit of either multiplicity or change. "Transition, becoming, anything which permits us to say that being is not yet what it will be or that it already is what it is not—all that is forbidden on principle. . . . From this point of view, we shall see later that it [being-in-itself] is not subject to temporality."[14] One could scarcely find a clearer example of how the principles of deductive logic yield a conception of being as timeless.

On the other hand, Sartre emphasizes the temporality of human experience. And he undertakes to show, at some length and with considerable subtlety of detail, that the structure and dynamics of time are *dialectical*. But, he argues, since being-in-itself is atemporal and undialectical, this temporal dialectic must have its source in some other type of being. The experience of time thus points to the existence of a species of being that is dialectical and exempt from the law of identity that defines being-in-itself. Only a

---

13. See esp. the "Interlude" in *The Philosophical Fragments*.

14. Jean-Paul Sartre, *Being and Nothingness*, trans. Hazel E. Barnes (New York: Philosophical Library, 1956), lxvi. My parenthesis.

being that is *not* what it is, but that is always at a distance from itself, can supply the negativity that is necessary to dialectic and temporality. Thus, Sartre argues that temporality presupposes the existence of a being that is *not in*-itself or self-identical, but that is "ekstatic," or has its being outside itself.[15]

We ourselves are just such beings. Because he is a self-conscious being, a human being is never simply identical with himself, but is always *present to* himself. As self-conscious, man is a witness of his own being, and this means that there is a "rupture," or inner gap, in our being that is the source of negativity and dialectic. But this is also the source of human freedom, according to Sartre. Because self-consciousness opens a fissure, or gap, that separates the self from itself, man cannot simply be what he is. Rather, he "is what he is not and is not what he is." His identity is not assured or given with his being, but is always a burden and a task to be completed through freely constituting himself. But the task can never really be completed, so that man's existence is a perpetual effort to restore his sundered identity through self-determination. Consequently, Sartre says that man is "condemned to be free." This inner dialectic of man's being in pursuit of his own being is the source of temporality.

Does Sartre's ontology promise to resolve all the issues currently before us at once, in a single solution? It does seem to bring together all that we need to prove that human beings are free. The temporality of human experience contradicts the deductive ideal of reason upon which the argument for determinism ultimately depends. But the temporal processes exhibit another, dialectical form of reason, while freedom supplies a dialectical mode of being to generate this temporal dialectic. All that is wanting, then, is some clear link between time, dialectic, and freedom, on the one hand, and human existence, on the other. Sartre, following Hegel, locates that link in human self-consciousness, which is the basis for freedom, dialectic, and time and which forms the link among all three. This solution also answers quite well to my own analysis of the structure of freedom. Human self-awareness allows the individual to place a distance between himself and his world and even places him at a distance from himself, as Sartre insists. And freedom, as self-determination, requires just such an inner distance within the self as this, just such a reflexive, dialectical relation of the self to itself as is inherent in self-consciousness.[16] Thus,

15. "Only a being of a certain structure of being can be temporal in the unity of its being . . . temporality can only indicate the mode of being of a being which is itself outside itself. . . . Temporality exists only as the intra-structure of a being which has to be its own being; that is, as the intra-structure of a (being) For-itself" (ibid., 136).

16. Cf. Chapter 5, pages 114–16, above.

human self-consciousness constitutes a sufficient condition of freedom and the necessary foundation for the temporality of our experience.

Moreover, this solution also points to an answer to the question whether freedom is an exclusively human characteristic, and thereby seems also to dispose of the question of the *range* of freedom. If self-consciousness is the necessary condition of freedom, then it seems to follow not only that human beings are free, but that *only* human beings are free, or at least that we are the only free beings we know about. For although other species of animal may be conscious of their surroundings, only man appears to be explicitly conscious of himself, aware of his own awareness. We are able to regard, contemplate, and even criticize our own perceptions and feelings, our own desires and fears. No other species of animal appears to be capable of such detachment and such refinements of reflection. All of this points to the conclusion that human beings, alone, are free.

Examination of Sartre's philosophy seems well worth the effort. It seems to lead to a resolution that knits together all the topics and problems that have concerned us in this chapter. Sartre's philosophy exhibits both the link between deductive reason and an atemporal conception of being-in-itself and the link between time, dialectic, and freedom. Moreover, he supplies a clear explanation of how freedom and time are possible by showing that both are founded in human self-consciousness. Taken all together, this seems not only to complete the proof of human freedom, but also to show that human beings alone are free, thereby settling at one stroke all of the problems raised at the opening of the last chapter.

Unfortunately, this resolution really only displaces the problems it appears to resolve, so that they reappear in a different guise.

First of all, Sartre's own analysis of consciousness raises serious problems for the argument that only human beings are free because we are the only self-conscious animals. For Sartre argues quite vigorously that there can be no consciousness whatsoever *without* self-consciousness. That is, he argues that self-consciousness is a necessary and indispensable condition of consciousness, "for if my consciousness [of a table] were not consciousness of being consciousness of the table, it would then be consciousness of that table without consciousness of being so. In other words, it would be a consciousness ignorant of itself, an unconscious—which is absurd. This is a sufficient condition, for my being conscious of being conscious of that table suffices in fact for me to be conscious of it."[17] Sartre does not mean by this that every consciousness must involve an explicitly *reflective* consciousness *of* itself, only that there can be no consciousness that does not include an immanent or inner self-awareness, a *"pre-reflective cogito."* "This

17. Sartre, *Being and Nothingness*, lii. My parenthesis.

self-consciousness we ought to consider not as a new consciousness (which would have the original consciousness of an object as *its* object, as in the case of reflection) but as the only mode of existence which is possible for a consciousness of something."[18] Thus, apart from all explicit *reflection,* every consciousness must be reflex*ive,* or self-related, since a consciousness that was *not* self-conscious in this prereflective sense would be an unconscious consciousness, which is self-contradictory. But if all consciousness must be self-conscious and this self-consciousness, in turn, entails self-determination or freedom, as Sartre also argues, then every conscious being must also be free. And insofar as any other animals are conscious, they must also be free.

Sartre himself does not draw this last conclusion. On the contrary, his argument seems to assume the very opposite, that only human beings are either conscious or free. For, having argued that consciousness *must* involve a prereflective self-consciousness, he proceeds quite systematically to show how the whole complex fabric of human existence and experience follows inevitably from this prereflective self-awareness. But, taken all together, his argument overreaches itself and proves too much. For, in the end, he must either deny that other animals are conscious or insist that they are also self-conscious, and must ascribe to them all of the dimensions and subtle intricacies of human freedom and experience that he has shown to be *consequences* of that prereflective self-consciousness. It is difficult to see how he could both acknowledge that animals are conscious *and* allow for any differences whatsoever between human beings and other animals.

As a matter of fact, Sartre never explicitly addresses the problem of the consciousness or freedom of animals. Indeed, the reader of *Being and Nothingness* may well wonder whether Sartre has ever noticed that there are other animate species on the planet. But the details of his argument clearly point to a denial that any other species of animal is conscious in the only sense in which Sartre can allow that consciousness might exist. Again and again, Sartre argues that it is "human reality" that introduces negativity and dialectic into a metaphysical or ontological context that *would be* exhaustively defined by the self-identity of being-in-itself were it not for the existence of human beings. Specifically, for example, he argues that multiplicity, totality, value, possibility, and temporality all enter into being *only* because of human existence. Apart from human reality, then, there would be no values, no possibilities, no time, but only being-in-itself, whose cohesive identity does not admit of any such ambiguous and dialectical forms of being.

We here encounter the most serious consequences and problems for

18. Ibid., liv.

Sartre's view and for the "resolution" developed above. For if the existence of time and dialectic depend upon freedom and humans are the only free beings, then it follows that time is a purely human phenomenon. This is actually Sartre's position in *Being and Nothingness,* and it is at this point that all the problems encountered in the last two chapters erupt again. Despite the fact that he conceives of being-in-itself, apart from human experience, as a timeless self-identity, Sartre is able to explain the existence of time by ascribing it to human self-consciousness and freedom, which supply the negativity that is necessary to the dialectic of temporal succession. He thus escapes the inconsistency of those philosophers who, under the spell of deductive reason, with its principle of tautology, conceive of reality as timeless and are therefore forced to resort to an irrational principle in order to account for the *phenomenon* or *experience* of time. Time is not unreal or irrational, according to Sartre, because concrete reality is the totality composed of being-in-itself and freedom, or being-for-itself, and this is a *dialectical* totality and in that sense is rational. Nonetheless, time is still only a *phenomenal* reality for Sartre because it exists only by virtue of and in relation to human awareness and human freedom and would *not* exist apart from human consciousness.

This result is hard to swallow. The notion that apart from *Homo sapiens* nature is completely timeless, without change or becoming or evolution, scarcely seems acceptable. For now it is the existence of the human species, rather than that of time, that confronts us with a hopeless enigma. And indeed, the problem of accounting for the existence of time is simply replaced, in Sartre's metaphysics, by the mystery of the origin of man, a mystery rendered insoluble by his explanation of time. Sartre's view makes an *evolution* of man inconceivable, since "before" the existence of human consciousness, there is only being-in-itself, which cannot alter or evolve, because it cannot become something other than what it is. Indeed, one can only speak of a "time" before the existence of man by a fiction whereby human consciousness projects itself and its temporality back beyond its own origins. Thus, just as Plato resorted to a myth in order to explain time, Sartre lapses into language that he concedes is mythical in order to explain the origin of being-for-itself, or human freedom. He writes that it is "*as if* the in-itself, in a project to found itself, gave itself the modification of the for-itself."[19] But he is well aware that this is inconceivable, given his conception of being-in-itself. By restricting consciousness and freedom to man and by conceding all of being *except* human existence to the principles of deductive reason that define being-in-itself, Sartre has cut humanity off

---

19. Ibid., 621.

from nature as decisively as the older, Cartesian dualism between mind and matter. An evolution of consciousness and freedom from being-in-itself is as impossible as an evolution of thought from matter, as Descartes conceived the two.

Far from resolving all our difficulties, then, examination of Sartre's view leads to a whole new horizon of problems. It seems that any philosophy that undertakes to do justice to the reality of time must introduce the concept of freedom into its account of the universe. But if freedom is regarded as a distinctively human characteristic, then time is relegated to the status of a merely phenomenal reality. In that case, the existence of man and of freedom are unintelligible or inexplicable in principle, and this means that the existence of time, too, is ultimately inexplicable. Evidently the notion that only *Homo sapiens* is free needs to be more carefully and critically examined. Sartre's philosophy is peculiarly instructive, then, not because it resolves all the problems surrounding the question whether man is free, but because it exhibits with singular clarity the problems involved in the assumption that *only* man is free. That assumption must now be brought under more direct critical scrutiny.

The search for a different reason, a different model of intelligibility, has led us through a critique of historical determinism to the question of the evolution of freedom. It has forced us to articulate the relations between freedom, time, and dialectic. The shortcomings of dialectic as an instrument of deduction mean that it cannot fulfill the ambitions of historical determinism to establish the necessity of human events. But dialectical reason is therefore better able than deductive reason to acknowledge the reality of time. Its very deductive weakness and absence of necessity mean that dialectical reason is suited to cope with real temporal processes. Yet it also means that dialectical explanations are lacking and incomplete unless they can be grounded in free choice. Thus, freedom, time, and dialectic seem to form an interdependent triad, the intelligibility of each depending upon the other two.

The course of development from critique of historical determinism to the problem of evolution is itself significant and has led to the brink of questioning the dichotomy between human freedom and natural necessity. On the one hand, historical determinism would "naturalize" the course of human events, assimilating history to the predictability of natural processes. On the other hand, the theory of evolution "historicizes" nature, assimilating natural processes to the form of historical development and even laying the foundations for historical geology. And although the course of evolution is retrospectively intelligible, no one can predict where it may lead, or reconstruct the stages of the evolutionary sequence deductively.[20] (We await the discovery of "new" ancestors to shed light upon our own past and no longer cherish the illusion that the emergence of the human species was necessary from the very outset.) But if the intelligibility of time depends upon freedom, then we must assume that human beings are not the only free beings in the cosmos; otherwise we must be willing to believe that time "began" with the "advent" of our own species, which is unthinkable, since both that "beginning" and that "advent" presuppose a prehuman reality of time. So unless we are ready to boast that human beings have "always" existed, we must attend seriously to the question of the range of freedom and ask about what place freedom may have in the rest of nature. That question will offer an occasion to retrace our steps, to consider more carefully and positively the role of freedom in evolution and history and to try to understand the difference between evolutionary history and historical evolution.

20. Cf. James Gould, "Play It Again, Life," Natural History 95, no. 2 (1986): 18–26, for a lucid treatment of this theme by a contemporary biologist who has given long and careful attention to defending the historical character of the evolutionary process against those who would insist that it ought to fit the deductive model of scientific explanations, which would dictate that a process can only have one outcome.

❋10❋

Freedom and Nature

Mechanism and Organism

Ever since Descartes and Newton, since the very beginning of modern physics, defenders of *human* freedom have tended to concede the rest of nature to determinism, arguing that only man is free, while everything else in the universe is governed by mechanistic causal laws. Indeed, this is one of the primary motives for the long dominance of Western thought by the dualistic opposition between mind and body. The body was thought to be governed by the laws of physics, like all other material things. But human beings could still be free because the human *mind* was conceived to be an immaterial substance and therefore exempt from the laws of physics. This dualistic doctrine was carried to such absurd lengths that French physiologists defended the vivisection of animals on the ground that animals are merely intricate but mindless machines and therefore incapable of feeling any pain. The writhings and plaintive cries of the animals were dismissed as remarkable counterfeits of expressions of suffering. Thus, although the very derivation of the word "animal" from the Latin word for "soul" reminds us that the ancient world recognized that man is not the only species to possess a mind or soul, modern thought tended to set *Homo sapiens* apart as the only strictly "animate" species, the only beings not entirely conceivable in terms of mechanistic determinism. Conversely, one of the motives for the determinist's rejection of human freedom has been an understandable reluctance to acknowledge any such profound gulf between us and the rest of nature, a reluctance that has been greatly reinforced since the theory of evolution established that the human species is a late product of natural processes of biological evolution.

Surely, no one today would seriously argue that animals cannot experience pain. Whatever disagreements there may be about the nature of "mind," no one would try to maintain that consciousness is an exclusively human attribute and that animals are utterly unaware of their surroundings.[1] But if *Homo sapiens* is not the only "animate" or conscious species, is there still any reason to suppose that only human beings are free?

Having discovered that determinism is neither a necessary truth nor a scientifically proven hypothesis concerning human behavior, why should we concede the *rest* of nature to this theory? Since it is only a hypothesis, we certainly should not take it for granted that determinism holds true of all other species except *Homo sapiens*. When we turn from the psychology of human behavior to the scientific study of animal behavior, we do not suddenly find ourselves confronted with rigorously mechanistic, deterministic laws rather than probabilistic, statistical laws. The levels of probability obtained in the study of animals may be higher than those usually obtainable in the study of human behavior, but the results are still, typically, statistical and probabilistic. Such laws fall short of the deductive necessity demanded by strict determinism, while a qualified determinism that could be content with probabilities is not in conflict with finite freedom, which actually *presupposes* such a partial determinism.

So long as science was convinced that all physical processes are governed by strictly deductive, mechanistic laws, there was more reason to argue that animals must be determined, whether or not psychology or biology had

---

1. Well, *scarcely* anyone. The exceptions are those psychiatrists and cognitive scientists who link consciousness to the use of language. In the case of psychiatry, this seems to go back to Freud's 1915 essay "The Unconscious," in which he identifies consciousness with verbal ideation (in vol. 14 of *The Standard Edition of the Complete Psychological Works of Sigmund Freud*, ed. James Strachey [London: Hogarth Press, 1957]; see esp. 201–2). In the case of cognitive science, it seems to derive from the attempt to conceive of the mind as a "physical symbol system," which allows no room for a nonsymbolic, merely perceptual consciousness.

discovered similarly mechanistic laws of animal behavior. After all, since every elementary particle in the animal's body must be a material particle determined by mechanistic processes, the actions of the entire organism must also be so determined. The discovery that elementary physical processes must, themselves, be described by statistical, nondeterministic laws has shaken the foundation of that argument. Contemporary physics no longer supports the picture of the entire physical universe as a vast machine, determined through and through, down to its tiniest elements, by laws that admit of no exception. Where statistical laws prevail, scientific explanations do not satisfy the theory of explanation that is the ultimate source of the deterministic hypothesis. A statistical law only enables us to predict that, given certain initial conditions, the behavior of an entity will fall within a certain *range* of possibilities. It therefore only enables us to explain, after the event, why the individual's behavior fell within that range of possibilities, but not why it realized just *this* possibility within that range rather than some other. For example, it will allow us to explain why an electron fired at a target landed within a certain definite *area,* but not why it struck this one particular spot rather than some other spot within that area. The most that we can say is that if the result lies close to the statistical mean, then the individual electron did what was *most probable.* But we cannot say that it could not have realized any other possibility, as the deterministic ideal of explanation requires. Insofar as science has come to *accept* explanations based upon probabilistic, statistical laws as satisfactory, it no longer lends its authority to the deterministic ideal, which identifies sufficient reason with complete causal necessitation.

Of course, the determinist may argue that physicists *should not be satisfied* with statistical laws, that physics must eventually return to deterministic laws and explanations. And many scientists, unhappy with probabilities and physical indeterminacy, might agree. Witness Einstein's celebrated assertion that "God does not play at dice." To accept an irreducible margin of indeterminacy in any process seemed to him to leave the exact outcome to chance. And appeals to chance are a poor excuse for causal understanding. They merely disguise our failure of explanation by giving it a name, as though "chance" were an additional causal ingredient.

But are we really forced to choose between sheer chance and complete causal determinism? This shopworn argument constructs a false dilemma because it lapses into the fatal error of assimilating the explanation of temporal processes to the model of deductive proof, which is incompatible with the reality of time. Sheer chance is not the only alternative to causal necessity. In the course of questioning whether human beings are free, I showed that we can *both* accept a margin of indeterminacy *and* understand it by ascribing the outcome to choice rather than to chance. Since free choice is quite consistent with *in*complete causal determination and would be unintelligible *without* it, choice enables us to explain, without resort to the slippery concept of "chance," individual variations within the range specified by a statistical law. Therefore, we need not scorn a science that rests content with probabilities. We can be satisfied with a "partial determinism" that leaves a margin of indeterminacy, because we can ascribe the outcome to freedom instead of fate or chance.

Of course, indeterminacy alone is no proof of freedom—and it may seem utterly inappropriate to invoke the categories of freedom in order to explain the behavior of electrons. Most of us still find it easier to think of the physical universe as composed of tiny ball bearings pushing each other about than to believe that an ordinary ball bearing is only the relatively stable product of the interlocking patterned activity of tiny packets of energy whose individual behavior cannot be precisely predicted. Yet developments within modern physics seem to demand that we embrace the latter view and accept the uncertainties of quantum mechanics—and today we must contend with scientifically inspired philosophers like Whitehead, who *do* propose to ascribe freedom to the microphysical events that compose the natural world.

Whitehead reverses the terms of the classical argument that man must be determined because he is a part of nature and that his behavior must therefore be explainable in terms of those same mechanical processes and laws that prevail throughout the physical universe. Whitehead reasons, conversely, that because any occasion of human experience is a natural event, we should assume that all natural events share the characteristics exhibited by human experience in some manner or degree. Whitehead invites us to abandon the notion that the elements of the universe are enduring material particles, entirely determined by external conditions, with no inherent energy or purpose, taking no account of their surroundings in any manner. He dismisses such elementary entities as "vacuous actualities" and argues that we should replace that conception of the primary realities with a more dynamic, "organic" cosmology that would recognize that *events,* rather than enduring particles, are the elemental realities. Every such event inherits the objective state of affairs produced by prior events. But the objective situation out of which an event arises leaves the future partially indeterminate, so that the exact outcome is only "decided in the event." For if the end were fully present at the outset, the event would make no difference, and there could be no change, or even endurance. Whitehead argues that, on the contrary, every event is "decisive," whether it adds a novel determination to the world or simply reiterates and sustains the established order.

Whitehead's emphasis upon the primacy of events and processes and his introduction of the idea of freedom into the interpretation of events redirects attention from enduring particles and "eternal laws of nature" to the importance of temporality, novelty, and irreversible change. I have just shown that the concept of freedom provides the basis for a rational, dialectical understanding of these temporal features of experience, whereas the deterministic ideal of deductive reason entails that temporality is unintelligible. Failing some third alternative, any philosophy that is to do justice to the reality of time must introduce the idea of freedom into its account of reality. And if time is not to be regarded as a merely human imposition upon pure being, or upon a reality that is atemporal apart from us—in the manner of Kant or Sartre—then the idea of freedom must be introduced into the description of natural processes as well as of human history. If we deny that freedom and time have any place in nature, or in being as it is apart from human consciousness, then the very existence of the human species becomes a hopeless enigma, as it is in Sartre's philosophy.

No such enigma arises for Whitehead's view. According to Whitehead, our human experience of freedom and temporality only raises to a distinctive level of clarity and intensity a dialectic of becoming that is common to all natural processes. The introduction of freedom into his interpretation of the most elementary events in nature enables Whitehead not only to establish the reality of temporal process and therefore to supply a conception of nature in which genuine becoming and novelty are possible, but also to provide a basis in nature for the evolution of man, in whom freedom first becomes fully self-conscious. That is, he furnishes a conception of nature in which evolution *can* occur, because nature is temporal, and in which the evolution *of man* is possible, because human and natural existence are not essentially heterogeneous.

Whitehead's attribution of freedom to microphysical events makes his metaphysics the extreme antithesis of the thesis that only human beings are free. I cannot attempt a critical appraisal of this highly speculative and controversial hypothesis here. Fortunately, for my purposes, it is not necessary to reach a final verdict upon Whitehead's cosmology. I can take a shortcut. The key to the continuity between man and physical events in Whitehead's system is his interpretation of events as *organisms*. Rather than pursue the question of the freedom of physical events any further, we can follow the example of Socrates in Plato's *Republic* and turn our gaze to the same issue written in larger script by considering organisms of the more familiar, biological sort, where the evidence and the problems are much more accessible. In this way, we can concern ourselves with the general question whether organisms are free without having to settle the more controversial question whether microphysical events are organisms. If biological organisms are free, that would provide a basis in nature for the evolution of *human* freedom, whether or not Whitehead is correct in introducing organic concepts into the interpretation of physics.

Freedom and the Process of Life

Whereas we may hesitate to attribute subjective agency to microscopic events, it is difficult to think of biological processes in any other way. Even molecular biologists who are committed to discovering materialistic explanations of vital processes cannot seem to resist describing organic processes in terms that imply interacting subjects. They often describe cellular processes in terms that sound more political than physical, as they describe cells, or even parts of cells, as collaborating, competing, sending coded messages, waging battle, etc. An immunologist, for example, describes the education of T lymphocytes in the thalamus in the following terms: "These budding T cells are first taught how to recognise self. To enable self to be recognised, a collection of almost unique proteins is displayed by every cell in our own unique body. This display of 'self' provides the cells of the immune system with a biological mirror into which they can look to simultaneously compare 'self' with foreignness. From the very first development of the immune system, nothing is more important than making sure that we do not attack our own tissues."[2]

Or again, two Harvard researchers describe the neurological development of the brain in terms of daughter neurons leaving home to find a place in the world:

> "The mother cells do not impart specific information to their daughters about what to become," Dr. Cepko said. "They do not say to one cell, you go to the visual cortex and to another, you go to the motor cortex." Instead, the scientists propose that when the neurons arrive at their final location, they are hailed by other cell components—long feathery fibers called axons—which hook up to the neurons and instruct them on their assignment.
> "The neurons are greeted by axons coming from other parts of the

2. John Dwyer, *The Body At War* (New York: New American Library, 1988), 32–33.

brain, and the axons tell them precisely what to do," Dr. Walsh said. "One set of axons carries visual information, another set carries information about sensation."[3]

These may be metaphors, but they are "telling" metaphors. Biologists who use such metaphors can often back them up with clear biochemical analyses of how these subjective functions are carried out, explanations that require no appeal beyond material, physical processes. But in so doing, they show how to bridge the gap between physical processes and subjective reality. It would be easy to read the lessons of molecular biology backward, as evidence for a reductionism that would purge biology of every hint of real purpose or subjective agency and thereby establish the truth of mechanistic determinism. But to do so would be to reproduce Sartre's predicament of rendering the existence of *human* subjectivity an inexplicable mystery by banishing subjectivity from the rest of nature and by reducing the natural world to the aimless motion of material particles. It is far more instructive to read the evidence *con*structively, as explaining how physical mechanisms can implement functions that embody a subjective form of reality that transcends mechanism without invoking any mysteriously immaterial principles.

Such a constructive reading of the biological evidence reveals not only the source of subjectivity but the rudiments of the dialectic of freedom, as Hans Jonas has shown in *The Phenomenon of Life*.[4]

Jonas points out that an organism *cannot* be reduced to its material components, because the life of every organism depends upon a constant exchange of matter with its surroundings:

> In this remarkable mode of being, the material parts of which the organism consists at a given instant are to the penetrating observer only temporary, passing contents whose joint material identity does not coincide with the identity of the whole which they enter and leave, and which sustains its own identity by the very act of foreign matter passing through its spatial system, the living *form*. It is never

3. Natalie Angier, "A Brain Cell Surprise: Genes Don't Set Function," *New York Times*, January 28, 1992. The researchers quoted are Dr. Constance L. Cepko and Dr. Christopher Walsh.

4. Hans Jonas, *The Phenomenon of Life* (Chicago: University of Chicago Press, 1982). The discussion that follows here is deeply indebted to Jonas's book, which contains a subtle and complete discussion of topics that must be treated rather briefly and summarily here. Indeed, a full exploration of freedom in nature requires a book in its own right. I hope to return to the subject in a later work.

the same materially and yet persists as its same self, *by* not remaining the same matter. Once it really becomes the same with the sameness of its material contents . . . it ceases to live.[5]

The reality and identity of any organism thus necessarily transcends that of its material parts—*not* by the inclusion of some immaterial vital principle, but by appropriating new matter or physical energy, which it uses to sustain itself. An organism is no mere aggregate result of its transitory material ingredients:

> [I]ts very existence at any moment, its duration and its identity in duration, is, then essentially its own function, its own concern, its own continuous achievement. In this process of self-sustained being, the relation of the organism to its material substance is of a double nature: it coincides with their actual collection at the instant, but is not bound to any one collection in the succession of instants, "riding" their change like the crest of a wave and bound only to their form of collection which endures as its own feat. Dependent on their availability as materials, it is independent of their sameness as these; its own functional identity, passingly incorporating theirs, is of a different order. In a word, the organic form stands in a dialectical relation of *needful freedom* to matter.[6]

Thus even metabolism, the most basic and indispensable vital process, embodies the very dialectic of freedom and necessity that is central and indispensable to understanding freedom. Jonas emphasizes this very point, remarking upon "the thoroughly 'dialectical' nature of organic freedom, namely that it is balanced by a correlative necessity, which belongs to it as its own shadow and as such recurs intensified at each step to higher independence as the 'shadow' peculiar to that level."[7] Thus, the same metabolic process that *frees* an organism from dependence upon any particular collocation of matter also imposes upon it the *necessity* of incorporating new matter in order to survive and thereby entangles it in a world beyond itself—as we have found that freedom must inevitably be engaged in a surrounding world. This same dialectic can be traced at every level of organic function, as Jonas remarks. The animal achieves a freedom of movement that plants do not enjoy. But its freedom *to* move makes it

5. Ibid., 75–76.
6. Ibid., 80.
7. Ibid., 83.

necessary to move *on* in search of the food upon which its power of motion depends.[8] Meanwhile, the freedom to move about in search of fresh forage or prey would be aimless and useless if not complemented by *perceptual* powers that enable an animal to *direct* its motions and *control* its actions. Self-directed motion and activity must be balanced by a *receptivity* to the world—another condition we found necessary to freedom. Even amoebae and paramecia can thus take account of the world perceptually *without* ingesting or modifying it. And as the range of motility increases in the higher, multicellular animals, so must the range of perception, culminating in specialized organs of sensation that enable animals to survey an entire scene and to locate objects at great distances. Perception at a distance opens a horizon that is as much temporal as it is spatial. It extends the animal's grasp of possibility, enabling the predator to stalk or lay in ambush for its future meal—and the prey to flee a danger that is "still a long way off."

A wider horizon of possibilities brings a wider range of choice. And without choice, after all, the independence conferred by metabolism, motility, and perception would only supply negative conditions for freedom. Freedom is not merely indeterminism, but self-determination; the mere absence of causal constraint would be empty without the ability to choose. But organic life does balance independence with choice and self-control. We can trace the rudiments of choice all the way to the selectivity of the metabolic process, which does not simply absorb matter indiscriminately from the environment, but selectively admits and appropriates what the organism can use to sustain and reproduce itself, while excluding or evacuating what is useless or dangerous. This metabolic selectivity is self-directed in the double sense that it is both directed *at* and directed *by* the form of the organism. The immunological system further expands the organism's reflexive and selective functions, distinguishing "self" from "nonself" among the material constituents of the organism and attacking "foreign" substances that threaten the survival of the "self."

8. Cf. "Fourth Essay: To Move and to Feel: On the Animal Soul," in ibid., esp. 104ff. "Thus animal metabolism makes mediate action possible; but it also makes it necessary. The animal, feeding on existing life, continually destroys its mortal supply and has to seek elsewhere for more. In the case of flesh-eaters, whose food is itself motile, this need is increased in proportion and forces the mutual development of that agility in which so many other faculties of the animal must participate" (105).

The Animal's Range of Freedom

The evolution of mobile and sensitive organisms significantly transforms and enlarges these rudimentary functions of selectivity and self-control by shifting the scene of both from the interior of the organism to action in the world. Learning and memory transform them still further, as hindsight modifies foresight and the "light" of experience adds depth and meaning to the perceptual horizon. For though the very ability to perceive objects at a distance opens up a horizon of apparent possibilities, animals can only *fore*see beyond what they actually see or hear insofar as present perception evokes recognition or memory or learned affect. Animals that can "learn their way about" the environment and learn a whole repertoire of behaviors while young thereby diversify their options and enlarge their field of choice.

Where foresight fails, instinct must often prevail, spanning the gulf between what is perceivably possible and those more remote eventualities upon which the survival of the individual or the species may depend. Animals that cannot perceive the connection between copulation and reproduction would soon disappear if instinctive sexuality did not ensure the perpetuation of the species, for example. Wherever action is instrumental to some vitally necessary end that is too remote to be foreseen, the action cannot simply be left to choice. The urgency of the necessary behavior must be innate, or "hard-wired" into the organism. It is tempting, therefore, to conceive of instinct as "mechanical" and as precluding choice. But in fact, instincts do not operate like machines, and they *necessitate* choices as much as they preclude them. For although the distant end may be "built into" the organism at birth, so that no organism can choose its instincts, each individual organism must choose the means of realizing that end in the situation at hand. If the instinct left the individual organism no choice at all, then the species could not adapt to any variation whatsoever in its circumstances and would perish with the first minor change in the environment.

Survival thus depends upon a balance between instinct and choice, neither of which could suffice without the other. Only by placing ourselves within an organism's subjective horizon of possibility can we properly estimate or appreciate the balance between instinct and freedom in animal choice. Ethologists often describe organisms as adopting alternatives that will ensure the survival of their genes—without seriously supposing that any subhuman animal could possibly entertain any such purpose. On the other hand, it is all too easy to dismiss animal behavior as "ruled by instinct," because we can scarcely imagine a range of choice confined to possibilities that are immediately apparent to perception.

In order to deal justly with the question of animal freedom, we have to bear in mind that an organism's capacity to choose is always limited by the range of options available *to* that organism—and that this is always confined to the horizon of possibilities it can survey. And the range of animal choice is more limited than we can readily appreciate. We are apt to misjudge the issue because we thoughtlessly assume that all the options that *we* can see are also evident to the animal, and then reason that the animal is not a free agent because it did not choose some option—an option of which it could never have been aware in the first place. We are liable to underestimate both animal intelligence and animal learning because we forget how much our own learning and sense of possibility depends upon our use of language and other forms of symbolism. Symbolism enables us to represent what is absent, to frame hypotheses and formulate fictitious scenarios, to spin out long chains of possibilities such as no animal lacking symbolism could ever contemplate. But by denying freedom to animals, we lose sight of the source of our own freedom, misconceive the relation between freedom and nature. And we thereby misconceive the nature of our own freedom. For we can only properly recognize the genuinely distinctive character of human freedom against the background of a full appreciation of the reality and limits of the freedom to be found elsewhere in nature. When nature is conceived as unfree, freedom can only appear to be supernatural.

Part V

The
Value
of Freedom

I want to tell you, gentlemen, whether you care to hear it or not, why I could not even become an insect. I tell you solemnly, that I have many times tried to become an insect. But I was not equal even to that. I swear, gentlemen, that to be conscious is an illness—a real, thoroughgoing illness. For man's everyday needs, it would have been quite enough to have the ordinary human consciousness, that is, half or a quarter of the amount which falls to the lot of a cultivated man of our unhappy nineteenth century.

—Fyodor Dostoevsky, *Notes from the Underground*

To acknowledge the freedom of animals is not to deny the difference between human beings and other animals. For it is not freedom as such that distinguishes us from other animals, but our use of symbols, the wellspring of human culture and historicity. The human use of symbols transforms the character of animal freedom by vastly extending the range of possibilities that can figure in human choice. But it also carries the germ of an illness—that disease of self-consciousness of which Dostoevsky's underground man complains. In Part IV, I attempt to appreciate the distinctive reach of human freedom—and then try to reckon with the peculiar liabilities that result.

Chapter 11 analyzes that contrast between natural evolution and human history which arises from the difference between genetic and cultural change. Modern recognition of the historicity of culture spawns the awareness that traditional norms and institutions are not fixed by nature, but subject to deliberate alteration and choice. Hallowed customs lose their authority as historical self-consciousness breeds a self-awareness of freedom and the recognition of freedom itself as an ideal by which customary institutions and norms may be judged and condemned. Can the ideal of freedom fill the void opened by the withering of the authority of conventional norms in the light of historical awareness? Can an ethics of freedom meet the challenge of relativism and nihilism that arises from the recognition of the artificiality and malleability of culture?

Chapter 12 seeks an answer to this question among its own generative conditions—in the process of communication that arises out of the human use of symbols and makes human culture possible. Since communication subordinates causal interaction to communally shared meanings, it suggests the possibility of standards of free coexistence that transcend the contingency of historical conventions. If the very existence of culture is rooted in communication, then the conditions essential to communication deserve respect as standards of a genuinely *human* community. Granted, we may often employ the communicative process to manipulate, threaten, or deceive one another. But in so doing, we violate one another's freedom and controvert the very nature of communication by sacrificing meaning to causal efficacy.

An ethics of freedom must ask how freedom can be sustained amidst the interplay of coexisting freedoms. The answer must be sought in the conditions of a free communication that substitutes reciprocal recognition for mutual manipulation.

❊ 11 ❊

Nature, Norms, and Nihilism

The Evolution and History of Human Freedom

The human species does not introduce freedom into an otherwise mechanistic or deterministic natural world. Although the choices of animals may be confined to a comparatively narrow range of alternatives, they nonetheless establish a natural ancestry and basis for the emergence of human freedom. Indeed, taken all together, the above reflections on nature suggest the outlines of a long and gradual evolution of freedom. We have discerned the antecedents of animal freedom in that active independence which is characteristic of all organic existence. If microphysical events are also organic, as Whitehead argues, that would mean that the origins of freedom can be traced to the most elementary occurrences in nature. We need not commit ourselves to such a pervasively "organic cosmology." Whether or not such speculations are warranted, it is still possible to see human freedom as an outcome of natural, biological evolution rather than as an abrupt departure from natural processes or a characteristic that radically distinguishes *Homo sapiens* from all other species and from the rest of nature as a whole.

What does distinguish human freedom from its natural antecedents is primarily the scope of possibilities and options that man's conceptual and symbolic capacities make available to him. The use of symbols enables human beings to pass beyond what is immediately and perceptibly possible, to distinguish clearly between the possible and the actual, and to conceive of possibilities that are not evident in the immediate situation at hand. Through the use of symbols, we are able to contemplate, manipulate, and even fabricate possibilities that are not perceivably present, but only represented symbolically. In mathematics and logic, we are able to deal with pure, abstract possibilities that are almost completely divorced from the world we perceive as actual. Thus, symbolism serves to extend the range of possibilities human beings can envision, far beyond those imminent alternatives that are available in the presymbolic experience of either men or other animals.

But although the use of symbols marks a decisive difference between the most primitive human cultures and all species of animal other than man, this difference does not emerge abruptly and full blown in the most primitive human cultures, but is the result of a long historical development. The researches of Ernst Cassirer and Mircea Eliade show that mythic or "archaic" cultures do not understand the relation of a symbol to that which it symbolizes as one of mere signification or *meaning*. Rather, they assume that there is some actual connection uniting symbol and symbolized, a substantial ontological link, or bond of being. Archaic societies therefore believe that the manipulation of symbols is not just a way to convey mere meanings, but an effective way to manipulate the actual world. This belief justifies rituals and behavior that we would dismiss as "magical" or regard as "merely symbolic" because we distinguish more clearly and readily between meaning and being. But archaic cultures do not draw such a sharp distinction between what is actual and the order of mere possibilities and meanings represented by symbols.[1] In that respect, archaic culture seems to invite comparison with animal feeling, in which the actual and the possible

1. Of course, *individuals* within an archaic society may acknowledge differences that are ignored by their myths. Mary Douglas aptly warns against assuming that primitive societies are entirely and homogeneously composed of deeply religious "true believers"—or that skepticism and secularism are peculiarly modern phenomena. On the contrary, she urges, "The truth is that all the varieties of scepticism and materialism and spiritual fervour are to be found in the range of tribal societies" (*Natural Symbols* [London: Barry & Rockliff, Cresset Press, 1970], x). The remarks in this section should not be taken as generalizations about individuals or societies. They pertain to the way of thinking exhibited by archaic myth and ritual—and

are also fused, even though the use of symbolism has already carried mythic culture far beyond the limits of animal experience.

The result is *not* that the experience of archaic man resembles that of the animal, however, but that he *sees* his culture as "natural" rather than as artificial or conventional. That is, he does not recognize the language, myths, and other forms of symbolism peculiar to his society as artificial products of human imagination and thought, but sees them as belonging to the eternal and sacred order of the world. Social conventions are understood as having the force of cosmic or divine law, as part of a fixed and unalterable order of being. It is therefore entirely fitting that the violation of a taboo or custom be seen as causing a natural disaster, even if the error was unintentional—as the unwitting "crimes" of Oedipus were supposed to have brought famine and plague to Thebes. Thus, because archaic man *sees* his culture as part of what we would call the "natural order," it actually functions as a "second nature," almost literally so—confining the horizon of available alternatives much as does the nature of an animal species and resulting in a similar uniformity of behavior. Year after year and generation after generation, the members of an archaic society repeat the same ritual scenario, the same repertoire of activities, with much the same uniformity as is to be found among the members of a species of animals. The few undisturbed primitive cultures remaining in the world today, which even include some Stone Age societies, bear witness to the fact that such an archaic culture may endure for millennia without any very significant changes in its pattern of life.[2]

We are so accustomed by our own culture to think of human freedom in terms of "creativity," "novelty," and "individualism" that it is well to be reminded of the countless generations of human beings in many very diverse societies who have exercised their freedom within the limited range

---

apply to particular individuals or societies only to the degree that they accept such myths or believe in the efficacy of the rituals.

2. Or, at least, so they believe. Here again, Mary Douglas, in her discussion of ritual in *Natural Symbols*, offers a useful caveat to balance Eliade's analysis. She reminds us that in preliterate societies, changes in law, morality, or ritual, "being unrecorded, are unperceived." Belief in an immutable God-given law is therefore in practice compatible with changing practices. "However earnestly the anthropologist is assured that the worship of Gods follows an immutable pattern from the beginning of tribal history, there is no justification whatever for believing what the performers themselves believe" (idid., 2–3). Of course, before Darwin, Western theory projected the currently existing forms of flora and fauna back to the dawn of time in similar fashion—and believed that all species of life are as primordial, fixed, and immutable as the myths claim for the forms of human life. It was only as we began to "read the fossil record" that we could discover that there are no fixed species, that populations alter through gradual, thitherto imperceptible mutations.

of possibilities sanctioned by hallowed customs. Although symbolism opens the way to the envisionment of novel possibilities, archaic cultures discourage exploitation of this potentiality of the symbol. Eliade argues that such cultures are not simply ahistorical, but "*anti*historical," stubbornly resisting any novelty or change that might alter the customary pattern of life and refusing to acknowledge the reality of such changes as *do* occur. In a very important sense, Hegel was right in saying that such prehistoric cultures do not *know* that man is free.[3] Archaic man does not recognize that culture is a human creation, and therefore does not know that he is free to change it. For want of this awareness of the merely human origin of customs, he really is less free than modern Western man, though only in the sense that the range of alternatives within which his freedom operates is more limited.[4]

Gradually, in and through the course of history, human beings have come to appreciate and exploit the power of symbolism to disclose ever broader horizons of possibility. In this sense, human history may be regarded as an extension of the natural evolution of freedom. To be more precise, we should not say that freedom itself has evolved, but that both natural evolution and human history have served to extend the range of possibilities accessible at successive levels of organic and historical development. Still, this expansion of the scope of possibility also entails an increase in the relative importance of freedom in the life of the individual organism compared to the role of natural limitations imposed either by inherited physiology or by the environment. In the life of the most primitive organisms, these natural limitations leave the individual little or no room for significant choice. The evolution of the more versatile higher animals has opened the way to greater individuation within the limitations imposed by the nature of the species. In the case of man, the natural limitations common to the species as a whole tend to be eclipsed by the dramatic importance of social and cultural factors that are not innate, but the product of human activity.

At first glance, this difference may not appear so great. On the one hand, recent research has disclosed the rudiments of culture and technology

---

3. Hegel said this of Oriental culture, but the point is more justifiably applicable to more archaic or primitive societies.

4. Eliade argues that this restriction is balanced by archaic man's freedom to abolish time and history. But that freedom is evident only from *our* standpoint, whereas the purported abolition of time is valid only from the standpoint of archaic man. According to Eliade's own analysis, the abolition of time is achieved through an identification with a divine archetype, which abolishes the independence of the individual man along with time. In fact, this conjunction of the self-abnegation of human independence and freedom with the denial of time casts an intriguing sidelight upon the whole topic of the link between freedom and time discussed in the last chapter.

among chimpanzees and other primates. In general, the higher animals are remarkably flexible and adaptable, and there are sometimes striking differences between the behavior of one individual or population and another within a single species. On the other hand, a human society may be so custom-bound and inflexible as to maintain a uniformity of behavior that is strikingly reminiscent of an insect colony. Indeed, some cultures seem to be so rigid and confining that the chimpanzee might well be envied his individual liberty. Viewed in this light, the difference between animal and man does not appear so great as the differences among human cultures.

But the difference between biological species and human cultures is nevertheless a decisive one. For the uniformity and continuity of an organic species is "natural," whereas that of a primitive human culture is "artificial," even where it is not recognized as such. That is, the nature of a species is something "native," or inborn, transmitted through the genes and literally *embodied* in the physiology of the individual organism, whereas a culture is a product of human activity that must be learned or acquired, and is therefore sustained and transmitted only through the activity and example of individuals. Individual organisms cannot alter the nature of their species through their activities. Even activities that modify the *body* of the agent are not genetically transmitted to the next generation.[5] But individual humans can and do alter their cultures, often quite inadvertently, by linguistic or ritual "errors"—failures to reproduce exactly the very patterns they are seeking to preserve.

This difference between nature and culture reflects a correspondingly profound difference between biological evolution and human history. For the difference between genetic inheritance and cultural transmission—the means that assure uniformity and continuity in each case—is also the key to the difference between evolutionary and historical *change*. Whereas evolution develops through the emergence of new species, history develops within the career of a single species. Because the activity of organisms does not alter the nature of the species, evolutionary change *can* only occur through the appearance of new species. The novel forms of life that mark the successive stages of evolution are physiologically distinct from their antecedents. Insofar as this process has resulted in the emergence of more

---

5. Of course, the choices and activities involved in mating do play a role in genetic variation, since individuals who fail to mate are eliminated from the genetic pool. But these activities serve primarily to reproduce the existing species rather than to introduce novel forms. And if activity results in mutations in the chromosomes themselves, then of course the results may be inherited by the next generation. But thus far, such mutations have been largely unintended and unwanted. The controlled breeding of plants and animals provides the limiting case in which the processes of natural inheritance become topics of cultural concern and control.

intelligent and versatile species, it does extend the range of independent activity and enhance the scope of freedom. But evolutionary change is not a function of individual choice or action. The processes of mutation and genetic variation, the primary agencies of evolutionary change, are largely independent of the acts and choices of individual organisms, as are the environmental processes that "select" which novel forms will survive.

In contrast to these processes of biological evolution, human history issues in striking changes in the typical forms of human activity without any corresponding changes in human physiology, changes in the customs and culture that constitute man's "second nature" without any change in the "nature of the species." Although these cultural changes are partially a response to changes in the environment, and although they are often not the product of any deliberate intention, they do reflect man's ability to alter his own form of life. Because the customs and norms of a culture are only *sustained* by individual activity, they can also be *altered* by individual activity, unlike the genetically transmitted nature of a species. Customs, laws, and taboos can be violated or ignored, altered or abandoned, after all. And even though an archaic society may believe that its customs are sacred and eternal rather than artificial and conventional, it acknowledges that these norms are not *inviolable* by establishing rituals and sanctions for dealing with individual errors or infractions of its rituals, mores, and laws. However great the force of custom, the fact remains that even where cultural traditions are most rigorously enforced, the limitations imposed upon the individual by the "second nature" of custom and culture are *optional*, whereas those imposed by the nature of an organic species are not. That is why in the case of *Homo sapiens* there can be a history of a single species rather than an evolutionary sequence of different species. History is not simply an extension of natural evolution, then, but a transposition of the process of development to a fundamentally different plane, the plane of custom and culture, of norms and ideals.

Clearly, this difference between history and evolution implies an equally significant difference between human freedom and that which may be ascribed to any other species of organism. Since the exercise of freedom consists in choosing among alternative possibilities, human and animal freedom are *formally* the same and may be said to differ "only" in that human beings can envision a wider range of possibilities than any other animal. However, this difference in the scope of available alternatives has implications that are so extensive as to make a profound difference between human and animal freedom. Although an animal may be able to choose between alternatives that are immediately apparent, it cannot decide the remote or ultimate ends of its actions. Lacking language and other forms of symbolism, it cannot conceive or represent such distant possibilities to itself. Animals therefore cannot formulate long-range projects or strata-gems.[6] Although an animal's life may hinge upon a single choice, and although the series of its choices and acts may be said to constitute its individual career, an animal, so far as we know, can neither *conceive* nor *choose* an entire career or elaborate pattern of action in advance. Animal freedom extends only to proximate ends and acts. The more remote ends that are sometimes served by animal behavior—in building a nest or burying eggs in the sand, for example—*must* therefore be instinctive or innate rather than the result of any conscious plan or purpose. On the other hand, human beings can envision horizon after horizon of increas-ingly remote possibilities and can formulate elaborate projects and strata-gems for achieving distant goals because we can represent entire series of interlocking possibilities through the use of symbolism. This capacity extends the range of human purposes and options far beyond the horizon of immediate alternatives between particular acts to a choice among very broad and distant goals, and even enables human beings to decide about the ultimate ends of life and action. Thus, human freedom, like human history, is raised to the level of ideals and norms—of laws and patterns of behavior that are not natural or innate, but artificial, a function of human action and subject to human choice. Indeed, that is why the principles of stability and change in human history are so different from those of natural evolution. Man is able to *alter* his culture and adopt a wholly different pattern of life because culture and symbolism extend the range of human options beyond the horizon of immediate possibilities. If anything, indeed, human communities have to take special pains to preserve social and cultural patterns from the erosion of individual variation and change.

Culture and Self-Consciousness

Human awareness of self is as radically affected by these cultural and symbolic factors as is our consciousness of possibilities—and the two are

6. Cf. Jane van Lawick-Goodall, "Tool Using in Primates and Other Vertebrates," in vol. 3 of *Advances in the Study of Behavior* (New York: Academic Press, 1970). This extensive review of evidence of the use of tools by animals clearly shows that the definition of man as the only tool-using animal is untenable. But it also clearly spells out the limitations of the capacity of animals to formulate elaborate plans. In *Through a Window*, Jane Goodall describes some chimpanzee social strategies that seem quite elaborate, such as the tactics males adopt to lure females in estrous off on extended consortships. But although Goodall sees that successful consortships enhance the likelihood that a male will father more offspring, she does not suggest that male chimps can foresee or intend that result.

very closely implicated. I have already dismissed the thesis that only man is free because only man is conscious of himself; I have dismissed this thesis because a flat denial that animals experience any form of self-awareness seems unwarranted.[7] Animals must surely have some sense or sentiment of self. An animal totally oblivious of itself could scarcely experience fear or take steps to protect or preserve itself. Studies of animal social organization clearly show that an animal may even be aware of its own social status, its rank in a "pecking order." Modern ethological and psychological studies furnish compelling evidence of animal self-awareness. Perhaps the most dramatic example is provided by Washoe, the chimpanzee taught to use the deaf-mute hand language by Allen and Beatrice Gardner. When she was first asked, in sign language, "Who is that?" while she was looking in a mirror, the chimp signed back, "Me, Washoe."[8] Washoe's ability to recognize herself might be explained away as a very special case—a consequence of the fact that she had been "humanized" by learning to use language. But Gordon Gallup has amply demonstrated the same ability to recognize their own images in chimps and the apes who have not learned to use language.

The ability of chimpanzees to recognize their own images certainly knocks the pins out from under any presumption that human beings have a monopoly on self-consciousness. But that is not to say that there are not important differences between the self-awareness of a human being and that of an ape—as there are surprising differences between apes and other animals. The most startling result of Gallup's ingenious use of mirrors to test animal awareness was the discovery that although some species of animals can recognize objects in mirrors and many respond to their own mirror images as they would to other members of their species, clear evidence of self-recognition is encountered only among the great apes. Even other primates seem unable to recognize themselves. Gallup concludes that the great apes have a "self-concept," or a sense of identity (defined as a sense of continuity over time and space), that is lacking in monkeys and other animals.[9]

7. See Chapter 10 above.

8. Jane van Lawick-Goodall, *In the Shadow of Man* (New York: Dell, 1971), 254.

9. "The capacity for self-recognition, although influenced by learning, is predicated on a sense of identity [defined as a sense of continuity over time and space]. The unique feature of mirror-image stimulation is that the identity of the observer and his reflection in the mirror are necessarily one and the same. The capacity to correctly infer the identity of the reflection must, therefore, presuppose an already existent identity on the part of the organism making this inference. Without an identity of your own it would be impossible to identify yourself. And therein may lie the great difference between monkeys and great apes. The monkey's inability to recognize himself may be due to the absence of a sufficiently well-integrated self-concept" (Gordon G. Gallup Jr., "Self-Recognition in Primates: A Comparative Approach

The gulf between apes and men is as broad as that between apes and other primates, as Jane Goodall herself observes. On the one hand, she insists that Washoe's ability to recognize herself offers scientific proof that the chimpanzee has a primitive awareness of self. But she immediately adds that human self-consciousness is of a very different order:

> Man is aware of himself in a very different way from the dawning awareness of the chimpanzee. He is not just conscious that the body he sees in a mirror is "I," that his hair and toes belong to *him,* that if a certain event occurs *he* will be afraid or pleased or sad. Man's awareness of Self supersedes the primitive awareness of a fleshly body. Man demands an explanation of the mystery of his being and the wonder of the world around him and the cosmos above him. So man, for centuries, has worshiped a God, has dedicated himself to science, has tried to penetrate the mystery in the guise of the mystic. Man has an almost infinite capacity for preoccupation with things other than Self: he can sacrifice himself to an ideal, immerse himself in the joys or sorrows of another; love, deeply and unselfishly; create and appreciate beauty in many forms. It should not be surprising that a chimpanzee can recognize himself in a mirror. But what if a chimpanzee wept tears when he heard Bach thundering from a cathedral organ?[10]

This passage adumbrates the differences between animal and human self-awareness without pinpointing the exact character of those differences or explaining their origin. To strive to create beauty or to be able to weep in its presence, to dedicate oneself to others or to inquiry or to an abstract ideal—all this shows that human *self*-consciousness is as profoundly mediated and transformed by culture and ideals, and thus by symbolism, as is our awareness of possibility. A chimpanzee may be able to recognize its own image in a mirror, much as it can perceive a possibility that is immediately available and even make a simple tool in order to attain its end. But it is only man who makes images of himself, who represents himself to himself. By

---

to Bi-directional Properties of Consciousness," *American Psychologist* 32 [1972]: 334, parenthesis taken from Gallup's footnote; see also Gallup's "Self-Awareness and the Emergence of Mind in Primates," *American Journal of Primatology* 2 [1982]: 237–48). Gallup has tested, for their reactions to mirrors, quite a variety of species, including chickens, goldfish, parakeets, weaver finches, and assorted monkeys, as well as chimpanzees. He finds that although many species spend considerable time in front of the mirror, the evidence indicates that they do so because they react socially to the image—as to another member of their species.

10. Van Lawick-Goodall, "Tool Using in Primates and Other Vertebrates."

formulating such a representation of himself, man places himself at a distance. The reflexive relation to self, which is present in animal self-feeling and even in the simplest metabolic processes, widens into a definite breach as man contemplates his own image as an object. Whereas an animal may be curious and inquisitive about the surrounding world and a chimpanzee may have a sufficient sense of its own identity to be curious about changes in its own appearance, only man can stand back far enough from himself to question his own existence, to inquire about the mystery of his own being.

Moreover, man's representation of himself is rarely, if ever, a mirror image of what he actually *is,* or an accurate reflection of how he *feels* at a particular moment. Though not immutable, an individual's "self-image" is far more stable and constant than his momentary sense of self, and it may be far "better" or "worse" than he actually *is.* Indeed, this self-image functions as a sort of stable norm or standard against which he measures his momentary feelings and particular deeds and which reciprocally influences how he acts and how he feels *about* himself. This is because man's image of himself is a *symbolic* representation rather than a mere *copy.* The self-representative power of symbolism conjoins with its power to represent *possibilities* so as to produce an image or concept of an *ideal* or *possible* self. The actual self may or may not coincide with the ideal, possible self, which therefore functions as both a *goal* to be realized and as a *norm* that regulates feeling and action.[11] And insofar as the individual's self-image is formulated in terms of a symbolism that is rooted in a common culture, it introduces an intersubjective, public dimension into the very heart of individual self-consciousness.

This modification of human self-consciousness by the mediation of symbolic representation has profound implications for human freedom. Because he can formulate an ideal image or concept of himself and contemplate himself as a *possibility,* man is able to make decisions *about* himself at a level at which no other animal can. An individual may resolve to re-form himself so as to con-form more closely to his ideal, for example. Or, he can call that ideal self into question. He can decide to alter or entirely abandon a certain image of himself that *has* directed his actions and can pursue a new ideal, like the confirmed bachelor who finally decides

---

11. This does not begin to chart the full complexity of human self-consciousness, of course. For example, because human beings constantly judge themselves in relation to their ideal self-images, every individual tends to develop a habitual judgment of his actual self as good or bad, successful or unsuccessful, beautiful or ugly, etc. But it would require a separate inquiry to exhibit the interplay between an individual's immediate self-awareness, his ideal self-image, his awareness of his actual or empirical self, and his habitual self-judgment.

to discard his image of himself as a promiscuous playboy and to espouse, instead, the ideal of the faithful husband and doting father. Or he may choose the opposite metamorphosis, from conventional family breadwinner to swinging single. Consequently, man is not only able to choose among alternative particular *actions,* as animals can, but even able to choose among alternative possible *selves.* Man is thus able to determine himself in a way in which no other animal can. An animal may *in fact* determine itself through the series of its particular choices and acts. But for lack of any clear image or conception of itself, it cannot *choose itself.* That is, it cannot choose among alternative ideal or possible selves, or choose a program of actions or a career that aims at realizing such a possible self. Because man is able to decide about himself at this level, he is a free, or *self-determining,* being in a sense in which other animals are not.[12]

This extension of human freedom and self-consciousness into the domain of concepts and ideals introduces an ethical or normative dimension into human freedom that is missing in the case of animals. I can train my dog to stay off the furniture and out of the kitchen, and a young chimpanzee can learn to conform its behavior to the social patterns of its group. But this might be explained as a function of conditioning or habit formation rather than accepted as evidence that animals have any *conception* of norms or awareness of ideal standards. If we do not hold animals legally or ethically responsible for their acts, that is because we cannot reasonably expect them to recognize legal or moral norms and to regulate their actions accordingly. Weasels and foxes are "natural thieves"—and perhaps men are too. "Man is a wolf to man," according to an old Roman adage. But human

---

12. If an animal that has no self-concept cannot even *recognize* itself in a mirror, still less can the animal that lacks a clear image or conception of itself *choose* itself in the significant sense at stake here. That requires a concept of the self as possibility that is of an order different from the sense of identity Gallup ascribes to the great apes. We can better appreciate the levels of self-awareness involved here by attending to the design of one of Gallup's experiments for studying self-awareness in animals. He dyed parts of their faces with a bright, odorless stain while they were unconscious and then waited to see how they would react when they looked in the mirror upon awakening. Animals that could not recognize their own images could not recognize the difference, of course. Even chimps that had not been exposed to mirrors before did not react to the change, of which they were oblivious, since they could not recognize the brightly stained visages as their own—and had no basis for noticing the change. But chimps who had learned to recognize themselves in the mirror beforehand spent conspicuously more time inspecting themselves in the mirror and touching the dyed areas than did controls. It seems obvious that they were comparing their new images with a durable conception of their "normal" visages. That warrants Gallup's conclusion that they must have some conception of self that transcends the moment. But there is nothing to suggest that chimps can project their self-images into the realm of possibility so as to be able to choose among alternative self-concepts as human beings do.

thieves can be held responsible for theft and for violating social conventions, whereas we cannot reasonably hold weasels responsible for their predatory ways, or expect the fox to acknowledge the property rights of the chicken farmer.

There would be no point to passing laws or to debating about ethical standards of behavior were it not for our ability to base our choices and actions upon the concept of a law or ideal norm. Immanuel Kant saw this ability to base decisions upon the concept of a universal law as the very touchstone of human freedom and the fundamental presupposition of any objectively meaningful morality. But even apart from all considerations of *common* or universal ethical standards, a particular individual's ideal or self-image serves as a standard or norm against which he judges himself and in relation to which he may either condemn or commend himself for some particular action or feeling. It also influences his assessment of alternatives and directs his choices among them. This personal, individual ideal introduces a normative factor into the exercise of human freedom, even if it happens to appear eccentric or morally perverse in relation to the common standards of society.

But of course, the individual's personal norms and ideal image of himself are usually profoundly influenced by the common *ethos* and shared ideals of his society. This is not simply due to lack of imagination or to social pressure to conform to common standards. After all, the symbols that enable the individual to formulate a conception of himself are derived from that shared culture so that the very source of the individual's personal ideal is mediated by his culture. At this point, I come full circle in discussing the differences between human and animal freedom. For it is this conformity of individual norms within a culture that accounts for the peculiarly human uniformity of behavior within a society—so like the uniform repertoire of behavior of a biological species and yet so different because it is optional, subject to human questioning and choice. If individuals usually choose to conform to the norms of their society despite their freedom to violate them—or to reject them and embrace other ideals and standards—that is less because of external pressures for compliance than because their personal ideals and norms are already formed in the terms supplied by a common culture. The very cultural resources that liberate human beings from purely natural limitations and raise human freedom to the level of ideals and norms also tend to ensure community of purpose and uniformity of behavior within any given culture. People usually identify so completely with the ideals of their own culture that they don't even recognize the existence of any legitimate alternatives. When they encounter alien customs and values, they typically dismiss them as barbarous or false because they judge them by their own, native standards, which they regard as the only "natural" or "correct" values. Thus, although the diversity of human culture and the possibility of historical change hinge upon the *optional* status of cultural norms, men do not necessarily recognize that they are free to alter their norms or to adopt different standards. This is especially true where the customary norms are regarded as divinely ordained and sanctioned. Similarly, during much of human history, the individual's social status and role in life were not matters open to choice, but were assigned at birth on the basis of natural determinations of family, sex, race, order of birth, etc. Thus, although the mediating role of culture and symbolism in human self-consciousness greatly expands the scope of human freedom *in principle,* *in fact* they may play quite an opposite role by defining the individual's awareness of himself and his options in terms of conventional norms and ideals. The Inquisition does not recognize heretics as harbingers of progress, or as creative individuals who embody new human opportunities.

The Ideal of Freedom

However, in and through the course of history, man has become conscious of himself as historical and as free. Even the most custom-bound primitive individual can presumably recognize that he is free to *violate* the norms and taboos of his tribe. Though he may believe that those customs are divinely ordained and part of a sacred cosmic order, he can nevertheless see that it is *possible* to disobey them. In the myth of Eden, God himself forbids Adam and Eve to eat of the fruit of the tree of knowledge. But of course, that very prohibition confronts them with a choice between good and evil, or between obedience and sin. A taboo against incest does not make incest *impossible* or place it beyond the range of choice. If anything, such taboos tend to focus attention upon the forbidden possibility and lend it a certain dreadful fascination. Human beings have presumably always been aware of their "freedom to sin," to violate the customary norms and ideals of their societies. But they have not always been aware that they are free to *alter* those customs, or that there might be *legitimate,* nonsinful alternatives to traditional ideals and values. However, in the course of history we have learned that culture is neither natural nor sacred, but is the product of human history and activity. The human species is not confined by nature to a specific pattern of life, and once individuals recognize that, they become conscious of their own freedom. For once human beings see that their language and rituals, their customs and laws, their whole traditional pattern of life and values are products of *human* activity rather than of cosmic necessity or the acts and decrees of the gods, a whole new dimension of possibilities opens up to them, a horizon of ideals and norms of their own choosing.

At that point, man is not only free, but fully conscious of being free. And this self-consciousness of freedom opens a still more decisive gulf between human and animal freedom. For while there may be reason to grant that animals are both free and self-conscious in some degree, there is no reason to suppose that they have any other awareness of themselves *as* free than that which is implicit in the awareness of having to choose among immediately apparent alternatives. An animal can no more have an explicit conception of freedom than it can have an explicit conception of itself, since both require the abstractive and representative functions of symbolism. The conjunction of self-consciousness and freedom in an explicit awareness of oneself as free is peculiarly human. And even this self-conscious freedom remains incomplete so long as people regard the parochial customs and ideals of their cultures as norms that can be violated but not altered, as belonging to an eternal natural or divine order that is beyond the range of human choice and action. Only the consciousness of his own historicity, the recognition of the human origin of human culture and custom, brings man to complete self-consciousness of the entire scope of his own freedom.

What is important here is not simply the addition of self-awareness to a freedom that remains unaffected thereby. Rather, it is this self-consciousness itself that first effectively discloses to the individual a domain of purposes and ideals that are not supplied by either nature or custom but are self-conscious human conceptions or inventions. Human freedom thus transcends its natural and historical sources, sees both what is natural and what is historical as optional, and may even oppose itself to both. Human beings set themselves goals that are conceived in self-conscious opposition to their own natural inclinations and historical traditions. Rather than accept things as they are, or bow to the hallowed traditions of the past, they treasure novelty, individuality, and "progress," or dream of utopias and seek to find in an ideal future the norms and standards whereby the present and the past are measured and found wanting.

And because he is not only a free being, but a being who is *conscious* of his own freedom, man is able to make freedom itself an ideal. Freedom then becomes its own end, so that man not only exercises freedom in choosing, but chooses with respect to his own freedom and makes freedom itself the goal of his choice and action. Abstracted from its natural and historical origins, human freedom is raised to the rank of a norm or standard against which man's natural and historical condition may be measured and judged. For the sake of that ideal, men have denied their natural appetites, defied the customs and opinions of their societies, and even sacrificed their lives. Stoics and ascetics have sought to dissociate themselves from their own bodies and even to prove their freedom by making the body an instrument of its own torment and mortification. In the name of freedom, armies have been raised and wars have been fought. Revolutionary thinkers of almost every political persuasion have attacked the social and political institutions of their societies as oppressive of freedom and have undertaken to change the whole pattern of life of entire nations and civilizations in order to liberate them from that oppression.

The Abyss of Nihilism

But our modern "liberation from the bondage of custom" has its price, for it is inseparable from the collapse of the authority of those conventional norms that fostered community of purpose and the stability of shared values and ideals in customary cultures. The self-recognition of human freedom that accompanies modern historical self-consciousness is epitomized in Smerdyakov's statement, in *The Brothers Karamazov:* "If there is no God, then everything is possible." What he means, of course, is that if there is no God, then everything is *permissible,* for there is no sin. If there are no divine prohibitions, if the norms of human behavior are only artificial conventions, made by man and not by God, then they have no authority *over* man. And then, indeed, "everything is possible"! Every individual is free to reject customary standards and to establish his own goals and values. Indeed, the ideal of freedom seems to demand that every individual should break the bonds of custom, liberate himself from the tyranny of sheer tradition, and think and choose for himself. It is this ideal of self-conscious freedom that is at the heart of the Nietzschean ideal of the "overman," or the "authentic individual" of existential thought, the individual who wrenches loose from the herd mentality and from the tranquilizing conformity of the "everyday," "average" man so as to confront the problem of creating his own values and goals.[13]

But with the recognition of this freedom comes anxiety. For the self-conscious recognition and idealization of freedom thus threatens to do away with any common ethos or ethics and to reduce the normative dimension

13. Robert N. Bellah and his colleagues Richard Madsen, William M Sullivan, Ann Swidler, and Steven M. Tipton diagnose a distinctively American version of this modern predicament in *Habits of the Heart: Individualism and Commitment in American Life* (Berkeley and Los Angeles: University of California Press, 1985). See esp. chapter 3, "Finding Oneself."

of freedom to the individual's pursuit of his own quixotic dream. But the individual is thereby left without guidance, with no support for the ideal that he *does* choose to pursue except the authority of his own decision. And his own ideal of individual freedom gives him every reason to expect that his pursuit of his own purposes will clash with the equally idiosyncratic pursuits of others. In short, the full self-consciousness of human freedom seems to carry with it the dangers of moral nihilism, individual anomie, and social anarchy.

Can the ideal of freedom itself fill the void left by the collapse of conventional norms? Can it provide the foundation for an ethics to replace the customary ethos? Can freedom serve as a common ideal that will give individuals some community of purpose? Can it furnish social and political standards that will ensure some minimal stability of expectations? Can an individual, a society, or a civilization that has thrown off the yoke of custom and convention in the name of freedom really find in that new ideal the basis for values and norms that would be adequate to the needs of the individual and of society?

Unfortunately, the ideal of freedom has proved to be as elusive as Proteus. The ascetic seems to imprison himself in the austere self-abnegation wherein he seeks his liberty, while the self-indulgence that he denounces as slavery to lust is precisely the libertine's idea of freedom. The liberal of the twentieth century, who seeks to relieve social oppression through the action of the state, collides politically with champions of the laissez-faire liberalism of the nineteenth century, who denounce the growth of state power as oppressive. The revolutionary, who begins by overthrowing tyranny in the name of freedom, all too often ends by imposing a harsher tyranny in its place. Albert Camus, who insists that the ideal of freedom is the motive of every genuine revolution, also points out that revolutions usually adopt murder and terrorism as their means and that revolutions typically end by enhancing authority rather than freedom:

> All modern revolutions have ended in a reinforcement of the power of the state. 1789 brings Napoleon; 1848, Napoleon III; 1917, Stalin; the Italian disturbances of the twenties, Mussolini; the Weimar Republic, Hitler. These revolutions, particularly after the first World War had liquidated the vestiges of divine right, still proposed, with increasing audacity, to build the city of humanity and of authentic freedom. The growing omnipotence of the state sanctioned this ambition on each occasion. . . . The strange and terrifying growth of the modern State can be considered as the logical conclusion of inordinate technical and philosophical ambitions, foreign to the true spirit of rebellion, but which nevertheless gave birth to the revolutionary spirit of our time. The prophetic dream of Marx and

the over-inspired predictions of Hegel or of Nietzsche ended by conjuring up, after the city of God had been razed to the ground, a rational or irrational State, which in both cases, however, was founded on terror.[14]

Why is freedom such an elusive ideal, such a protean goal that those who have pursued it have so often succeeded only in achieving the very opposite of what they intended?

The answer lies in the very logic of freedom. The actuality of freedom consists in the exercise of choice among alternative possible actions or goals. But, for this very reason, the concept of freedom refers *beyond* the act of choosing to those further goals and possibilities between which the choice is to be made. While the choice itself is the act of freedom, *any* act that is chosen may be described as "a free act" simply because it *is* chosen and therefore embodies an exercise of freedom. The freely chosen goal or action becomes confounded with the act of choosing it. Thus, the idea of freedom may be attached to almost any content, any act or purpose that may be chosen. For the very nature of the idea of freedom is such as to point beyond itself to an indeterminate array of possible goals and purposes.

This explains how the ideal of freedom has come to be associated with so many diverse human purposes. For if the idea of freedom may be attached to any chosen action, then the ideal of freedom may be evoked to justify any purpose one chooses. That is, any individual may argue, in the name of freedom, that he should be permitted to pursue any specific goal that he happens to have chosen. The same holds true of any group, faction, or party. And so, it can easily happen that every party to a dispute can claim to support the ideal of freedom and come to see its particular program or ideal as the embodiment of freedom while denouncing its opponents' purposes as "oppressive." That is why, at the very outset of this inquiry, we found ourselves confronted with such diverse and conflicting doctrines of freedom.

It would seem to follow that the ideal of freedom is not only elusive, but downright *illusory.* For if every individual and every party can always claim to champion freedom, then the cause of freedom is always victorious and always defeated, regardless of who wins or loses. And in that case, the ideal of freedom is never more than a *pretext* that really disguises other, more definite purposes, even though it may not be explicitly and cynically recognized as such. To invoke the ideal of freedom "in itself," apart from any further determinate ends or goals, is to appeal to a vacuous and

14. Albert Camus, *The Rebel,* trans. Anthony Bower (New York: Vintage Books, 1956), 177.

self-contradictory abstraction. For there can *be* no freedom in the absence of further ends or goals, as there can be no choice without some end or action that is chosen.

It appears, then, that the ideal of freedom is an empty ideal, a pious label that can be affixed to any personal or political purpose, but that therefore cannot provide the basis or content for any definite ethical or political norms or prescriptions, or stand as a positive common goal that could unify diverse individual purposes. Indeed, it would seem that the very invocation of the ideal of freedom as a *goal* rests upon a confusion. If the mere fact that an act or purpose is *chosen*, and therefore the *result* of an exercise of freedom, warrants its association with the idea of freedom, then how can freedom be invoked as the *end* or *goal* that *justifies* that act or purpose? For if the freedom in question has *already been exercised*, it can scarcely be the end still to be attained through the specific action or purpose in question.

On one level, the answer to all this is obvious enough. It is not the freedom of *choice*, but the freedom of *action*, that people set up as a goal or ideal: our old friend "the freedom to do as I please," or the freedom of self-realization, which depends upon the absence of obstacles or constraining circumstances (see Chapters 1 and 2 above). The individual who has made his choice, and thereby exercised his freedom in the first sense, still has the problem of translating his chosen purpose into action. If he is unable to do so, his choice is abortive, and his freedom remains unrealized. Freedom of choice is empty and incomplete unless complemented by the freedom to *act*, to *do* as I choose (see the section "Action and Self-Realization," in Chapter 6 above). But freedom in this sense depends upon favorable circumstances, upon the absence of insuperable external obstacles to action. Men make freedom their purpose when their other purposes are thwarted. When confronted by obstacles that prevent them from doing as they choose or by limitations that allow them no alternatives that seem worthy of choice, they turn upon those obstacles and restrictions themselves. Cut off from actions and ends of their own free choosing, they then turn aside to make freedom itself their goal. Therefore freedom can stand as an ideal or goal, even for a being that is already free. To make freedom one's ideal or purpose is to set out to overcome those obstacles and limitations that restrict one's options and block one's other purposes. And that is why the content of the ideal of freedom gets defined in terms of obstacles to be overcome and limitations to be surpassed—because those obstacles and limitations stand in the way of realizing one's choices in action.

But this answer *relocates* the problem of the elusiveness of the ideal of freedom without *resolving* it. The shift of attention from positive purposes to opposing obstacles does not rescue the ideal of freedom from the threat of vacuousness. Defining the ideal of freedom by the obstacles and limitations to be overcome leaves its meaning as protean and elusive as ever. What counts as an obstacle is strictly relative to one's purposes, so that one man's obstacle is another man's purpose and vice versa. The Great Wall of China was an *obstacle* to invaders—which was precisely the *purpose* of the Chinese in constructing it. The chains of slavery and the repressive machinery of a dictatorship offer parallel examples. The desires and pleasures that the sensualist adopts as purposes are the very obstacles that the ascetic seeks to overcome within himself. And so it goes. We here rediscover the dialectic of competing definitions of freedom with which this whole inquiry began. If the ideal of freedom receives its content and definition only from the obstacles and limitations at hand, then it can have no univocal meaning and can supply no ultimate norms or common standards, because those limitations and obstacles will differ with the particular purposes and circumstances of each individual. And if we abstract the notion of freedom as absence of limitations or obstacles from *all* particular purposes and circumstances and set it up as an ideal in its own right, we are left with the vacuous and impossible ideal of an absolute and limitless freedom, as I showed in Chapter 4. That forces us to recognize, as it did in Chapter 5, that freedom presupposes an opposing world that limits and obstructs the exercise of freedom. Indeed, it is because freedom can only exist in such a world that freedom of choice is incomplete and must be complemented by the freedom to act, to *do* as one chooses.[15] In the absence of all opposition and resistance, there could be no action, no problem of translating one's chosen purpose from intention to reality, and hence no "purpose" at all in any proper sense of the term. For the very notion of purpose implies an intention that has still to be realized through action. Thus, the ideal of freedom *from* opposition or limitation can only have meaning within the context of specific purposes and specific limiting circumstances. It is, in fact, a merely *provisional* or intermediate goal. To act for the sake of freedom by attacking obstacles and oppressive circumstances is to act for the sake of being able to act in other ways, in pursuit of other, more ultimate goals.

This helps to explain why the ideal of freedom is such a will-o'-the-wisp and why its pursuit has so often proved self-destructive. For if freedom is only a provisional goal, then it can only be realized in a provisional and temporary form. If the ideal of freedom acquires definite meaning only from the particular purposes and obstacles at hand, then its attainment is limited accordingly. To be able to realize one's chosen purpose is not to be

---

15. Cf. the section "Action and Self-Realization," in Chapter 6 above.

able to realize *all* purposes, and the realization of any *one* goal is bound to make the realization of others impossible. To overcome the obstacles at hand is never to overcome *all* obstacles and achieve a condition of unlimited options, but only to exchange one set of limitations and obstacles for another. And these new circumstances may well prove to be even more confining, may allow even less room for choice and action than the old. That is why the very pursuit and successful realization of the ideal of freedom may prove self-destructive, may leave an individual or society less free than it was before.

But this points toward a solution to the problem of defining an ethics of freedom. The ideal of freedom remains elusive so long as it is narrowly identified with the realization of a particular purpose or, in an equally narrow fashion, is conceived in one-sided opposition to a particular set of obstacles and limitations. In either of these cases, it forever escapes those who pursue it, like the horizon, which always recedes just as we reach it. Nor can we escape this difficulty by resorting to the ideal of a completely purposeless or "gratuitous" act or the ideal of a complete absence of limitations and obstructions, for then it remains a completely empty concept that certainly cannot provide any positive standards, or yield any ethical or social norms that might fill the void left by the collapse of conventional values.[16] Indeed, such conceptions of freedom, which ignore its inherently dialectical character, simply become caught up in an external dialectic that leads to endless ambiguities and contradictions.[17] The dialectical tension between freedom and an opposing, limiting world is inescapable because it is necessary to the very possibility of freedom. It is only in choosing a purpose and in struggling to overcome obstructions so as to impose that purpose upon a resistant external world that freedom can be exercised and realized. That does not mean that it escapes all limitations and determinations, however, but that it *determines itself* through its own activity. But to determine itself is to *limit* itself. The dialectical relation of freedom to a limiting yet supporting world is thereby *internalized,* taken up into the very reality of freedom itself, as the free agent finds himself confronted by limiting determinations that are not alien impositions but the product and realization of his own free activity. And these self-created limitations, both external and internal, may be such as to severely restrict

16. Herein lies much of the force of Michael Sandel's criticisms of John Rawls's *Theory of Justice in Liberalism and the Limits of Justice* (Cambridge: Cambridge University Press, 1982). But Sandel's critique founders because he never manages to cope with the inevitable ambiguities of the relation of freedom to its own determinacy, whereas Rawls's veil of ignorance allows him to finesse that whole problem without attempting to resolve the ambiguities involved.

17. Cf. the section "Finite Freedom and the Dialectic of Freedom," in Chapter 5 above.

the scope of further options and actions and therefore may effectively curtail or even cancel the subsequent exercise of freedom. That is why even the pursuit of the ideal of freedom can be both a realization of freedom and yet, paradoxically, destructive of further freedom.

Here we reach both the source and the solution of the elusiveness of the ideal of freedom. For it is precisely this ability of a free agent to subvert or destroy his own freedom in the very process of exercising it that led to the distinction between ontological and existential freedom in Chapter 6. That precipitated an examination of the "categories" of freedom, the conditions under which freedom can be preserved or enhanced rather than nullified or destroyed by its own act. The ways in which a self-determining being relates to its world and to itself were formulated in terms of the categories of choice and character. Each of these categories has negative, or deficient, modes that express the ways in which the exercise of freedom may be self-subversive, whereas the positive mode of each category defines the conditions of the self-consistent exercise of freedom. Since the positive or normative forms of these categories simply formulate the conditions under which the exercise of freedom is not self-destructive of freedom, they seem to supply the ideal of freedom with a positive content—a definition that is not simply a pretext for some ulterior purpose, but that refers us back to freedom. Decisiveness of choice and integrity of character provide norms for realizing and sustaining freedom itself. I therefore noted, at the end of Chapter 7, that these categories establish the basis for that ethical conception of freedom according to which freedom depends upon living and acting in accordance with an ideal befitting the nature of the self—in this case, the self-consistent and self-sustaining exercise of freedom. Whether or not that ideal and those norms are adequate to the requirements of ethics is another question, postponed at the time, to which I now turn.

✻ 12 ✻

Coexistence and Communication

A Demonic Note

Do the categories of freedom define an "ethics" of freedom? After establishing the categories of choice and character, I remarked at the end of Chapter 7 that the very logic of freedom vindicates the basic claim of that traditional ethical view of freedom, which argues that an individual is only free insofar as he lives and acts in accordance with the moral law or an ideal befitting human nature.[1] Since man is free, he has no "nature" in the usual sense. But the categories of freedom do constitute the conditions of his *remaining* free, and thereby define an ideal that is in accordance with his *being*. Since he can violate those conditions, their status is normative and

---

1. Cf. Adler's generic formula for this type of view: "To be free is to be able, through acquired virtue or wisdom, to will or live as one ought in accordance with moral law or an ideal befitting human nature" (*The Idea of Freedom* [Garden City, N.Y.: Doubleday, 1958], 1:606).

optional: They are standards of free existence that he can freely ignore—at the cost of his freedom. Does this mean that decisiveness of choice and integrity of character supply the basis for an ethics of freedom—or that these categorical conditions of freedom provide the general foundations for an ethics? Kant argued that we could readily deduce the fundamental principle of morality, or moral law, *from* human freedom—if only we could prove that man is free.[2] Granted, he also argued that no such proof is possible. But we have seen that his reasoning would make the temporality of human action and natural events unintelligible. I have tried to prove that, on the contrary, we must understand man and nature to be free if we are to understand them at all. Does that vindication of the hypothesis that man is free pave the way for establishing an ethics, as Kant supposed? Does my "deduction" of the categorical conditions of existential freedom in Chapter 7 provide something like the deduction of a moral law? Do the categories of freedom have the moral authority of Kant's "categorical imperative"?

It is tempting to suppose so. Unfortunately, I am in no position to draw such ambitious conclusions. For I only established in Chapter 7 that choice and character are conditions of existential freedom, not that we have any moral obligation to satisfy those conditions. To show that they are morally binding categories, it would be necessary to prove that freedom is a supreme value or fundamental norm. Otherwise, these conditions are only what Kant called "hypothetical imperatives," since they are only necessary in order to maintain freedom, a task that has not been shown to be obligatory or morally binding. If there is no obligation to seek the end, there is no obligation to adopt the means thereto. But is freedom an absolute end or a supreme moral goal to be fostered at all costs? Nothing I have said so far proves that it is.

And if we ask whether the positive forms of the categories of choice and character define a cogent ethical ideal, a little moral reflection will show that they do not. For they do not rule out behavior that most of us would regard as patently immoral. The terms I have used to describe the categorical modes of relation of the free self to itself and to its world have certainly carried ethical overtones. But these overtones may be deceptive. The very phrase "integrity of character" seems to imply moral virtue, for example. "People especially admire integrity of character," says Rameau's nephew in Diderot's dialogue. But his words are entirely ironic, for he is an amoralist, a pimp and parasite who is advocating deliberate wickedness: "If there's one realm in which it is essential to be sublime, it is in wickedness. You spit on ordinary scum, but you can't deny a kind of respect to a great criminal: his

---

2. See *The Critique of Practical Reason*, trans. Lewis White Beck (New York: Liberal Arts Press, 1956), 28–30.

courage amazes, his ferocity overawes. People especially admire integrity of character."[3]

He is right, of course. The popularity of the "antihero" in literature proves his point. Here is a possibility that cannot be overlooked. The categories of existential freedom described in Chapter 7 might very well be fulfilled in the life of a person we would not hesitate to brand as evil. Indeed, an immoral individual who displayed the decisiveness in choice and flexible continuity of character that I described there as the positive categories of freedom would be a sublimely wicked person, a demonic figure. That possibility has long fascinated the literary imagination, for such a person would be the consummate villain. Romantic authors were particularly intrigued by the possibility of the perfectly evil life, a life devoted to evil with all the deliberation, resoluteness, and consistency of purpose that the perfectly virtuous person would display in pursuit of the good. Dostoevsky describes Stavrogin, in *The Possessed*, as a man who has "experimented" with this inverted ideal. Gide's Lafcadio is a similar figure, and this possibility was a persistent preoccupation for Jean Genet.

Shakespeare's Richard III is probably the most familiar example of such "sublime wickedness." Richard is certainly a resolute, decisive man who chooses—and chooses knowingly. Nor can his decisions be relegated to the deficient modes of choice: withdrawal and surrender. His own misshapen body and his circumstances as a public figure might well have prompted him to withdraw from the world and seek an obscure or monastic life. Instead, he chooses to confront and overcome the world. But although he certainly becomes entangled in worldly intrigues, it would hardly be accurate to describe Richard as "surrendering" himself to the world and to worldly goals. True, he does commit himself to the pursuit of power and the throne. Yet he is no Macbeth, urged on by the overpowering ambition to rule. It would be more fitting to say that what appeals to Richard is the very process of acquiring the throne, of triumphing over those who had humiliated him and overcoming, through deceit and treachery, the obstacles that stand in his way. Surely, there is a certain integrity and style to his entire career, which seem to answer to the demands of the category of character. And, correspondingly, Richard's career does seem to be one in which freedom is exercised in such a way as to preserve and enhance its own scope rather than to cancel or subvert itself. Indeed, if some vestiges of moral scruples do arise to afflict his dreams at the end of the play, these only seem to curtail his freedom, to interfere with what had theretofore been a steadily expanding range of freedom and power.

---

3. Denis Diderot, *Rameau's Nephew and Other Works*, trans. Jacques Barzun and Ralph H. Bowen (Indianapolis: Liberal Arts Press, 1964), 58.

What are we to make of such a demonic figure? Or, again, how are we to contend with the suggestion that the freest act of all is the gratuitous *crime*—the theme of Gide's *Lafcadio's Adventures*—or with Genet's notion that the act of betrayal is the freest action of all? The arguments that lead to decisiveness of choice and integrity of character as conditions of existential freedom do not seem to rule out such resolute wickedness. But if these categories are consistent with such a combination of freedom and evil, then they certainly do not supply us with an adequate definition of morality. At the very most, they might be necessary, but not *sufficient,* conditions of morality. An adequate account of morality would require some other criteria or conditions than these.

What is missing? Why don't these categories allow us to distinguish between the virtuous and demonic individuals, the perfect hero and the perfect villain? The answer should not be hard to find. We have only to ask what it is that makes the actions of a Richard III or a Stavrogin or Lafcadio so obviously immoral, even though they may satisfy the categorical conditions of freedom discussed above. And we don't need any very subtle moral discrimination or detailed analysis of each case to recognize what it is about such men and such deeds that makes them so obviously immoral. Their wickedness is easily recognized in their treatment of their fellow men. One may admire a certain genius and strength of character in Shakespeare's Richard. What marks him as evil is certainly not his employment of these qualities in the pursuit of his political ambitions. Presumably, we would prefer men of genius and strength of character as our rulers. In these respects, Richard is surely far better qualified to rule than his brother Edward. What stamps him as evil is his unscrupulous treatment of the other persons he tramples under on his path to the throne.

The categories of choice and character developed in Chapter 7 do not encompass this interpersonal dimension of the exercise of freedom. They may furnish standards for the relation of a free individual to his world and to himself, but they define no limits or criteria for relations between free agents. Yet it is precisely upon relations between persons that the most delicate and urgent problems of human morality seem to center. Perhaps an individual *can* fail morally in his relation to himself or to the nonhuman world, but most people are surprised by the suggestion that they have duties to themselves or to animals. The most obvious and difficult moral issues seem to center on relations between persons.

The limitation in my earlier account of the categories of freedom is now quite obvious. I dealt only with the case of an isolated freedom, alone in its world. Perhaps the opposition between the ethical and the demonic would not arise for such a solitary freedom. But an account of freedom that does not embrace relations between free individuals and offers no limiting criteria regarding them could scarcely provide a sufficient foundation for any ethics that would be recognizable as adequate to the human condition. The most heated debates and battles over freedom have to do with political and social affairs, with issues involving relations *among* individuals. Even a minimal account of the nature and conditions of freedom must look beyond the isolated individual to the community of coexistent freedoms. Yet the transition from solitude to community is not a simple one. Indeed, one must question its very possibility.

Solitude, Solipsism, and Coexistence

A single free being, or self, *might* be alone in its world. Freedom does not necessarily presuppose a world populated with more than one free being. For although freedom cannot exist without a world, there appears to be no necessity that its world should contain other freedoms. Therefore, the case of an isolated free individual is not impossible. Such a solitary self would be *solus ipse,* alone to itself. Hence, a philosophy that envisions such a world, containing only a single self, is described as solipsistic. The mere suggestion of such a total solitude seems somewhat uncanny and foreboding. It evokes echoes of the voice crying out in the wilderness where there is no one to hear, images of the last man on earth in the wake of a nuclear holocaust. To offset these desolate associations, one might do well to recall that isolated selfhood would also describe the situation of God before the creation of any other self. And yet, even the religious imagination seems almost to shun the thought of such a lonely divinity, preferring to surround the creator with other gods or with a heavenly host of angels so as to provide God with a community of eternal, immortal companions even before the act of creation. The problem of a community of free individuals most engages our interest, since this is the possibility that pertains to the human condition. The possibility of an isolated freedom seems to be a highly abstract and speculative construct by contrast.

And yet, the unhappy image of a solitary self, alone in the cosmos, has haunted modern Western thought. Not that solipsistic doctrines have been frequently propounded or popularly embraced. But the problem of solipsism has plagued modern thought because it is bound up with the sharp distinction between mind and body that Descartes bequeathed to his successors and that has proved to be such an enduring feature of our intellectual landscape ever since. Serious thinkers have rarely, if ever, denied the existence of other selves or minds. But they have had trouble explaining how one mind or self can possibly know another, or even be aware of the existence of any others. This is because the mind and its thoughts have been understood to be essentially private and unperceivable. The problem for modern thought has not been one of wondering whether I am alone in the world, then, but one of perplexity about *how* I know that I'm *not* alone and of explaining just how a number of essentially private mental substances can possibly form a community.

Rather similar problems arise for any attempt to conceive a community of *free* individuals. For what could be more private than a choice or decision in which the self determines itself? In every exercise of freedom, the self is involved in a reflexive relationship with itself. I cannot make your decisions or choose *for* you, nor you for me. Or rather, insofar as an individual *does* let others make his decisions, he alienates his own freedom in so doing. Indeed, the very nature and possibility of relations between two freedoms is extremely problematic. I have already noted, in Chapter 6, that the relation of a free self to its world is inherently problematic and indeterminate. Relations between any two free individuals must be even more so. The self's relation to its world is always a problem because that relation is never simply *given* or entirely settled: It is up to the free individual to define his relationship to the world in choosing among the opportunities that the world makes available. Insofar as the other beings encountered in the world are not free, however, there is no reciprocal problem about how *they* will choose to relate to the self. But where *two* free individuals are involved, the relationship between them will be *doubly* problematic and ambivalent, since it will depend upon the choices of both parties. Neither individual can determine unilaterally what their relationship will be. Any discussion of relations among free individuals is therefore faced with multiple and compound ambiguities.

Yet none of this will make any difference at all to either of the two individuals involved unless each can take account of the freedom of the other. Otherwise, the ambiguities inherent in their relationship will not exist *for* the individuals involved themselves. There will be sheer discrepancy. Each might reckon with the other as a determinate part of the world, yet remain oblivious to the ambiguities introduced into the situation by the other as a source of free decisions. Clearly, if it is to make any difference to one free self that there are other free beings in its world, then there must be some way in which that self can encounter those others and encounter them as free. For of course, a freedom that never encountered another freedom would be *effectively* alone to itself, even in a world populated by other free individuals. (What difference could it make to Adam if God had created Eve, but set her down in another Eden at the opposite end of the earth? At most, Adam might notice that he was missing a rib. But Eve would not exist for Adam, nor he for Eve. They would *co*exist only for God, but not for one another.) If individuals are to coexist as free and if that coexistence is to make any difference to them, they must at least be present to one another. But mere contiguity or presence together in one spot is not enough. For it does not ensure that either individual will encounter the other's freedom *as* such. On the contrary, the very conditions of coexistence in the world seem to raise problems about the possibility of any such contact between freedoms.

In order to see *why* this is so, we need only examine the conditions of objective coexistence in the world. I found it helpful to contrast choice and character, the categories governing freedom's relation to itself and to the world, with Kant's discussions of cause and substance, the corresponding categories of objective relations. The same contrast will prove useful here. In his third category of relation, "The Principle of Coexistence in Accordance with the Law of Reciprocity or Community," Kant attempted to formulate the necessary condition under which things may be known to coexist with one another objectively. His original statement of this principle is the clearest for my purposes: "All substances, so far as they coexist, stand in thoroughgoing community, that is, in mutual interaction."[4] Kant's point here is that reciprocal causal determination is a necessary condition of objective coexistence, that coexistence cannot consist of a mere juxtaposition of entities that are otherwise completely unrelated and unaffected by one another. Anaxagoras had long since stated the principle involved in more colorful terms: "The things in the one Cosmos are not separated off from one another with an axe."[5] A more modern formulation would state that there are no completely closed or isolated systems within nature. This is sometimes referred to as the principle of the unity of nature, which requires that the whole of nature be regarded as a single closed system of interdependent entities.[6]

The details of Kant's explanation and proof of this principle are untenable.[7] But in the present context, a somewhat different account of the

---

4. *Critique of Pure Reason*, trans. Norman Kemp Smith (New York: St. Martin's Press, 1961), A211, p. 233. The title cited above is from the second edition, B256.

5. Diels Fragment 8. I quote the Freeman translation.

6. Kant himself says that the three categories of relation taken together declare the unity of nature (*Critique of Pure Reason*, A216, B263). But since he also sees the category of coexistence as combining the other two (B210–11), it really is itself the principle of the unity of nature.

7. Kant's explanation is incompatible with contemporary physics, a serious defect in an account that is supposed to be valid for all possible objective knowledge. However, the details of the account are also incompatible with Kant's own analysis of causation—and for rather similar reasons. By coexistence, Kant clearly means contemporaneity. In his explanation of the principle, Kant makes coexistence depend upon mutual causal determination, whereas

principle is available, one that will also help to highlight the problem of the coexistence of freedoms. Like all of Kant's categories, the principle of coexistence expresses one of the necessary preconditions of objective knowledge. Now, objective knowledge has been described in Chapter 7 as that special opportunity or project which aims at ascertaining the structure of the world as a completely determinate realm in its own right, rather than as an arena of action. That is, objective knowledge attempts to apprehend the nature of the world as it is independent of freedom. I have already suggested how the categories of substance and causation formulate the requirements of this purpose as it applies to single entities and particular determinations. The category of coexistence, or principle of reciprocity, is simply a way of formulating this purpose as it applies to the world as a whole. For purposes of objective knowledge, the world must be regarded as a single, fully determinate domain or system of coexistent entities, in which there can be no gaps or cracks of indeterminacy. Where the specific determinate relationship between entities is not known, it must be assumed to exist nevertheless. Thus formulated, the category of coexistence should be as valid for an Einsteinian universe as for a Newtonian one. It should also be broad enough to apply to either a dynamic, physical world or a "world" of pure Platonic forms or Whiteheadian eternal objects. In a world of pure forms, the reciprocal determinations of entities would also be purely formal, whereas in a dynamic, physical world the mutual determination would be defined causally.[8] In either case, entities may be said to coexist only by virtue of the fact that each is determined by the others.

This definition of coexistence in terms of mutual determination or causal interaction places the very possibility of coexistence among free entities in doubt. For it is not hard to see that this principle would define a deterministic universe in which there is no room for freedom as *self*-determination. It is a principle of the coexistence of *unfree* beings, though, again, this only articulates the very purpose of objective knowledge, which is to ascertain the nature of the world as it is *apart* from freedom. Nevertheless, the dependence of objective understanding upon this "law of reciprocity"

---

modern physics requires that contemporaneity be defined by mutual causal *independence*. (Cf., e.g., M. Capek, *The Philosophical Impact of Contemporary Physics* [Princeton: Princeton University Press, 1961], chaps. 12 and 13.) But insofar as Kant's account seems to require a relation of mutual *simultaneous* causation, it is circular and contradicts his own analysis of causation as involving temporal succession. Cf. R. P. Wolff, *Kant's Theory of Mental Activity* (Cambridge, Mass.: Harvard University Press, 1963), 291–92; on the problems of Kant's treatment of simultaneous causation, see 280–82.

8. That is, as causal independence if strict instantaneous simultaneity is meant, but as causal interdependence in the case of enduring entities.

underscores the problem of understanding coexistence among *free* entities. Let us state that difficulty as sharply as possible. Entities can be said to coexist precisely insofar as they are determined by one another. But an entity is free only insofar as it determines *itself*, that is, insofar as it is *not* determined by others. It would seem, then, that an entity can be said to be free just insofar as it *violates* the necessary condition of coexistence and that entities can be said to coexist only insofar as they are not free. How, then, can we even conceive of a coexistence of freedoms?

The very statement of this dilemma in these terms points toward its solution. For the dilemma revives the notion of a pure and absolute freedom that would be uncontaminated and unconditioned by any limiting world. Such an absolute freedom could not coexist with *any* other beings, whether free or unfree. It would have to be not only solitary, but worldless and disembodied as well. But this ideal of absolute freedom is illusory; no such freedom can exist. Freedom can only exist in a world, and it can only *be* in a world by having a body that belongs to that world. By the same token, free individuals can coexist only insofar as they are together in the same world, and they *can* only be together in the world insofar as they have bodies. A *community* of worldless, disembodied freedoms is impossible because a *single* worldless, disembodied freedom is impossible. But as bodies in the world, free individuals are *in part* describable deterministically, in terms of Kant's law of reciprocity. The body must be a part of the world if it is to serve as an organ of receptivity that gives the self access to the world. As such, it must be determined and determinable by all the other parts of the world, including the bodies of other free individuals. There is some force, therefore, to the objection that a coexistence of freedoms depends upon a reciprocal determinism and hence upon unfreedom. Even free beings can coexist only insofar as they are not *absolutely* free, that is, insofar as they are not wholly *self*-determining, but are also externally determined as bodies that belong to the world and mutually determine one another. But insofar as they are determined by one another, they are *not* free, not self-determining. How, then, can there be any encounter between them as free beings?

Such an encounter is possible because the body belongs to the self as well as to the world. *As* free, the self must transcend the alien determinacy imposed upon itself by its world and its body and determine itself through its own choices and actions. The body is not only a passive receptivity that exposes the self to external determination. It is also an instrument of action that enables the self to modify the world and to realize its choices. Insofar as the free self both acts upon the world and is acted upon by the world, it satisfies the demand of reciprocal interaction of the category of objective coexistence. But insofar as action in the world *is* a realization of freedom, it brings free individuals into direct contact with one another. It is the process of reciprocal determination between free individuals acting upon one another causally as bodies that gives them access *to* one another.

Communication

But causal interaction merely makes an encounter between freedoms *possible*. It does not guarantee it, any more than does mere juxtaposition. Free individuals may interact causally without ever taking any account at all of one another's freedom, even though each is affected by the other's actions. If there is to be any encounter between individuals *as* free, then their causal interaction must not be a mere determination of each by the other, but must become a vehicle of *communication* whereby each takes account of the freedom of the other. Just what forms that communication might take may remain an open question at this point. For the moment, we need only recognize that if no such communication occurs, then the two individuals only affect one another causally. For lack of some form of communication, each would only encounter the other as a body, as one determinate part of the world completely determined by other parts of the world.

Reciprocity among freedoms therefore strictly presupposes communication. Whereas the coexistence of unfree beings depends upon reciprocal *causation,* then, the coexistence of freedoms depends upon reciprocal *communication.* But causal reciprocity and reciprocal communication are not *opposed* to one another, since it is the process of causal interaction that makes communication possible by giving free individuals access to one another in the first place. If communication is to be achieved, this process of causal interaction must be appropriated by freedom and made to serve as the organ or medium of communication. The merely *causal* reciprocity must be transformed into an instrument for the realization of a reciprocity of *choices.* Let us consider more carefully how this can come about.

Any overt action of another individual *may* serve as a means of communication if I choose to regard it as an expression of the other's freedom rather than merely as an event in the world. If someone jostles me sharply in the street, or if my wife's foot strikes my shin under the table at a supper party, I may wonder whether these events are mere coincidences, or whether they are expressions of choices. But this role of choice is clearest when the actions taken are those we would normally think of as vehicles of communication, such as speech and writing. These actions have negligible causal efficacy so long as we only regard them as perceptible *events*. The little sounds and marks we produce scarcely have much causal impact if we only regard them as sounds and marks and not as words. They are important only insofar as an individual chooses to *make* them significant by taking them as meaningful expressions of another self. To "attend" to the other is to *choose* to be receptive in relation to the other, not simply to be causally affected by the other's acts.

On the other hand, to be active in communication, to choose to communicate, is to choose to act upon the other in a way that is not simply causal. It is to choose to act upon the other, not simply as a body in the world, but as free, since it is *as* free that the other can "attend" to my actions and interpret them as expressions of a free self. Thus, communication is possible because a merely causal reciprocity can be transformed into a medium of communication through a reciprocity of choices, because free individuals may not only affect one another causally, but can choose to relate to one another as free. And since communication depends upon choice, a refusal to communicate is always possible—whereas one individual cannot similarly refuse causal interaction with another, since that is a function, not of choice, but of the fact that the two individuals coexist objectively in the same world.[9]

Reciprocal communication between free individuals therefore constitutes a third category of freedom. The exact nature of the communicative process has been left open thus far for several reasons. First, it is important to describe the *category* in perfectly general terms in order to demonstrate that it is, indeed, a necessary condition of *any* relations between free individuals *as* free. Whether and how this may actually be achieved is a separate question. The point is to recognize that if no communication occurs, freedoms never encounter one another. Second, it is important not to bias description of the category of communication from the very outset by freighting it with assumptions drawn from familiar features of *human* communication. For, on the one hand, we should not blind ourselves to the

---

9. Of course, this only accounts for the barest possibility of communication among free individuals. It leaves unresolved many venerable problems and controversies concerning the nature and limits of communication: whether it works through empathy, analogous inference, direct intuition, etc.; whether human beings alone are capable of communication or whether animals and even insects are also able to communicate in more limited ways; and so on. An attempt to do justice to all these problems would require such a long digression as to seriously sidetrack the issue at hand. No such digression is necessary, however, since in any case coexistence among freedoms as free *presupposes* reciprocal communication, just as, for purposes of objective knowledge, coexistence among unfree beings presupposes reciprocal *determination*. Where there is no such communication, there is no effective coexistence of freedoms as such.

possibilities of communication among other sorts of free individuals, among animals, for example. And, on the other hand, not every form of human communication would really be pertinent. The mere fact that human beings are communicating with one another in some manner does not mean that they are relating to one another as free. A mere transfer of objective information or instructions can occur without necessarily achieving any reciprocity between freedoms as such.

Finally, and most important, we must bear in mind that each category of freedom has deficient modes. The fulfillment of the categories of freedom is never guaranteed, because the very exercise of freedom may be self-canceling. The self can determine itself in ways that contradict its own freedom. Alongside the categorical forms of freedom's relation to itself and to its world, therefore, are the deficient modes of those relations, which reflect the possibility that a self-determining being may cancel the conditions of its own being in its existence. This same possibility must be acknowledged in the case of relations of one freedom to another. Even if reciprocity and communication between free individuals are *possible,* nothing guarantees that that possibility will be actualized. And even where communication does take place, deficient forms are bound to subvert any genuine reciprocity between freedoms. Indeed, the possibilities of failure are multiplied in the case of relations between freedoms. For in this instance, *either* of the two individuals may subvert its own freedom *or* that of the other self, *or* may refuse to communicate *or* ignore the other's attempts to communicate. These are not strictly exclusive alternatives, but any one of them would suffice to prevent the realization of a reciprocity of freedoms.

In dealing with the categories of choice and character, I described withdrawal and surrender as deficient modes of those categories. Withdrawal and surrender are ways of relating to the world and to self that are self-destructive exercises of freedom because they dissolve the dialectical tension between self and world that is inherent in freedom. These same alternatives can be discerned in the present case. Refusal to communicate is the counterpart of withdrawal from the world and might be described as a withdrawal from the *social* world. We regard a total refusal to communicate with anyone as a symptom of extreme human pathology. Refusal to communicate with one particular individual may be rude, but we regard it as anyone's right to do so, though it is just as much a violation of this category in the context of that particular relationship. Either a total or a selective refusal to communicate involves a rejection of others or of a particular other, an attempt to avoid entering into a reciprocal relation with the other *at all.*

But even where individuals *do* communicate, some modes of communication represent forms of withdrawal. After all, communication only satisfies the requirements of reciprocity insofar as it provides each free individual with access to the other *as* free and as an individual. But communication may be employed precisely so as to frustrate that requirement. I may attempt to *deceive* others, using the very process of communication to defeat its own purpose, so as to *prevent* others from gaining genuine access to my intentions. The very revelatory function of communication carries with it the possibility of this misuse for purposes of concealment. A deceiver communicates, yet refuses to communicate, both at once. On the other hand, one individual may choose to misinterpret another, a phenomenon quite familiar to students of group dynamics and of families as dynamic systems. What the listener chooses to hear may depend more upon his or her own purposes and fears than upon what the speaker actually said. In its extreme form, such willful misunderstanding invites comparison with withdrawal into a realm of fantasy, since the misinterpreter may thus contrive to substitute a meaning of his own choosing for the other's real meaning, even to fabricate a character and personality of his own invention that has little to do with what the other person really is and does.

To choose either to deceive or to misinterpret the other is to attempt to dissolve the dialectical relation of self and other by attempting to control *both* poles of the communicative relationship. This strategy directs attention to a deficient mode of this category of free coexistence that has no parallel in the case of choice or character. In those cases, there could only be a question of the self's subverting its *own* freedom in the course of its existence. But in the case of relations between freedoms, there is also the possibility that the self may attempt to subvert the freedom of another individual by manipulating or dominating the other self. In its most obvious form, the attempt to manipulate or dominate the other may employ sheer force alone, exploiting the other's vulnerability to direct external determination by attempting to cancel the other's freedom through coercion rather than through communication. But attempts to coerce others directly are likely to backfire by provoking reprisals. However, the very process of communication may also be employed to manipulate or dominate the other, perhaps far more effectively than would be possible through more violent forms of coercion, as Sissela Bok stresses in her book on lying: "Deceit and violence—these are the two forms of deliberate assault on human beings. Both can coerce people into acting against their will. Most harm that can befall victims through violence can come to them also through deceit. But deceit controls more subtly, for it works on belief as well as action. Even Othello, whom few would have dared to try to subdue by force, could be brought to destroy himself and Desdemona through falsehood."[10]

While violent coercion may invite the other to a contrary exercise of freedom in response to treatment as a mere thing or instrument, communication may achieve a more subtle domination by seeking to direct or control the other's exercise *of* freedom. Because communication provides access to the other self as free, it can be employed in order to subvert that freedom.

But if communication can serve as an instrument of domination and oppression, it can also serve as a means of surrender or submission. I have described surrender as an existential subversion of freedom in which the self allows itself to be entirely determined by the world. However, the very word "surrender" suggests relations between free individuals, since it is most commonly applied to situations in which one party yields to the domination of another. Yet surrender is possible even where the other makes no corresponding attempt to dominate or suppress. In order to subvert his own freedom, a submissive individual may exploit the access to other selves that communication offers. Communication makes it possible for the individual to evade choice by submitting entirely to the freedom of others, becoming a willing slave to the other's desires, perhaps even an unwanted one. ("Your wish is my wish, your will is my command.") The individual who becomes a mere dependent organ of another's freedom furnishes the simplest, most conspicuous example of submissiveness. But freedom may also be surrendered by submerging oneself in the general flow of communication, as Heidegger so forcefully showed by analyzing how readily and completely we abandon ourselves to ordinary talk. The everyday self is typically so absorbed by prattle, gossip, and public communication, he charges, that choice and responsibility are surrendered to an anonymous other, the "one" or "they," who is everyone and no one. Where this occurs, we may describe an individual as "surrendering to the dictates of custom," or as becoming "a slave to convention." But whether he surrenders to a particular individual or to such a generalized other, the submissive individual thereby chooses to avoid the dialectic of reciprocity between freedoms by relegating all freedom to the side of the other.

These examples of withdrawal, deceit, manipulation, domination, and surrender should serve to illustrate the range of deficient modes of the category of communication without pretending to furnish an exhaustive analysis. Nor are they mutually exclusive options. The same individual may be submissive to officials and a tyrant to his family, or withdrawn with

10. Sissela Bok, *Lying: Moral Choice in Public and Private Life* (New York: Vintage Books, 1979), 19.

women but "one of the boys" in the locker room or at the VFW post. Contrasting alternatives may even be combined in a single relationship, since submissiveness may be an effective manipulative strategy, forcing choice and responsibility upon the other. Except for the case of complete withdrawal or refusal to communicate, they are all forms of coexistence in which communication may occur, but in such a way as to prevent or subvert a reciprocal relationship between individuals *as* free. Instead of bringing freedoms into mutual contact with one another, such deficient modes of communication establish a unilateral relationship by suppressing either the freedom of the self or the other's freedom—or both.

In contrast to these deficient modes, the positive mode of this category will be a form of communication whereby free beings are able to relate freely to one another's freedom. How is this more genuine form of communication possible? This problem has been an important theme in recent thought. Twentieth-century German thinkers, especially, from Karl Jaspers through Hans Gadamer, Jürgen Habermas, and Karl-Otto Apel, have sought to develop theories of free and undistorted communication as a basis for both ethics and critical social theory.[11] A thorough exploration of this problem that would do justice to their contributions would be entirely out of proportion here. The present context calls for—and allows—only a succinct categorical analysis, an attempt to identify the key constitutive ingredients of a positive form of communication that can establish reciprocity between free agents. How, then, is this positive form of communication to be characterized?

Free Communication

First, we should consider how communication relates to the other two categories of freedom: character and choice. Reflection on their role in

---

11. Communication is a central theme of Jaspers's philosophy. He distinguishes *existential* communication from all merely objective and utilitarian forms of communication because it is a communication that engages individuals as free. Cf. esp. Karl Jaspers, "Communication," chap. 3 of *Existential Elucidation*, vol. 2 of *Philosophy*, trans. E. B. Ashton (Chicago: University of Chicago Press, 1970). In *Truth and Method*, rev. ed., trans. J. Weinsheimer and D. G. Marshall (New York: Sheed & Ward, 1989), Gadamer proposes to displace methodological theories of hermeneutics with a dialogical model of interpretation. Apel and Habermas would found a critical social theory in a critique of systematically distorted communication that assumes a model of pure free discourse as normative. Habermas has discussed this in many places, but his major work on the subject is *The Theory of Communicative Action* (Boston: Beacon Press, 1983). See also Seyla Benhabib and Fred Dahlmayer, eds., *The Communicative Ethics Controversy* (Cambridge, Mass.: MIT Press, 1990).

communication will lead to the basic conditions of free communication, much as the positive forms of choice and character referred to one another. For as character depends upon choice and choice depends upon character, communication depends upon both choice and character. Free communication can only occur by choice and between characters. Individuals only communicate freely insofar as they do so by choice. That much is obvious. On the other hand, communication cannot be established between pure, undefined freedoms, but only between freedoms individuated by the actual exercise of freedom—that is, between characters defined by their choices. That is partly because pure freedom is an abstraction that stands for the bare *possibility* of self-determination, a possibility that is *realized* only in choice and action. It is also because free individuals can make contact with one another only by acting in a common world, and in so acting they define and limit themselves.

But if individuals have exercised their freedom only in such a way as to cancel it, then they cannot freely relate to one another's freedom. If I have used up my freedom by surrendering to the world, I cannot freely relate to another individual. And if I have withdrawn from the world, then I have also cut off my access to other free individuals. Only the self that is freely related to itself and to the world can sustain its own side of a reciprocity of freedoms. This means that the fulfillment of the positive mode of the category of communication depends upon the positive fulfillment of the other two categories of freedom. Thus, communication between freedoms demands decisiveness of choice and integrity of character on the part of both individuals. This is a stringent requirement, but an unavoidable one, since communication between free individuals requires that they be existentially as well as ontologically free. But free communication will impose still further requirements, since it must define how their freedom can be sustained in their relations to one another. Let us consider more exactly how free communication depends upon each of the other two categories of freedom: choice and character.

It should scarcely be surprising to find that the quality of communication between individuals depends upon their choices. Surely, if free individuals are to communicate freely, then they must choose to do so. But it is not enough for them to choose to communicate with one another, for either party might choose one of the deficient modes of communication described above and thereby foreclose the possibility of reciprocity between them. If their communication is to establish a reciprocity of freedoms, then they must choose to communicate in a specific manner. Each must choose to be *open* with the other, since deception, dissimulation, and inhibition of expression tend not only to coerce the other but to foreclose the other's free access to the coercing self. In simpler terms, this is only to say that genuine communication requires sincerity or candor. Granted, just as individuals may interact without choosing to do so, so may they exercise their freedom so as to interact and influence one another even when they misrepresent themselves to each other. But obviously, insofar as their deceptions succeed, they do *not* genuinely communicate themselves to one another.

But candor would be futile if the other person is unreceptive. If effective and free communication is to occur, the individuals must not only be open *with* each other, they must also be open *to* one another. The most candid expression effects no communication if it is ignored. Thus, if individuals are to communicate, they must choose to be *receptive* to one another. *Expressive* openness must be complemented by *receptive* openness. Without open self-expression, the other is denied access to the freedom of the self. Without receptive openness, the self does not gain access to the freedom of the other. Clearly, both individuals must choose to be open in both ways if communication is to establish a reciprocity of freedoms.

However, to be receptive is not only to be passively attentive to what the other has to communicate, but to choose to be open to the other's freedom. The category of choice requires that the self determine its relation to the world rather than allow the world to determine itself; in Kantian terms, it requires autonomy instead of heteronomy. But no simple alternative between autonomy and heteronomy will suffice in the case of communication, because to determine my relation to another self autonomously and unilaterally is precisely to deny the other's freedom. To be open to the other's freedom instead of denying or canceling it is to choose to let the other choose. Conversely, simply to allow the other to decide everything unilaterally would be to surrender my own freedom, which is heteronomy. And that would also subvert any possible reciprocity of freedoms. To be receptive to the other's freedom is not to abdicate one's own choice, but to decide to relate to the other in such a way as to make room for the other's decision.[12]

Communication, then, is a function of interrelated choices. In this respect, it resembles character. In the case of communication, the choices are those of *different* individuals, of course, whereas character depends upon how the choices of a single individual are related to one another. But in many ways, the problem of an individual's relation to another freedom echoes the problem of the relation of each self to its own freedom. In the case of character, each choice determines the self and thereby places

---

12. Cf. Heidegger's contrast between an inauthentic "leaping in" to take over *for* another and authentic solicitude, which "leaps ahead" to "help the other become transparent to himself *in* his care and to become free *for* it" (*Being and Time,* trans. John Macquarrie and Edward Robinson [New York: Harper & Row, 1962], 158–59).

conditions upon subsequent choices and how they are made, perhaps restricting or broadening the range of alternatives available. This is most conspicuous where the self chooses in such a way as to cancel its freedom and preclude future choices. Very similar relations also obtain between the choices of different individuals. The choices that one individual makes may be decisive for another individual, restricting or expanding the range of alternatives available to the other. The domination of another individual, effectively subverting his freedom, is a relation between the choices of two different individuals that is exactly parallel to the choice whereby an individual subverts his own freedom and preempts his own further choices. Conversely, the specific sort of choice just described as necessary to free communication is exactly parallel to that which has already been shown to be necessary to the self's maintenance of its *own* freedom. In that case, existential freedom requires the choice of a mode, or "style," of existence that is open both to the world and to further choice. Freedom destroys itself either by withdrawal from the world or by a surrender to the world that leaves no room for future choices. The choice necessary to genuine communication simply demands this same sort of openness in relation to the other's freedom. It is a choice that leaves the other room to choose. The choice of character and the choice to communicate openly are thus parallel. Both hinge upon how choices are interrelated. In the one instance, it is the quality of character and the existential freedom of a single individual that are at stake. In the other case, it is the quality of communication and the relation to the other's freedom that hinges upon these relationships between choices. In an important sense, of course, the existence of freedom consists entirely in single acts of choice, and the other categories of freedom depend upon the ordering of these choices. The problem of character depends upon the serial order of the choices of a given individual, while the problem of communication has to do with the parallel series of choices of different individuals.

Actually, however, we must consider both types of relation together. There are not, after all, two kinds of choices, one whereby each individual determines his character and another whereby each determines his relations to other selves. The ways in which individuals choose to relate to one another determine their character, and their characters are of decisive importance to the possibility of communication between them. Communication is not an instantaneous occurrence that might be merely the product of two single momentary choices. Rather, it is a process that depends upon interrelated series of decisions, and relations *within* each series will determine relations *between* the two series. Therefore, we must consider how character bears upon communication.

I have already noted that communication between freedoms demands integrity of character of both individuals because free communication requires existentially free individuals and integrity of character is a categorical condition of existential freedom. But I must now examine more specifically how the requirements of these two categories of freedom are related.

An individual's choices are constitutive of the character of that individual because the self determines *itself* through its choices. The character determined through prior choices conditions subsequent choices in turn, so that the self does not make each new choice in a vacuum, as a completely undetermined capacity to choose. Rather, its choices are those of a determinate individual self and tend to be characteristic of that individual. Existential freedom depends upon integrity of character, which is defined in terms of both consistent choice and the self-consistency of an individual's choices. That is, what integrity requires is not that the individual evade the demands for consistently choosing in each novel situation by rigidly adhering to an antecedent choice, but that he choose so as to accept the decisiveness of prior choices in determining himself.

How do these relations among the choices of a single individual bear upon the possibility of communication between free individuals? In the first place, it must be reemphasized that the choices an individual makes not only condition his *own* subsequent choices, but those of the other as well. But if B is to base his choice, the exercise of his freedom, on A's choice, then he must be able to *rely* upon A. And that presupposes not only that A has been open with B and has not deceived B about his own choices, but also that A's choices are reliable, that A will not turn around and choose the exact opposite at the next occasion. The maiden who refuses her hand to a prince because she has pledged herself to the stable boy should be sure that the stable boy will not decide to marry the miller's widow the following week. If communication is to establish reciprocity between individual freedoms, then, those individuals must be not only candid but reliable or responsible in their relations with one another. This demands just the kind of consistency of choice required by integrity of character. Without this reliability, even the most open communication would become vacuous and futile, since what was communicated at one instant might be nullified at the next by a contrary decision. If a man's word is not trustworthy or reliable, then communication becomes pointless. And if a man's word is to be trusted, he must not only be candid or sincere, he must also be consistent or steadfast, ready to assume responsibility for what he has chosen and "to stand behind his word." It matters very little to the aggrieved young maid of the ballads whether her lover was insincere or merely fickle, whether she has been deceived by her trust in his words or by her trust in his character. Just as integrity demands that the individual accept the decisiveness of his own choices in determining himself, communication requires that each party accept responsibility for his choices in relation to the other. Thus, we may say either that the self-consistency of choice demanded by integrity of character becomes responsibility and reliability in relation to another self—or that the responsibility demanded by communication between free individuals requires integrity of character.

But integrity of character requires consistent choice as well as self-consistency among choices. Acceptance of the decisiveness of prior choices must not become the excuse for evading subsequent choices and adhering to a narrow consistency that is not open to the demands of new situations. Where the choices of two different individuals are involved, a parallel requirement emerges. For each individual must not only be able to rely upon the other, but must be able to anticipate that his own choices will *make a difference* to the other. Otherwise, again, communication becomes vacuous and pointless. Communication can scarcely establish a reciprocity between two freedoms if each is indifferent to how the other exercises his freedom in making choices. The self-consistency of responsibility to the other must not pass over into an inflexible rigidity toward the other. Responsibility to the other must be balanced by responsiveness to the other. Moreover, a receptivity toward the other that was not completed by responsiveness would surely be fraudulent. ("I'll *listen* to you, but it won't make any difference to me what you say.") Responsiveness is therefore the necessary complement of receptivity, much as reliability is the necessary complement of candor. That is, communication requires not only that each individual choose to be open to the other's choice, but that each be responsive to the choices of the other, adjust his choices to those of the other, even make the other's choice decisive for his own. So, whereas the self-consistency of integrity requires that I choose to accept the decisiveness of my own prior choices without being rigidly bound by them, the responsiveness demanded by communication between freedoms requires that each party choose to accept the decisiveness of the other's choice, yet without simply submitting passively to the other's decision. To be responsive is not to be acquiescent, but to allow the other's choice to make a difference to my own.

Communication and Ethics

At the beginning of this chapter, I asked whether the categories of freedom can provide the foundation for ethics. Might an ethics of freedom furnish a set of values and standards capable of filling the moral vacuum left by the collapse of conventional norms in the face of modern man's self-consciousness of his own freedom and historicity, or overcome the threats of nihilism, anomie, and anarchy that are posed by that self-consciousness? My search for the conditions of free coexistence has led to an account of communication that has obvious moral connotations. Have I thereby laid the basis for an ethics?

Receptivity, candor, reliability, responsibility, responsiveness—these are the necessary ingredients of the categorical mode of communication. Like integrity of character and decisiveness of choice, these terms all resonate with moral or ethical overtones. And as conditions for the self-consistent exercise of freedom, these categories do establish the *possibility* of an "ethics of freedom." Of course, they only suggest the outlines for such an ethics, at best. A fully developed ethics of freedom would require a far more ambitious and detailed inquiry. Whether such an inquiry would be worth the effort depends upon a more fundamental question, however. Given that an ethics founded upon the categories of freedom is *possible,* could such an ethics be *adequate* to the requirements of human morality? At the beginning of the chapter, I demonstrated that the categories of choice and character do *not* yield an ethics that would be humanly recognizable as complete. They would not allow us to distinguish between a perfectly ethical person and a demonic individual or perfect villain. But this was because they provided no limits or standards defining the way in which one free individual should deal with another. At the very most, I acknowledged, the first two categories of freedom might supply an ethics for a completely solitary freedom.

The addition of communication as a third category pertaining to the coexistence of freedoms fills this hiatus. Does the addition of communication entitle me to claim that I have defined an adequate ethics of freedom? That is, can the conditions of existential freedom as enlarged by the conditions of free communication define an adequate foundation for ethics? Do the conditions of free communication described above adequately define a *moral* relationship between free individuals?

The first two categories of freedom do not rule out the possibility of the demonic individual who exercises his freedom in the pursuit of immoral ends. Do the conditions of free communication rule out the demonic couple or community? Or is free communication compatible with complicity in evil? What about a couple like Kate Croy and Merton Densher in Henry James's *Wings of the Dove,* whose remarkable "subjective community" leads them eventually into a sinister conspiracy. Offhand, free communication seems to provide no obvious ironclad guarantee against the common adoption of immoral purposes and might even foster cooperation for their successful execution.

But to acknowledge that the conditions of free communication can be satisfied in the case of complicity in evil is only to admit that there may be honor even among thieves—which is certainly not to license theft, but only to recognize that the same individual may be honest and moral in one relationship, but wicked or deceitful in another. The question is not whether conspirators in evil may communicate freely, but whether they would still be evil if they satisfied all the demands of free communication in *all* their relationships, and of the other categories of freedom as well. The evil done by Kate and Merton does not arise *between them,* but in their deceitful manipulation of others. And in the end, their own intimate community of minds is infected and destroyed because they find that they cannot honestly share the fruits of their duplicity. As for the demonic community, the constrictions and distortions of communication in Nazi Germany, probably the most demonic community in human history, are too well known to require any comment.

Of course, to show that the categories of freedom rule out the most extreme forms of demonic evil is only to show that they may provide *minimal* conditions for ethics, not that they can adequately define a moral life and moral relationships. Nor does it even begin to prove that they deserve to be regarded as ethical imperatives or norms. For although receptivity, candor, reliability, and responsiveness may evoke ethical associations or overtones, it must be admitted that they have been established without any appeal to moral considerations. No arguments have been offered to establish that these categories are morally prescriptive. That is, I have not even attempted to show that free individuals *ought* to adhere to these conditions. Without such a proof, they cannot be advanced as moral or ethical requirements. Failing that, I can only claim to have shown that the categories of freedom are conditions of the existence or coexistence of freedoms, and I have never attempted to establish more than that. My argument has been designed solely to describe the conditions of existential freedom or of the coexistence of free individuals. That leaves the further question whether these conditions define how freedom *ought* to be exercised, or prescribe which alternatives it would be *best* to choose?

An observation made at the opening of the chapter bears repetition here. The categories of freedom are only necessary to the maintenance of freedom. But is freedom the highest good, or the sole end of a moral life? The positive forms of these categories only deserve to be respected as prescriptive norms if freedom merits such a special status as a fundamental or ultimate moral value. After all, if an "ethics of freedom" is possible, so is an "ethics of pleasure," or of power or profit—or even an "ethics of cruelty," since there seems no reason to doubt that one might define "categories" or necessary minimal conditions for realizing and sustaining any of these ends. But that would scarcely prove that anyone *ought* to pursue any one of those goals rather than another.[13]

Failing some evidence that existential freedom is a moral goal that ought to be pursued and preserved, the categories of freedom can only found what Kant called "hypothetical imperatives" and conditional obligations. That is, they dictate that *if* you choose to realize and preserve your freedom, *then* you ought to act or choose in accordance with these standards. But that leaves open the question whether there is any moral obligation to preserve one's freedom at all costs, or whether it might not be best to sacrifice freedom for the sake of some higher moral good. To attempt to base a complete ethics upon the categories of freedom would seem to presuppose that freedom is the ultimate moral value.

But why should freedom deserve such an elevated status? No doubt, many people *do* place a high value upon freedom, but that does not even prove that it is a *moral* good, still less that it is the supreme human good. Indeed, the very logic of freedom seems to point to the opposite conclusion. For since freedom is the ability to choose between alternative possibilities and to strive to realize one's chosen purpose, there is no getting around the fact that the very concept of freedom points beyond itself to further purposes and goals. Doesn't this mean that freedom cannot serve as an ultimate ideal or standard, but only as a *provisional* goal, which is worth pursuing only for the sake of those other ends to which it opens the way? To make freedom an ultimate end, to cultivate and preserve it for its own sake, would seem to be as pointless as cultivating and preserving inedible fruit or grain. The worth of a canned peach is in the eating, and the value of freedom is in its *exercise,* which lies in the choice among ends and values *other* than freedom. But if that is the value of freedom, then it clearly cannot provide a standard for *assessing* those other purposes or furnish any guidance regarding what ends we *ought* to pursue. How, then, can it serve as the basis for an ethics? Surely, the basis for an adequate ethics must be sought in an ideal that is not merely provisional, but that defines the

---

13. Cf. Richard Double's argument that although free will is a *normative* concept, it is not a *moral* one. At the end of a chapter that asks, "Does freedom require morality?" Double concludes: "I believe that free will is a normative concept, but it is not normative in the sense that free agents need to be moral. Free will is normative in the way that any human excellence is normative—viz., to exercise it, one must satisfy qualitative standards, in this case standards of rationality. But since the morality of the resulting actions depends upon different variables than the norms for free choices, the strong conclusion of this chapter follows. Free will does not require morality, not even a little bit" (*The Non-Reality of Free Will* [Oxford: Oxford University Press, 1991], 74). However, Double's "internalistic" strategy rules out consideration of problems of communication, since it involves adopting the standpoint of methodological solipsism in order to deal with choices in isolation from the world.

ultimate human good, and the ideal of freedom cannot qualify as that highest human good, the ultimate aim that every human being ought to pursue.

It might be answered that even if freedom is not the ultimate good, it is nonetheless a fundamental moral value, even the most basic of all moral values. Many philosophers have claimed that *any* ethical or moral value whatsoever presupposes freedom. They argue that it makes no sense to say that an individual *ought* to act in a certain way or adhere to a specific standard if he is not free to do so—and that it is even more nonsensical to hold that an individual is morally guilty or responsible for an action if he was not free to act otherwise. This argument is often advanced as a proof of human freedom. Even Kant, who insists that for purposes of objective knowledge we must regard ourselves as unfree, as completely determined by external causes, nevertheless maintained that our moral experience, our sense of responsibility and obligation, is completely unintelligible unless we assume that we *are* free. Determinists respond to this argument by attempting to show that they can furnish a consistent and intelligible account of moral obligation without invoking freedom. There is no need to pause here to develop and assess the two sides of this controversy, since the issue of freedom versus determinism has already been disposed of on other grounds. It is sufficient to point out that if morality *does* presuppose freedom, then the categories of freedom do have a normative ethical status. For in that case, as necessary conditions of a free existence, they would also be necessary conditions of a *moral* existence.

But would this really answer to the issue at hand? After all, to show that the categories of freedom are necessary conditions of morality is not to show that they are the *sufficient* conditions of an adequate or complete human ethics. Even if it is true that I must be free in order to be morally responsible or obligated, that still doesn't tell me what I ought to do. The very argument that freedom is a presupposition of *any* moral obligation whatsoever leaves the exact *content* of particular obligations unspecified. Granted, the positive modes of the categories of freedom do supply a more specific set of standards of free existence. But even as more exactly defined by those categories, the ideal of freedom remains ambiguous. The categories of freedom do not seem to promise any univocal guide to action. Although they do spell out the general conditions of the self-consistent exercise of freedom, they remain extremely open and ambiguous. That is because the ideal of freedom does not dictate what goals or purposes men ought to choose to pursue, but only the conditions under which those choices and pursuits will not mean a sacrifice of freedom. But does that mean that I ought to preserve my freedom at all costs? After all, there are other, more ultimate purposes and ideals for the sake of which men have been willing to sacrifice their freedom and to which they have even freely sacrificed their lives. Surely, the basis for a complete human ethics must be sought among these more final purposes.

Evidently, the attempt to found an ethics upon freedom cannot escape this one crucial deficiency in the ideal of freedom: it leaves unanswered the question of what ends men should choose. Therefore, freedom cannot be the highest human good, the ultimate purpose of human action. But if the ideal of freedom thus remains mute and ambiguous regarding the highest good, then how can it furnish a complete account of what is good for man? And if freedom doesn't furnish an answer to that question, then how can it possibly found a complete ethics or serve to replace those customary ideals that the full self-consciousness of human freedom has displaced from their former positions of authority?

In fact, it is precisely the assumption that there *is* a single ultimate good or goal of human activity and striving, a single definition of human perfection upon which ethics must be founded, that has to be called into question here. This assumption *must* be questioned because it inevitably *will* be questioned. For there is probably no single point of which contemporary thought is more skeptical than of the existence of a single absolute good or ultimate human purpose. Skepticism about moral ideals is nothing new or peculiarly modern, of course. It is almost as old as philosophy itself. But the modern perspective of a developed historical consciousness, clearly cognizant of the role of custom and convention in defining men's ideals, has deepened that skepticism into an abyss of doubt. And, indeed, it is this abyss of skepticism and moral relativism that has motivated the present stage of this inquiry by raising the question whether an ethics of freedom could be adequate to fill the moral vacuum left by the collapse of the authority of traditional values and ideals occasioned by modern historical consciousness. For it is the same historical consciousness of the human origin of human ideals that makes man fully self-conscious of his own freedom.

But this very recognition that man is free raises still more serious problems about the possibility of defining a single ultimate human good or purpose. For if human beings are free agents, we cannot look to *human nature* for the basis of such an ultimate human good, since to be free is to have no fixed nature. To acknowledge human freedom is to acknowledge that although there may be common human *needs* that are natural because founded upon the innate exigencies of bodily life, there is *no* single natural aim or purpose of human activity. For it is of the very "nature" of freedom to refer beyond itself to a diverse array of possible further ends.

In short, the notion that a complete ethics must be founded upon a single vision of the ultimate good is doubly questionable. On the one hand, it is exposed to the doubts raised by awareness of the diversity of human ideals and purposes. We are no longer prepared to dismiss alien ideals and customs as "barbaric" or "unnatural," or to claim a divine origin for our own parochial mores and morals. On the other hand, this historical diversity of human norms and goals testifies to man's freedom and thereby undercuts the very foundation of the idea of a univocal human nature or a single ultimate human good.

Of course, to call attention to these doubts and difficulties is not to *prove* that there is no one ultimate good and no single definition of human perfection. That would require a comprehensive review of moral philosophy and a systematic critique of all the alternative ideals and solutions that have been propounded in answer to these difficulties. But if the definition of the ultimate good cannot be based upon mere convention, or upon "human nature," then where *are* we to seek its foundation? An appeal to the revealed will of God may satisfy the man of faith, but for the philosopher this only displaces the locus of the problem from man's freedom to that of God, which does not resolve the dilemma.

To this "crisis of values" and moral skepticism, which are so characteristic of contemporary culture, the ideal of freedom actually provides a peculiarly apt and promising answer. For, if it is indeed true that there is no single ultimate human good, no one final purpose of all human activity, then what I have been calling the "deficiency" of freedom as a moral ideal is really a singular asset. For then the fact that freedom cannot be an ultimate end, because the very logic of the concept of freedom points beyond freedom to whatever further ends and purposes men may freely choose, proves to be a virtue rather than a defect. In the first place, this means that freedom is an ideal that can allow for and accommodate the manifold diversity of actual human purposes and therefore does not collide with those facts of history and comparative anthropology upon which customary ideals and purportedly "naturalistic" ethics have foundered. For although attempts to base ethics either upon parochial mores or upon a timeless and universal "human nature" founder upon human freedom and historicity, that itself means that the ideal of freedom is the one ideal that is both in accordance with man's being and consistent with the historical diversity of human purposes and ideals.[14]

At first, this may seem to be a rather dubious and precarious advantage, one that really only serves to revive and underscore the charges of ambigu-

---

14. Thus, one could say that the ideal of freedom is the one ideal that *is* founded in human nature, except that to be free is precisely *not* to have a fixed and determinate universal "nature," since it is to be self-determining. Thus, an ethics of freedom cannot properly be described as a naturalistic ethics, though one can still claim that it has an *ontological* foundation in man's *being*.

ity raised above. Doesn't the ideal of freedom escape these objections and doubts simply because it fails to meet the problem of what ends men ought to pursue and is therefore too ambiguous to provide adequate ethical standards?

But ambiguity is not necessarily a shortcoming in a moral ideal. A precise and unambiguous moral code, one that offers an exact recipe for every action and situation, can never really do justice to the demands of the human condition in all its variety and diversity of historical circumstances. Neither honor nor justice nor happiness nor piety—nor any of the other ideals that have been held to be the ultimate moral goal—provides an unambiguous guide to action. The ideal of freedom is peculiar only in that it cannot pretend to be a final good or ultimate goal, so that its ambiguity accommodates not only a diversity of circumstances, but a diversity of ends and purposes as well.

But it is precisely this ambiguity regarding ends and purposes that makes the ideal of freedom so aptly suited to meet the moral quandary of contemporary culture. For, again, if there *is* no single ultimate human good, then ethics has no business prescribing one, and any ethics is at fault that either presupposes such a single, univocal definition of the good or holds one up as a universal end for all men to pursue. Accordingly, the fact that the ideal of freedom does *not* dictate any final human purpose or prescribe any single ultimate goal is not a defect, but an eminent advantage. Not only does it thereby escape the doubts and objections that a skeptical historical consciousness raises against other moral ideals, but it also offers a positive alternative: an ethics that does *not* presume to dictate what aims men ought to pursue, but which dictates, instead, that they ought to be free to choose their *own* ends.

But this does not mean that an ethics of freedom boils down to the simple but useless maxim "Do as you choose," or that such an ethics would be *too* ambiguous to provide any real moral guidance or clear ethical standards. Even a very cursory review of the positive modes of the categories of freedom will show that although they do not prescribe any final human purposes, they are nevertheless extremely demanding standards. They require decisiveness of choice, integrity of character, and receptivity, candor, reliability, responsiveness, and responsibility in interpersonal relations. This constitutes an imposing set of demands that includes, or at least adumbrates, many of the classical moral virtues. But these are only the most fundamental requirements of the preservation and maintenance of freedom, the minimal conditions that must be met if the individual's exercise of freedom is not to prove destructive of either his own freedom or that of others. A completely developed ethics of freedom would have to go much further in specifying the individual conditions of free coexistence and the social and political conditions of a free community.

Indeed, the ethics of freedom opens a broad vista of normative political questions. To forestall the dangers of a demonic complicity whose evil resides in the refusal to respect freedoms outside a restricted circle of communication, we must pass beyond communication to community, beyond the limits of relations between two communicating freedoms to collective problems of how to organize a free community. I cannot communicate with everyone at once, yet my choices and actions eventually impinge upon other free agents, some of whom I may never have met, yet whose actions impinge upon me in turn. The active exercise of freedom alters the world in which others have to choose and act, and the social interplay of individual actions alters the world in unchosen and unexpected ways that determine the scope of options available to each agent. A complete account of the conditions of free coexistence would therefore have to pass beyond ethics to contend with the broad horizon of problems concerning social and political liberty that have inspired so much thought and debate since the Renaissance. I certainly cannot explore that horizon here. Others have attempted to derive standards of political and social freedom from reflection upon the conditions of unconstrained communication or open, neutral dialogue, and I cannot do justice to the subtlety of their reasonings within the confines of the present inquiry.[15] For present purposes, it suffices to point out that a fully developed account of the conditions of free coexistence would have to extend beyond the limits of private communication into the public domain of social processes and economic and political institutions.

A full-blown ethics of freedom would therefore not be lacking in rigorous or demanding norms and standards. And yet those standards could never be assailed as "too restrictive" or too narrow and confining, since they are precisely the conditions that are necessary to maintain and foster a maximum of individual freedom. It would therefore be an ethics that every person could follow for the sake of his own purposes, since it would impose limitations only for the sake of assuring that every individual should be free to pursue purposes of his own choosing. This is not to say that an ethics of freedom would place no limitations at all upon human purposes, of course, but that it would limit them only insofar as they were incompatible with the freedom of each individual to determine his own ends. Consequently, the

15. In addition to the works by Habermas and others cited in note 11 above, see Bruce Ackerman's attempt to develop social and political norms out of neutral dialogue, in *Justice and the Liberal State* (New Haven: Yale University Press, 1980), and John MacMurray's *Persons in Relation* (Atlantic Highlands, N.J.: Humanities Press, 1991).

ideal of freedom is one in which all can share, no matter how diverse their conceptions of the good or their individual purposes. And, if there is no universal ultimate human good that every individual ought to pursue, then each individual has an inherent right to pursue the good as he sees it, for there can be no overriding reason or value that could obligate him to forgo that freedom.

However, it follows that every individual has an *obligation* to respect the freedom of others, for he can never be justified in imposing his personal purpose or vision of the good upon others or in abrogating their freedom to pursue their own ends. Consequently, the statement above must be modified to read that every individual has a right to pursue the good as he sees it, *insofar as that is consistent with his obligation to respect the freedom of others.* But this means that each individual is obliged not to sacrifice or destroy his own freedom, for that is a necessary condition of remaining responsible and responsive to others. Of course, this means that every individual's freedom must be "compromised" to some extent. But it is important to remember that to *exercise* freedom is inevitably to compromise it in that sense, since self-determination is self-limitation and every free act imposes limits upon the freedom of others as well as upon the agent. However, the goal of an ethics of freedom is not unlimited freedom (which is impossible in any case), but a self-limitation of freedom for the sake of the preservation of freedom for each and for all. An ethics of freedom has obligatory force, then, not because freedom is the absolute and ultimate good, but precisely in the *absence* of any such overriding ultimate good that could justify the sacrifice or destruction of freedom.

All this has been stated in a hypothetical manner because no attempt has been made to *prove* that there is no single ultimate human good. I have only called attention to the motives of the profound skepticism concerning ultimate norms and values that is so prevalent in contemporary thought, a skepticism that is rooted in an awareness of the historical diversity and mutability of human mores and ideals and that so readily evokes moral relativism or nihilism. Whether that skepticism is justified, whether there *is* a single ultimate human good, is a not a question I can answer here. But, whether justified or not, that skepticism and the crisis of moral conscious- ness that it engenders are present cultural realities. On the other hand, those who do not share in that skepticism, those who are confident of the rectitude of their own ideals and values, do not agree in their conceptions of the good. Whether we like it or not, we live in a pluralistic society and culture where there is little or no moral consensus or agreement about ultimate ends. It is a situation that holds very real dangers. For, on the one hand, the lack of the moral consensus that once characterized more homogeneous and conventional cultures tends to foster discord and even a degree of anarchy, while, on the other hand, these very tendencies tempt those who are certain of their own rectitude to impose a rigid conformity upon everyone through the power of the modern state.

In the face of this situation, the ideal of freedom acquires a status of decisive moral significance. For although freedom is not a *final* good or end in itself and therefore cannot be the ultimate good, it may be for that very reason the highest *common* good, the one ideal that obligates all human beings, regardless of our differences, just because it allows us to preserve and contain those differences within the framework of an ethics of mutual respect and responsibility. Where there is no accord about final purposes, there is an obvious danger that adherents of one vision of the good will impose their purposes and values upon all others—or that the partisans of different values will engage in mutually destructive bickering and warfare that serves no one's purposes. An ethics that leaves the choice of final purposes open is the best protection against both of these dangers, and the ideal of freedom is the one value upon which all can agree.[16]

There is, however, another way to view this case for an ethics of freedom. It would rest upon a more positive recognition of the diversity of human values, a recognition that, instead of drawing skeptical conclusions, would simply accept the existence of a multiplicity of human goods, each of them quite real, each of them an ultimate value in the sense of being intrinsically valuable or good in and of itself. In that case, the highest good, or *summum bonum,* would literally be a sum of goods, a composite of all these particular goods. Yet no individual can possibly attain so composite a perfection. The attainment of any excellence requires selection, limitation, and concentra-

---

16. Cf. Robert Kane's definition of "the moral point of view" in terms of mutual respect between finite free agents, in chapter 7 of *Free Will and Values.* Indeed, Kane argues that freedom *depends* upon a plurality of goods, which presents the individual with incommensurable sets of reasons for action, so that there is no single "best" action in any given situation. Which act is best or right depends upon which good one seeks, and that can only be settled by a free choice that establishes the set of reasons relevant to evaluating one's specific options. "The moral point of view" stems from the recognition that in the absence of any single ultimate good in terms of which to rank diverse goods and reasons, any other project deserves as much respect as my own.

Still, there is an important difference between equal respect and communication. Equal respect does not reconcile differences, but only acknowledges them and requires that we refrain from imposing our values upon one another. That leaves open the kinds of problems that communitarians find with liberal individualism, whereas the standard of communication seeks to reconcile differences in a larger whole—though *not* necessarily under a single conception of the good. Kane does address these issues in a discussion of "second-best strategies" involving bargained compromise, and a fully developed communicative ethics would certainly have to consider what second-best strategies would be called for in cases where partisans of different goods refuse—or simply fail—to communicate.

tion. In that case, the highest good would best be served by a pluralistic community of individuals, each striving for some single value or partial constellation of values and enriching the whole by his own particular achievements. In such a community, every individual and every group of individuals who share the same goal will tend to see one particular value or spectrum of values as deserving primary importance. Plato thought that such a community could best be realized and harmonized through the rule of a group of philosophers whose knowledge of the ultimate form of the good would enable them to organize and coordinate all the individual pursuits of particular goods. Unfortunately, the history of philosophy gives us no reason to hope that a group of philosophers could ever reach agreement about the nature of the ultimate good or about how all particular and partial goods are to be coordinated and integrated. In the absence of any such comprehensive wisdom or consensus of the sages, the ideal of freedom would remain the highest *common* good, not because freedom has any value in itself, but because it is the condition of the accessibility of all other values. For only if every individual is free to pursue his own good, or to enter into cooperation for the sake of a shared value, can there be any assurance that the entire spectrum of human goods will be served or that the partisans of some partial and parochial vision of the good will not seize power and subvert all other values for the sake of their own.

In sum, whether we view the multiplicity of human values cynically and skeptically or in a more positive and appreciative manner, an ethics of freedom seems to offer the best answer to the problem posed by that diversity. To the skeptic, who concludes on the basis of that diversity that there are no real ultimate values, it offers the alternative of an ethics that would be nonetheless rigorous and binding, even if all other values are merely subjective and personal. For the realist, who is prepared to embrace a diversity of human values as real and legitimate, an ethics of freedom would supply the best guarantee that the entire range of human goods shall be served, and the solution to the problem of coordinating men's several individual pursuits of different ends. I have laid the foundations for such an ethics of freedom here. It would require another book to complete the structure. But the task is not entirely novel, after all, and it is not as though the further outlines and details of such an ethics had to be left entirely to conjecture. For the inquiry into the conditions of individual freedom and of a free community of individuals has occupied liberal thought and liberal politics for three centuries. The present inquiry into the concept and conditions of freedom might be regarded as an attempt to furnish a new preface or prolegomenon to that liberal tradition, a tradition that is now assailed, as it always will be, by those who would subvert or sacrifice freedom to their particular ends or to the ephemeral expediencies of the moment.

Even the term "liberal" is all too often appropriated or attacked by partisans of one or another special purpose until it has become a vague and empty epithet, too ambiguous to communicate any clear meaning that could stand as a value above partisan passions and policies. Yet the authentic task of liberal politics and liberal thought is to rise above such special pleading and partisan strife and seek to reconcile and integrate disparate and conflicting freedoms.

Epilogue

To reconcile and integrate disparate and conflicting freedoms: that has also been the task of this book. Indeed, "this is where we came in." We seem to be back where we began, but somewhat wiser for our wanderings. Controversies about the meaning of liberalism echo the controversies about freedom raised at the beginning of the book. These philosophical wanderings were provoked by disputes about freedom that appeared to be endless. It was soon obvious that arguments about the existence of freedom could not be answered without contending with conflicting conceptions of the nature of freedom—or conflicting conceptions of the meaning of "freedom." But by the end of the second chapter, the idea of freedom threatened to dissolve into a haze of ambiguities that seemed to defy resolution.

I remarked at the outset that philosophical disputes about freedom evoked echoes of the political arena, where every party to every conflict claims to be "the party of freedom." Now, at the end, those same echoes seem to emanate from the other side of the valley. Perhaps I can take advantage of those echoes to recall what has been accomplished in the meantime. By heeding the political echoes of the themes developed in the course of the work, I can consolidate the lessons learned along the way into a brief closing reprise that will also suggest how the resources of liberal political thought might prove useful in the more complex exposition of an ethics of freedom and how the philosophical reconciliation undertaken here bears upon the seemingly endless task of moral and political reconciliation among free agents.

For whereas the political task of reconciling individual freedoms is indeed endless, the task of conceptual reconciliation that has occupied this inquiry is finite and may now conclude. The political process of harmonizing freedoms can never come to an end, because new choices will always evoke new conflicts among free individuals, so that every resolution must be temporary and provisional. But this book *can* come to an end because the freedoms it has undertaken to reconcile are not disparate decisions of individual agents, but disparate conceptions or definitions of freedom— and because a general and durable resolution to that problem has emerged in the course of the inquiry.

For although competing definitions of freedom may seem to threaten to proliferate as endlessly as individual choices, the source of that proliferation is no longer a mystery. In Chapter 12, I showed how fecundly the meanings of freedom increase and multiply by taking the freedom of the choice *among* options and imparting it to the particular option that is chosen, so that freedom comes to be identified with any purpose, policy, or means that has been freely chosen. So long as controversies about the nature of freedom are carried out at this level of diverse and conflicting purposes, no final conceptual reconciliation is any more possible than a final political reconciliation among free individuals is possible—and for much the same reasons.

The important work of conceptual reconciliation began with the recognition that all these appeals to freedom on behalf of specific purposes are simply diverse projections of a single concept of freedom: the ordinary idea of freedom as being able to do as I choose, or the "freedom of self-realization." Where freedom is understood as the ability to do as I choose in the absence of obstacles and constraints that would frustrate my purpose, it is easy to slide over into identifying freedom with the ability to realize the particular purpose I have chosen. The single conception of freedom as self-realization is thereby projected into an endless array of particular goals. But to recognize that fact, as I did in Chapter 2, is to resolve all those competing claims under the single concept of self-realization.

That did not resolve *all* the disputes about the nature of freedom, of course. It still left the deeper, more stubborn conflict among three major competing views: the three perennial philosophical conceptions that Mortimer Adler and his associates distinguished in *The Idea of Freedom:* freedom as self-realization, freedom as self-determination, and freedom as self-perfection. But the ensuing inquiry has also reconciled those three forms of freedom and integrated them into a comprehensive philosophy of freedom. First, the ordinary conception of freedom as self-realization, or the ability to do as I choose, proved to be inherently incomplete. Critical analysis showed that self-realization is not self sufficient, but must be grounded in self-determination, or freedom of choice. We can appreciate why by appealing to a celebrated political parallel that illustrates that same point in larger terms. The ability of a colonial administration to execute policies and purposes imposed by an imperial regime scarcely counts as the freedom of the colony or its subjects; "Taxation without representation is tyranny," to invoke a celebrated example—and the more tyrannical, the more effectively the taxes are collected. It is obvious that in order to enjoy genuine and meaningful freedom, a nation—or an individual—must also be able to determine its own policies and purposes for itself. Self-realization is empty without self-determination.

The colony that rebels against imperial rule and wins the right to determine itself may well find that it lacks the power to carry out its own policies and purposes after the revolution, however. Self-determination has proved to be as empty and incomplete without self-realization as is self-realization unfounded in self-determination. The two are not to be understood as disparate and competing forms of freedom, but as distinguishable moments or aspects of a single process of self-determination that is only abstractly and incompletely conceived when the two are separated and opposed to one another.

The former colony that has won the right of self-determination may also find that liberation from foreign rule has not left it free—local tyranny has displaced imperial rule. Whether a people is genuinely free depends as much upon the internal constitution of its system of government as upon whether it is governed by Rome or London—or New Delhi. "National self-determination" does not issue in real, substantive freedom if the people submit to rule by a military dictator or revolutionary junta. To choose to submit to a popular dictator like Napoleon or Juan Perón is as subversive an exercise as an individual's decision to use addictive drugs, since both mean abdicating the power to govern oneself.

This recognition—that the freedom of self-determination may be self-destructive—led to a reconciliation of Adler's third form of freedom, the freedom of self-perfection, with self-realization and self-determination. According to that conception, whose most celebrated exposition is to be found in Kant's ethics, freedom depends upon acting or choosing on the basis of a moral ideal or principle, or in accordance with the true nature of the self. Since the self is free, the one moral ideal that accords with the nature of the self is the ideal of freedom. Only by acting or choosing in accordance with the conditions of freedom itself can freedom be sustained in the course of its own exercise.

A complete understanding of freedom must therefore incorporate all three of these perennially popular, competing philosophical ways of thinking about it, including a version of the freedom of self-perfection as well as self-determination and self-realization. That recognition completed the conceptual reconciliation and integration of diverse and conflicting freedoms into a durable and comprehensive philosophy of freedom. In each case, the parallel political issue has provided a useful illustration of the conceptual issues motivating such a resolution.

Reconciliation of competing claims about the nature of freedom, however, does not answer the claim that the very existence of freedom cannot be reconciled with the natural order. According to that claim, the whole of nature is hostile environment, a realm of determinism that forbids freedom entirely. On this assumption that freedom and nature are essentially incompatible, some have argued that to be free is to be outside the natural order, while others have argued that freedom cannot exist at all. Once again, a political parallel may prove helpful. To be independent, a community must secure some viable natural habitat. It must inhabit some part of the world that supplies the natural resources it needs to survive. A community that can find no place in the world cannot constitute a free state. By the same token, if nature excludes freedom, then freedom is impossible.

But the account of the nature and conditions of freedom that emerged in the course of my conceptual analysis has not only reconciled diverse and competing conceptions of freedom. It has also reconciled freedom and nature—and thereby settled the dispute about the existence of freedom that provoked the whole inquiry to begin with. First, it showed that freedom cannot exist outside of some world or natural habitat. For just as a free state must command the territory upon which it depends for survival, freedom must have a body that lodges it within the world, a body that is a part of that world, yet subject to control by the self. Second, by showing that other organisms also satisfy the fundamental conditions of freedom, I have laid to rest the notion that human freedom constitutes an anomalous exception to a deterministic natural order. The difference between man and animal is not a metaphysical frontier between freedom and determinism, but is due to the role of culture in human life—to the decisive roles of language and other forms of symbolism in human existence.

By thus locating human freedom within a natural setting, this interpretation also "liberated" nature from the deterministic hypothesis. The idea that nature is a realm of strict determinism was shown to be incompatible with our experience of natural processes—because it is inconsistent with the occurrence of any temporal processes whatsoever. For a deterministic order has no room for the emergence of anything new, anything that was not already implicit in antecedent conditions. The liberation of nature from that hypothesis allows us to understand the evolution of human freedom as the emergence of a novelty—but a novelty that has natural antecedents. The emergence of human freedom is therefore not a mysterious metaphysical leap, but only an extension of the range of animal freedom by the power of cultural symbols to represent remote possibilities and devise unprecedented options.

But the expansion of freedom afforded by the use of symbols is not simply an extension of the range of foresight, to be compared with the extension of sight by a telescope. The use of symbols dislodges *Homo sapiens* from significant natural constraints that limit other species and raises human freedom to a new and different plane. To acknowledge that animals are free is therefore not to deny the depth and breadth of the differences between human and animal freedom. By locating that difference at the border between nature and culture and by exploring that frontier carefully, I was able both to reconcile human freedom with the natural order and to appreciate the sense in which human freedom transcends nature, all in a single stroke. For culture alters the terms of human existence in two decisive ways.

First, it transposes human existence from the milieu of natural evolution to the domain of historical activity, where the conditions of survival and change are very different. Once patterns of life are stored in symbols rather than in chromosomes, historical change becomes possible because human beings can adapt their inherited patterns of behavior to meet altered conditions without changing physiologically. Indeed, historical change now becomes all but irresistible, since a cultural pattern is at the mercy of individual usage and only survives insofar as individuals choose to perpetuate it. Even when they do, the most treasured ceremonies, customs, and laws are subject to erosion and transformation through a succession of ritual errors—or judicial decisions. The "force of custom" is powerful; yet in the absence of the innate physiological mechanisms that sustain the repetition of instinctual patterns, language and laws and other cultural patterns are fragile and can be sustained intact only by very deliberate effort.

In such cases, human culture doubles back upon itself to become an object or value for itself, as also happens when a society sees its own customs as outmoded, as needing to be modified or abandoned. Of course, many societies have denied the difference between nature and culture by presenting their own customs as part of a natural or sacred order—and hence as immutable. Yet human beings are always aware that cultural forms are optional insofar as they know that it is possible to sin—to violate the customs and conventions of the tribe. But once they recognize that those customary norms and practices are not natural and immutable, but artificial and historical, they can see that they are free not only to sin, but to rebel against inherited customs and to change the very pattern of their lives. With this recognition that the customary patterns of human existence are not natural and innate, but optional, human freedom also doubles back upon itself to become its own object. That leads to the second way in which culture decisively alters the terms of human freedom.

Human freedom can double back upon itself to become recursive or reflexive because the resources of culture enable freedom to represent itself to itself symbolically. Without that capacity, freedom would still be conditioned and limited by its own exercise, but could not make the preservation and enhancement of freedom its own object or value. Only the peculiarly human powers of symbolic self-representation enable freedom to confront itself and its own historicity, to *recognize* that freedom is at risk through its own exercise, and to adopt the ideal of freedom as its goal. Once freedom thus doubles back upon itself, it collides with the same problems of freedom raised at the outset, though at a new level. For then, as I noted in Chapter 7, the dialectic of freedom is recapitulated at the existential or practical level. The ontological conditions of freedom reappear as conditions of the preservation of freedom through its own exercise. And that opens the way to an ethics and politics of freedom.

Indeed, an ethics of freedom becomes not only *possible,* but *imperative,* once freedom becomes its own object. An ethics and politics of freedom become *possible* once the free agent recognizes that freedom, like custom, can be preserved, diminished, or destroyed through its own exercise. For then freedom may become its own goal as well as its own object, since free agents may seek to preserve and enhance their freedom rather than to destroy or curtail it.

An ethics of freedom also becomes *imperative* once free agents fully recognize their own freedom and historicity. Once fully aware that they are free, they will no longer have any reason to acquiesce to hereditary social roles or to accept inherited customs as inherently binding and legitimate. For once it is clear that no way of life is natural or necessary, that all human ideals and norms are optional, an ethics of freedom is the only option. For then, *only* an ethics that accepts freedom as its source and standard can command respect. Free agents who know that they are free will insist that the ethical and legal norms governing their lives not to be based upon the order of nature, but be founded in the free consent of the governed.

Index